5, 6, 7,

SIR WILLIAM BUTLER

SIR WILLIAM BUTLER

AN AUTOBIOGRAPHY

BY

LIEUT.-GENERAL THE RT. HON.
SIR W. F. BUTLER
G.C.B.

WITH FOUR PORTRAITS IN PHOTOGRAVURE

NEW YORK
CHARLES SCRIBNER'S SONS
1911

CONTENTS

a 2

CHAPTER XV

CHAPTER XVI

CHAPTER XVII

CHAPTER XVIII

CHAPTER XIX

CHAPTER XX

CHAPTER XXI

CHAPTER XXII

CHAPTER XXIII

ILLUSTRATIONS

FOREWORD

My father began this Autobiography in March 1909, and worked leisurely at it up to within a few days of his unexpected death on 7th June 1910.

The manuscript breaks off in the middle of the last chapter, which deals with the end of his command in South Africa ; and though, on his deathbed, he entrusted the task of completing this chapter to me, I was unable to learn his wishes as to the sources of information among his papers to which I should apply.   On finding the detailed ' Narrative of Events,' which he wrote shortly after his return from the Cape, I thought I could not do better than adhere solely to this record.

The reader will understand the onerous nature of my task, for, while keeping closely to the 'Narrative,' I have realised the necessity for abbreviation and condensation, without omitting what appeared to be essentials.   Whether my father would have wished for more or for fewer omissions, I cannot say ; but I have inclined towards few, for fear of losing anything he would have wished retained.

EILEEN BUTLER.

SIR WILLIAM BUTLER

AN AUTOBIOGRAPHY

CHAPTER I

Earliest recollections   The Irish famine.   'Butler's country.'
School.   Gazetted ensign to the 69th Regiment.

HAD it been possible for any one child to tell us exactly what
he saw when he first opened his eyes, that earliest impression
of the world would probably have proved the most interesting
brain-picture ever given by an individual to the general public.
Nothing like it could ever have been told by him in later life

'We awake at our birth,' somebody says, 'staring at a
very funny place.   After serious examination of it we receive
two fairly definite impressions—delight and fear.'   He puts the
sensation of delight first, that of fear second.   That is right;
but do they keep these places always ?   I think the verdict of
humanity would be that Life was a longer or shorter process of
the change of place between these two predominant powers.

Our delight at the first sight of earth we are able to recall
only dimly in after time.   The fear is bound to grow.   Once
at St. Helena there came a huge avalanche of rock, loosened
from an overhanging mountain, in the dead of night, crashing
down upon the poor straggling single street of Jamestown.
It crushed to powder two houses, killing instantly sixteen men
and women.   When daylight came, the frightened neighbours,
climbing through the ruins, found a three-months-old baby
lying on its back close by the mountain boulder, alive, kicking
and crowing—every other thing was dead.   To the baby the
rock was only a new possession.   That is the whole point.

Anyway, *our* child-world was a happy one.   Everything was
ours—the green foreground where the spotted pet rabbits
nibbled and nuzzled together ; beyond these, long glimpses of
green grass seen between lime and beech trees , then a glisten-

A

ing river, with shimmering shallows and bending sallows ; beyond that, more green fields ; and then a long blue mountain range, which grew bolder and loftier as it stretched westward, where it ended in two peaked summits, behind which the sun went down only to come up again next morning at the east end of the range—our sole unquestioned property still. Such are my earliest recollections of the home of ' the little sallow ' —Ballyslateen, where I first saw the light on the 31st of October 1838, the seventh child of Richard and Ellen Butler.

The world, as the young child saw it, was a very different place from the world which the older child was to hear and realise a few years later. The early 'forties gave no warning word of what the decade would do in Ireland before it closed. I was about eight years old when the crash came. The country about where we lived in Tipperary was swarming with people. Along the road were cabins or little thatched mud-cottages at every hundred or hundred and fifty paces. I had been taken at the age of four years to live with a maternal aunt and uncle at Artane, near Dublin, a charming spot three miles from the city ; and in this second home, with the kindest relations that child could have, I spent the years from 1842 to 1846 These years are, of course, only a bright hour in memory now, but one or two events stand out in clearest light. I still retain the recollection of being taken into a large building, the name of which I knew only in after years. Richmond Penitentiary it was called. We passed through big gates and doors, and came out into a garden which had a very high wall around it. Following a walk to a spot where another walk crossed ours, we found a group of strange men, with one very big burly man among them. I remember the scene particularly, for the reason that there were a good many apple-trees growing on either side of the walks, and the fruit was sufficiently large upon them to rivet my attention while the older members of the party were conversing with the burly man and his companions. All at once the big figure moved forward, and, taking me in his arms, lifted me above his head, while he shouted in a great strong voice, ' Hurrah for Tipperary ! ' The big man was Daniel O'Connell, and the time must have been in the June of 1844 ; for he was in Richmond Prison from May to September of that year.

Early in 1846 I was taken from these loving relations at
Artane back to the Tipperary home. It was a two days' coach
journey, of which I remember little beyond the grief of the
first day at parting from these beloved ones ; and the grey
monotony of the second day passing slowly through long
stretches of bog until at last, as evening was closing, the great
towers and battlements of the Rock of Cashel rose before the
post-chaise in the gloaming ; but another weary hour had to
pass before home was reached. When we were quite near
home, my sister, who knew the road thoroughly, began to name
the persons whose cottages we should have to pass before our
gate was reached. She repeated about a dozen names. I being
terribly tired, the list gave me the idea that we had still a long
road to travel, and I heard it with dismay ; but my alarm was
needless, the distance was only a few hundred yards. I passed
along that same road a few days ago : not one house, not even
the site of a house, can now be discerned there. In that
month of March 1846 the famine which was to sweep four
millions of Irish peasants out of Ireland was about to begin
its worst slaughter. The following winter brought ' the black
forty-seven.' It was a terrible time. Everywhere the unfortunate people sickened, died, or fled. There was no preparation, no warning ; the blow fell straight. The halting and
creaking machinery of the State could not cope with this
sudden onslaught. A second or third rate despot could have
at least parried the blow ; but a constitutional government
face to face with a sudden crisis is as helpless as a stranded
whale in an ebb-tide.

My father and the better-endowed neighbours flung themselves bravely against the advancing plagues of famine and
fever. Their purses were none too flush ; but they gave
liberally. They bought meal in the nearest town where it
could be got, carried it fourteen miles by cart, and, under
escort of police, gave it to the famishing people. I have some
of the old books still which hold the record and keep the
accounts of these weekly distributions. They are pitiful reading.
They range from early February to the end of July 1847. The
little entries opposite the names of relief recipients are more
striking in their briefness than elaborate descriptions of misery
could be. Here are some of them.

'Kitty Marony and three children. Her husband has gone from her and she doesn't know where he went.'

'The widow —— and five children, two and a half stone weekly.'

'Nicholas Murphy and four children; has an old cow.'

'Edward Mockler of —— "the Idiot" is receiving.'

'The cost of the Indian meal varies between 1/4 and 1/10 the stone.'

Sometimes a name disappears from the list, and the entry column knows it no more.

The records end in July 1847, perhaps because the Government machinery had then got into working order, or because the earth had begun to yield some stray bits of nutriment again.

In September 1847, things looking somewhat brighter I suppose, I was sent with two older brothers to a school in the King's County called Tullabeg. This establishment was conducted by the Jesuit Fathers. It was situated in the midst of a great region of bog-land, as the name implies—Tullabeg, the little bog—in contradistinction, I suppose, to the great many big bogs which surrounded it. My recollections of this school are not happy ones. I was nine years old, and thin and delicate; and the cold of the winter, in that elevated marsh-land which lies to the north of the Slieve Bloom Hills and almost in the centre of the island, seemed to strike into the heart and soul of a frame such as mine. All the more did the climatic conditions tell against a small boy because the majority of the other boys were strong. Many of them were rough, and, it is needless to say, were as merciless to their smaller and weaker fry as though the school had been of pilchards. My mother's death in the summer of 1849 caused us to be taken from school. Things had grown worse over the land. If actual famine had lessened, its after effects had spread and deepened. Sickness of many kinds prevailed everywhere, and contagion carried death into homes of rich and poor alike. The winter of 1848-49 dwells in my memory as one long night of sorrow. I was only ten years old; two children still younger than I was were both stricken with the long wasting fever which was ravaging the country. It was at this time that my mind began to take impressions which time has not been able to impair, and to form thoughts which experience of life has only tended to deepen.

In what manner my father was able to weather the storm which had so suddenly broken, in which so many stronger craft had gone down, I do not know, but he was a brave man. The strange part of it was that it was all new work to him. He had not fought these foes before, and he was at this time not far off his sixtieth year. This is where religion comes in. Gradually things grew better. Youth soon rallied, and even when things were at their worst, we youngsters had the fields, the river, and the mountain still with us—the country of which Spenser had said that it was ' the richest Champain that may else be rid '; and the mountain that he speaks of as ' the best and fairest hill that was in all this Holy Island's heights.' Nor had he forgotten the river : he calls it ' the gentle Shure.' But that was saying little : gentle it was, no doubt ; but many things besides—grass-banked, willowy, winding, pebbly, with deep limpid pools and silvery shallows—' the fishful Swire,' another old writer calls it. Our old home lay at the other side of the river, and its name told the sylvan story of the beautiful stream, ' the town-land of the winding river '—Ballycarron. My father had been born there, as had some eight or nine generations of our family, since the time Black Tom of Carrick[1] had settled his brothers and a lot of his followers west of the Suir after the destruction of the Desmonds in 1584

The family traditions were almost as extensive as the family purse was limited. I think that there was a somewhat similar antithesis of thought with us between purse and pride, not uncommon in cases of the kind—as though nature had put into old blood some antitoxin to neutralise the effect of the bacteria of poverty. Be that as it may, the river, the mountains, and the family history were all interwoven together.

The old peasants still called the great plain that stretched from Slieve-na-Man to the Galtees, ' Butler's country.' The name alone survived. The possession had long since shrunken to narrow limits. Cromwell had ridden over it, and William had crossed it again forty years later, harrowing where the other had ploughed. A century of penal law had bitten out

[1] Thomas Butler, tenth Earl of Ormond.

many a broad acre from it as the devil was said to have bitten out the big gap in the ' Devil's Bit ' Mountain, that bounded our range of sight to the north as the Galtees stopped it to the south.   What ups and downs of life had all these ups and downs of land surface seen !   Some very old men had survived the famine and fever years, and they were always ready to spin a story of ' the good old times ' for us young people.

Cromwell's war was not such a far-away event in 1850 to men or women who could reckon eighty or ninety years of existence.   They had heard, as children, old men and women of fourscore years telling their tales by the winter's fireside— 1850, 1770, 1700, 1630—when Oliver Cromwell was farming and brewing in Huntingdon.   A hears a story from B who had heard from C what D was told ten years before the time when forty of the Butlers fell at Kilrush fighting under Mountgarret in Wexford—that time when a riderless horse belonging to one of the forty, with broken bridle and saddle topsy-turvy, came galloping into the castle ' bawn ' on Kilmoyler Hill, a short mile across the fields to the south of our river.   The church-yard lore, too, seemed to have survived the wreck of life and estate longer than other traditions.   Our family burial-place was by the old ruined church of Killardrigh, half a mile beyond the hill of Kilmoyler.   A fragment of an old headstone, lying among debris near the east window of the little ruin, said that in this place several generations of the Butlers of Kilmoyler, descendants of the ninth Earl of Ormond, were interred. Before Killardrigh, the old people said we had buried in Lough Kent, four miles to the east ; and before that at Clerihan, about the same distance to the south-east.   This showed the steps which the course of incessant tribal fighting between the Butlers and Desmonds had caused the family outposts to follow, as the Desmonds were being slowly pushed back towards the west   If Desmond had ' wine from the royal Pope ' and guns from the King of Spain, ' Black Tom,' in his great house at Carrick, had had many a boat-load of arms, powder, and bullets from his ' cousin ' the Queen of England.   Her likeness and royal cipher are still to be seen in Italian stucco work in a dozen medallions round the ruined banqueting-hall of the castle at Carrick.

In the old times neither chief nor clansman went far to marry or to bury. Wherever you find one of those lonely, lofty, square stone towers, called 'castles' in Ireland, you will also find, close by, the ruined church, with mounds and mouldering headstones around it—Mullaghnoney, Woodenstown, Kilnacask. Cromwell's soldiers smashed them all to bits, but the dead steal back to the ruined churches still.

Looking back now at the early days of my boyhood, I often think with keen regret of all the opportunities lost for ever of hearing more and still more of what those grand old people had heard or read of in their day. My father had been educated at Ulverston in Lancashire, at a school kept by Bishop Everard, a refugee from France in the time of the Revolution. This remarkable ecclesiastic, afterwards Archbishop of Cashel, had, with the aid of some of the old highest Catholic families, started a private school in the little Lancashire village in the last decade of the eighteenth century. We were related through marriage with the family of Everard, and thus had arisen the connection between teacher and student at Ulverston. What mines of historic interest here lay entombed ! An Irish-French bishop getting away from the south of France before Napoleon had taken Toulon My father used to tell us of delightful evenings spent at the house of a Catholic lady who had lived at Ulverston at this time—Barbara, Lady Mostyn. She had early separated from her husband, Sir Piers Mostyn, for some incompatibilities, one of which I remember. Sir Piers was sitting late with his foxhunting friends one night shortly after the marriage. My lady was in her own apartments. It was proposed that she should be 'blooded '— this ceremony consisted in drinking a cup of claret in which the brush of the fox last killed was put. My lady was sent for. Seated at the table, the rite was explained to her, and the noxious draught placed before her. She refused to drink it. 'By G——, madam,' thundered Sir Piers, 'you will have to drink it ; you must be " blooded." ' Lady Mostyn drank the cup, and left the castle, to which she never returned.

Another Ulverston story I also remember. One of the young men at the school (they were all of university age) came in from the garden one evening showing signs of great mental distress. A strange form, he said, had appeared to him on a garden walk. It tried to utter some words : the light was

good, he could not have been deceived.   Next day he adhered
to his story   He was advised to go back again to the spot.
He did so.   The form again appeared at the same place.   It
spoke.   It was the form of a relation who was abroad in some
distant place.   A ship had gone down at sea , he (the relation)
had been lost.   There was a sum of money owing to some
person : the form had come to ask that this money might be
paid ; that was all.   Months later came the news of shipwreck.

My father had lived too in the time of Napoleon Bonaparte,
and of that still more successful warrior, King George the
Fourth, whose charge at Waterloo, when Prince Regent, as is
well known, had smashed the French army to pieces.   Of this
last hero he (my father) had seen something : he saw the First
Gentleman of Europe standing up in his carriage, either in
College Green or at the Curragh—a cap of green velvet with a
long gold tassel on his royal head, and a tumbler of hot whisky
punch in his royal hand, pledging the health of his true and
loving Irish subjects with whom he had determined to spend
the remaining days of his life.   I will not here indulge in any
speculations as to what the course of history might have been
had this royal intention been carried out.

I was never told, nor do I know to this day, how it had
happened that our family had been able to hold on to Ballycarron through all the vicissitudes of the Penal times.   So
long as a Stuart was on the throne they had friends of some
sort at Court ; but after the accession of the House of Hanover
the family anxieties must have been considerable.   Among the
fourteen main clauses of confiscation and persecution in the
penal code, there were at least three which must have made
the life of a Catholic gentleman in the eighteenth century a
very doubtful blessing, and a most precarious possession.

11. Any Protestant seeing a Catholic tenant at will on a
farm, which in his opinion yielded one-third more than the
annual rent, might enter on that farm, and by simply swearing
to the fact, take possession of it.

14 Any Catholic gentleman's child who became a Protestant
could at once take possession of and assume title to his father's
property.

7. Any two justices of the peace could call any man over
sixteen years of age before them, and if he refused to abjure

the Catholic religion, they could bestow his property on the Protestant next of kin.

With provisions of spoliation such as these, and there were many more of similar impact, making, every morning, poverty a 'possible contingency' before evening, the lives of some of my progenitors in Ballycarron must have been somewhat Damoclesian ; but Nature has many ways of correcting the errors of the law-maker, and no doubt she used them at this period along the winding river. The habit of seeking wives near at hand had caused a very numerous cousinship to spring up in the valley of the Suir. One mile down the river there resided, sometime about the year 1750, a certain 'Mosh' or Tom Butler, of desperate fighting tenacity. Tradition said that he was always ready to fight anybody , but the descendant of a Cromwellian settler had ever first claim on him, and the great duel between him and one Sadler at a place called Ock-na-Gore (the ford of the goat), close by where I am now writing, was a favourite subject for spirited recital by elderly black-smith folk and old fishermen along the river when I was a boy. Large crowds had assembled to see the fight. The point of the story was that Sadler was reputed to wear under his clothes a suit of chain mail, impervious to the bullet of that time. In loading the pistols, 'Mosh's' second contrived to insert a silver coin as the wad between the powder and the bullet. The word was given ; the combatants fired Sadler was seen to wince ; 'Mosh' was untouched : the seconds declared themselves satisfied. Both combatants mounted their horses to return to their respective homes, but when Sadler reached the ford at the little stream of the Fidogtha, and his horse bent its head to drink, somebody observed blood running down the leg of Sadler and into his boot. Examination could no longer be deferred ; but while preparations were being made for it the Cromwellian champion fell from his horse, and then there was found outside his net of steel a flattened bullet, and inside the mailed shirt a small incised wound, through which the silver coin had found its way into a vital spot. The old blacksmith, who used to love to relate this story and many others of a similar kind, was a philosopher of no mean contemplative power ; and often when pursuing some train of thought he would sum up the lost Cause by carrying it into the other world, and he would suddenly ask me such a question as, ' Where 's Cromwell now ? ' or, ' Where 's Ireton to-day ? ' I was always careful not to anticipate the supreme point by giving direct answer to his question ; but I would just say, ' Where ? ' Then his eyes would flash like the sparks from his own anvil. ' I 'll tell ye,' he would cry. ' He 's where he could kindle his pipe with his elbow.' Then there was nothing more to be said.

By means of a cousinship of the kind exemplified by ' Mosh,' and a numerous family of the O'Doherty clan, a member of which had moved into Tipperary from Innistown towards the close of the seventeenth century (whose son married a Butler of Ballycarron early in the eighteenth century), the eleven hundred acres that lay within the town-lands of the winding river had remained tolerably secure throughout three hundred years of penal confiscation.

It was about 1778 that Catholics were given the legal right to hold estates. Through the same relaxation of the penal codes during the American War a large number of these fighting cousins found their way into the army.

Some half-dozen of those family feudatories appear in the Army List of the end of the eighteenth century—one of them Colonel Richard O'Dogherty in the 69th Regiment of Foot, which regiment he saved from capture by the French in 1795. A nephew of this man, another Richard, got a commission about ten years later ; but his name appears as ' Doherty '—the ' O' ' and the ' g ' omitted. What 's in a name ? A good deal, sometimes. Richard had a brother Theobald, who also got a commission in the 40th Regiment after the rupture of the Peace of Amiens. Theobald had a wellnigh unequalled fighting record : he fought at Roleia, Vimeira, Talavera, Busaco, Badajoz, Salamanca, Vittoria, Pyrenees, Orthes, and Toulouse. He only attained the rank of captain ; and he was compelled to leave the army years later because, under cir-cumstances of very gross provocation on the score of his religion, he had challenged a senior officer to fight a duel. The elder brother, Richard, saw active service only at Guadaloupe and Martinique : he had those two bars to his war medal against his younger brother's ten ; but he gave up his faith as well as the obnoxious ' O' ' before his name.

Nevertheless, to Richard I owe the fact that I was a soldier, and that I was posted to the 69th Regiment. I remember well a visit which I paid to this old kinsman in 1856 or 1857. I was under inspection. It was an anxious moment. He was reserved, graciously solemn, and of the type of veteran not uncommon at that time, but now rarely to be seen—the type of Gough, Napier, Harry Smith, and a dozen others. He wore a high black silk stock, behind the stiff shelter of which he seemed to be able at times to withdraw a good deal of the lower part of his face in order to regard me to greater advantage from the upper portion. But I anticipate by a few years, and I must go back to the years succeeding the great famine.

When things became financially safer, we boys were sent to school again—this time to Dublin, where, in a large house in Harcourt Street, once the residence of the notorious John Scott, first Earl of Clonmel, a Doctor James Quinn had established himself as president, assisted by a staff of teachers, nearly all of whom, like their chief, attained celebrity as bishops in the colonial ecclesiastical world. I often wondered in after life how the balance of the account lay, between the loss of school education caused by those famine years, and the gain of that other lesson of life—its necessities, its sorrows, its hard bed-rock facts which that terrible time had implanted in my mind. In particular there was one scene in the theatre of that time which did more, I think, to shape the course of thought than years of study could have done.

One day I was taken by my father to the scene of an eviction on that road of which I have already spoken as being so full of the cottages and cabins of the people who were called cottiers—peasants with three or four acre plots of land. I have never forgotten the pity of that day. On one side of the road was a ruined church, the mounds of an old graveyard, and a few of those trees which never seemed to grow any larger but remained stunted and ragged deformities, nibbled at by goats below and warped by storms above, and left to find voice for the wind as it whistled through them ; on the other side, and beyond the old church, stood some dozen houses which were to be pulled down on this day, and their denizens evicted. At this time the weakening effects of the famine were still painfully evident in the people, and the spirit of opposition which in after years was to become so strong was not in being. The sheriff, a strong force of police, and above all the crowbar brigade—a body composed of the lowest and most debauched ruffians—were present.

At a signal from the sheriff the work began. The miserable inmates of the cabins were dragged out upon the road ; the thatched roofs were torn down and the earthen walls battered in by crowbars (practice had made these scoundrels adepts in their trade) ; the screaming women, the half-naked children, the paralysed grandmother, and the tottering grandfather were hauled out. It was a sight I have never forgotten. I was twelve years old at the time ; but I think if a loaded gun had been put into my hands I would have fired into that crowd of villains, as they plied their horrible trade by the ruined church of Tampul-da-voun (the church of the east window).

Singularly enough, it fell out that, after twenty-five years, I should meet at Highclere an ex-colonial governor who had filled many positions of trust and authority in his day—Sir Arthur Kennedy. He had been in early life one of the Famine Commissioners in the County Clare, and not the least tragically interesting in the gloomy Blue Book which has collected the reports of these officers throughout Ireland are the reports sent in by the then Captain Arthur Kennedy of his experiences in Western Clare during the famine years.

One day the conversation turned upon Ireland and the Irish famine. Something was said which caused the old veteran's face to flush. Turning full towards his host he said, ' I can tell you, my lord, that there were days in that western county when I came back from some scene of eviction so maddened by the sights of hunger and misery I had seen in the day's work that I felt disposed to take the gun from behind my door and shoot the first landlord I met.' ' Strong words, Sir Arthur,' was all that the then Colonial Secretary could say. ' Not stronger, my lord, than were my feelings at that time,' answered the old soldier.

While I was at school in Dublin the Crimean War began ; and as the regiments in garrison were all sent to the East, their departure for the seat of war was an event of great interest to the schoolboys. Daily we used to accompany some regiment of horse or foot, cheering them as they marched through the streets. In one of these infantry regiments there marched a subaltern officer who was afterwards destined to rise to great distinction, and with whose career I was in after life to have the honour of being associated on many occasions.

In the *Story of a Soldier's Life*, Lord Wolseley has graphically described the departure of his regiment, the 90th, from Dublin ; the scenes of the streets ; and the sympathy of the men and women with the eight or nine prisoners who were under his charge as subaltern officer of the day. ' Many purses were handed to them, and they had a real ovation. I found myself the centre of a crowd that regarded me as a jailer. " Poor boys ! " I heard on every side, whilst men and women scowled upon me. They (the prisoners) were assumed to be England's enemies because thus guarded, so of course they became the heroes, the dear friends of the Dublin rabble.' For my part, I have found this feeling of sympathy with prisoners a very general one through the world, and I do not think that human nature has any reason to be ashamed of it. Nor is the sentiment of sympathy, even when it is misdirected, peculiar to the people of Ireland I remember once seeing a naval picket in Plymouth carrying, or endeavouring to carry, a very turbulent sailor to his ship. A crowd of women were following the cortège, and cries of ' Ah ! don't hurt the pore sailor ! ' were frequent. As the picket passed, I noticed that the ' pore sailor ' had got the petty officer's thumb into his mouth and was vigorously engaged in the attempt to chew it off, but the greatly suffering petty officer had no pity expressed for him. Here undoubtedly was a case of sympathy so misdirected that there was not even a rule of thumb about it.

The Crimean War was over before I left school. A short interval of aimless expectation followed it. My father was not keen that his son should enter a profession in which the disadvantage of the absence of money could only be overcome by the surrender of one's religion—for that at least was the lesson which the cases of his relatives in the army had taught him.

In June 1857 came the news of the Indian Mutiny. I have already spoken of a visit paid to the old kinsman, Sir Richard Doherty, and of ' the inspection ' then undergone. It appears to have been tolerably satisfactory, because not long afterwards a letter arrived from him to my father enclosing a communication from the Military Secretary, nominating me to a direct commission without purchase. In July 1858 I passed the qualifying examination at Old Burlington House, and on the 17th of the following September was gazetted ensign in the 69th Regiment, the corps which had been saved from capture by the French through the instrumentality of another Richard O'Dogherty some sixty-three years earlier. My new corps was stationed in Burmah, and its dépôt was at Fermoy, in the County Cork, some forty miles at the other side of the Galtee Mountains. At that time there was no railway to this military station, so I proceeded thither by a roundabout journey on a long-car which ran from Kilmallock to it through a wild hilly country dividing the valley of the Blackwater River from the waters flowing into the Shannon and the Suir. It was a dull November evening, the 17th, as we reached Fermoy. I carried a letter from Sir Richard Doherty to the commandant of the dépôt battalion — a Colonel Egerton, who had once been my venerable cousin's adjutant. There is a certain aspect of awe about the interior of a barracks when it is entered by a young officer for the first time ; and the square of the old barracks at Fermoy made no exhilarating-looking picture as it appeared to me in the gloom of a damp November evening when I made my way across it to the house of the colonel commanding. But how kind and bright was my reception at the hands of Colonel Egerton and his wife ! I was to come and lunch with them the next day. I was to dine at the mess that evening just as I was. The colonel took me himself to the officer commanding my dépôt, and then I went back to the little hotel to get ready for the mess dinner.

Ensign W. F. Butler.
At the age of twenty on joining the Service in 1858.

CHAPTER II

I HAD had but little acquaintance with the world up to this time. Fifty years ago boys were very far removed from the intercourse with older persons which is now so common among them. The thing, therefore, that struck me most strongly was the kind and familiar manner with which I was treated from the first moment of joining at Fermoy. Nearly all the older officers had seen service in the Crimean War, which was then only a recent event. The majority of them were splendid fellows ; that long siege had been a wonderful school for the forming of manly characters. They had a type and manner of their own   Their hair was not cut short, as in the present day, but was worn long over the ears , and they had large fuzzy whiskers, with moustaches that went straight into them. They smoked much, and some of them drank a good deal , but they carried their liquor well, as it used to be said. There were the dépôts of six different regiments in the battalion—two companies from each regiment (twelve in all on parade), with a colonel, two majors, an adjutant, and quartermaster specially attached as battalion officers. Some of the captains had been promoted from the ranks for distinguished conduct on the field. The colonel, Isaac Moore, had risen from the ranks. He was an old officer, with the profile of an eagle, the voice of a Stentor, and a heart of great goodness. He was exceedingly strict on all matters of duty, a splendid drill after the manner of the time, and he rarely left the barracks except to take the battalion out to the drill field. His pronunciation of some military words was peculiar. He was warned not to exert his voice too much on parade, but he persisted in giving the long-drawn-out cautionary commands of the old Peninsular drill days, such as, ' The battalion will change front by the wheel and countermarch of subdivisions round the centre ' ;

15

following it in lower key by, ' Close up the suppernomerrary ranks ', then, louder than ever, ' Right subdivisions right about face, the whole right wheel ' ; and ending by a ' Quick march ' that could be heard in the town square at the foot of the barracks hill. One day, after one of these excessive throat exercises, the old man was seen to lean forward upon the neck of his old horse, and they carried him to his quarters to die. He had burst a blood-vessel in the lungs.

The soldiers of the different dépôts could be divided into two absolutely distinct lots : about half were old soldiers finishing their twenty-one years' service, the others were young recruits who had recently joined. The difference between these two divisions was as the difference between a sixteen-hands trained hunter and the pony of a costermonger. The Crimean War had virtually put an end for ever to the old army. Here were the few survivors of that unequalled infantry which had carried Wellington from Vimeira to Waterloo, whose ' charging shouts ' had been heard on fifty European and Asiatic battle-fields. More than half of them were Irish, no matter what might be the county title borne by the regiment to which they belonged.

I was soon established in the old barracks, being duly drilled in the balance step without gaining ground, the manual and platoon exercises, the science of turning, wheeling, and moving in file, in sections, and in subdivisions ; until at the end of three or four months I was dismissed drill and declared a fit and proper person to command a company on parade. When that event took place, I was able to resume many of the sports and pastimes of the old home life. The Blackwater was noted as a salmon river, and its numerous tributary streams, Funcheon, Araglin, and Bride, were famous trout streams

In May 1859 a General Election took place. A riot in Limerick having led to some trouble between the mob and the police, which had ended by the police firing upon the mob, an urgent call for military assistance was received one evening, and two hundred men were told off to proceed next morning to Limerick. The 13th and 68th Light Infantry Regiments supplied the entire portion of the detail, being mostly composed of old soldiers. It was a source of great satisfaction to me to find myself selected, by the captain of the 13th Regiment who commanded the party, for duty with his detachment. We marched to Buttevant the first day—a longish march of about sixteen Irish miles ; and got to Limerick the next day. Our work was to guard the approaches to the courthouse where the polling was carried on, and to prevent the mob from storming that edifice. The supporters of the obnoxious candidate had to be protected through the streets ; for those were the days of what is called open voting, and the free and independent electors were marched, under escort of horse, foot, and dragoons, to register their votes by order of their landlords. There were a few broken heads ; but, on the whole, the mob and the soldiers got on remarkably well. The ladies of the town came up with the most delightful freedom of expression to the line of soldiers which had closed across the streets after a batch of terrified voters had been got through from an outside wilderness of screams, and mud and stone throwing. Then the chaff would begin on the part of the ladies—any officer or soldier of exceptional size or feature being especially selected for the tongue target. The old soldiers looked stolidly out upon the viragoes, though one could see at times in their eyes that some shaft of ridicule, which usually took the form of a remark addressed by one virago to another, had struck home.

From Limerick we were marched to Ennis, where another contested election was being fought on similar lines of mud, mischief, and drunkenness, to all of which the simple adoption of the ballot by our sapient legislators would have put an immediate end.

When we got back to Fermoy early summer was over all the land, and the valley of the Blackwater was in radiant beauty. One evening I set out from barracks to fish for trout in the Funcheon, where it enters the Blackwater. Passing from the junction along the larger river until opposite the old house of Careysville, I saw the rise of a salmon in the centre of the river. I had a salmon fly among the trout flies, and I took off the trout cast and put my single salmon fly on the trout tackle. The near half of the river was shallow at this place, so I was able to wade until I came within casting distance of where the salmon had risen. I threw the fly on the spot, and in an instant my little trout rod was bent nearly double by the weight of the fish. I played him at first from the

B

shallow where I was standing, expecting every moment to smash rod, line, and wheel ; but luck was on my side   Nothing broke, and in ten minutes or so my fish was boring quietly in some deeper water nearer shore.   Then I waded back to the bank, and getting his head down stream, took him down to where an eddying backwater, close under the bank, had collected on the surface of the water a lot of white foam.   Into this little circular pool I steered my salmon.   I had no gaff, and he lay just beneath the surface.   I could see that he was no small fish, but a salmon of ten or eleven pounds.   What was to be done ?   No one was near to help   I had a pocket-knife of ordinary size with me.   I opened its larger blade, got down to the lower ledge of turf close by the pool, and as the now tired fish came slowly round in the eddy and the foam, close against the bank, I struck the little knife with my right full into his shoulder, holding the rod in my left hand bent in towards the shore.   The fish gave one great plunge ; but the blow was straight and sure, and I found that my stroke had pinned him against the bank.   Then, dropping the rod from my left hand, I got my fingers under the gills and lifted the salmon safely in to the shore.   He was a beautiful fresh-run fish.   I got back to the mess as the long June evening was closing—wet, tired, but very proud of my feat ; and as the dépôt battalion had many good anglers among its numbers, I had to go through the scene in the ante-room with all the original paraphernalia of the performance shown in action.

There was an old captain of the 95th Regiment in the battalion who had his quarters on the opposite side of the passage where I lived—Captain Robert Weild—'Old Bob Weild,' as he was popularly called amongst us youngsters. He was a very quaint specimen of a soldier now quite extinct. He drank a good deal, and smoked pipes of many kinds and colours   He spoke the broadest Lowland Scotch.   He took a fancy to me, and would often come into my room with his long cherry-stick pipe and sit smoking at the fire and telling me of his early life and former service   He was a native of the town of Wigtown, where his father had been the principal baker, and young Bob's business had been to deliver the bread through the town.   He preferred to try his fortune as a soldier, and enlisted in the 95th Regiment   He went to the

Crimea as a colour-sergeant, was at Alma and Inkermann, and did his full share of trench service. One day a round-shot hopped over the parapet and struck Colour-Sergeant Weild in the chest. Fortunately a wave of wind which came a little in front of the ball had turned the man slightly on one side, so that the mass of iron only carried away two or three ribs, laying bare the heart below them. To all appearances he was killed; but there was a spark of life still left in him: the heart had not been actually touched. ' As they were carrying me back through the trenches,' he used to say, ' we met a surgeon who had a well-filled box of medical comforts, and the first thing this good fellow did was to empty a pint of strong brandy down my throat; that kept the heart going and saved my life.' It must be said that old Bob never forgot the liquid to which he owed his salvation. Sometimes he would stay late in the little club at the foot of the barracks hill, and as I would be crossing the square to the mess, I would encounter my old friend making the best of his way from the gate to his quarters, walking straight to the front, but gazing at the ground with a fixed stare and an expression in his eye that told me it would not be safe to speak a single word to him. He had taken his line from the gate, and he was steering for his door upon a mental compass bearing so fine that the smallest whisper might have deranged it. On other occasions we passed each other like ships in the night. Orders for India came in the early summer of 1860, and we went our several ways—old Weild to India, I to Burmah. Six months later I heard of his death in Central India.

I was very active in those days. A month before we started for the East there were foot races in Limerick, where I won the two hundred and fifty yards hurdle race against the south of Ireland garrison.

Our 69th draft—three officers and one hundred and twenty men—embarked at Queenstown in the ship *Coldstream* for Madras in July 1860. There were also in this little vessel of eight hundred tons sixty men of the Royal Irish Regiment and three officers After a delay of three days in Queenstown Harbour, for laying in provision for a long voyage, we were towed out beyond the mouth of the harbour and cast off. It blew a stiff gale that night, and we kept plunging into a heavy head sea, for land was on the lea and there was no sea room. It was the 11th of July, a Wednesday ; I remember the day of the week because from the midday of that Wednesday to the evening of the following Sunday no food passed my lips. I was then nearly dead of starvation.   For one hundred and twenty-four days we continued to crawl over the ocean, and in those four months saw but two specks of land— Madeira, and St. Paul's Island in the Southern Indian Ocean.   We lay becalmed in the vicinity of the equator for three weeks.   The drinking water was horrible — the colour of weak tea and with a taste that was nauseating.   It had first rotted in the barrels, then fermented, and after it had gone through that cleansing process it was declared to be wholesome.   Bad as it was, the men became mutinous because they could not get enough of it to satisfy their thirst when we were lying becalmed in the tropics.   After some forty days we caught the south-east trade winds and shaped a course towards the coast of South America ; then by Tristan da Cunha, which was hidden in dense masses of clouds ; and round the Cape of Good Hope, but some four hundred miles to the south of it.   Here, towards the end of September, we entered upon a vast ocean of gigantic rollers, a grey limitless waste of waters that came surging after us in stupendous billows as though they would overwhelm the little speck of ship that carried us.   Vast flocks of sea-birds circled high above our masts.

The captain was a most excellent man ; the crew of twenty-nine hands were strong and fearless fellows.   It was often a splendid sight to see them aloft, double reefing topsails on a night of storm and lightning in the Southern Indian Ocean— black darkness everywhere, then a flash lighting up the deck, masts, and spars, and showing the black specks aloft in the rocking rigging, clewing in the flapping canvas to the topsail yards.

We kept night-watch like the crew, and wretched work it was ; the ship leaked badly from the beginning, but it was only when the stormy southern latitudes were reached that the leakage became really serious.   The ship was then making several inches of water every hour.   We had one pump near the mainmast on the quarter-deck ; and it used to take the men of the watch, with the pump handles fully manned, a full hour's hard work before the water was got out of the vessel. Three times in the night this work went on. The soldiers hated it so much that it was no easy matter to get them up from the lower deck out of their hammocks to the wet and slippery quarter-deck.

With the sergeant of the watch one had to creep along the odour-reeking deck under the hammocks, shouting, and often unslinging the hammock lines before the men would turn out Then, when the handles were manned, they would vent their ill-humour upon the wretched pump by working it like demons up and down—until the captain, hearing the banging, would rush out from his cabin behind the little ' cuddy ' vociferating to the men that if they broke the pumps the ship would sink in thirty hours. This miserable work went on until the ship's course was turned northwards from the little island of St. Paul's, and as smoother latitudes were gained the leakage lessened. We did not know then, but it was afterwards discovered, what was the cause of the leakage. The ship was carrying a very dangerous cargo, and one that should have made it impossible for her owners to obtain a commission for the carriage of troops—railroad iron. She had six hundred tons of iron rails down below the other ordinary cargo. It was this dead solid weight that had caused her timbers to open in the gale and heavy seas into which we plunged the night after leaving Ireland. Fortunately the rent was just at or above the water-line, so when the sea was fairly smooth the intake of water was small , but whenever bad weather came, and the vessel's bows went down into the waves, the water came in in quantities, and for six hours in the twenty-four the men were at the pumps. There was no Plimsoll in those days : the shipowners could do as they pleased , and a five-pound note placed in the palm of an inspector between decks by the agent from the office in Leadenhall Street could lighten the duties of inspection and remove many doubts and difficulties.

My kit was a small one, but I had managed to include in it one box of books, and I was able to borrow other works from brother officers on board. I read a great deal in the long weary months, sailing the great circle to India.

In a little book which I wrote more than forty years ago, subsequent to that voyage, I was comparing the sailing ship of the old bygone times with the steamers of to-day, and I wrote that it was then 'the great circle, but now it was the short cut.' A London literary review, with the well-known infallibility of the editorial armchair, which embraces everything in knowledge from a needle to an anchor, pointed out that I was in error, inasmuch as 'the great circle' and 'the short cut' were synonymous expressions. But he forgot that we were dealing with sailing ships, and that the trade wind was the chief factor concerned in the question. From England to India by the short cut via the Cape is about ten thousand miles ; but no sailing ship attempting that passage in the teeth of the trade wind could get to its destination under a term of years. The great circle, which the sailing vessels still follow *en route* to India—making a fair wind of the south-east trade by running towards the coast of South America from the Line and thence, before the powerful western winds, by Tristan da Cunha to St. Paul's and Amsterdam Islands, where they turn north for India—is some eight or nine thousand miles longer in distance, although it saves many months in time.

Now and again on that long voyage we had some incidents that gave us, at least, a subject for conversation at the little 'cuddy' table where we gathered for meals. One morning, in the early watch, strange sounds were heard as of some one singing under the bottom of the ship. No one could locate the sound. It was fitful and indistinct, hilarious and despondent by turns. Men looked at each other. At last the morning roll was called, and it was found that there was a man missing. All the decks were searched, the cook's galley, the long-boat, where the six or eight sheep and the dozen pigs were, and the forecastle wherein the crew had their bunks—no man could be found ; but still the mysterious sounds rose at intervals. At length it was discovered that a person looking down the square hole through which the long chain cable was passed into its box below, could hear the strange noise with greater distinctness than elsewhere in the ship. This discovery soon solved the mystery : the missing man was far down in the chain locker. Some one descended the shaft. A very fat soldier was found near the bottom of the aperture, stretched upon some cargo in the hold. Fresh discoveries followed. The captain and the mate descended. From where the fat man was found a track led over piles of general cargo to a bulkhead, which was directly under the stern part of the ship. This bulkhead had had a hole cut through it into the spirit-room. This hole passed through, a still stranger sight was revealed : many cases of gin and other strong spirits, which had been destined for the consumption of Asiatic committees in general, were found opened and rifled , a comfortable straw-lined tap-room was next found among the cases, and many small candle ends, some of which, in lieu of candlesticks, had been stuck on to the ship's side, the timbers of which the lighted candles had in many places charred. Here had been the chosen meeting-place of a select few among the crew and soldiers. Night after night those faithful fellows had descended the chain locker and sought the seclusion of this spirituous paradise. At last, in a happy moment for the remainder of the uninitiated, the fat soldier was bidden to the feast. He had descended easily ; but when the hour came for reascending to the cold upper world, either his size or the quantity of liquor he had swallowed prevented the ascension. His companions could not drag him up the locker, and he had to be left at its base : elation or terror did the rest. The fatness of this particular male siren had probably saved the good ship *Coldstream* from a fate worse than any shipwreck ; and the hardest part of the thing was that he was the sole man of the wrong-doers whom it was possible to punish. Instead of being the recipient of many Humane Society's medals for saving the lives of about two hundred and fifty human beings, he spent the greater portion of the remainder of the voyage in leg-irons.

At daybreak on 2nd November land was in sight. We had been heading for it a day or two before, and there it was at last —a low coast beaten by a white surf, fringes of palm-trees, some white houses, and a range of hills beyond the Coromandel coast. Some forty miles north of Madras we anchored in the open roadstead of that town about noon. A high surf was running, and only a naked Catamaran man on his three logs lashed together could come out to us with letters and orders carried in his skull cap of oiled wicker work. After three or four days' rolling and pitching at anchor we were allowed to land, and when evening came we all marched to a place called Poonamallee, about twelve miles west of Madras. Everything was new and strange to us—the people, the trees, the fireflies in the bamboo hedges, the cicadas in the feathery palmtrees, the bull-frogs in the grassy fields, the endless multiplication of life human and animal everywhere to be seen, heard, or felt. Poonamallee was a delightful old cantonment, built in the days of Clive or earlier—an old semicircular messhouse with mango-trees surrounding it, and a broad verandah raised two feet above the ground, supported along its outer edge by pillars of snow-white ' chunam '; three hundred yards away a Moorish fort with a broad ditch around it full of bull-frogs; and beyond it the village or town of Poonamallee, a very extraordinary assemblage of Hindoo temples and houses, the former representing, with an effrontery not to be abashed, the lower and most disreputable lines of the Hindoo worship.

This old dépôt station was commanded by one of the most interesting veterans it was ever my good fortune to meet in life — Colonel Impett, formerly of the 71st Foot, in which regiment he had fought at Waterloo. He was now in his sixtieth year, tall and spare, the most lovable old soldier who ever drew to him the heart of man or woman. What days I had listening to this man ! After Waterloo he had marched to Paris, when he was not yet fifteen ; then later he went to Canada. He had been at Fermoy in the 'twenties, and now for thirty years his service had been wholly in India. Before I was a week at Poonamallee he had taken me out to shoot snipe with him in the paddy fields, five miles from the station. In the gharry going to and coming from the ground, and in drives to and from Madras, he often used to speak about his early experiences—particularly of the day at Waterloo. He was given a commission at either Eton or Harrow, and had been hurried out to Belgium in the spring of 1815 to join his regiment there cantoned—part of that vast force of about a million men which those brave fellows, the kings and emperors of Europe, had gathered round the French frontiers to fight the single soldier whose army two months earlier had numbered a bare five hundred all told. He described the repeated charges of the French cavalry upon his regiment in square on the windy slope of the ridge behind the hollow road that ran from La Haye Sainte. When night fell the wearied men, already half asleep, lay down where they stood. Impett caught a black horse which passed by without a rider ; he tied the rein to his wrist, and then sank into a deep sleep. When he awoke in the early June dawn, the horse was gone. ' It was a lump and a line all day,' he said : ' a lump to resist the cavalry, a line to avoid the havoc wrought by the round-shot.' That was certainly a baptism of fire for a boy of fourteen.

Many incidents of lesser interest in his life he used to speak about in those little shooting excursions—of days camped on an island in Georgian Bay, Lake Huron, fishing and deer hunting, of long walks in the mountains I had lately left near Fermoy. One day, in a glen somewhere in those hills, he and his companion, Captain Markham, a noted shot, came upon a still in full work. No information was given to the excise officers in the town, and a couple of weeks later Markham and Impett found a small keg of poteen whisky laid outside the door of their rooms in the old barracks.

After two or three months in Poonamallee the draft moved on to Burmah by steamer from Madras. We touched at several ports on the east side of the Bay of Bengal. Boats carrying fruits and lunka cheroots surrounded the vessel at one of these places. After a time many men were found to be drunk on board ; this was strange, because care had been taken to prevent the bringing of spirits on board. But the attack usually beats the defence. We found on close examination that the oranges in many cases had a small round hole drilled in the rind, through which the juice of the fruits had been extracted and the vacuum filled in with arrack, the rind plug being again inserted.

In due time we reached Rangoon, and shortly afterwards we embarked in Burmese boats for the Pegu River, and marched thence across the twenty miles of low-lying jungle and high, grass-covered waste which divided the Pegu River from the larger Sittang.

A very perfect pagoda, one of the loftiest and most gracefully tapering structures of the kind in Burmah, lifts its ' thay ' of many bells three hundred feet and more above this wilderness of grass. Our camp was at the base of this beautiful object,

now the sole survivor of everything that had made Pegu one
of the greatest cities of the East in the early days of Portuguese
commercial enterprise. It was not easy to look up at this
glittering musical spire in the hot glare of daylight ; but when
evening was closing over the landscape, which everywhere
showed evidences of ruin and retrogression, the eyes were
instinctively drawn upwards to this triple tiaraed crown of
tinkling bells, whose lark-like music fell soft as dew through
the cooling air. Gone was everything else of that once proud
kingdom of Pegu ; this, the work of some old Buddhist saint
or hero, was left alone with its own music in the wilderness.

We marched at night across the twenty miles of grass and
jungle, and at a spot called Khyatsoo, on the Sittang, found a
flotilla of boats ready to embark us for a long journey of twenty
days up that river. The wide river was here still subject to
the tide, which at times forms a ' bore ' of a very dangerous
character. A few years earlier the entire half-battalion of a
native infantry regiment, with all its officers, baggage, etc.,
had been swamped near this place by the tidal wave—the
' Caligima Yeh,' the bad water of the Burmese. We soon
passed the wide, tidal part of the river, and entered the narrower
stream, which was still high and turbid after the monsoon rains.
At first the strangeness of the scene, and above all the boats
and boatmen, gave occupation to the mind. The boats were
of a shape and structure unlike any other craft in the world :
about twelve feet of the stern end of the boat was thatched
with strong reeds, the remainder of the boat was open, the
stern sloped high above the water, and at its extreme end
a high wooden chair gave the steersman a lofty seat, from which
he was able to move a big spoon-shaped oar, by a simple turn
of his hand, to the right or left. He thus looked over the
thatched cabin and well beyond the bows and the bamboo
platform from which the crew worked the boat. The crew of
four men took it in turns to propel the boat with long poles,
which they worked by going forward to the bow, placing the
pole against the hollow of the shoulder, and in this bending
position walking down the narrow bamboo platform to the
thatched cabin ; then, releasing the poles from the bottom,
they went back again to the bow to repeat the toilsome journey.
The current, swollen by the rains, ran strong, and during quite

half of the day the boat was brushing against the tall reeds that covered the banks, sometimes on one side of the river, sometimes on the other. One would have thought that after their long work at this laborious poling, the men would have been glad to lie down to rest when we tied up at night against the bank; but that they seldom or never did When the rice was boiled and eaten play of some sort began, and often in the grey morning light I have looked out from under the thatched roof of the boat and seen the crew still hard at work at cards, or stones, or some queer game of chequers. In the damp fog which then hung over shore and river, they would get up from the little fire by which they had squatted all night, unfasten their 'loongies,' and take a plunge in the yellow waters of the river, diving about like ducks, and coming up wet and glistening to resume the long bamboo poles for the day.

Our average rate of progress was about ten miles a day. Now and again the boat would tie up a little earlier than usual, or the pace would be arranged so as to arrive at some village where a ' pooay ' or play was going on in celebration of a local marriage or funeral.

At some of the larger villages a peculiar smell would manifest itself when the cooking hour arrived : this was caused by the preparation or consumption of the celebrated Burmese delicacy known as ' Napee.' As the river was now falling quickly, these napee nights became more frequent, because the time had come to unearth the deposits of fish, buried in the sandbanks of the river before the torrential rains of the monsoon began to fill its wide bed. A deep pit is dug in the sand and filled with fish of many kinds , the sand is pressed down upon the mass of fish , a long pole is driven into the bar to mark the spot. The river rises, and water overflows the cache for six months ; then, when the waters subside, the cache is dug up, a terribly pungent effluvium is evolved from the opened pit, and the napee is carried off by the villagers to be eaten as a special delicacy during the next twelve months. The traveller is conscious of a napee night while he is yet at a considerable distance from the place of entertainment. But, after all, has not man, even in his most civilised state, some bonne-bouche of this kind—a venerable Stilton, a mite-riddled Roquefort, a semi-liquefied Camembert ?

After three long weeks of this slow travel our boats reached . the bank of the river at the top of which stood Tonghoo. We had been twenty-one days doing these two hundred miles ; but at the end of these three weeks one had gained a knowledge of Burmese life, labours, and manners which was an asset of much use to one in many ways.

At this station of Tonghoo I found my regiment, the 69th. They had been here more than three years—one might say buried in the Burman forest, for communication was at that time so tedious that a letter took two and a half months to come from London, and a voyage by the long sea route was, as we have just seen, a matter of about six months' actual travel.

Under conditions of life such as these, rust of mind and body must be the prevailing features of European life. The seasons, too, helped the distance and environment. Tonghoo led to no place ; it was the end of the track . beyond and on every side was forest. This month of February was the middle of the dry season. In three months the clouds would sweep up over the tree-tops from the sea, and in terrific thunder and lightning the ball of the monsoon would open. Then for nearly six months it would not be possible to stir beyond the roads of the cantonment. All the forest would be a swamp ; the river, which was now thirty feet down in its channel, would be running level with the tops of the banks ; the bull-frogs would croak outside every compound ; and all the creeping things that love heat and damp—scorpions, centipedes, huge spiders, strange lizards, beetles, cobras, and pythons— would hold general carnival.

With these climatic conditions in view, it became necessary to do something in the way of exploring the surrounding country in the next couple of months, while the forest tracks could still be travelled by a pony. Once the monsoon began, only the elephant could manage to plough through the deep black mud. Daily rides were therefore taken in many directions. Tonghoo, like all Burmah, has had better days. A huge walled city had been once here ; the rectangular wall, measuring one mile on each face, alone remained with its enormous ditch, now a jungle-grown swamp. Inside this great brick wall, which was thirty feet thick, a little wicker town of bamboo and rushes occupied about a twelfth part of the original city site. The pagoda again remained the sole remnant of the old glory, and a beautiful pagoda it was, though not equal to its Pegu rival. Beyond this great city wall spread mingled spaces of low jungle and paddy fields, all of which were now quite dry. As one galloped along the sandy jungle tracks there would open out at sudden intervals some little village scene— a dozen bamboo huts ; a small pagoda with its glistening spire ; a teak-wood rest-house for travellers ; a little Poongee monastery, the cocoa palms and mango-trees about it, and its shrine piled with little figures of Buddha, cross-legged and long-armed, with long pendent ears, and big dreamy eyes looking out upon a big dreamy world.

It would be impossible not to like the Burmese people— good-natured, nice-mannered, pleasant people. They never scowled at one nor shouted some unknown word of abuse ; they were glad to render any little service of the wayside without thought of ' backsheesh ' ; everybody smoked big cheroots made up in a large green leaf; everybody seemed happy.

But the life of the forest was the one I was most anxious to see ; and late in May I managed, in company with a brother officer, to induce the official in charge of the Forest Department to lend us three elephants (their purchase was quite beyond the reach of our subaltern purses), and loading these animals with our supplies, we sent them to a place some sixty miles south, there to await our arrival by boat This time the craft selected was a long ' dug-out ' canoe of teak wood. With ten or a dozen men paddling, we travelled by the light of a full moon, and went gaily down-stream, expecting to reach our landing-place by daylight, and to find the elephants awaiting us with our supplies, and breakfast ready. But it was noon before our destination was reached : there were no elephants, no food, no anything. We sat all day in a Burman bamboo hut, expecting that every hour would bring us refreshment. Evening came, still no food. Next day it was the same ; then hunger began to assert itself, for rice and napee were not encouraging, so my companion, who spoke a little Burmese, essayed to get a fowl in the village ; but the people were all good Buddhists, and no one would sell us a fowl, much less kill one. The day wore on, and we were becoming ravenous.

My friend sallied out again with his gun.   There was an old cock on the outskirts of the town, and this antiquated bird he was allowed to shoot   The woman of the house where we had taken up our abode plucked the bird in some form, and boiled it in an earthen vessel.   It was then served up half hot, but very tough.   I tried it, but had to forbear at the third bit ; my companion, with a braver digestion, performed an unhappy despatch upon his victim, while I looked on.   Just as the melancholy meal ended, I heard what seemed to be the solemn sound of the elephant bell in the neighbouring forest.   Yes, it was our belated beasts coming slowly into harbour with all our good things on board   That evening we went on about twelve miles into the forest to a place called Banloung, and camped there in absolute freedom—neither house nor village was near.   Some previous hunting party had put up a rude shelter of bamboos.   A lake close by had water ; round the lake there were large spaces free of forest.   We began to beat for big game next morning   It was a hunter's paradise : bits of high grass almost level with the shoulders of the elephants alternated with stretches of splendid forest ; there was low jungle, high jungle, and no jungle.   To these varied covers all sorts of animals had come—sambhur, bison, themming, and jumping deer.   It was often like rabbit shooting in bracken, only the rabbits were sometimes sixteen hands high, and the bracken six feet.   The themming were in grand herds in the open spaces, the old stags with heavy brow antlers always keeping on the outskirts of the herd.   We saw the tracks of many tigers, but the bodies of none—the cover was too dense. The monsoon broke while we were yet in the forest, and when we moved back the elephants had to swim across a dozen nullahs, which had been dry as dust a fortnight earlier.

The monsoon ran its dreary course during the next few months.   The rain pattered in big straight drops all night long upon the broad leaves of toddy palm and plantain, and the whole land was streaming and steaming with water. Everybody went to mess with lanterns carried in front, for snakes were very numerous, and they had a disagreeable habit of getting up from the wet lower ground on to the little raised tracks of brickwork which led from the bungalows to the mess-house.

Among the senior officers in the station there were some strange and interesting survivals of an earlier generation. At times, when the Madras troops paraded with our regiment, one occasionally heard strange words of command given to the brigade, such as, ' The brigade will prime and load.' All the drill formations were those which old Davy Dundas had designed in the days before the Peninsular War , and although the flint-lock musket had disappeared twenty years earlier, the recollection of its cumbersome processes of combustion still lingered among our seniors. All the same, they were fine old gentlemen, and it was to one of them that I am indebted for my first quasi-staff appointment.

The regiment was inspected in December 1861 by a medical officer of high degree, whose official report declared it to be suffering from a too prolonged sojourn in the enfeebling forests of Burmah, and who recommended its early removal to the drier climate of India Orders were received in January 1862 for our removal to Madras. The battalion was to descend the river in two separate bodies each of five companies. The old colonel who was to command the last of these detachments appointed me as the staff officer of the wing, and all at once I found myself adjutant, paymaster, and quartermaster of some four or five hundred men. A month later we moved in a great fleet of boats down the Sittang River. The water was now very low, and at one or two places elephants were used to shove with their heads the flat-bottomed boats over the sand-bars in the stream. Where the river ended and the estuary began we had some exciting experiences of the dreaded ' bore.' Our boatmen were fully prepared for it, and the boats were all taken out from the banks and anchored in mid-channel ; bow-men, crew, and steersman were all at their posts ; the ' Caligima Yeh ' was constantly uttered among them. After we had been some time thus moored a low noise became audible far down stream ; this sound gradually grew in depth and volume, but neither the water around our boats nor the reach of the river below us showed any sign of motion. The sound increased rapidly ; it was now coming to us across the neck of reed-covered land round which the river disappeared at the end of the last reach which our sight commanded. All at once a great white billow of water appeared, sweeping round this

neck of land. At the banks the splash of this white wave
rose several feet in the air ; but when the entire wave had
rounded the turn, one could see that in the central part of
the river the wave was comparatively low, yet all of it was
curling forward almost in a straight line up-stream. It struck
our boats full on the bows ; all of them rose well to the impact ;
but some were torn from their moorings, making confusion as
they ran amuck among the others. It was a fine sight—
the 'bore' itself, and the manner in which the boatmen bore
themselves.

The next night we marched across the low ground to Pegu.
At the moment of starting from Khyatsoo an incident occurred
which fortunately ended happily. A man of recalcitrant
character in the regiment, who had been a prisoner for some
time, refused to march. As I was acting as paymaster as well
as adjutant, the prisoners and the cash chest of the regiment
were in my charge. I had come to the guard to see the cash
chest safely put into a Burmese buffalo waggon, and the guard
and prisoners moved with it after the column. As the first
battalion was moving off, the prisoner in question suddenly
refused to budge. What was to be done ? The only course
possible was to tie him to the rear of the waggon ; he would
then have to march perforce. But in this arrangement the
buffaloes had not been reckoned with. These curious animals
have never taken to the English invaders. You will see a
small native boy leading or driving a pair of enormous blue
beasts with perfect command over them, but they will shy from,
and sometimes charge at, any European who may approach
them. On this occasion, no sooner was the word to march
given, than the buffaloes attached to our treasure waggon,
seeing that the other end of the waggon had an English soldier
attached to it, began to behave in a very excited manner ;
and to make matters worse, our prisoner still refused to march.
The only thing then to be done was to lift the man bodily
into the waggon, and put him in company with the cash chest.
This was done in a twinkling ; but now the buffaloes, growing
quite beyond control, started off across country over dry paddy
'bunds,' deep ruts, and many other obstacles. The guard was
quickly left behind ; the infuriated buffaloes, with their driver,
the waggon, the cash chest, the prisoner in tow, were careering

madly over the plain, making the most horrible noise possible
to imagine.　Being on horseback I was able to keep up with
this tornado ; and I could see that in the stampede the prisoner
and the regimental cash chest seemed to be having a tremendous boxing match in the interior of the conveyance, as they
were shot up and down and about by the incessant joltings
of this primitive vehicle.　The prisoner, as a light weight in
the contest, got a good deal the worst of it.　There was a hole
in the wicker bottom of the waggon, and at last the prisoner's
legs got into this opening, and the unequal fight was terminated
by his whole body following its legs through the aperture,
leaving the regimental cash chest alone in its glory.　The rope
which tied the prisoner to the waggon quickly ran its length,
and then he was dragged along the ground after the waggon
in a very alarming manner.　All I could do was to hack at
the ropes with my sword as I galloped along, and between the
cutting at the line and the strain upon it the man was soon set
free.　He was black, and bruised, and bleeding, but the first
words he uttered when the guard had overtaken us soon reassured me of his safety.　' I 'll march now,' he said.

About the beginning of spring the wing embarked at
Rangoon for Madras.

CHAPTER III

From Rangoon to Madras. A hurricane at sea. The Nilgherry Mountains.
The Carnatic Plain. The lives and thoughts of Eastern peoples. Leave
spent on the western coast.

WE were carried in two vessels—a steamer and a sailing ship,
the first towing the second. As my lot fell to the sailing vessel,
I will deal with it only. For two days all went well with us,
but on the morning of the third day a change began to show
itself in the aspects of sea and sky. A curious grey gloom
spread itself quickly over the circle of the ocean ; everything
became the same colour ; there was little or no wind, but the
still, unbroken surface heaved a little. This undulation grew
more perceptible as the morning passed, until it began to lift
our ship uneasily, and made her rise and fall upon the tow-line.
The barometer began to fall. Whatever it was, we appeared
to be going to meet it, and it seemed that it was coming to
meet us also. Our captain was a rather elderly man of the
Indian Marine Service, and he appeared to be suffering from
marked depression of spirits, which one of the junior officers
explained was the result of the death of a brother, who had
been drowned a couple of weeks earlier in the Rangoon River
through the upsetting of his boat as he was proceeding from
the shore to his ship lying in the river. During the two days
we had been on board he had kept to his cabin, and had not
taken his meals with us in the saloon. The second officer, a
gentleman named Salmon, impressed us all as being the
moving and governing spirit of the ship's company. These
latter were all Lascars from the Chittagong side of the Bay
of Bengal. They were a poor lot, but, so far, there was little
or no occasion for their services on the deck or aloft, nor did
it seem likely that there would be any ; all the sails were furled.
The chain cable had been left in great coils along the deck, for
the run across the Bay of Madras in the wake of the steamer

even at the slow rate of towing was not expected to occupy more than five or six days. The *Tubalcain*, as our ship was named, was an old and cranky craft, half transport, half warship. She mounted a couple of guns on the main-deck. The strong suns of the Bay of Bengal and the Persian Gulf had not improved the seaworthiness of her timbers.

At the head of the native crew there was a powerful and masterful-looking ' Syrang,' or mate of Lascars, in whom both European officers and Indian crew seemed to have complete confidence.

We passed the Cocos Channel between Burmah and the Andaman Islands, and were now well into the centre of the Bay of Bengal. Suddenly the gloomy murkiness of the sea and sky became lit to the westward with vivid lightnings, and the rumbles of an incessant thunder struck the ear , there was still hardly any wind, but hot puffs of storm came at intervals from ahead, ceasing as quickly as they arose. Then all at once a storm began, and a vast commotion manifested itself among the crew on deck. The motion of the ship on the tow-line had become more and more uneasy as the sea rose. All at once a big wave sprang like a panther upon the bows of the *Tubalcain*, scattered the Lascars that were on the forecastle, and jumped again into the sea, carrying with it our splendid Syrang. The Syrang swam bravely, and as he passed beneath the stern of the ship he caught at the log-line that was hanging from it, trailing in the wake of the vessel ; but the rate at which we were being towed, slow though it was, was too fast for the man to let him get a firm grip on the thin line, and it ran through his fingers to the end where the patent brass log was twirling like a fishing minnow ; that, of course, was impossible to hold, and we saw the poor fellow still swimming bravely on the tops of the waves behind us. There was a shout to cut the tow-line, but that could not be done without orders from the steamer, which all this time had been tugging us into the jaws of a hurricane, for that was what all this strange turmoil, and thunder, and gloom of the afternoon had really meant.

The captain of the steamer seemed now to realise what he was in for, for he shouted through a trumpet, ' I am throwing off the hawser,' and in a couple of minutes more we were separated from him. I shall never forget the look of things that evening when we found ourselves left alone in that deepening light and rising hurricane, as we saw our hitherto guide and leader steaming off into the black gloom of the coming night. There was a great deal of confusion for a moment, but the best men stepped instinctively to the front, and discipline soon reasserted itself. It had all happened so suddenly that it was inevitable the parting of the ways should have found us unprepared. The second officer, whose name I have given, showed himself master of the situation in a moment. The first thing he had to do was to restore spirit and confidence among the Lascars, shaken as they were by the recent loss of their leader. Fortunately, we were as yet only on the outer edge of the main whirlwind, that still lay to the westward, and the lightning and thunder were all ahead of us. Four of the strongest of the Lascars were now lashed to the tiller, a few sails were set on the lower yards and booms, the decks were cleared of some of the loose rubbish that encumbered them, and a course was laid which gave the ship greater ease in the now boiling cross-seas that were showing themselves. When night closed we were running towards the north-west, amid a rapid alternation of blinding flashes of lightning and inky darkness. The hatches of the lower decks had all been battened down upon the soldiers and the women and children, the deadlights fastened, and only the reefed foresail and some other light fore-and-aft canvas set. The barometer was still falling. A couple of hours later the full crash of the hurricane came. No one can ever describe such a scene accurately. There are things in it that when put into words are bound to appear exaggerations. There is no sea and no sky, and no air. They have all become one vast, black, solid, gigantic animal, compared to which the lion is a lamb, the whale a minnow, the biggest cannon a child's popgun. There is no sea running as in an ordinary storm ; beneath this awful wind the sea crouches for a time like a lashed hound, and that is exactly what it is. It cannot get up and run before that vast wall of wind. It lies down at first and the wind mows it like grass, shaves it off in swathes of white foam which are caught up into the rushing wind itself, so that no eye can open against it, and no face can face its saltness. But the roar is the thing that lives longest in memory ; it seems to swallow even the thunder, as though that too, like the sea, had been brayed into it.

As the night wore on the damage grew; there was no attempt made to take in sail, and one by one they were blown away into the night. The ship then was put before the wind, and we ran as the hurricane listed. Fortunately, there was sea room on every side. At times we seemed to get thrown into the trough of the seas. No man could stand on the poop-deck, and on the quarter-deck the rolling of the vessel set the guns free from their lashings, and caused them to go rolling from one side of the deck to the other, until they broke through the bulwarks and shot out into the sea. The chain cable also got adrift on the deck, and began to roll its immense links from side to side as the ship lurched to and fro. The watch could not live on the deck; they were brought into the saloon, where they lay on the floor so beaten that one could walk over their bodies. Our boats, too, were torn from their davits, one wave carrying away the long-boat and some live-stock that were penned within it. Towards morning the upper foremast went with a great crash, and the wreck of it could not be cleared. Just before daybreak some one discovered that the barometer had lifted a shade above the extraordinary depth to which it had fallen. This news infused life and vigour into many, who amid these long-continued crashes and disasters had begun to give up hope, and had made up their minds that the ship must founder. The unfortunate captain had shut himself up in his cabin, the Lascar crew were completely demoralised, half of us landsmen were lying in the most exhausting pangs of sea-sickness, and the ship herself was only a floating wreck—boats, yards, gone; booms broken, guns disappeared. When daylight came it was seen that the hurricane was going down as quickly as it had arisen. There was one man who had fought the elements undauntedly throughout that long night, Salmon, the second officer He had lashed himself securely to the mizzen-mast before the worst came, and from there he called his orders to the steersmen. Undoubtedly, he saved the ship.

A dead calm succeeded the rage of storm, the sun came up bright in the east. Away to the north-west a vast bank of hurricane was driving towards the Orissa coast. We were about one hundred and fifty miles out of our true course, a dismantled wreck upon the heaving ocean. By the afternoon things were got into some shipshape, and we were able to bend some sails and rig up a little canvas again. Then, when observations had been taken, a course was set for Madras. Meanwhile the women and children had been brought up and laid out on the deck; they had suffered much. The seams of the deck had opened, the strained timbers had let floods of water into decks and holds—everything was water-soaked.

A week later we crept into Madras; the steamer had got in four days earlier. She gave a bad report of the chances of the *Tubalcain* ; we were given up as lost, poor chaps ! The Army List page of the 69th Regiment had to be revised, and then it had to be revised again ! We were quartered in Fort St. George, a four-company detachment being sent to Wellington in the Nilgherry Hills. A new colonel and several officers joined, and fresh drafts were awaiting us. I closed my accounts with the paymaster and the quartermaster, handed over the wing documents to the adjutant, and started for the hills with a wonderful little Pegu pony, which had escaped injury on the deck of the steamer. He had been thrown out of his crib and rolled about the deck, but had picked himself together again and again, and escaped with a few cuts and bruises. Some other horses had to be cast into the sea.

I know no change so satisfying to body, soul, and sense as that which a man experiences when in the month of May he passes from the Indian plains to the Indian hills. No transformation scene can equal that change. Every wearied sense, exhausted in the intense heat of the lower lands, springs at once into life. The air of India, when it is breathed at an elevation of six thousand to eight thousand feet, is purity and freshness and life itself, and nowhere does it combine all those attributes in a higher degree than in the Nilgherry Mountains, the Blue Hills. Blue they are when seen from a distance, but green when reached, and what is more, green with all the verdure and scent of the grasses and flowers of Europe. That is the touch which makes us at once at home in these beautiful hills. Through the rose hedges at Coonoor flits the small brown wren ; blackbirds and thrushes build their nests in the gardens at Ootacamund, and the lark sings high and clear in the radiant atmosphere over Dodabetta. All our rare shrubs are there, too, in tree form—the heliotrope, azalea, myrtle, magnolia, gardenia grow to forest heights. From fifty to sixty inches of rain fall annually on this lofty tableland, from which innumerable streams and watercourses wind their opposite ways to rivers which fall into the Bay of Bengal on one side and the Arabian Sea on the other. Once the level of the upper hills is gained the ground is practicable for riding almost in any direction, and from the ramparts which look down on the plains of the Carnatic on the east to those which overhang the coast of Malabar on the west some six hundred or seven hundred square miles of rolling tableland lie open to the traveller. If the Garden of Eden was not here, it might well have been. There are points on the eastern ramparts of this paradise from which, in gardens hung with roses and jessamine, one can sit and look down from a clear and bracing atmosphere upon a hundred miles of the fevered, quivering plains of Southern India seven thousand feet below.

In this delightful spot I spent a couple of months, the Burmese pony enabling explorations to be made in many directions through the hills. The change back to Madras in the hottest time of the year was, however, very trying, and unfortunately the heat disabled so many of our officers that those who were not on the sick list found themselves almost incessantly detailed for garrison or regimental duty. Many of the men fell sick too, and cholera appeared among them. The ground upon which Fort St. George stood was a very hotbed of disease. In October came a welcome change, for the musketry training began, and I moved to a place called Palaveram, about twelve miles to the south-west of Fort St. George, for that practice. It was here possible to see a good deal of the lives of the people of Southern India—the outdoor people, they who bend and toil in the paddy-fields; who dwell in mud huts without the commonest articles of household furniture; who have scarcely any clothes; who are lean of leg, and shrunken in body, and hollow of stomach, whose women work at water wheels all day long; who are patient beyond any limit of patience known to white men; who live and die scratching the hot soil and pouring water upon it; the poor, starved race, the feeble foundation of all the wealth, splendour, and magnificence the very name of which has made the hungry mouth of the rapacious West water for the last four hundred years. How long will it go on ?

Looking back on the lives of the toiling millions of the Carnatic plain through fifty years, one can see many things which were not then visible. In the fulness of his animal life the British subaltern in a marching regiment is not overmuch given to philosophic inquiry. He drops easily into the belief that he represents the highest form of civilisation, and that he has only to snipe-shoot or pig-stick his way through the world, while at the same time in some mysterious manner he is bearing aloft the banner of British freedom and Western culture. It would be better, perhaps, for the continuance of the ' Raj ' which he represents if the British officer could by inclination, or even through compulsion, put himself in closer touch and sympathy with the lives and thoughts of the masses of the Eastern peoples with whom the greater portion of his service has to be spent under the conditions of army life now existing in the Empire. I will not pretend that I was different from my fellows in this respect, but even at that time I think I had an instinctive knowledge that the work we were engaged upon in India lacked the greatest element of stability—sympathy with the people of India. I find myself writing at this time, ' It has yet to be proved . . . in our rapid development of intellectual power among the people of India . . . whether it be possible to graft upon the decaying trunk of an old civilisation the young offshoot of a newer and more vigorous one. For my part, I am inclined to think that the edifice we are uprearing in India has its foundation resting upon sand. We give the native of India our laws and our scientific discoveries ; he sees that they are good, and he adopts them and uses them as some counterbalance to the misfortune of our presence in his land. . . . He knows that the white man came as a suppliant trader to his shores and begged humbly for the crumbs of his riches. He believes our religion to be a thing of yesterday compared to the antiquity of his own. He knows that by violence and bribery, oftentimes by treachery and fraud, we obtained possession of his lands. He knows that by force of arms and strength of discipline we hold our possessions; nevertheless, he hates and fears us, and while he adopts and uses the discoveries of our civilisation, he still holds that civilisation in contempt. We pull down the barriers within which his mind has hitherto moved, but the flood of his inquiry being set flowing, we cannot stay or confine it to our own limits. I can see signs that this great structure we are building will be a ruin before it is completed. I can find no instance in history of a nation which has possessed an old and completed civilisation of its own being able to fuse it, imperfect though it may be, into a newer and a foreign one.' When I re-read these words now I see better what was wanting in the edifice.

There was another subject, and one which appears to have reached a crucial stage in the political outlook of our present day, but which my old notebooks show was very evident to my subaltern comprehension just fifty years ago. Notwithstanding all I have heard and read about the superiority of voluntary enlistment over conscription, it is still, I think, an open question. In a few years the old British army will be extinct—the rocks of the Crimea and the sands of India have covered all but the last of it. How will voluntary enlistment work then ? While the army remained small and select, as it was prior to the Crimean War, all went well, strong men were easily obtained, and no soldiers equalled ours in strength, courage, and endurance. That day is gone. We have now to garrison India with three times the number of men that used to suffice there, and our home army has to be considerably increased. Already the result is visible : the standard has to be reduced ; men are now taken who would have been rejected with scorn a few years ago ; we get recruits no longer from the rural districts, but from the slums of the big cities, and even from these sources we find it difficult to obtain them in sufficient numbers. I believe that a serious war to-morrow would prove to our cost that the army is not of the old stamp. At present enough is still left of the old stuff to counterbalance the admixture of the new element, but that will soon cease, and then England will have to elect between a bad army and conscription. I shall never forget the sorry contrast that presented itself on the bank of the Sittang River at Tonghoo, where one draft of a hundred and

twenty men of the new model formed up on the high shore from
the boats.   The old soldiers had come down from the big teak
huts a couple of hundred yards away to see the new arrivals.
The contrast between the two sets of men was not flattering
to the newcomers.   The 69th Regiment had been in the West
Indies during the Crimean War.   The men were thus of the
old type, the men of Meeanee and Sobraon, men of splendid
physique and well-chiselled feature.   The flank companies
were still in being, the Grenadier and Light Infantry Companies.   I often look now as soldiers pass and marvel what
has become of those old Greek gods, for not only are the figures
gone, but the faces have also vanished—those straight, clean-
cut foreheads, the straight or aquiline noses, the keen, steady
eyes, the resolute lower jaws and shapely turned chins.   What
subtle change has come upon the race ?   Is it the work of
railroads ?   Free Trade ?   the   Penny   Press ?   Democracy ?
Education ?   All I know is that they are gone as the buffalo
are gone from the prairies, or the Red Man from the American
continent.   I sometimes think that if these men were bred
amongst us to-day there need have been no suffragettes.

In 1861 and 1862 little was occurring in India to make residence there interesting to a soldier.   Profound peace had followed
the close of the Mutiny.   A great conflict had broken out in
North America ; but ocean telegraph cables were still unknown,
and the news of all the desperate fighting upon the shores of
the Rappahannock and the Potomac and in the Shenandoah
Valley took a long while to get to Madras.   Only in one sense,
and that a strange one, was this gigantic conflict brought
immediately home to us on the Carnatic coast.   One hot season,
when Madras lay gasping for breath, there were no cooling
drinks to be had—the ice-ship from Boston to Madras had not
arrived.   The *Alabama* was known to be out, and to her
account the fact of the ice-ship's being missing was at once laid.
The Southern cause had many supporters among us at the
time, but this supposed interference with our thirst by the
celebrated Confederate cruiser was a thing which had not
been reckoned with when the balance between the rival combatants had been struck in our community.   Had not our
Mess rights just as pressing to us as those of Alabama or the
Carolinas to the Southerners, and had they not been violated in

this matter ? So for a time, at least, there was pause in debate among us, until one day the ice-ship was seen in the offing, and the Federal cause went down again to zero like the temperature in our tumblers.

We were seldom quite free from cholera at this time in the fort at Madras. It seemed to strike at random among us. Although the disease had been the scourge of India for more than thirty years, little was known about its treatment, and still less about the science of its cause Certainly the condition of the fort was at this time so bad as to make it unnecessary to look for other sources of disease anywhere else. At about 2 A.M. the outlet of the terrible main drain of Black Town was opened, some five hundred yards to the north of the fort, and a frightful flood of pent sewage was discharged into the sea The current set down shore, and thus this horrible black mass was carried slowly down along the shingle in front of the quarters, filling the entire air of night with a stench so penetrating that it caused the wretched inmates of our barracks to start instantly into wakefulness, no matter how sound might be the sleep into which nature, wearied by the excessive heat of the day and early night, had at that hour fallen.

Our colonel, a most estimable man and an excellent officer, was one of the first to fall a victim to this scourge ; his own child was also taken on the same day. Several of the finest men went too. The blow fell without any warning. A strong man went down all at once ; he was carried in a dhooley to the hospital ; and all was over in six or eight hours. Certainly the 'finest appanage of the British Crown' levies heavy toll upon the Crown's subjects. 'The Pagoda Tree' has its roots in the graveyards of India's military cantonments.

In May 1863 I set out with two other officers to spend our sixty days' 'privilege leave' in visiting the western coast of the peninsula. We were to cross by railway to Beypore, and there, taking bullock bandies, proceed northward to the falls of Gairsoppa, near Honore, a journey of two hundred miles by road. The falls are said to be the most remarkable in India, the River Sheranditty precipitating itself down the face of the Western Ghauts in leaps of eight hundred and a thousand feet. As the south-west monsoon would break in

June, the river was likely to be in full flood by the time we reached Gairsoppa. Such was my plan, but when one travels in a trio there is always a chance that you will have two to one against you. We reached Salem in the evening, and, as the train stopped there for the night, we made our beds on the station platform. It was not a lively experience, as a coolie died of cholera close by us during the night. The heat was excessive, and, bad as the fort at Madras had been, this was worse. Next morning our train continued its western progress, and the evening found us at Palghaut. We got into the travellers' bungalow at that place. Palghaut lies in the bottom of a great rent or fissure in the Western Ghauts, which gives easy and level access to the Malabar shore from the Carnatic On either side of a very long defile the mountains rise steeply. Great forests of teak, blackwood, and green undergrowths take the places of the burnt, cindery hills and arid plains of Salem and Coimbatore.

A magnificent storm, the prelude to the opening of the monsoon, burst upon Palghaut that night, and the forest dripped rain for many hours; but the morning broke bright, and again our train resumed its slow march for Beypore, the terminus on the Malabar coast. We got to Calicut that evening. This old town, the first spot in India reached by Vasco da Gama, and described as being then a place of great magnificence, is now poor and decayed, a straggling town hidden in cocoa-nut palms, its old harbour silted up, a big sea breaking ceaselessly upon its straight sandy shore. Here preparations were to be made for the journey of two hundred miles along the coast to Honore, but, alas for the permanence of our projects, things fell out badly for us.

The senior member of our little party was an old colonel whose military career of close upon thirty years had been spent in India. He had an old native servant, 'Sam' by name. Sam liked his ease as much as did his master. That night on the railway platform at Salem had checked the travelling ardour of both master and man. Under date 10th May I find this entry in my notebook, 'Calicut. Sam lost.' What really happened I don't know. Sam turned up in the night, but his master's spirits did not rise with the return of this ancient native. I find the following entry in my notebook :—'Calicut. Various and conflicting plans,' and then : ' Scene, the Bungalow in Calicut, time 10 P.M.

' H. Well, out of this infernal hole we must get, so let us decide at once.

' M. (from his bed) Go anywhere. I don't care where.

' B. Why not Gairsoppa ? Mangalore is only one hundred miles from here.

' H. I vote for Palghaut.

' M. I think Palghaut a capital place.

' H. We can stay there and eat our stores.

' B. Well, we can never show our faces again in the Mess if we do that, that's all I say.

' M. Oh, d—— the Mess !

' B. (anxious at all costs to save the ignominy of Palghaut). What about Sissapara ?

' H. Of course, Sissapara.

' B. Or Cochin ?

' H. Cochin. I always thought it an excellent place.

' M. (very sleepy). Palghaut, Palghaut.

' B Let's try to get bandies for Cannanore.

' After a short discussion this proposal is agreed to, and Sam and other servants are despatched for bandy-wallahs. Silence until arrival of bandy-wallahs. M sleeps. Enter the wallahs and servants.

' B. (through interpreter). How much charge to Cannanore ?

' SERVANT. Twelve rupees each bandy (General consternation, during which M. wakes.)

' H. We will give him ten rupees. (Animated dialogue ensues in Telugu between servants and wallahs. Offer refused. Exit wallahs. M. falls asleep murmuring " Palghaut.")

' Arrival of a second batch of wallahs, who after a protracted discussion agree to take three masters to Cannanore for ten rupees eight annas each master An advance of eight rupees on each bandy is now made, and general harmony appears to prevail. This is shortly broken by fresh outbreak of Telugu tongue.

' SERVANT (interpreting). He says " Bridges," Sa.

' TRAVELLERS. What bridges ?

' S. Five bridges, Sa. Master must pay five bridges.

' M. (from bed). It's all rot.

' Exit second batch of bandy men. Debate adjourned until next morning, when a last effort is to be made for Mangalore and Honore *en route* to Gairsoppa, failing which all agree to turn south for Cochin and Travancore.

'N.B.—The rocks I have to guard against are first a return to Palghaut, there to consume our stores Second, a retreat to Pulicat, a place on the coast south of Madras, said to be famous for fish, but not otherwise of any interest.'

The next entry is made at a place called Trichoor on the 15th May, so I had succeeded in getting my companions south of the railway line which led back to Madras, and their heads were now turned towards Cape Comorin Trichoor was a quaint old place; the Portuguese had been there, and the Dutch, then had come Hyder Ali and Tippoo Sultan. Like all the other towns and villages on this coast, it lay deep in palm trees. Here began that remarkable series of backwaters which run south for nearly two hundred miles. Three lakes of salt water are separated from the Arabian Sea by a thin ridge of the cleanest and finest sand, sand such as might be put into an hour-glass without further refinement. Upon these sands which the sea has cast up grow beautiful groups of palm trees and many flowering shrubs. The lakes widen out at intervals into large expanses of open water, and at other places narrow to channels of canal width, fringed with mango trees and spice plants. Large water-lilies spread themselves from the shores, and water-fowl of many kinds and plumage float or fly over the sparkling waters. Our boat carried ten oars, and under their strokes, and often with a sail to aid the rowers, we sped along, and, travelling through the night, reached Cochin at sunrise next morning.

Cochin was in its way the most mixed and variegated-looking spot I saw in the East. Once everything in commerce, it had now shrunken to next to nothing in the world of barter. The Portuguese had had it, and the Dutch had taken it from them, and made much of it in their peculiar ways of business. It used to be said of old that the Portuguese began their colonial settlements by building a church, that the Dutch inaugurated theirs by building a fort, and that we commenced ours with a public-house. In Cochin this triple transition can still be seen. The old cathedral of da Gama or Albuquerque is turned into a fort, and the public-house has been superimposed upon both, but not even these several transitions had kept trade true to its old centre It had fled from Cochin. Eighty years earlier the town had 'a harbour filled with ships, streets crowded with merchants, and warehouses stored with goods from every part of Europe and Asia '; now the cocoa palms hid the desolation that followed the destruction of the fortifications and public buildings by order of the British authorities in 1806. One curious survival remained : there were still to be seen here representatives of the old polyglot population which had once made it famous. St. Thomas the Apostle is supposed to have come here in the earliest days of Christianity, and two distinct races of Jews are still here, the black and the red Jews. It is strange, too, to find in this place two distinct bodies of Christians, the descendants of the early Syrian proselytes of St. Thomas, and those who acknowledge the jurisdiction of Rome. These do not worship together, no more than do the black and the red Jews.

But however desirous I might have been to make longer stay in this museum of almost extinct Eastern races, one dominating factor forced me forward. Another wild night of rain and storm broke upon us as we sat in the verandah of the travellers' bungalow. It was a grand sight to watch the thunder-breeding clouds come whirling in from the Indian Ocean, giving out rain deluges, lightnings, and storm gusts as they swept over the roaring beach across the great lagoon and up into the rocks and forests of the range of the Ghauts, which rose immediately above the inland waters. But those displays of fire and water had a fatal influence upon the spirits of my companions. Again they proposed a retreat to Madras. Fortunately, in a moment of exuberant expectation, when the weather had been fine a day or two earlier, I had been made the paymaster and treasurer of the expedition. I held the common purse. There was no use in any further expostulation or pronouncement as to what the Mess would say about the ignoble policy of retirement to Palghaut, so I waited my opportunity to answer, and remarked quietly that ' I would crack on alone for Quillon at twelve o'clock next day, and had engaged a large boat for the journey.' There was another pause, several looks at the weather to windward, and then came the final plunge. ' Well, we won't break up the party. Let's all go together to Quillon.' So at noon next day we embarked in a fine boat with fourteen rowers, and favoured by a fair breeze we sped bravely through the water. The day was glorious with sunshine, the water clear and smooth. At first our course was through the middle of the great blue lake, the shores of which in some places were not visible, and in others just marked by a fringe of trees which seemed to be growing out of water. After sunset the shores closed in towards us again, and we pulled all night under a brilliant moon, arriving at Quillon at nine next morning. A mile before making the landing-place, we came on one of the many mimic promontories rising from the water which has a stone monument built upon it. It has a history. Many years ago a certain Colonel Gordon was resident at Quillon. He was the owner of a large Newfoundland dog. One morning Gordon was bathing in the lake off this promontory ; the dog lay by his master's clothes on the shore. Suddenly he began to bark in a most violent manner. Gordon, unable to see any cause for the animal's excitement, continued to swim in the deep water. The dog became more violently excited, running down to the water's edge at one particular point. Looking in the direction to which the animal's attention was drawn, the swimmer thought that he could perceive a circular ripple moving the otherwise smooth surface of the lake. Making for the shore, he soon perceived that the ripple was caused by some large body moving stealthily under the water. He guessed at once the whole situation a very large crocodile was swimming well below the surface, and making in his direction. The huge reptile was already partly between him and the shore. The dog knew it all. Suddenly he ceased barking, plunged into the water, and headed in an oblique line so as to intercept the moving ripple. All at once he disappeared from the surface, dragged down by the huge beast beneath. When the dog found that all his efforts to alarm his master were useless, he determined to give his own life to save the man's, and so Colonel Gordon built the monument on the rock above the scene, and planted the casarina tree to shadow it.

We spent a couple of days in this remote but beautiful cantonment of Quillon. Here under date 23rd May 1863 I find the following entry ·—'Dined with the officers 23rd Madras Native Infantry in their delightful Mess. Heard rumour of war with America.' What particular rumour of war this referred to in the long civil strife I cannot now identify, but undoubtedly during those years of the early 'sixties there were many times when the question of peace and war with the Northern States hung in very delicate balance.

Our southward course now led to Trivandrum, the capital of Travancore. This small native state, the most southern in the peninsula of India, probably combined within its five thousand square miles a larger diversity of scenery and race, and a more extraordinary variety of social manners and customs, than any other part of the world known to me.

It is a long and narrow strip of territory lying between an impassable mountain range and a sea upon whose shore huge breakers are almost always beating. The mountain barrier rises to heights of seven thousand and eight thousand feet, and, with the exception of two gaps or ghats, one at the north end, Palghaut, the other at the south end near Cape Comorin, it is unbroken and untrodden by man. Every animal from the tiger to the tiniest monkey is in the forests of these mountains ; the rivers and the backwaters are full of fish, birds are here in vast varieties and of rainbow colours, and reptile life is as plentiful as heat, moisture, and underbush can make it ; but above all other life that of man is the most varied and interesting. The Nairs and Tiers of old Hindoo origin are generally of fine figure and handsome face, graceful in carriage, and of a rich, light olive complexion. A limited but very fierce race of Mohammedans are found in the towns along the coast, Moplahs by name , these are descendants of old Arab traders settled on the coast long before da Gama appeared from Europe. High up in the wild glens and secluded ' sholahs ' of the mountains are an extremely rude race, who dwell in little round beehive-shaped huts and live upon wild animals, and cultivate a few patches of the castor-oil plant. Of these people I shall have occasion to speak later.

Out of a total population of more than one million souls Travancore numbers some one hundred and fifty thousand Christians of Syrian and Portuguese descent. Here, as elsewhere in India, the dominating note of the land is life. This great fervid sun, these sweeps of rain, this rich soil, these limpid waters, have all combined to call forth in forest, plain, island, lake, and shore an all-pervading sense of human, animal, bird, fish, and insect existence In these countries you cannot

D

get away from this fact of life ; it jostles you in the towns, it roars at you in the forest, it flies and hums about you in the air, it swims around you in the waters. These graceful Nair and Tier women with their rich golden skins and black, silky tresses, wading in the warm inland waters, or working in their island gardens amid all the spice plants of the earth, are, no doubt, the descendants of the people whom Camoens saw on this coast, and sighed after, and wrote about in the dread days of misfortune and captivity.

Continuing our southern course from Quillon, we reached the end of the greater or northern backwater, and crossed on foot a low range of hills separating it from a shorter lake which runs to Trivandrum, the capital. At sunset we were on the height of land between the two long reaches of water ; to the right as we marched was a magnificent ocean prospect. The sun had burst forth from masses of cloud on the horizon, and in rich folds of hill and forest the land lay green and golden in the level rays, backed by the glorious Ghauts, tree-covered to their summits. Looking back we saw for many a winding mile the water track we had followed from Trichoor. A little distance to the westward of our road lay the old city of Anjengo, once a place of importance in the early Portuguese trade. Some forty years after this evening of glorious sunset views, I read in St. Helena the following entry in the old island records :—

'June 27th, 1757.—I, Mr. Scott, Your Honour's Resident at Anjengo, transported to this island in the *Clinton and Hector* ten Malabar men who it seems were officers to the King of Travancore, to serve you as slaves here, one of which died on the passage. The other nine were landed and clothed. A few days after they were sent into the country five of them hanged themselves, and one of the remaining four has since died. The other three threaten to destroy themselves if they are put to any kind of work.'

Well done the British trader as a missionary of civilisation ! This sample of his peculiar methods occurred a hundred years prior to my visit to Travancore, but in the fifty years which have since elapsed I have seen enough of our missionary trader to make me think that he might be still at his old methods of civilisation, if there had been no French Revolution to give him pause in his calculations. The 'Records' from which the above extract is taken contain many reverential observations on humanity in general and the Bible in particular.

The lake which lay south of this ridge between the two backwaters carried us into Trivandrum, the capital. Here, after a couple of days' delay, we quitted this delightful mode of water transport, and held our way by road towards Cape Comorin.

The monsoon had not yet broken, the sun was straight over our heads, and the heat sufficiently great to make night or early morning travel preferable to the march by day. The country was rich and undulating, mountains grand and bold to our left, and to our right the sounding Indian Ocean. 'How,' I find myself asking in my notebook, ' has it happened that the All-grasping Company kept their hands from this fertile province ? True, they got eight lakhs out of it, and they kept in their hands the civil and military power. I suppose the reason was that Hyder Ali never conquered Travancore, for we seem to have usurped all his usurpations as a matter of course.'

On the second day from Trivandrum we reached a quaint old place called Oodagherry. A crumbling fort built round the base of a steep rocky hill, and half covered with jungle growth, gave us shelter in one of its bastions, upon which the travellers' bungalow (that last remnant of the old regal hospitality of India) had been built. A few miles south-east of this spot began the Aroombooli Pass in the mountains, the southern gateway through the Ghauts It was through this gate that the British column marched in 1809 to the conquest of Travancore, and here at Oodagherry the last effort of resistance was made by the Travancoreans. My own corps, the 69th Regiment, had formed the principal European portion of this force. We found the tradition of the old conflict still living, and some old natives, having scraped away the tangled foliage below our bastion-bungalow, showed us the graves of Europeans who had fallen in fight or died of disease at this place ; but the rains of fifty years had rendered the names upon the gravestones quite illegible.

Here, close to Cape Comorin, and one thousand five hundred miles northward and east and west, from Orissa to the Arabian Sea, they lie in countless graves, these old, forgotten, heroic soldiers, unthanked and unthought of by the millions to whom their deaths gave untold riches and unequalled empire.

CHAPTER IV

Down to Cape Comorin, and back to Madras. The scene of a
bygone massacre. Starting for England. St. Helena.

BEFORE continuing our journey to Cape Comorin our little
party broke up, and two of us turned aside into the Ghauts
to seek for sambhur and bison in these wonderful forests
which had so long flanked our line of march on the eastward,
revealing, when the sunset light struck full into their countless
glens and 'sholahs,' innumerable parks and game preserves.
The spot selected for our incursion was called the Ashamboo
Valley, at the extreme southern end of the range of Ghauts
and only a few miles north of Cape Comorin. In this glen a
couple of gentlemen of the London Missionary Society had
built themselves two small bungalows for retreat in the hot
season at a height of between five and six thousand feet above
sea-level. Very steep and rough, a narrow pathway wound
among rocks and jungle from the lower level, and after two
or three hours of heavy toil we gained the entrance to the
valley. It was a wild and picturesque spot, looking right down
upon the southern point of India. Higher mountains enclosed
the glen on three sides, but to the south the eye ranged over
the immense expanse of ocean which surrounds the cape.
Two little thatched cottages stood on a rising ground some
three or four hundred yards from the entrance gap in the
hills ; through this gap the gathered waters of the glen plunged
down the mountain-side. The lower slopes of the valley were
free of forest and grass-covered ; the higher ridges were seamed
with belts of deep green forest — 'sholahs,' as they were
called.

A missionary in Nagracoil, at the foot of the mountain, had
kindly given us the key of his mountain cottage, so we marched
straight to it. The house had not been occupied for many
months, and the lock was rusty and difficult to open ; but at

last entrance was effected, and then a strange sight met the first man that went in. Underneath a charpoy, or coir bedstead, in one corner of the little room, a large brown mass was seen, like a piece of old bedding folded and put away. The man came running out, exclaiming that there was a very big serpent lying coiled under the empty bedstead. We now got a side window open to give us more light, and then it could be easily perceived that the bundle was a huge snake lying in a semi-comatose state. It was not easy to make out where his head was and where his tail, but I took the bulkiest part of the coil for aim, and gave him a bullet, at ten feet distance, full into the middle of it. Then a great upheaval and disentanglement began, during which I retreated to the door to await developments, for with the smoke and the rumpus one could not tell what the next move of the reptile would be When the thick smoke cleared out of the little room our sleeping python was quiet ; the ball had broken his body in halves at its thickest part. He was about twelve feet in length, and thick as a man's leg   A big figure 8 repeated itself along his back in a sort of purple tint upon a brown background. He had done us one signal service : there was not a rat in the bungalow.

Next morning we were out before sunrise. We first crossed a steep ridge called ' Bison Point,' and descended into another valley ; again we climbed a hill, and, crossing another glen, reached at noon a place called by our guide ' The Hillmen's Valley ' Here some half a dozen little black men were collected out of about the same number of little beehive huts. These strange dwarf-like people were the first and last of their kind I met in India. They were all much under five feet in height, very black in colour, and almost naked. Their instinctive knowledge of the habits of wild animals, and their power of following a trail across all kinds and conditions of ground, were equalled by their noiseless and yet rapid methods of moving through dense jungle.

With these men we now plunged into some very thick forests, and soon separated. I was following my particular little man through this jungle, when suddenly he stopped his rapid steps and pointed to some object in advance and slightly to the left of where he stood. A step brought me beside him.

Following his ' point,' I could discern, at a distance of about twenty or thirty paces, a huge head that was looking at us over and through some lower jungle. It was a bison. I carried a short rifle which loaded at the breech in some strange fashion long ago obsolete. I aimed at the big head that was looking at us, but before I could pull the trigger the beast threw himself half round from us. Dropping the muzzle below where I thought must be the level of his shoulder, I fired There was a great crash, and I heard and saw no more Fearing the beast was off down the slope, I rushed forward, my black friend remaining where he was. On his side lay the bison, struggling hard to get on his legs again. I fired at twelve feet from him two more shots into his huge carcass, neither of which seemed to have any effect ; but the first wound was mortal, and after a last struggle he lay still. All the hill-men now came together, and with their keen knives the big head was severed from the body, poles were cut, and we all marched back, bringing the head in triumph to the hut. The bison was one of the largest the little hunters had ever seen. He measured eighteen hands at the shoulder, and his girth was ten feet. We slept that night in a sort of porch belonging to the largest of the beehives, and the little men, and the little women, and their yet smaller children, were soon inside their hives.

After nine days of this wild life, but with no sport to equal that first day's, we said farewell to our good friend Mr. Cox, who was about to attempt coffee-planting in Ashamboo ; and descending again to the low country pursued our route to Cape Comorin. The heat was now great, and felt particularly trying to us after the cool days and really cold nights of the upper mountains. The country was now covered with old forts and ruined temples. At night, when it became too dark for the bullocks to make their way, we would tie up beside some old temple and sleep until day came, lulled by the sea winds whistling through the broken masonry and dilapidated figures of Vishnu or Parasu Rama. The last-named Brahminical deity was the favourite god of the Travancoreans ; for they say that it was he who created this country by hurling his axe from the summit of the Ghauts into the ocean, which then came to the foot of the mountains, and that the waters, receding from the space over which the weapon sped, left bare the rich region of this province.

Early on the morning of 16th June we reached the cape. Here India slanted quietly into the sea, in gently sloping shores upon which the waves had washed up three distinct kinds and colours of sand—puce, garnet, and black. An old bungalow stood at the extreme point, facing south, and three big rounded granite rocks marked the southmost bit of land. The bungalow was very large; it had been built by a former resident at Trivandrum, and even at this hot time of the year was cooled and freshened by winds that were always from the waves.

From this point our bullocks had their heads turned northeast to Tuticorin, a port on the coast of Tinnavelly, facing Ceylon. Slowly they dragged us through the Aroomboli Pass, and out once more into the blinding levels eastward of the Ghauts. I look over the old notebook, and read :—

'At length we are turned towards Madras. I liked Comorin much; wild, secluded, and scarcely ever visited. What a place for study! The quaint old house with the roar of the surf echoing through its lofty rooms, and the sea winds whistling round the gables, making even noonday dreamy. Halted for the night six miles from the cape, on the frontier.'

Then we pushed on through Tinnavelly, by Palamcottah, and a dozen other places ending with 'ary' or 'gully,' and late on the 24th reached Tuticorin, after having covered in the last stage thirty-three miles in twenty-six hours. The heat was very great during those seven days' travel, and the country scorched and sandy, and with many salt marshes. The day following our arrival at Tuticorin is marked, 'Sick and seedy all day.' It was really a day of intense illness. The Carnatic climate had begun to tell upon me, and for some time past a recurring day of horrible sickness came upon me at intervals of about a month. The doctors could not make out what it was, and as it usually happened that there was a full moon when these violent night attacks occurred, I had begun to think the moon was in some way answerable for them.

At Tuticorin we hired a native boat called a 'dhoney,' and set sail through the Gulf of Manaar for Madras, following the general line of the coast northward, anchoring at sunset, and going on at sunrise next day.

It was a new experience of Indian life, and therefore of great interest, despite the general condition of discomfort that necessarily pervaded it. The ' dhoney ' was of about twenty tons burden , the crew—a whole family and a couple of followers—was Mohammedan. My companion and myself had a small after-hold for our mattresses, and an equally small space on deck to sit in during the day. A big lateen sail towered above and gave us shelter from the sun ; forward of the sail the crew, of all ages, was huddled together on jute bales. The craft itself was old, and its planks were simply held together by coir ropes and stitches.

On the 28th June we passed through Adam's Bridge and anchored at Paambaun. Many islands were scattered about these narrow seas between India and Ceylon. The coasting trade was large, and native craft were numerous. Passing through Palk's Straits on the 29th, our ' dhoney ' was all but run down by a two-masted native vessel of ten times our tonnage. I had seen under the lateen sail this big craft coming towards us more than a mile away, and had pointed her out to our ' Ries,' for the courses on which we were both running must bring us close together. Then the sail had intervened, and I ceased to watch. All at once there was wild shouting from our crew before the mast, and a more distant bellowing from the people on the brig. How we scraped by each other I don't know ; but amid all the bellowing and gesticulation the big craft brushed past us a few feet distant on the starboard side, our joint speeds giving a rate of perhaps twenty miles an hour.

On the 30th we passed the tall lighthouse on Point Calymere at noon, were off Negapatam at three, and anchored at Carrical at sunset just as the tricolor was being hauled down from the French flagstaff. Then to Pondicherry for one day on shore, and to Madras on the evening of 4th July. It had been well timed. Our sixty days' leave would expire next morning. We had travelled some twelve hundred miles by rail, boat, bullock, bandy, dhoney, and on foot in these fifty-nine days.

At Madras we found the orders for home had arrived ; we were to sail in the following February.

But there was one spot in the Carnatic which I had not yet seen, although it had been of particular interest to me since I had read the early records of my regiment as they were told in a large folio MS. volume in our Orderly Room. This spot was Vellore, a fortress and town lying some eighty miles to the west of Madras. Not even in the cindery plains of the Carnatic is there to be found a place of more intense heat ; red rocky hills surround it, the radiation from which makes the night almost as fevered as the day. In the splendid fort built by early Mohammedan conquerors of the Carnatic four companies of the 69th Regiment, together with nearly all their officers and families, were shot down one hot night in July 1806 by the native troops who were in garrison with them. The mutiny of Vellore had been a very notable occurrence in its day ; it was now entirely forgotten. All the greater reason for going to Vellore.

I arrived there in the end of July, when it was about as hot as the sun and the hills could bake or make it. The fort, a magnificent structure of early Moslem work, stands intact and entire, as sound as the day it was built, and it will probably remain in that condition for another thousand years. The immense ditch is hewn out of solid rock, and the walls and bastions are of great square stones quarried from the ditch. Almost in the centre of the large square which is enclosed by these massive walls, a very lofty Hindoo pagoda, covered with sculptures and carvings of Khrishna and Rama and his monkey armies, lifts its head.

The object of my visit was to see this scene of a bygone massacre, and the graveyard where the bones of so many old soldiers of my regiment had been laid at rest. Strangely enough, I found in the fort a dépôt of old European pensioners of the Indian army, and to their little huts within the fort I first went. Men were there whose service dated back to earlier years than even 1806, and among them there was a survivor of the battle of the Nile, the only one I ever met. He had been a boy on board a ship in Nelson's fleet in that celebrated fight, and had afterwards served in the Company's service for many years. He was very old and very deaf ; but his brain was still going. ' What was it like ? ' I roared into his better ear. ''What was it like ? ' he answered, gaining a little time for his reply before he uttered it.   ' Well, it was like the sound of the water-wheel of a big mill.'   That was all I could get from him.

Other old pensioners were tried as to the mutiny with greater success.   Two or three of them knew from hearsay all the sights of that memorable night and morning at Vellore in July 1806   The old barracks through the windows of which the mutineers had fired on our men as they were lying asleep in their cots ;   the rampart and bastion to which the survivors had escaped, and which they held until the arrival of the gallant Gillespie from Arcot at the head of his avenging cavalry ; the flagstaff, from the summit of which the green flag of Mysore was torn down, under a murderous fire, by two splendid soldiers of the 69th ;   the spot on the ramparts over the great gateway from which Sergeant Brady first descried the hero Gillespie riding far in advance of his leading squadron ;   the gate blown in by the fire of ten galloper guns of the King's 19th Dragoons — all these places we visited ;   and finally we reached the graveyard where, shaded by an old decaying tree, stood the square mound of brick and mortar, without date or inscription, and broken with rents, through which wild plants grew luxuriantly, marking the ground where so many of the old regiment rested.

It was late at night when I got back to Madras.   A subscription was soon set on foot, the Government of Madras helped with a grant, and six months later, when the regiment embarked for England, they left a fitting monument in the graveyard at Vellore to the memory of the gallant men who lay there.

I was sorry then to leave India, and I am sorry still that I did not labour more when I was there to know better its people and their history.   India is a bad school for the young soldier in many of its aspects.   There are some of our race to whom contact with the native spells retrogression ;   there are others to whom this old civilisation, these vast edifices of power decayed, and wealth squandered, and religion degenerated, teach lessons which are not to be found in the school-books. Cradle of all things !   Tomb of all things !   Gorgeous, starved, degraded, defiled, debauched, mysterious East !   I wish that I had studied you more deeply when I dwelt with you.   And yet

I can well believe that we of the old army, snipe shooting, and bison hunting, and serving and even romping with the people, knew more of them and their ways than did our rich cousins of the Civil Service. The gulf between the European fighting man and the Indian is shallower than that which divides the ruling man from the ruled man. I used to meet in my wanderings many highly paid civilians—commissioners, collectors, judges, and all their deputies of so many degrees; but now, looking back upon it all, I think that the men who impressed me most favourably in the Civil Service were those who had begun their careers in the army, and had subsequently passed from military life to civil administration. Wherever the Mohammedan is found, the love of arms inherent in his nature will make him regard the man who carries them in a sense different from that in which he regards a purely civilian superior. The Asiatic fighting man quickly sees through the 'superior person' of our time. It is Colonel Newcome and the Collector of Boggly Wallah over again; and it will remain so to the end of the chapter, even though the colonel should always die in a Charterhouse Hospital.

I am not quite sure that our new superior person, governor or collector, is a better ruler than the old-type civilian who was still to be found in the out-stations in my time in India.

Bungay Smith was a type. He possessed one marked social accomplishment, and to this it was said that he owed his fortune in the Civil Service. He could buzz like a bumble-bee. One evening at a reception in Government House somebody mentioned to the governor-general the fact of Bungay's accomplishment. By special desire he was requested to give a performance in the rôle of the bumble-bee, a screen being provided to render the performance less arduous. From behind that screen Bungay poured forth such variations of buzzing that the company were delighted beyond the measure of words. He buzzed as the bee approaching the flower; he buzzed as the bee leaving the flower; he buzzed as the bee who has struck against your hat and become violently irritated and enraged at his own stupidity; and he buzzed as the bee dreamily dozing amid the scents of linden trees. From that moment his success was assured. He went up country to a collectorship, which unfortunately was in a part of India where tigers were numerous. From a love of nature in the humbler lives of the striped bumble, he passed to the higher levels of striped animal life. He would hunt the tiger. A collector finds many willing hands to aid him in compassing his wishes. It was soon arranged that a ' machan,' or stage, should be erected at some spot frequented by the lord of the Indian jungle. Upon this stage Bungay was to take his seat, a bait or lure for the tiger was to be fastened underneath, and the remainder of the proceeding would, it was said, be almost automatic : the tiger would come to eat the bait, Bungay had only to discharge bullets down upon him from his ' machan,' and the desired end would be achieved. The whole arrangement fulfilled all the conditions known as ' a dead certainty.'

The ' machan ' consisted of a sort of strong double step-ladder, having a stage at top upon which Bungay with his head shikaree was to be seated. Everything promised well. Before darkness closed over the forest Bungay and his shi-karee were in position ; a small buffalo calf was tied to a stake underneath the structure. Night and silence followed The tiger was now the only actor wanting in the piece, and he had to appear under the staging, and not on it. It was here that the hitch came in.

It was late when he appeared, with the stealth and caution common to his kind. There was something suspicious about this buffalo calf, and what was the meaning of this curious wooden pyramidal thing placed straddling its legs over the jungle pathway ? It required examination. He approached the scene. His back had been giving him trouble in the matter of mange ; this sloping arrangement of wood offered a con-venient means of getting on even terms with some parts of his own person which had previously defied his attempts to scratch them. All at once a thing never calculated upon by tiger or collector happened , there was a crash, a roar, a going off of firearms, the thud of falling weights ; full upon the tiger's back fell Bungay straddle-legs. Away went the tiger, scared as he had never been scared before ; tight to the tiger clung Bungay, roaring for all he was worth ; shikarees descended from neighbouring trees, firing promiscuously in all directions ; a spring from the tiger, wilder than anything he had yet achieved, flung Bungay into the jungle, from whence his roars served to guide his followers to the rescue of their chief. He was taken back to his palace practically unhurt, but with nerves so shaken that severe mental complications ensued. He imagined himself a tiger, and, as before he had hummed as a bee, he now broke forth in the roars of a tiger. After a period of prolonged treatment these fits of imagination lessened in severity, and the intervals between them grew longer. But they never quite left him, and a powerful native servant always accompanied him carrying some yards of strong light rope, which, upon a warning note sounded by Bungay, he had orders to tie quickly round his master's arms and legs, for unfortunately, under the stress of the delusions, he felt impelled at times to act the part, as well as to utter it.

There was a favourite story told in the club at Madras of how upon one occasion when Bungay was proceeding at night in his gharry along the Mount Road, the tiger delusion suddenly came upon him as they approached the long bridge over the Adyar River. Something had gone wrong with the rope, and before the servant could reach his master the fit was fully developed. The servant turned and fled ; the master pursued ; down they went into the dry bed of the wide river ; from arch to arch the chase went on ; the servant hid himself behind a buttress ; Bungay growled on all-fours till he found him ; then the solitudes rang with the roar of the king of the forest, as in and out of the arches the master followed the man. I have forgotten how this strange rendering of the poet's ' Hound of Heaven ' ended.

In the month of February 1864 the 69th Regiment, or what was left of it, embarked for England in two vessels of the famous line of ' clipper ' ships owned by Messrs. Green of London.

The right wing of the regiment sailed on the 10th February. There were ten days between the sailing of the two vessels, the *Trafalgar* and the *Lord Warden*. Both were noted sailers, and there was much excitement as to which of them would do the thirteen or fourteen thousand miles in the quickest time. Both were to call at St. Helena, and then to make for Plymouth. I was with the left wing of the regiment in the *Lord Warden*.

It is interesting to compare these old logs of sailing ships

with the ' runs ' made by liners to-day. We kept a journal
on board — the *Homeward Bound* by name — and in its
pages I find the record :—

' In the first fortnight after leaving India we averaged only 80
miles a day ; in the second fortnight the average was 124 miles ;
the third fortnight saw us out of the tropics and into the
latitudes of strong winds, and our average increased to 184 miles ;
then when the stormy seas of the Cape of Good Hope were entered
we ran up to 197 miles in twenty-four hours ; finally we attained
in the run from St. Helena northwards an average of 212 miles,
and covered in one day 320 miles between the Azores and the
Lizard.'

The only event in the long three months that is worth
remembering is a short stay of two days at St. Helena—15th
and 16th April ; but they were days so steeped in thoughts of
glory and of grief that if I lived for a thousand years they
would live with me. Our ship had been standing off the
island in the late night, and long before dawn I was on deck
to catch the first glimpse of the rock. It came in the west
as the stars were going out in the east Nothing like this
black berg is elsewhere in the world. Nothing so lonely, so
gaunt, so steep, so age-riven, so thunderous with the sound
of seas, so sorrowful in the wail of the winds, so filled with the
sense of blank distance, so sombre in desolation. Béranger
said that where some older earth had been ruined in the great
conflict which the powers of Good and Evil had waged, the
rock of St Helena had been left at the special prayer of the
vanquished spirits of Evil as a memento of their having been
once supreme upon earth. And he makes the Almighty ask
the reason for the request thus made.

' I ask this boon,' answers the spirit, ' in order that one day
in a far-distant age of this new world there may be brought to
that dark ocean rock a mortal all but godlike in his genius,
who shall undergo there upon that black altar a lingering death
at the hands of evil men.'

I got on shore at the earliest possible hour, and was soon
riding up the steep road that led from Jamestown to the tomb
and to Longwood. At St. Helena one quickly masters the
chapter of St. Helena. These gigantic rock walls, these im-

passable precipices, and all this environment of charred desolation in the midst of which the miserable farmhouse is perched,
gaunt and alone, tell in the space of a three-mile ride the entire
story of the captivity. When the summit level above the
tomb is reached at Hutt's Gate, the 'altar' craved of the
Demon lies outspread before the traveller, and the word
'prison' is read in gigantic characters on sea and sky, on peak
and precipice of that grey, gloomy circumference, in the centre
of which is Longwood. Here all the names known in the
history of these five or six years of suffering cease to have any
individual meaning. 'Rupert's,' 'Deadwood,' 'Longwood,'
'the Flagstaff,' 'the Barn,' 'the Valley of Silence,' disappear,
and there only remains the all-pervading sense of an inner
prison, surrounded by even more impassable boundaries of lava,
chasm, and rock wall than the ocean and the outer sea face of
the island had already provided.

I had stood by the tomb, had seen the house, and looked
long on the features of the marble bust within the black-railed
space which marks the spot where the little camp death-
bedstead stood on the 5th May 1821, and now it was time to
leave Longwood Perhaps it was because one had asked the
French sergeant who was in charge questions which he was not
able to answer, or perhaps from some other reason, but as I
was about to depart he volunteered the information that there
was still living, at only a little distance from Longwood House,
an old soldier who had been on the island during the captivity.

'Monsieur might care to see him ?'

'Yes, very much.'

'He lives close by, monsieur, in a little hut, there below the
dip of the ridge between us and the gate of Longwood.'

Five minutes later I was at the hut. An old man was at
spade-work in a little garden.

'Well, old friend, they tell me you were here in Bonaparte's
time,' I say, speaking very loud, for he is deaf. 'Can you tell
me anything about him ?'

He looks up from his work, leans on his spade handle, and
says nothing. I put the question again in a louder voice.

'Is it Bony ye mane ?' he says, in an accent which, notwithstanding a lapse of forty or fifty years, still tells of Ireland.
'To be shure I remember him, and so I ought, for many the

day and the night I mounted guard over him, and stood sentry beyond the gum trees there by the house.'

' How long have you been here ? ' I ask.

' Fifty years come October next,' he says.   ' I came out with the 53rd Regiment, and when it left to go to India I exchanged into the 66th, and I married and settled here.   Did ye ever hear tell of Sligo ? ' he went on.

' Yes, often.'

' Well, that was my country.   I wonder now how it 's getting on, and if there 's any of my people living.'

So anxious was I to follow the thread of the guard and sentry memory that I could at the moment have consigned Sligo to the deepest bottom of its own bogs ; but it was wiser to dissemble a little, so after a few words about Sligo I got the old fellow's memory back again to Longwood, the guards, the sentries, and the old times of the captivity ; and as a starting-point I asked him where the line of sentries used to be placed by day and by night.

' The sintries is it ? ' he says.   ' There 's the field over where the sheep are grazing ; that 's where the big camp stood.   By day the sintries were kept below the ridge, along the far side of the valley ' (pointing across the depths of Fisher's Ravine), ' and by night they were drawn in, and they closed up around the house.'

' Did you ever see the Emperor ? '

' Who ? '

' Bonaparte.'

' Yes, often.   I used to see him of times working in the garden at the house, or throwing crumbs to the fish in the pond near the door.   When he got too bad to walk out in the garden, I used to see him sometimes in the house ; for I was told off to look after the Chinamen that were employed there, and to see that they fetched up the water every day from the spring down by Torbutts, where the tomb is now.'

Then we spoke of the house and the dwarf gum trees that grew on the level ground just above his cabin.

' There were more of them there in them days,' he said, ' but the storm that blew the night before he died—the awfullest wind that was ever on the island—knocked most of them down.'

Then, after some other talk about St. Helena, his mind

wandered off again to Sligo. and he soon ceased speaking. The old man's brain was tired

I could have remained a long while there, but it would not have been of any use This curious, old, time-rusted link in the chain between past and present, dressed in a soldier's tattered coat, had said his say ; and the well of his memory had run dry. What things had these old eyes looked at ! Old friend, good-bye

I mounted and rode away, thinking over the words, ' closed up around the house.' All these vast precipices, from the edges of which the passer-by recoils in instinctive horror ; these gloomy rampart rocks , all these camps of soldiers—one there at Deadwood, one hundred yards in front of the farmhouse , another at Hutt's Gate, where the sawback ridge begins which just suffices in its width at the top to carry the road on to Longwood between the prodigious rents in the earth plunging down, one thousand feet in depth, below the narrow roadway ; these were not wards and guards and barriers sufficient, placed though they were with thousands of leagues between them and the nearest land, but the line of sentries must ' close up at sunset ' around the walls of the miserable house itself.

The news that reached us at St. Helena was full of interest. The Civil War in America seemed to be drawing to a close , but a little speck of conflict was showing in Northern Europe. Two great Powers had invaded little Denmark. To us poor homeward-bound soldiers, anxious for service, it seemed that this wanton and cowardly proceeding must produce the general war which some of us, at least, wished for. I find in the pages of our little sea journal some lines entitled ' War's Whisper,' the concluding verse of which ran thus :—

> 'Ho ! babblers of "peace," ye who boasted in pride
> That the sword in its scabbard for ever was tied !
> Did ye hear that low murmur waft over the main
> Its tidings of battle in the land of the Dane ?'

But alas for poetic flight and bellicose imaginations ! No sword leaped from scabbard either in France or England, and the massacre of Düppel passed unnoticed by either of the Powers whose one great chance in modern history it was. These things do not happen twice. Louis Napoleon might

E

easily have saved Sedan and Paris had he then struck for the Dane, and there would, in all human probability, have been no ' Dreadnought ' scare to-day had there been a single soldier-statesman in England in that year 1864.

There was no Suez Canal in 1864, and the roadstead at St. Helena had always plenty of shipping in it, vessels taking in food and water on their homeward route from India and China. At the time of our visit it held other craft—American whalers from the Antarctic hiding from the *Alabama*, which was still at work of destruction in various seas. I went on board one of these whalers She was three months out from Maine ; her captain and crew in beards and clothes like so many Robinson Crusoes. It was early morning. The captain insisted upon my having breakfast with him—a black bottle of terrible spirit and a plate of hard-tack biscuits, on a table that had been lubricated with blubber. It was sufficient.

Our sister ship, the *Trafalgar*, conveying the right wing of the regiment, had gained a week upon us in the run from Madras to St Helena. She had left the island with a clear seventeen days' start. The race home now seemed hopeless for us.

We left St Helena with the south-east trade blowing strong, and it bowled us along before it during the next sixteen days. No halt from calms on the Line , the northern tropic proved equally propitious, and the ' roaring forties ' sent us flying along from stormy Corvo to the Cornish coast in glorious style. On 21st May we anchored at Plymouth, ninety days out from Madras. An hour later a full-rigged ship was visible on the horizon from beyond the Eddystone Lighthouse. Our captain, who had only one eye (but, like Nelson's, it was a very good one) laid his glass upon the distant vessel. ' It 's the *Trafalgar*,' he said ; and so it was That three hundred and twenty mile day on the 17th had done its work ; we had gained some seventeen days upon our sister ship in the run from St. Helena.

When we entered the Channel a thing foretold by the ship's officers happened. We carried some seventy or eighty invalid soldiers from India, the wrecks of the Carnatic climate. ' You will see many of these men die when we get near the English coast,' the officers and doctor used to say. So it fell out. We buried several of these poor fellows almost in sight of the Lizard. For them the 'chops of the Channel' had a sinister meaning.

On 22nd May the two sisters, now in company, sailed before a delightful westerly breeze along the coasts of Devon, Dorset, and Hampshire to Portsmouth. Very fresh and beautiful it all looked ; hawthorn blossom holding out welcome to us ; scents of spring from the shores, and May-green on the hills for the rest and refreshment of our sun-seared eyes. To understand all the loveliness of an English spring you should spend a few summers in the Carnatic.

CHAPTER V

WE were stationed at Gosport after arrival, and then we went to Aldershot. These south of England town garrisons made bad stations for soldiers lately arrived from abroad; that harpy the Jew jeweller, and the betting or gambling man have there a wide field for the exercise of their various greeds, wiles, and villanies. Before we were a year at home half of our officers were in debt, and many of them had to exchange or leave the service.

After a short leave of absence at home, I was sent with a party of men to Hythe to learn out of books that theory of musketry in the practice of which I was already no mean proficient. But Hythe was no exception to the rule which I have found existing in every part of the world—namely, that a man will find something of interest, something that is worth knowing or seeing, no matter what the spot may be on the earth's surface where fortune has cast him.

Visiting Dover one day, I turned into the Ship Hotel for lunch. At a table in one corner of the public room four men were sitting. The waiter informed me that they were officers of the American Federal cruiser *Kearsarge*, which was then lying in the harbour. Over at Calais lay also in harbour, and afraid to stir from it, the Confederate cruiser *Alabama*. The Federal agent in Calais kept the captain of the *Kearsarge* constantly informed of the doings of his rival. The *Kearsarge* lay in Dover with steam always up. The truth was, the *Alabama's* game was up, unless some extraordinary freak of fortune should again befriend her, for the *Kearsarge* had ' the legs of her,' and whether the brave Semmes headed out into the North Sea, or went down Channel, he must be overhauled by his enemy.

Suddenly the door of the coffee-room opened, and four gentlemen, dressed in rather peculiar suits of 'mufti,' entered the room. They stopped short, stared hard at the occupants of the table in the corner, turned abruptly round, and left the room. They were officers of the *Alabama*, who had crossed from Calais by the mail-boat that morning, probably to have a look at their enemy from the pier. A couple of weeks later the Confederate slipped out from Calais at night, and with something of a start made her way down Channel; but the *Kearsarge* was soon upon her tracks.

Cherbourg afforded a last refuge for the little warship whose career in all the oceans, and even in the corners of seas, had cost the Northern States such enormous loss. When the time limit was up she had to put to sea. A few miles off Cherbourg the two cruisers met for the first and last time. It was all over with the *Alabama* in an hour. Semmes and his crew were picked up by an English steam yacht—I have forgotten her name—but curiously enough she had steamed close alongside for many miles, a month or two earlier, when the two clipper ships were racing each other along the south coast of England from Plymouth to Dartmouth.

Early in 1865 we moved to Aldershot, then in a very different condition from what it is to-day. Great expanses of sand stretched from beyond the Long Valley up to the doors of the wretched huts in which we were housed. All the verdure and foliage which chiefly owe their origin to the labours of Colonel Laffan of the Engineers were then unknown, and when a south-west wind blew one might have imagined that Cæsar's Camp was a koppje in the Sahara.

But the thing that made the Aldershot of 1865 a place of delight for memory to recall was the individuality of the military characters one met there. Not one solitary vestige of these old vanished heroes can now be found in our army. Truly can it be said that the entire military type and bearing of that time is gone, 'lock, stock, and barrel.' The stock still clung to the soldier's neck, the lock and barrel were of the old percussion muzzle-loading model, 'fire-lock' it was still called by the older drill sergeants

Our regiment 'lay,' as the expression used to be, in the North Camp, and very uncomfortable 'lying' it was for all

concerned. When I marched the company to which I belonged
to the group of huts assigned to us, I heard one of the old
twenty-one-year men mutter as he entered the hut, ' Twenty
years all round the worruld, and in a —— cowshed at the end
of it.'

All the drills, movements, and manœuvres were exactly
what they had been fifty years before. There might just as
well have been no Crimean War, no Mutiny, no anything.
Most of the old officers swore as their ancestors had sworn on
the fields of Flanders one hundred years earlier. I think the
men liked them all the better on that account. The general in
command was a splendid veteran. It was he who, a quarter
of a century earlier, had told his men at Meeanee to ' turn the
fire-locks ' as they drove their bayonets into the enemy when
these brave Belooch swordsmen were hacking at the Twenty-
Second over the levelled bayonets. He had borne at Inkermann the worst pressure of the Russian attack in the early
hours of the fight. When the first reinforcement—Cathcart's
Division—came up, that general had ridden forward to ask to
what part of the field he should direct his troops. ' Anywhere
you like, my dear sir ; you 'll find plenty of fighting all round.'
And indeed he found it, for within a couple of hours Cathcart
and about half of his division were dead on the slopes that lay
to the right rear of the famous Sand-bag Redoubt.

I can still see this old hero sitting his charger on the top of
a knoll over the Basingstoke Canal, across which the engineers
had, in manœuvre language, ' thrown a pontoon bridge '
(two pontoons and twenty planks). Over this structure our
brigade had to go, and the great point was that they should
not keep step as they crossed, but the poor fellows had been
so mercilessly trained to keep step that they couldn't break
it to save their lives ; and as the canal was only about four
feet deep in the centre of its twenty or thirty feet width, it
didn't matter a pin whether they fell in or not.

But from the general's excitement you might have thought
that the operation was quite on a par with that of the Russians
retreating over their bridge of boats from the south to the north
side of Sebastopol. Up we came to the canal in solid, serried
ranks. The more he swore at us, the more his staff roared at
us shouting ' break step,' the more our men stepped ' as one

man,' as they had been taught and drilled and bullied into doing for years : tramp, tramp, tramp. I can never forget the sight of that fine old soldier ; the reins dropped on his charger's neck, his hands uplifted as far as they could go, and a whole torrent of imprecations pouring from under his snow-white moustache. Two ladies who had ridden out with the staff thought it prudent to retire from the scene. The two pontoons stood it all.

Among the old officers of lesser rank the one who gave us youngsters the most unvarying entertainment was the colonel of a distinguished Fusilier battalion, a North Briton. All the manœuvre formations were then in close order ; a modern dynamite shell bursting in a brigade would inevitably have ended the collective life and entire martial capacity of that military unit This view of the question, however, had not occurred to any of our superiors ; and to us subalterns in the ranks these close formations had, at least, the merit of enabling us to get all the mounted officers of three or four battalions within easy range of our ears and eyes. We knew, in fact, everything that was going on in the brigade. Old Colonel R. S. was our central point of interest. He had a profound contempt and dislike for a staff officer, and in this feeling we were with him to a man.

An A D.C. or a Deputy A D C. would ride up to the brigade, salute, deliver his orders, wheel his horse round, and gallop away. Colonel R. S., being a very senior officer, was frequently in command of the brigade. He would never move a muscle as the staff officer went through his message. He would then gravely turn to one of the old ' fizzer men,' as they were called (pensioners who had the privilege of hawking ginger-beer among the troops), and ask him, ' What did the d—— fule say ? '

' He said, yer honour, that the brigade was to move to the right '

' Did he ? Third brigade, fours left.'

Or, again, he would on occasion, when he had had words with the messenger of movement, take all the men into his confidence by turning in his saddle, and remarking with a most comical expression of face, ' He 'll nae puzzle the Fusiliers, I can tell ye ' And indeed, I am quite sure that nothing which

the most conceited young staff officer could do would ever
have ' puzzled ' that splendid body of men. They would
have died to a man with that old Scotsman.

I had one resource at Aldershot of inestimable value to me.
It was the Prince Consort's library. Many an hour I spent in
that cool retreat reading of the wars on land and sea, and of the
men who fought them. By hook or crook I must go to Belgium,
and see some of the scenes themselves. The few pounds I had
put together in India were now gone. Aldershot was an
expensive station at that time, for regiments and battalions
were constantly arriving, and the reputation of the ' Old 69th '
for hospitality had to be kept up, literally at all costs. But
I managed to get together about twenty pounds, and one fine
evening I was off, knapsack on shoulder, for Lille, intending
to leave the train at Tournay, and begin to work the ground
on foot from that place.

I reached Tournay early on the second morning, picked up
a guide on the steps of the cathedral, and was soon on the road
to Fontenoy. The guide was a ghastly failure. He professed
to know the battlefields around Tournay, but I soon found
he knew only the public-houses. ' You know the field of
Fontenoy ? ' I said as we cleared the old town. Certainly he
knew Fontenoy, he answered , was not his father in that
battle, and did not the Emperor decorate him when it was
over ? Astonished by this information I merely said, ' Go
ahead '

It was a very hot afternoon, the road was deep in dust, and
the knapsack still a new burden to my shoulders. Whenever
we passed a beer shop he looked longingly at it , but I held
steadily on, taking a most malicious satisfaction in the situation
that was now developing, for I soon saw that the fellow was
soft as butter. At last he craved a halt and a drink. These
I gave him, even though he still adhered to the story of the
decoration of his father on the field of Fontenoy by the Emperor
himself Then I thought, ' Are we not now in the Cockpit
of Europe ? ' There were so many battles fought here that
this man may well have got a bit mixed among them, and
perhaps in this matter of the decoration he had only inherited
an ancestral antipathy to the truth. So we went again along
the dusty road

It was getting towards sunset when we approached Fontenoy.
I had a map of the ground, and was on the lookout for the
wood of Barri. Passing that, we entered the scene of the
battle A large country waggon, full of women and girls
returning from work, came along 'Fontenoy ?' I asked
inquiringly They laughed, and pointed away to my left
front, where the ridge bent down into lower ground, and over
the curve could be seen a church spire, some white houses, and
trees. They asked me to join them, and made room for me
in the waggon, laughing and talking, under large lace or fringe-
bordered caps, all the while I was clearly a puzzle to them ;
but all the same they seemed disposed to accept my presence
as that of an old friend Another time I might have accepted
the seat offered in their midst, but as there was less than an
hour's light in the sky I thought it wiser to keep my feet, and
made straight for Fontenoy. The ground was all familiar
to me, for I had studied the map of it well. I paid off my
guide. He had brought me to Fontenoy, even though he had
failed to convince me of the decoration bestowed upon his
father in the battle.

On every side where the land was clear of wood the ground
lay open and unfenced . stubble interspersed with grass. Three
miles away on the right, Antoing showed its church top above
the valley of the Scheldt ; then the higher ground upon which
the French army had stood curved round towards Fontenoy
about two miles, and then ran in on the same easy circle to
Barri, the semicircle making altogether about four miles along
its circumference from the wood of Barri on the left to Antoing
on the right.

In front of the village of Fontenoy the ground dropped
quickly into the valley of Voyon. Never was there easier field
upon which to identify the events which took place there on
the 11th May 1745 Save that the French redoubts have
long ago been levelled by the ploughshare, everything is unchanged Between the village of Fontenoy and the wood of
Barri all the fighting took place. There Ligonier led on his
column of fourteen thousand English and Hanoverian troops
and twenty guns into the left centre of the French position
Shot at by cannon, charged by cavalry, fired into by infantry,
they go slowly forward, until meeting the French Guards the

two columns exchange first compliments and then volleys,
until half of the whole are down in the young corn.

The battle began at five in the morning, and it was all
over by one o'clock. At noon the allies were in full retreat
on Ath. Some fifteen thousand dead and wounded covered
this gently rolling ground. History has given half a dozen
versions of this once famous fight; but what is assured as
fact is that Cumberland's column under Ligonier had all but
won victory when it was wrested from their grasp by the
terrible onslaught of Saxe's reserve troops, among which six
regiments of Irish infantry, under Count Lally, formed the
most potent body and struck the most decisive blows.

I made my way across the field of Antoing as the dusk was
gathering over Fontenoy, and a white mist was coming up from
the Voyon Valley, creeping like a great ghost of battle across
the ridge where this wild slaughter had been wrought. The
partridges were calling briskly to each other in the cool twilight;
the smoke of supper was going up from many cottage chimneys.
How was I to fare in that way at Antoing? I struck straight
for that little old Flemish town, and at the inn kept by Monsieur
and Madame Roger Dubois the question was most satisfactorily
solved. After a little preparatory delay, a fillet, a partridge,
a salad, an omelette, a bottle of Bordeaux, grapes, coffee, and
a *petit verre*—what more could mortal ask on the evening of
a hot day? Heroes of Fontenoy, old, forgotten, long-waist-
coated grenadiers of England, France, and Ireland—Saxe,
Cumberland, Ligonier, d'Auteroche, Richelieu, and Lally—
I pledge all your memories in silence as the clock in the old
church tower outside strikes the hour of nine! To you in
particular, Madame Roger Dubois, I lift my glass and take off
my hat! If history tells truth, your husband's very remarkable
namesake, the Archbishop of Cambray, received a cardinal's
hat through the friendly intervention of George the First,
whose son was to lose this fight at Fontenoy some few years
later. Well, if the first George was to get a cardinal's hat
for anybody, it was perhaps meet that it should have been for
that 'little thin meagre man with the pole-cat visage, in whom
all the vices . . . contend for mastery'; but perhaps the royal
victor of Fontenoy would have had a better place in history to-
day had he hanged him.

The following day came oppressively warm, and I had a long march before me. I was to sleep at Mons, for I wished to see the field of Jemappes, that opening scene of the conquering revolution, and another great field of former fight which lay near Mons—Malplaquet. The sun was beating down on the narrow paved streets of Antoing almost with the fervour of the Carnatic as I cleared the town and took the road Mons-ward. It lay along the valley of the Scheldt, sometimes hot and dusty, sometimes under shade of rustling poplars, cool and refreshing after the glare. It took me long to get out of sight of the spire of Antoing and the tall tower of the old chateau, but at last I reached Jemappes very tired. No 'field' here for thought or study; nothing but a dry cinder-heaped hill, with smoking chimneys above it and coal-mines below. Nothing to show where Dumouriez placed his troops for the attack, where Clarefait's fourteen heavy batteries were ranged, where young De Charteris led his blue-coated volunteers up the hill of Cuesnes to assault the Austrian batteries; no chance, even, of identifying the three particular coalpits down which the victorious French put their own and their enemy's twelve thousand dead men and horses. The black country in Stafford is scarcely more cinder-heaped and smoke-grimed than is this spot where the first act of the greatest drama ever played in human history began.

At Mons next day I had better luck. From the top of the high tower of St Wadru, that old town of neither toil nor traffic, the eye could range far over this south end of the great 'cockpit,' over Malplaquet, over Frameries, over Bavay, over Jemappes. There yonder, between Sars and Tenniers, on the 11th September 1709, fell some thirty-five thousand French, English, Dutch, Danes, Germans, and Italians. 'Those who were not killed,' wrote Eugene, 'died of fatigue. I gave some rest to the remains of my troops, buried all I could, and then marched to Mons.' Of all the battles of Queen Anne's wars, this of Malplaquet was the most deadly. Although the Allies won the honours, the French got the tricks. 'The plunder of France was the general discourse in Germany, England, and Holland at the opening of the campaign of 1709'; but the loss of the twenty-five thousand of the best of the Allied troops saved France from serious invasion, and so crippled the attacking power of the Allies that it practically led to the conclusion of the war. 'If it pleases God,' wrote Marshal Villars after the fight, 'to favour your Majesty with the loss of another such battle, your enemies will be destroyed.' That was about the truth

I rambled along for another few days, and finally found myself on the road which led north from Fleurus to Ligny. The hot weather still continued, but notwithstanding the heat and foot-travel, the days were pleasant in themselves and delightful now to look back upon. I kept a notebook, and I find in it little bits of the life in town and country that read freshly now :—

'Stopped to rest in a clump of trees crossing a little mound on the right of the road, where there was an image of the Crucifixion, and underneath the inscription which poor Tom Hood wove so well into the ode that made Rae Wilson famous and ridiculous in his generation :—

> The pious choice had fixed upon the verge of a delicious slope,
> Giving the eye such variegated scope.
> "Look round," it whispered, "on that prospect rare,
> Those vales so verdant and those hills so blue .
> Enjoy the sunny world so fresh and fair :
> But" (how the simple legend pierced me through),
> "Priez, pour les malheureux."

'Yes, it was a fair world, and a delightful thing to wander over it. No anxiety for the morrow, no care for to-day, no regret for yesterday ; eating when hungry, sleeping when tired, reading the leaves of the trees, seeing the sunny half of the great round peach which we call the world. When I repine at poverty and wish for money, it is not for love of the gold thing itself, but for the love of all the golden scenes which the want of it hides from me. And then so little would suffice for what I long to do. The money which thousands waste without anything to show for it would carry me through the length of this glorious world. Men talk of knowledge of the world, meaning only knowledge of the human town mites that are on it, but of the true world they know nothing.

'*Evening.*—Halting in a sheepfold. The sheep have gathered in for the night. They stare at the strange intruder, first with awe, then with surprise, then with indifference or contempt. One, older or bolder than the others, presumes upon his ten minutes' acquaintance to approach close, look straight into my face, and stamp his foot at me. "Be off out of that," he says.

'*Sunday morning.*—The chimes in the old church tower have been busy for some time, and the inhabitants of the village are going past my open window in their best bib and tucker. I looked into the billiard-room of the inn last night, and now I can scarcely recognise in the black-coated churchgoers the players of last evening. I begin to be ashamed of my single tweed suit, now looking dusty and travel-stained ; but when a man has to carry his own baggage he cuts his clothing, not to his cloth, but to his knapsack.'

This day at Ligny was the longest and hottest of any in my rambles. All the names on the milestones were like the faces of old dead friends seen in a dream—Ligny, St. Amand, Sombreffe, Bry, Quatre Bras, 'To Genappe,' 'To Namur,' 'To Waterloo.' I had been reading of these places, great hinges of history, graveyards of human glory, for years in all sorts of places, trying so hard to transfer their printed names into brain pictures, that now when I came upon them, not in the flesh but in corn ridge and pasture slope and cottage plot, it seemed impossible they could be what the milestones and fingerposts said they were—themselves.

I passed through the little village of Ligny, and got to the higher ridges of Bry immediately behind it. The old windmill at Bussy, where Blucher had seen his centre broken in the twilight of the June evening, was there still, and near it stood a single old walnut-tree, offering most grateful shade under its branches. From this point, the events of the 16th June 1815 could be seen in a single sweep of vision. It was another of these Fontenoy fields, readable from a single centre, a thing never to be possible again One hundred years ago men stood six hundred yards from their enemies ; now they stand six thousand yards away. Below where I sat ran the little streamlet of Ligny, its valley forming an almost continuous line of hamlets from St. Amand on the right to Sombreffe on the left.

All along this valley, for a distance of some four miles, a terrible combat was waged on the afternoon of 16th June 1815 Villages, hamlets, and farmhouses were taken and retaken again and again ; while above, on the parallel ridges which front each other before either side of the rivulet of

Ligny, some four hundred and fifty guns thundered over the combatants.

I had to sleep somewhere near Quatre Bras that night, so after a rest of about an hour I struck the main line of paved road between Namur and Nivelles, near Sombreffe, and held westward towards Quatre Bras.

About halfway between the two places there is some high ground on the right of the Chaussée which commands an extensive prospect upon either side   You can see Fleurus and Charleroi to the south, and the half-dozen white houses of Quatre Bras to the west, while where you turn north-west the top of the cone of the lion-mound on the field of Waterloo is visible in this direction.   You can see, too, a little to the east of north, the smoke of Wavre.   At Marbais you stand nearly in the centre of the square which has for its corners the four battle-points of Ligny, Quatre Bras, Waterloo, and Wavre, and all the grand but simple strategy of Napoleon's campaign of 1815, planned in Paris, is apparent, magnificent in conception, simple when it is once understood.   The armies of his adversaries, Wellington and Blücher, were cantoned facing the northern frontier of France from Namur to Ath, along a distance of some fifty miles.   They numbered a total of about two hundred and thirty thousand men, with more than five hundred guns

The Emperor Napoleon could strike at this great array with a total of only one hundred and eleven thousand men and three hundred and fifty cannon.   It was an enormous, almost a hopeless, disparity of force, but it had to be faced, because at least another four hundred thousand men were moving from all Europe against the French frontiers.

From east to west, and through the centre of the Allied cantonments, ran a great paved highway (the same we are now on at Marbais), affording the easiest means of concentrating both armies, either separately or together.   This great road was bisected at Quatre Bras by another main road leading from Charleroi to Brussels, running nearly north and south   If Napoleon could seize Charleroi, he would be within striking distance of the great central road from Namur to Quatre Bras and Nivelles.   Here at Marbais we are at the spot which marked the point where the left of the army under Wellington touched the right of Blücher's army. Napoleon's plan was to strike this road at two places—one Sombreffe, which we have just quitted , the other Quatre Bras, to which we are going. If he could gain these two places on the main road, he had cut in two the direct line between his powerful enemies, and as neither of them had as yet concentrated their armies, he might hope to engage them separately and beat them in detail.

At daybreak on the 15th June he launched some seventy thousand men in three columns upon Charleroi. They were all to meet at or near that city. By noon the heads of these three columns had crossed the Sambre, carried Charleroi, and were pursuing the Prussian corps of Ziethen back to the great road at Sombreffe. On the same evening the French left column under Ney, following the bisecting road from Charleroi to Quatre Bras, had reached Frasne, less than three miles from Quatre Bras, driving the Allied troops of the Prince of Orange back to Quatre Bras. When night closed on the 15th the position of the three armies was as follows : the French head-quarters were at Charleroi, the centre concentrated round that place, the Prussians at Namur, the English at Brussels. Not until midnight on that day (the 15th), did the Duke of Wellington know that his enemy, whom he believed to be still in Paris, was in reality at Charleroi, thirty miles south of Brussels. Blucher, seventeen miles east of Namur, was in equal ignorance of Napoleon's movements, and of the concentration of his army on the frontier, one march distant from Charleroi, until the night of the 14th June.

It was a master-stroke of strategy, among the most brilliant in the records of war. One incident had alone interfered with its complete success—it was the desertion of the traitors, Bourmont and Cluet, on the 14th June, to the Prussians at Namur. Bourmont was the chief of the staff of Gérard's Corps forming the right wing of the French army. Cluet was an officer of Engineers, and there was a third officer of lesser rank. These three traitors carried to Blucher, on the night of the 14th at Namur, the first news he had received of the French move-ment ; and Bourmont, from his high position on the staff, was able to impart secret information of the highest moment.

It is now certain that if it had not been for this traitorous act the whole Prussian army would have been quiet in its

cantonments on the morning of the 15th June, and it would
then have required a clear forty-eight hours to assemble even
three corps of the Prussian army in front of Charleroi   With
the information given him by Bourmont, Blücher was able to
beat the ' Générale ' in his various cantonments on the night
of the 14th June, and to get his scattered corps in movement
in the direction of Fleurus at daybreak on the 15th.   Bourmont's treachery had robbed Napoleon of about twelve precious
hours.

Nevertheless, the chances were all in his favour at midnight
on the 15th.   Ney had actually reported his occupation of
Quatre Bras.   Napoleon himself was within striking distance
of Sombreffe.   Thus the main road commanding the two
Allied armies would probably be in his possession on the 16th,
and the two armies would be cut asunder.

The next day's work was to be this :

With his centre and right massed together, Napoleon would
attack the Prussians at or near Sombreffe.   Ney was to attack
Quatre Bras eight miles west of Sombreffe, whatever might be in
his front.   The result of the 16th June is easily told.   Napoleon
performed his part of the programme by smashing the Prussians
at Ligny ,   Ney failed in his much easier task at Quatre Bras.
On that morning of the 16th he had more than forty thousand
men, and over a hundred guns under his command, between
Gosselies and Quatre Bras.   Only a weak, mixed brigade of the
enemy held that important post.   Nevertheless, Ney let the
precious morning hours slip away in total inaction at Frasnes,
and it was past two o'clock in the afternoon when he moved
on Quatre Bras.   That position had then been heavily reinforced, and every hour of daylight that remained saw fresh
accessions of force arriving from the English reserve at Brussels,
and the scattered cantonments to the west   Here occurred
the first loss of the campaign of 1815 for Napoleon.   The
essence of this tremendous problem he had set himself to solve
was time.   In war, time must inevitably be often lost ; but
for this loss of at least eight hours before Quatre Bras there
was neither reason nor excuse.   It was the most gratuitous
waste of opportunity that the history of war affords, unless,
indeed, it be found two days later in another inexplicable loss
of ten hours on the part of a French marshal on the other

side of this great square, of which the four corners held the campaigning ground of 1815 Grouchy, on the 18th, will repeat, with still more disastrous results to his master, this terrible inaction at Gembloux, at Tabaraque, and at Wavre, which Ney is here practising at Gosselies, Frasnes, and Quatre Bras.

I must resume my own march upon Quatre Bras, and see the ground for myself. So, taking up the knapsack again, I trudged westward along the high road. I reached the little hamlet at the cross-roads as the sun was getting low towards the horizon. There was the field untouched: the wood of Boissu, the farm of Gemioncourt, rising into the higher ground behind which lay the village of Frasnes, the half a dozen white houses standing bare about the point of intersection of the two great highways.

The stubble was crisp under foot as I held on by Gemioncourt and Frasnes. A few ploughmen were unyoking their teams and turning homewards. Of all the fields of Flanders this of Quatre Bras had the strongest personal interest for me. Just there below the ridge of Gemioncourt the 69th Regiment had fared badly at the hands of Kellermann's Cuirassiers on the afternoon of that 16th June It was not their fault, poor fellows. The Prince of Orange had insisted upon line being formed from the square into which a careful colonel (who was killed two days later at Waterloo) had put them, the Cuirassiers had simply rolled up the line from right to left, killed and wounded a hundred and fifty officers and men, and taken the regimental colour back with them to Ney on the ridge of Frasnes.

Before I left Aldershot, one of those excellent men who have learnt to laugh at everything out of England asked me why I was going abroad to look at a lot of turnip fields; 'You know that here in England they say you can't get blood out of a turnip.' I answered . 'But in Belgium you can get plenty of turnips out of blood ; that 's why I 'm going there '

I reached Frasnes very tired after sunset. The day had been hot and hard, and I was badly in need of supper and rest. I found both in a clean little cottage here at Frasnes. When the homely supper was served on a snow-white cloth, I found another guest at table He was the head of the village commune, an excellent specimen of the Flemish peasant. There

F

was a dessert of grapes and two or three peaches, one of the latter being redder and riper than the others. My companion had the plate of fruit in front of him ; he turned it carefully round until the big peach was facing where I sat, and then courteously offered the plate to me. It was a simple thing, but I have never forgotten it. Civility goes a long way, they say ; in the case of my peasant friend at Frasnes it has gone more than forty years. Liberty, equality, fraternity, and the greatest of these is fraternity ; and perhaps if people practised it more frequently they need not have troubled themselves so much about the other two.

I walked from Frasnes to Waterloo on the following day. It was quite as hot and hard as any of the other days ; but by this time I was hard too.

I have said enough about these old Flemish fields of fight. We are not yet one hundred years from Waterloo. It is quite possible that there are thoughtful people in England to-day who are not quite so keen as their fathers were upon the ' leg up ' on the high horse of Europe which we gave Germany in that memorable campaign ; and neither am I sure that there may not be ' a good few ' in other parts of Europe who rather regret that flank march from Wavre to Waterloo, which saved Wellington from defeat, and made the rock of St. Helena famous.

CHAPTER VI

The Channel Isles   Victor Hugo   The Curragh   To Canada.
Leave in the West.   Buffalo hunt

THE 69th went from Aldershot to the Channel Isles in the
summer of 1866, and my lot fell to the beautiful little island
of Guernsey, where two companies were quartered in Fort
George on the crest of the hill above St. Peter's Port. The
view from the rampart of this old fort was very striking—
islands near and far on what was usually a blue and sparkling
sea, and beyond the islands the coast of Normandy from Cape
La Hogue to Coutance. It was a very happy spot, this island·
no very rich people and no very poor people in it ; moderate
comfort everywhere ; fruits and flowers everywhere ; the land
and the sea giving a two-handed harvest to the inhabitants.
It had, however, one serious drawback : intoxicating drink
was as plentiful as it was cheap. The island had a copper
currency of its own , unfortunately, a depreciated one   If a
man tendered an English shilling in payment for a glass of
brandy, he received twelve Guernsey pennies back. This
was too much for old soldiers, particularly for the men who
had served in tropical countries—a glass of French brandy
and twelve Guernsey pennies given in return for one English
shilling ! No soldier in his senses could understand a rate of
exchange based on such principles, even before he had drunk
his glass of brandy, and after that event the problem became
still more abstruse. It was impossible not to love these old
soldiers, for, notwithstanding this failing, they had so many
splendid qualities. I call these men old ; in reality they were
all under forty years, but they were old in every other sense of
the word. If you asked any of these men when they were in
hospital what was wrong with them, they would usually
answer, 'Only them pains, sir', and if you asked again what
had given them those 'pains,' they would invariably say it

was the heavy belts and cumbersome pouches they had to wear
for twenty-four hours on guard. It was true. Our stupid
regulations broke down those fine soldiers long before their
time. Men said that there were other causes, but I don't
think there were. There was not a regimental band in the
service in which you could not have found some old bassoon
or trombone player, who had sampled in his time every intoxicating fluid from cocoanut toddy to methylated spirits,
but who, nevertheless, was still going and blowing strong,
simply because he had not done a night's guard duty in his
twenty years.

A short road led to St. Peter's Port from our fort on the hill.
Half-way down the slope one passed a rather gloomy-looking,
solid, square house, standing on the right of the road. This
was Hauteville House, in which Victor Hugo had lived for
several years. He was absent from Guernsey at this time,
on a visit to Belgium. I had but recently finished reading his
Les Misérables. I thought his description of Waterloo the
finest piece of writing I had ever read. It had been constantly
in my mind during the recent visit to Waterloo, and I had felt
all that time the want of a practical acquaintance with the
French language. The first thing I now thought of doing in
this French-speaking island was to learn it.

A chance inquiry about a tutor gave me the name of a
M. Hannett de Kesler, who lived in a small house at a little
distance below Hauteville. It was thus that I made the acquaintance of one of the most delightful human beings I have
met in life. He lived in very straitened circumstances with
only an old woman servant to keep house for him. He
had had a remarkable career. Editor of a Republican newspaper in Paris in 1848, he had all the courage of his convictions,
and had stood beside Baudin on the barricade in the Faubourg
St. Antoine on the memorable morning in December 1851.
Then he had gone into exile with Victor Hugo and others.
When an amnesty was offered later he refused to accept it.
'Never,' said Victor Hugo, at poor Kesler's grave two years
after the time I am writing of—' Never was there more profound and tenacious devotion than his. He was a champion
and a sufferer. He possessed all forms of courage, from the
lively courage of the combat to the slow courage of endurance ;

from the bravery which faces the cannon, to the heroism which accepts the loss of home.' He was a deep and sincere Republican, and his love and devotion to Victor Hugo were an extraordinary thing to see. He literally worshipped the poet. But above all that anybody could say of him, stood his honesty and his simplicity of life. I look upon the hours spent in the society of this dear old man with unalloyed pleasure. He was broken in health, and was already showing symptoms of the slow form of paralysis of which he died two years later. He wrote poetry, simple and touching little verses, inspired, I think, by the antics of a minx of some sixteen summers who lived opposite, and who used to make eyes at him across the street. He used to read these verses to me. I remember one that began

'Elle a le charme, elle a la grâce'

He was, as I have said, in very straitened circumstances; but he kept it all to himself, and would not even let Victor Hugo know of his wants.

A month or two after I had begun to take lessons from him, in August I think it was, I had to go away for a few weeks. I was settling his modest fee for tuition, and I wanted to pay in advance up to the end of the year   I put the gold pieces on the table, but he would only take what was due to him at the moment, and insisted upon returning the rest of the money to me   It was some time after my return that I discovered the cause of this refusal. He had determined to go on board the Jersey steamer, and drop quietly overboard in front of the paddle-box on the voyage. He did not want to be a burden upon anybody. That was the reason he had returned the few sovereigns I had wished to give him in advance ! Meanwhile, somebody told Victor Hugo of the pecuniary straits of his devoted follower, and provision was at once made to meet his simple wants.

Shortly after the return of Victor Hugo to the island, I received a very courteous invitation to Hauteville House. 'Il a ajouté, "J'aurais le plus grand plaisir à voir Monsieur Butler, et j'espère qu'il ne tardera pas à me faire cet honneur."'

There was a District Court-martial that forenoon, which I was obliged to attend, and I went to it with feelings not easy to describe Something went very wrong with the proceedings shortly after we assembled, and I took advantage of the adjournment to fly to Hauteville House. I found there a party of some eight or ten persons assembled in a room which had many curious conceits in its furniture and decorations. Four carved seats were let into the wainscoting, with paintings done on their high straight backs in the old Dutch style. Three of these stiff chairs were for the living, and one, which had a chain across its arms, was marked ' For the dead ' The paintings represented ' The End of the Soldier,' ' The End of the Lawyer,' and ' The End of the Priest.' I have forgotten how the two first were supposed to come by their ends, but in the last picture a woman was laying a birch broom across the shoulders of a French cleric who was in the act of disappearing through a doorway.

During the *déjeuner* Victor Hugo spoke a great deal. I was able to follow what he said with difficulty. What struck me most was the extraordinary sonorous tone of his voice, its modulations, and, if I might use the word, its ramifications It seemed to run up and down through words as the fingers of a great musician might range through notes of music

He frequently repeated the invitation to me to attend these little weekly parties, and I used to meet him also in his walks to Fermain Bay, a beautiful little secluded sea cove between very high rocks, not far from our fort. At times he used to be full of fun and raillery, but the general tone of his mind was grave and serious. I kept no regular diary at this time, but I find in an intermittent little notebook some references to these meetings.

' *22nd Octr.* (1866).—At breakfast with Victor Hugo. After looking at me for some time, he suddenly said " I have examined your face, and if I was ever to be tried I would wish to have you for a judge."

' *26th Nov.*—To-day at Victor Hugo's. He said : " I also am an Irishman. I love Ireland because she is to me a Poland and a Hungary, because she suffers. . . ." Later he asked me if I would accompany him the following year through Ireland. " I want to see that island and its people. You shall be my guide there The only stipulation I will make is that we shall drive everywhere, and that you will not ask me to travel in a train." '

But the next year I was far away in Canada !

'4th Dec.—Dined this evening in company with Victor Hugo at Monsieur Le Bers'. He was full of fun. "Take care of him!" he said, pointing at me ; "he is an *enfant terrible*."

'10th Dec.—Breakfasted at Victor Hugo's. He said that there were two English words which he hated one was "Respectable," and the other "Ragged." "Ragged School! think of that," he went on ; "does it not make you shiver ? " '

Of the many curious things to be seen in Hauteville House, the master's sleeping-room was the strangest He had built it on the roof between two great blocks of chimneys. You ascended to his workshop bedroom by stairs which somewhat resembled a ladder : quite half of the room was glass, and the view from it was magnificent ; the isles of Jethou and Sark were in the middle distance, and beyond lay many a mile of the Norman coast. Alderney lay to the north, and beyond it one saw the glistening windows of the triple lighthouses on the Casquet rocks, and still more to the right the high ridges overlooking Cherbourg. The bed was a small camp bedstead, with a table on one side of it, and a small desk chest of drawers on the other, with pens, ink and paper always within reach. Near the bed stood a small stove, which he lighted himself every morning, and on which he prepared his *café-au-lait* ; then work began at the large table which stood in the glass alcove a few feet from the foot of the bed. This work went on till it was time to dress and descend to the *déjeuner* in the room on the ground floor already described.

As the sheets of writing-paper were finished, they were numbered and dropped on the floor, to be picked up, arranged, and put away in the drawer-desk at the end of the morning's labour. He called the writing-table his 'carpenter's bench,' and the leaves which fell from it his 'shavings.' It was at this table and in this airy attic that most of the great work of his later life was done Here were written *Les Misérables, Les Travailleurs de la Mer*, and many volumes of poetry. Among the few things which have survived the tossings and travails of life I have still managed to retain in my possession some of the 'shavings' from that 'carpenter's bench,' which he gave me as souvenirs of his friendship.

Nowhere in these islands is the sea more delightful than at

Guernsey. Victor Hugo has told us that when he and his son found themselves exiles in the Channel Isles, the son asked him what he proposed to do. ' I shall look at the sea,' replied the father ; ' and you ? ' ' I will translate Shakespeare,' answered the son. In this little conversation we get the key to two of the poet's works, *Les Travailleurs de la Mer* and *William Shakespeare*—the last little known, but nevertheless the work of which its author was proudest.

It is a wonderful sea that laves the feet of these beautiful island rocks. I bathed in it through the winter months of 1866-67.

Suddenly, at the end of the winter, ' the route,' as it used to be called, came. The 69th was ordered to Ireland. So, in March 1867, we sailed away from Guernsey, leaving with many regrets its kind, gentle, and generous people. The soldier is but a ' toiler of the sea ' and the land, and that means many partings in his life But this life of changing scene has several sides to it. I have sometimes thought that a marching regiment filled in our social system the place taken by a comet in the solar system when it comes along and the people run to the window and look out.

We spent the early summer of 1867 at the Curragh ; but in August ' the route ' came again suddenly, and we embarked for Canada on the 19th of that month in the transport *Serapis*, then making her first voyage. It was a very uncomfortable experience ; the vessel had little or no ballast, and she bobbed about among the Atlantic rollers for thirteen days before getting to Quebec. After a delay of one day we were transferred to boats plying between Quebec and Montreal, and again transferred to other river craft bound for Hamilton, at the western end of Lake Ontario ; finally getting to a little town in Western Canada called Brantford, about midway between Lakes Ontario and Erie. This district had been the scene of some recent incursions at the hands of armed bodies of Fenians who had formerly served in the Northern armies of the now once more United States, and who, finding their occupation gone on the Potomac and the Rapahannock, had elected to carry on war on their own account on the St. Lawrence and the Welland Canal. Hence our rapid movement to Canada.

The whole character of the new scene of service was so novel to me, and so full of the virility of a youthful people, that it would be impossible to give expression to the sense of the freshness of life that went with it to us who now beheld it for the first time. The approach by the mighty estuary of the St. Lawrence River, the gradual drawing in of these great shores, the immense width of the stream when it is still six hundred miles from the open sea, the varied scenery of lake and rapid along the upward course to Ontario, and then that beautiful expanse of water itself, all combined to strike the mind of the newcomer with the sense of size and majesty which is the dominant note of the American continent.

In boyhood I had read the novels of Fenimore Cooper with an intensity of interest never to be known again in reading. 'Leather Stocking,' Lucas, Chingaghook, the Mohicans, the Hurons, the scenery of the Thousand Islands— all these had been things quite as real to me in imagination as the actual scenes through which we were now passing Only the Indians and the wild animals were wanting. Where were they ? Gone from this West Canada, but still to be found west of the Mississippi and the Missouri, I was told. It was now the middle of September. I got three months' leave of absence and, in company with another old friend of the Indian forest days, started out for the great West. Three days after leaving Brantford we were at Omaha, west of the Mississippi. Fortune had favoured us. We knew nobody, nobody knew us, and yet it was simple truth to say that everybody befriended us. You met a man on board the train going to Chicago . he couldn't do enough for you ; he passed you on to some other good fellow who knew somebody else five hundred or a thousand miles nearer to the setting sun ; and when you alighted at the longitude of that particular location, you found that man as friendly as though he had been expecting you for years.

This was exactly what happened to us. We struck upon a general going west in the Chicago hotel, and he at once offered his good services to and at Omaha on the Missouri, where he was then stationed. At that period the soldiers of the armies of Sherman and Grant seemed to be all either in the West, or going there The new railway to California was just opened to Omaha ; and it was said that a train ran as far over the Nebraska prairies as Fort Kearney on the North Platte River, three hundred miles west of the Missouri, where the garrison of the fort was largely rationed, so far as fresh beef went, upon buffalo-meat. This was indeed news to us, and we set off from Chicago in high spirits. When the next evening came we crossed the Missouri over a very crank-looking temporary wooden bridge to Omaha. We found that city a very lively place ; railway navvies, gold-diggers, speculators abounded. Shooting went on pretty briskly in the gambling rooms and drinking saloons, of which there appeared to be an unlimited number. Every man policed himself with a sort of murderous solemnity that was most impressive. At one of the principal saloons, a day or two before our arrival, a miner had quietly drawn a bead upon a man who had just entered and was walking up towards the bar. ' What did you shoot him for ? ' asked his mate. ' Wall, I just guess that if I hadn't done that he might have hurt somebody,' was the plea of justifiable homicide entered by this voluntary preserver of the peace.

Our friend, the Chicago general, called early next day at our hotel, and asked us to go with him to the headquarters of the command. We went, and were introduced to General Augur, a very distinguished officer of the regular army who had held high command in the Civil War. Augur was of that splendid type of gentleman which West Point has so long given to America, and I will venture to hazard the opinion that if America keeps her military school at West Point in the future as she has kept it in the past, she need not fear that either foreign or domestic enemies will do her serious harm. West Point will give her captains for many wars , and the class to which that ' peace preserver ' belonged, whose peculiar methods of discipline I have already described, will give her the rank and file of fighting men.

The general had already been informed of the object of our journey to the West, and he entered warmly into our plans. He would telegraph at once to the commandant at Fort Kearney as to the whereabouts of buffalo on the Platte prairies, and if the answer proved favourable to our hopes he would send his aide-de-camp, Captain Russell, with us to the Fort, to smooth difficulties and facilitate our progress. The reply came quickly. Yes, there were several herds on the prairies near Kearney. So the next morning, in company with Captain Russell, we took the train for Fort Kearney Station on the new Union Pacific Railway. Some other officers and soldiers were proceeding west to join garrisons in the Indian districts of the Platte and Republican Rivers We were a very merry party. All the officers had served in the Civil War—some with Sherman, others with Grant. We had the end of the Pullman car to ourselves.

There was no want of refreshment, and nobody thought of retiring to the sleeping compartment until the night was more than half over. Story followed story. A major of the United States Infantry named Burt told the best; but the general's A.D.C. was a good second. I remember one of these stories which had a touch of historical interest in it.

General Grant was carrying out on the Mississippi, previous to the battle of Shiloh, one of the most hazardous operations known in war—crossing his army from one shore to the other, within striking distance of his enemy on the farther shore. He had only three river steamers to ferry his troops over. On the third day the operation was almost completed, and the general and his staff were on horseback on the enemy's side of the Mississippi, watching the passage of the rearmost battalions in the three steamboats. Grant sat his horse, silently smoking a large cigar, which he rolled a good deal between his lips. A staff officer in the group happened to observe that if they were licked in the next day or two they would want more transport to take the army back to where it had come from than those three little boats could give them. Rumour said that the general had consumed a good deal of Bourbon whisky that day, as was his wont at the time, I have heard ; but be that as it may, it did not unlock his lips ; he continued to roll and bite the big cigar in grim silence The staff officer repeated his observation about the scantiness of transport. After a bit the general seemed to have become aware that somebody had spoken, and that he was himself expected to say something in reply. Then the big cigar rolled quicker than before, and from the compressed lips the remark issued, ' Guess them three boats will be enough to take back what 's left if I 'm licked to-morrow ! '

We reached Kearney Station as day was breaking, and found a six-team army mule-waggon awaiting us. The fort was still some six miles from the railway, and on the other side of the Platte River. Things were soon fixed up, and away we went across a prairie as level as a billiard-table, just as the light was making the surrounding scene visible. Here was the mystic word ' prairie ' at last a veritable reality. Since my early boyhood that word had meant to me everything that was possible in the breathing, seeing, and grasping of freedom

We came suddenly to the Platte River, a huge, sandy bed more than a mile in width, with several streams running through portions of it. A mile from the south bank stood Fort Kearney.

The sun was now on the horizon, and the mists were lifting. As we approached the wooden palisades of the fort, we saw two big black objects standing on the prairie about a thousand yards on one side of the buildings. Buffalo ? Yes, there they were. Another minute, and we were drawn up at the door of the commandant's house in Fort Kearney. He was at the door to give us welcome, in full uniform, and with a broad-brimmed, steeple-crowned hat on his head ; and a very cheery welcome it was.

' Colonel,' he said to me, ' these early Fall mornings have chills in them , we have some medicine here which we find very effective against Platte fever.' A large bowl of hot Bourbon whisky egg-flip was on the table, and he ladled us tumblers of this fever-killer all round. The commandant was one of the most typical American figures possible to imagine—tall, thin, gaunt, wrinkled many years in advance of his age, he might have stood as the model for a picture of a primitive New England Puritan in the second generation from the *Mayflower*. Every now and then there came some word into his speech giving at first rather a shock to any ideas of complete Puritanic perfection, which his outward semblance and strong nasal utterance might have occasioned. He belonged to the 18th Regiment of Infantry. He had been many things in his time. He had run a newspaper in Pittsburg, made three sections of the Indiana and Memphis Railway, had kept a store in Lake Street, Chicago, had fought the Confederates for three years as a volunteer colonel, had been in as many general actions as the Duke of Wellington, and when the Northern army was reduced at the end of the war, he contentedly accepted a lieutenancy in the regular service of the United States. England must have seen many men of his type in the army that was drawn up on Blackheath as Charles the Second rode past to London in 1660.

The sight of the two big buffalo bulls within a mile of the fort was so strong in our minds, that we proposed to proceed at once in pursuit of them. This proposal for immediate action before breakfast seemed to tickle his fancy He at once abandoned Salem mannerisms, and descended into congregational colloquialisms 'Boys,' he said, bringing us down with a run to our proper levels from previous field rank, 'Boys, don't you trouble about them darned two bull-buffaloes. We 'll have breakfast in half an hour, the horses will be ready at nine o'clock, the shooting irons all fixed up, and we 'll have the hull day for the buffalo ' He was right. There was plenty of time and plenty of buffalo before us.

We set out shortly after nine—the old commandant leading —six or seven men on ragged-looking but very serviceable American army horses. The course taken led across the dead level prairie which surrounded the fort towards a low line of sandy ridges due south Our two bulls had vanished. Nothing but our own seven or eight horses moved within the wide circle of our vision.

We were now at the foot of the sandy ridge, and five or six miles from the fort. The commandant stopped. 'Colonel,' he said, again reverting to service form, 'Colonel, ride up that slope , before you get quite to the top of it take some place where grass is growing, so as to let you look over without showing your heads ; get the shooting irons ready, and then I give the word " go." '

We did as he directed, approached the top of the hill cautiously, and looked over Before or since 1 never saw the equal of that sight, and, what is more, no man can ever see it again. The ridge on which we rode dropped down at the far side into a prairie that quite dwarfed that over which we had come ; but the sight that struck us with astonishment was not the vastness of the scene, but the immensity of the animal life that covered it. From a spot three or four hundred yards from where we stood, far off to a remote horizon where sky and prairie came together on a line that was visible to us only by the small black specks of life that were on it, a vast herd of grazing buffaloes stretched away to the south ; huge animals in the foreground, gradually lessening in size as the middle distance was reached, and then dwindling down into the faint specks I have spoken of. A rifle bullet might have reached the nearest of the herd ; two hours' hard riding would not have carried you to the farthest animal where the earth limit was a line of buffalo backs   The commandant gave the word, and over the top of the hill we went spreading out to right and left, as we rode down the other side. The mass of animals was so vast that there was no picking or choosing of group or ground.

It was strange to see the wave of alarm pass from the edge of the vast herd that was nearest to us, on through the mass itself. The buffalo has (or we should say *had*, for he is now practically an extinct animal) a way of throwing himself away to the right or left from the heavy forepart of his body, pivoting as it were on his fore legs, and swinging the remainder of his body to either side. In an incredibly short space of time the part of the herd we could see was in motion straight away from our advance, ploughing at full gallop over the prairie. It was now a case of each man for himself. I was soon at the heels of a very big old bull, tearing at full gallop after him. The commandant had given us each a short and handy Spencer carbine, the then cavalry arm in the United States Army. It loaded through the butt, by an action of the trigger guard ; the magazine held seven cartridges , and as the process of reloading was easily effected in the saddle, it formed a very handy weapon in attack, pursuit, or retreat. All these a buffalo hunt afforded.

When my particular bull found that he was outpaced, he began to swing from side to side in his gallop, so as to eye his pursuer first from one eye and then from the other   I took advantage of one of these side surges to give him a shot, the only effect of which was that he planted his forefeet well in the light soil of the prairie, and pivoting as I have said, swung round upon me in a second   It was now my turn to fly and his to pursue ; but again finding I had ' the legs of him,' he swerved again and made off after the still flying herd. It was some little time before I caught him up again and got a second shot at him, and again came the same tactics and the same result. At last, after a couple of miles had been run, and some four or five shots fired, he turned for the last time, pawed the ground, bellowed, and fell on his knees to the ground.

I had now time to look around ; a change had come upon the scene in that two-mile gallop. My companions were not visible on any side. The great herd was still careering south, and from out its dust came the sounds of a few distant shots. I continued the pursuit, and soon came up again with the nearest animals. They were all bulls—some old, some young The same firing, charge, and pursuit were again enacted, and another big bull was on the ground. The tail and the tongue were taken, one as a trophy, the other for the table, and again the chase went on southwards ; then fatigue of horse and man called a halt, and after a rest one turned back towards the north to look for the ridge from which the fort would be visible.

Some of our party came together at the ridge, others turned up singly, and in the evening we were all united at the fort.

At this time Nebraska was still a Territory of the United States. Settlement had not yet penetrated into these great wilds. Indians and buffalo were still numerous , and the line of forts from the Missouri westward was maintained for the protection of the line of real conquest, the railway, which had now reached this central spot of the United States on its progress to the Pacific. The four years' Civil War had arrested for a time the opening up of this vast region, and now the wave of settlement was in motion again, with a force, a directness, an energy, and, I might add, a sense of empire, to all of which the long and costly war seemed only to have added strength and power

What impressed me most strangely about the men I now came in contact with was the uniformity of the type which America was producing—northern, southern, eastern, western, miner, hotel-keeper, steamboat-man, railroad-man, soldier, officer, general,—the mould was the same ' There has got to be ' seemed to be the favourite formula of speech among them all, whether it was the setting up of a saloon, the bridging of a river, or the creation of a new State. ' There has got to be ' this railway, this drinking bar, this city, this State of the Union. Nobody dreamt, except when he slept , everybody acted while he was awake. They drank a good deal, but you seldom saw a man drunk, and you never saw anybody dead drunk. They sometimes shot each other, they never abused each other ; they were generous, open-hearted, full of a dry humour, as manly as men could be ; rough, but not rude ; civil, but never servile ; proud of their country and boastful of it and of themselves. That day and evening, and all the other days and evenings I spent at Fort Kearney, were the same—good fellowship, good stories round the festive board at night, hard riding and hunting all day over the glorious prairies.

The accommodation of the fort was limited; and we four visitors had one room for sleeping in. At about six o'clock every morning the fort doctor used to enter this room with a demijohn of Bourbon whisky on his shoulder, from which he poured four doses of ' medicine ' for the guests. ' It will wake you, boys,' he would say ; and sometimes when his gait was not quite as steady as it had been previous to the dinner-hour of the evening before, he would lurch forward a little while he was preparing to pour the prescription into a tumbler, and send a liberal dose of it over the bed-clothes. ' It will do you no harm, boys,' he would then say ; ' it 's good outside and inside.' Later in the day he compounded several other draughts from his demijohns, the secrets of which he told us he had discovered when he served on the Upper Mississippi ; but I do not remember to have ever detected the flavour of that or of any other water in any of these many compounds.

Before returning to the Missouri we visited North Platte, the extreme point to which the Pacific Railway then ran. Civilisation, as it moves west, is compelled to halt at intervals, rest itself, and collect its stragglers before it moves on again. The construction of the line was proceeding at the rate of four miles a day, so the terminal station was constantly moving on, and the strangest part of this condition of movement was the effect it had upon the motley crowd of saloon society which had congregated to supply the wants of the army of navvies, constructors, engineers, etc , at work at this point. These people moved like the baggage carriers of an Indian column, carrying on their own backs, in waggons, or on the backs of animals the household gods (or demons) of their various trades.

At North Platte we found a distinguished officer of the army in command, Colonel Dodge, one of the foremost frontier men of his time, and the descendant of officers who had prepared the road for the army of settlement in the West. He was a mighty hunter too, and had killed every variety of big game from the Rocky Mountains to the Missouri. We told him of the week's hunting we had had on the Platte prairies. More than thirty buffalo bulls had been shot by us, and I could not but feel some qualms of conscience at the thought of the destruction of so much animal life , but Colonel Dodge held different views. ' Kill every buffalo you can,' he said , ' every buffalo dead is an Indian gone.' It sounded hard then, and it seems hard now , but seven years after this time I crossed by railway from California to New York, and looking out at this same Platte valley I saw it a smiling plain of farms, waving crops, and neat homesteads. The hungry crowd from overcharged Europe had surged into settlement over the old buffalo pastures of the Platte. ' Blessed are the meek, for they shall inherit the earth.' It was right. These Crows, Cheyennes, Sioux, and Blackfeet Indians were no doubt splendid hunters, and fierce raiders, and crafty foemen, but no man could say they were meek.

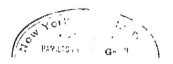

CHAPTER VII

WE were back in Omaha again. I was the paymaster of the
party, and carried the purse. It was literally a bag bulky
and weighty with greenbacks and a depreciated silver currency
at that time used in the States. To avoid the dual dangers
of carrying it with one in this rowdiest of Western cities, and
of leaving it in one's trunk in the hotel, I tried a middle course
one evening by concealing the bag inside a large shooting boot
placed casually in the trunk. Then we went out with our
United States Army friends to do the sights of Omaha. It
was late when we got back to the hotel, and I was tired and
sleepy. Before getting into bed, I bethought me of having
my boots cleaned, and never thinking of the bag of money
hidden in one of them, I took the boots from the trunk and
put them outside my door in the passage. Next morning I
awoke to an instant consciousness of what I had done. To
make certain, I sprang out of bed and went to the trunk :
there were no boots in it. 'Molloy,' I said to my room companion, 'we are ruined ; we have no money. I have lost
the purse.' Then I opened the door and looked out : there
stood the boots cleaned. It was not always a certainty that
you would find them thus polished ; but unfortunately, as it
seemed to me, on this occasion the negro boot-boy had come
along in the night and done his duty. I stooped down ; the
bag was in the boot ; but was there anything in the bag ?
That was the question. 'Molloy,' I said to my friend, 'the
bag is still in the boot ' ; but here I stopped, because the poor
fellow was leaning on his elbow, just awake, and regarding me
with an expression of face that plainly told me he thought
I was quite mad. I opened the bag. Out came the bundle
of greenbacks, out came the depreciated dollars and other

currency ; all there untouched to the last ' red cent.' I had scarcely finished counting the money when the door opened and a woolly-headed black appeared. ' Boots ! ' he ejaculated in a frightened manner, and then vanished. That much elucidation of the mystery I got, and no more. The only explanation I could arrive at afterwards was that some youthful understudy in the blacking business of the hotel had got the boots in the first instance, and finding the bag of dollars in the boot when he was cleaning it, had been frightened at the discovery, and thought it better to replace them at the room door as if nothing unusual had been discovered ; that, later on in the morning. he had related his strange experience to the head boss black bootblack , and that that functionary had rushed at once to the door of the room where we were, only to find the boots inside the door instead of outside, hence his wild ejaculation and rapid exit.

Returning by the route we had come, we had a few days' excellent wild-bird shooting in Iowa, and got further experience of the settlement of the West in what might be called the second line of the army of invasion. Iowa was one of the States which had adopted the law known far and wide as the Maine Liquor Law No intoxicating liquors could be bought or served within the limits of the State except by order of a doctor. On the evening of our arrival at the little town of Boone, a leading citizen came to visit us. He was friendly and familiar from the first, and he made no secret of the object of his visit. The prohibition law was a shameful interference with the liberty of the American citizen ; tea was not a beverage upon which the hunter could successfully pursue his vocation, and therefore he had come to show us an easy means by which this injustice could be set right, and a door through which access might be obtained to the hunter's proper paradise—that door being the apothecary's. If we would enter the apothecary's shop that evening, ask for a small bottle of Perry's pain-killer, he, our visitor, would be in an inner room behind the shop ; a prescription would be duly prepared by him, for ' he was a member of the medical profession,' and the apothecary would do the rest. We would only have to sit round and swallow the draughts thus prescribed for us.

We did as we were told, and soon found ourselves in an inner apartment of the apothecary's residence, in which some eight or ten persons were already assembled, excellent patients all of them ; they took their physic without a wry face. Instead of the bottle's being shaken before it was taken, it was the patient who underwent the shaking process, in repeated convulsions of laughter, after he had swallowed the compound.

As at Omaha, we found that the high rank with which we had been invested upon our arrival soon underwent reduction. We were all colonels, some of us even generals, at the commencement of the examination and when the prescription was being written ; but when we had paid our fees and were about to quit the professional room, our medical adviser whispered, ' To-morrow evening at the same hour, boys ! ' But we were far away to the north after the duck, the wavies, and prairie fowl when the next evening came. These men were largely ex-soldiers who had served under Grant or Sherman, and who had come out West when the war was over. They were very fine fellows, despite the little idiosyncrasies and failings to which I have alluded.

Youth does not concern itself much with tracing back facts to causes : it accepts the facts it sees ; the causes can keep. When I look back now upon that tremendous struggle through which America passed in the early 'sixties, I can see in it many things which were not then visible. It seems to me that the back of human nature must always be ridden by somebody. Victor Hugo in his breakfast-room thought that these riders would eventually be dismounted and driven out : I cannot think that hope will ever be fulfilled. Meanwhile I have come to believe that the soldier is not always the worst rider that human society can put into its saddle.

When we returned to Western Canada, the beautiful season known as ' the Fall ' was still in being, and the woods were glorious in all the colours of their dying foliage. But that was soon over, and November brought fogs and chills from the great lakes by which the peninsula of Upper Canada is almost surrounded. It would be difficult to picture a more desolate scene than the aspect presented by a Canadian half-cleared forest landscape when the leaves are gone and the snow has not yet come. Gloom has followed close upon the heels of glory ; the wreck of the forest lies on every side in fallen

trunks and blackened remnants ; the remaining squares of
uncut forest trees stand bare and leafless, flinging out great
ragged branches into the cleared spaces, as though they were
stretching arms of sorrow over the graves of their fallen comrades. The settler has here fought this forest giant for forty
years , the battle is now over ; the newcomer is the victor ;
but the dead still lie unburied, and the twilight of the coming
winter is closing upon the battlefield. Here and there, at long
intervals, the log-shanties of lately arrived immigrants are seen
interspersed with the more comfortable frame-homesteads of
the older inhabitants. The fight which has cumbered the
ground with the dead giants of the forest has at least given
to these homesteads a spoil of the finest firewood for defence
against the rigours of a Canadian winter. At the time I speak
of, practicable roads were few in this region. They were of
three kinds—'gravel,' 'corduroy,' and 'concession' roads, the
latter being only the surface of the ground cleared of wood.
The corduroy roads were of rough trees laid together over
swamps and boggy places. The gravel roads were alone
possible for travel at all seasons. One of these gravel roads
led from Brantford south-east towards Lake Erie, following
the high left bank of the Grand River to the little port of
Maitland. During my absence on the prairies an old veteran,
Colonel Cotter, who had been in the 69th Regiment sixty-five
years earlier, visited the regiment in Brantford. He lived now
on the shore of Lake Erie, some forty miles from Brantford.
He had fought as a captain at Quatre Bras and at Waterloo,
and had even served in the short war in Travancore (of which
I have spoken in Chapter IV.) in 1809. I was now engaged
in completing a history of my regiment, begun at Aldershot
two years earlier, so I was very anxious to meet this old veteran
with as little delay as possible. At eighty years of age the
sand is running out of Life's hour-glass very quickly. I set
out for Port Maitland. Twenty miles from Brantford a little
wooden town stood on the north side of the Grand River,
called Caledonia. At this village settlement a long wooden
bridge crossed the Grand River, and at the farthest side an
Indian reserve had been marked off in the forest for the
remnants of the once powerful Six Nation Tribes.

I have described at some length the aspect of that particular

spot in Western Canada as I saw it in the early winter of 1867.
I was at that time full of energy, of a boundless desire to do
something. Nothing tired me, nor damped the ardour that
was in me ; but a distinct and single purpose of life I had not.
To go seemed enough ; it did not matter where. Here amid
the desolate scenery on the Grand River a new conception of
life seemed all at once to open before me. I must achieve a
definite thing. When that resolve is once fixed deep and solid
in the mind, the opportunity is certain to come.

I found the old veteran 69th officer in a very dreary domicile
at Lake Erie. Although he had been so long away from home,
and was so far removed from those early years of service in
India and Belgium, his mind was clear and his memory of the
campaign of Waterloo was most retentive. As we sat that
night over the fire, he told me of many episodes in those
famous distant days. He described the rush of the Cuirassiers
in the rye-field at Quatre Bras, the retreat next day upon
Waterloo, and the night of rain and mud. ' It was so cold,'
he said, ' and as the ground was ankle-deep in mud, I preferred
to stand and walk about rather than to lie down. Soon after
daybreak I was ordered to take my company to the village
of Waterloo, to mount guard at the inn occupied by the Duke
of Wellington. As we marched along the front of our line,
the soldiers were busy drying, cleaning, and snapping off their
firelocks which had rusted during the night. Arrived at the
inn I drew up in front, and stood at ease. Presently an
A.D.C. came out and told me to return to the regiment, as
the Duke was about to leave his quarters for the field.
Shortly after I got back the first gun was fired from the
French position.'

Many other little episodes he spoke of, the following among
them.

When the 69th had formed up in column, a commissariat
waggon drove up with a supply of rum for issue to the men ;
and with it came the quartermaster, Matthew Stevens, the
same man who at St. Vincent, eighteen years earlier, had broken
the stern gallery of the *San Nicholas* and led the way for
Nelson to the quarter-deck of the Spanish vessel. When the
rum was serving out, a round shot struck the waggon and carried
off the head of a pioneer employed at it. ' Weel noo,' said the

quartermaster gravely, 'it's aboot time for a peaceable non-combatant like myself to gang awa.'

It was strange to hear on the shore of Lake Erie in Canada, from the lips of this veteran, these old stories of the great battle fought on the plains of Belgium fifty-two years earlier. But the stories were not all of Waterloo. He described at length an encounter forced upon him on his return to his native County Cork after Waterloo. Some local hero of duelling celebrity determined to try his mettle at twenty paces, near Mallow. The challenge was, of course, accepted, the whole countryside flocked to witness the fight, and a field of a couple of thousand spectators was ranged in two long lines, extending far on either side of the combatants. Shots were exchanged, no one was hit, honour was satisfied, and shouts and shillelaghs rent the air.

Cotter had entered the 69th in 1804. Like many other officers, he settled in Western Canada after the close of the war, and had remained there ever since.

But the strangest part had to come. Six months after this interview, on the 18th June 1868, the old gentleman came to see his former regiment, then in London, Canada West; and we put him standing between the colours in the front rank, exactly fifty-three years after he had stood in square with them at Waterloo. He died a few months later.

These military settlers had not been happy or fortunate in their new homes. The glamour of the forest life, as it appeared in the pages of a romance, was a very different thing from its actual reality in the backwoods of the West. The greater number of these old soldiers drifted into the towns or came back to Europe. Some of them perished miserably in the backwoods.

In the spring of 1868 I was appointed officer in charge of the 'Look Out' on the Canadian frontier, in succession to Lieutenant Redvers Buller of the 60th Rifles, who had held the billet for more than a year. Thus began an acquaintance which lasted upwards of forty years, and which was destined to run through many distant lands and strange scenes. At this time Redvers Buller was the best type of the regimental officer possible to be found. Young, active, daring, as keen for service as he was ready to take the fullest advantage of it, he stood even then in the front rank of those young and ardent spirits who might be described as the ruck of army life which is waiting to get through. We had met at Brantford during one of his monthly visits to the 'Look Outs.' These were small, detached parties of old and reliable soldiers, selected from the regiments in Western Canada, and placed at certain points along the frontier for the purpose of intercepting deserters to the United States.

Early in May 1868 I relieved Buller of this frontier duty. Needless to say that the work was congenial to me in every respect. I had to visit the various posts along the frontier once in every month. They were about fifteen in number, some in places that could be reached only by road, and in the circuit of the whole entailing a round of about fifteen hundred miles each month. The circle, which had London as its centre, embraced forts on Lake Huron, Lake St. Clair, and Lake Erie, thence inland to Caledonia, and northward to Paris, Stratford, and Adelaide.

Summer was now over the land, and the forest country was as beautiful in June as before in November it had been dreary. To the west of London great tracts were still in forest, and through these the railway ran in a vast avenue, cut deep and straight through woods of beech and maple. South of the line at a place named Watford, a region known as the Brooke Swamp extended for miles. It had the reputation of holding deer, and it was said that even a few bears were still to be found in it. I determined to explore it. In the inn at Watford I was directed to the house of an inhabitant who was said to be the village sportsman. Yes, he knew the swamp, and he had heard of that bear So we started together next morning. In the evening we had reached a log-hut in which a couple of lumbermen were at work. We slept there, and spent all the next day from morning to night seeking anything we could get, and finding neither deer nor bears. In the afternoon we happened to meet a solitary Indian hunter ; my friend the village sportsman shook his fist at the lone stranger and cursed him. 'What has he done to injure you ? ' I asked. 'Injure me ! ' he answered, 'the devil will never stop until he has killed that bear.' 'But the bear is as much his as it is ours,' I said ; 'probably that poor devil's ancestors have

hunted bears in this forest ever since it has been a forest.'
'Wall, I wouldn't leave a red-skin alive in the land if I had
my way,' he answered Here in this Canadian backwood
as in the prairies of the Platte, twelve hundred miles farther
west, the sentiment was precisely the same.

I got back to Watford very tired after this fruitless chase
of three days, and was glad to find in the little wooden inn
supper ready. At the table with me there sat a curious-
looking man of that peculiar type of American known as the
'down-Easter'—sharp, determined, of restless eye, straight
upper lip, and firm-set lower jaw. 'Stranger,' he said, after
a bit, 'you 'ave bin to the Brooke Swamp ; now don't tell me
'twas arter bars you were for three days in that darned hole.
No, sirree, 'twas arter lumber, or petroleum oil, or some other
fixen, I guess you were. I don't want to go into that thar
swamp myself, for I 've got a wife and family ; but as sure as
my name is Horatio Nelson Case, thar 's money in that swamp,
and you 've bin arter it those three days.' It was with considerable difficulty that I could persuade my chance companion
that it was a real live ' bar,' and not a bar of gold I had been
after ; and then I think the very absurdity of the idea seemed
to strike him as so original that he quite ' cottoned to me,' as
being entirely out of his own line in thought and action. He
first told me every detail of his own life and family—who his
wife was, the number of children they had, the various occu-
pations he had filled, and he finally wound up by asking if I
was disposed to join him in a speculation which would have
for the theatre of its effort this same swamp of Brooke ? He
had been told that, back in the swamp, there were fine ridges
of higher ground which bore heavy timber ; and he was very
desirous of getting some trustworthy information upon these
tracts of higher ground. I told him that what he had been told
was correct ; there were many such ridges well-timbered, where
the land was as dry as that on which the village stood. This
seemed to banish the last shred of doubt from his mind. If I
had had speculative outlooks regarding the swamp, I should
have kept this knowledge to myself : I might be a fool, but
it was clear I was not a knave. He ended by proposing a
joint partnership in the purchase of some thousand acres in
the so-called swamp. I was to find the money ; he would

furnish the brains. I told him I didn't like the arrangement ; that it was liable to end in his getting all my money, and in my having only a portion of his brains. This seemed to tickle his fancy. We exchanged names and addresses, and I left Watford at midnight with a large card in my pocket on which was printed Horatio Nelson Case, Postmaster, City, Ont. A few weeks later I received a letter from Horatio, proposing another scheme for my consideration. It was the purchase of a square block of forest lying further to the west in the neighbourhood of a place called Petrolia, where oil in some quantity had already been discovered. Horatio had visited this new oil field, and had fixed up in his mind some distinct theories about it. The forest was so dense that it was not at all easy to determine the general set and direction of the subterranean oil stream which had been tapped here and there ; but his observations had led him to think that the trend of the oil was in the direction of this square of forest-land, which he proposed to acquire at a cost of eight hundred pounds. Had I that sum of money ? No. Not in the least disconcerted by this negative, he asked how much I could command. Perhaps four hundred. Was there any other officer in the regiment who would be willing to put down a similar sum ? I went to the ground and saw for myself the correctness of the general idea upon which he was working. The well in which oil had been struck did seem to follow a rough sort of line through the trees. If you stood at one end of the hideous line of scaffolding, which marked the mouth of a well, you saw that while to the right or left of that line wells were doing little, the general continuation of the line had along it more prosperous borings. Our proposed block of two hundred acres lay on that line of continuation about a mile deeper in the forest. The end of the matter was that another officer joined me in this oil venture ; and Horatio Nelson Case, Lieut. W. F. Butler, and Ensign Albert P. Wodehouse became the joint owners of two hundred acres of forest in the vicinity of Petrolia, Ontario, sometime in the early part of 1869.

Before the purchase could be effected, however, the regiment had moved from London to Montreal. My delightful roving occupation at the ' Look Out ' was over, and I was once more ' cribbed, cabined, and confined ' within the limits of a big city in the depth of a Lower Canadian winter. As soon as I could obtain leave, I was back again in Western Canada. Horatio was more sanguine than ever. The line of wells in which oil had been struck was slowly but steadily drawing nearer to our dark block in the forest. Only two other blocks of forest-land now intervened between our possession and the latest find in the new oil field. The money must be got at once, or all our anticipations would be dashed to pieces.

The tendency to change the stations of our regiment still clung to us, and in the spring of 1869, while I was still in the West, we were moved from Montreal to Quebec.

I rejoined at the latter place in June. Two years had not elapsed since I had landed there for the first time ; but what a change had these few months wrought in the aspect of life to my mind !

This America was a great mind-stretcher. All these lakes, these immense prairies, these deep forests, these rivers of which the single lengths are greater than the width of the ocean between Canada and Europe; all the throbbing of the life that one saw everywhere, on road and river, in the cities, on the plains, this great march that was ever going on—all seemed to call with irresistible voice to throw one's little lot into the movement. It all seemed the exact opposite of the profession to which at this time I had given ten years of my life. There one seemed to be going round in a circle ; here the line of march was straight to the west. I had seen a sunset over the prairies of Nebraska, and the dream of it was ever in my mind—a great golden mist, a big river flowing from it, a dark herd of buffaloes slowly moving across the prairie distance to drink at the river, and the sun himself seeming to linger above the horizon as though he wanted to have a longer look at the glory he had made below.

In my ' Look Out ' wanderings I had frequently to visit a little lake—the Blue Lake—which lay in the forest a few miles north-west of Brantford. I had a cotton-wood canoe and a tent, and with these in possession youth has a ' free pass ' wherever water flows, or trees grow. The Blue Lake was a very beautiful spot ; no one had built above its shores or bored beneath them ; the larger forest trees were mostly gone, but another growth had sprung up, and the sheet of clear blue winding water lay in as perfect repose and reflection of shore and foliage as though no white man had ever placed his burden upon the land of Canada. ·

I determined to cross the Atlantic ; raise the four hundred pounds necessary to begin a partnership with Horatio Nelson Case, and, even if we failed to strike oil, to strike out some line in life other than that military one which, so far, seemed to lead to nothing.

I sailed from Quebec early in September in the *Moravian.* We took the northern channel between Newfoundland and Labrador, saw lots of icebergs after passing Belleisle, and reached Ireland after the usual rough passage. I have sailed in many good and bad vessels in my time, but I can truthfully declare that I never sailed with a bad sea-captain. I do not mean only in the mere sense of his profession ; I mean the man himself. He is the very best man this Empire produces ; the salt of the sea and the soul of the land are in him. He is as superior to the men by whom he is employed as the army officer is better than his departmental chief, and the naval officer is above his official administrator   These three classes of captains stand for the honour of English commerce, the fame of England's arms by land, and her naval superiority at sea. Men may cozen in the counting-house, be witless at the War Office, and play Dreadnoughts or Donnybrook in Whitehall ; but if England holds on to her captains by sea and land she will pull through in the end. In the Services the servants have ever been better than the masters.

After my arrival at home, I made every effort I could think of to prevent what was then looked upon as the worst of professional disasters from happening to me—namely, being purchased over by junior subalterns for the rank of captain. It was useless. At that time I had neither friends at the Horse Guards, nor money at the bankers'. My father was in very bad health ; my colonel was a complete military nonentity ; my captain, once a very able man, was getting softening of the brain, and had been obliged to retire from the service. Altogether, the outlook was about as hopeless as it could well be ; and to crown the catalogue of misfortune, a long space of regimental stagnation in promotion had just broken, and many purchase steps in rank were going.

With some difficulty I was able, through the kindness of relations, to raise the four hundred pounds required by Horatio Nelson Case for the purchase of the block of forest-land at Petrolia ; but whether that venture was destined to pour oil upon the troubled waters of my fortune, or to add yet another item to the already long list of professional calamities, had still to be proved.

In the midst of those disappointments I received an urgent message from my old captain, then residing in England, to go to him I found him in a deplorable condition of mental illness. He who had been a model of all the military virtues, a strict disciplinarian, and a most high-minded gentleman, was now filled with the wildest delusions. His friends could do nothing with him. To relieve the strain upon his family, and to try what change of scene would do in his case, it was proposed that he and I should go to Paris We proceeded thither At first everything went well. It was my first visit to the French capital, and my poor friend appeared to take pleasure in showing the sights to me. In December 1869 Paris was in the meridian hour of her glory ; Baron Haussmann had put the finishing touches to the great streets and edifices of the Second Empire. I shall never forget the effect of the blaze of light which the Place de la Concorde presented as we turned into it on a clear frosty December night, the last of the year, an hour after our arrival from dull, grimy, leaden London. All the long lines of sparkling streets radiated from this brilliant centre ; the Imperial Court was in residence at the Tuileries, and the windows of that famous palace shone through the leafless trees.

We turned into the Place Vendôme, and stood at last at the foot of the Roman column, with all the bronze of Austerlitz wreathed round it, and the figure of the great captain dimly discernible in the starlight above To-morrow the first visit of daylight would be made to his tomb beyond the river. It all seemed so real on that closing night of the old year ; and yet all this panorama of pride and power, seemingly fixed and solid as the earth upon which it stood, had at that moment little more than six months' lease of life.

Less than a year and a half later I was destined to stand in this Place de la Concorde again, and to see the palaces in smouldering ashes, the statues rent with cannon-shot, and the great column and its mighty figure lying prone in the dust of the Place Vendôme. But that is anticipating.

The mental affliction, which seemed at first to have calmed down in my poor friend, soon began to show itself again. One night we had come back to our hotel in the Rue St. Honoré from the Porte St. Martin theatre, and had retired to our rooms. I occupied a room inside that in which my old captain slept. We were speaking to each other through the doorway, and some trifling difference of opinion had arisen in our conversation. Suddenly he raised his voice and shouted, 'Now I 'll have it out with you for bringing my brother over from Cork.' (When his illness had reached an acute stage a fortnight earlier in England, I had thought it necessary to telegraph for his only brother, who was in garrison in Ireland.) Then I heard a thud on the floor of the outer room, the door was flung open, and in came my old commander, mad with rage, and shouting, ' I 'll throw you out of the window.'

I was a much younger as well as a stronger man, and quickly as he had come I was out of bed and on the floor ready for him. He came to within a few feet of where I stood, then stopped short, rushed to the window, flung it open, crying, ' I 'll throw myself out.' The drop looked ugly, for we were two or three floors up, and the courtyard below was hardly visible in dim lamplight. Then he rushed back to his room. Next morning he met me as though nothing had happened. But I had had enough of the undertaking now we squared up accounts, and I left Paris. A few days later the poor fellow got into an altercation with a Frenchman, whom he accused of having pushed against him as they were leaving the door of some theatre. My friend drew a sword from a cane which he carried, and lunged at the Frenchman, who fortunately received the blade through his gibus-hat. That matter was settled in some way or other , but a night or two later he joined a demonstration got up by the partisans of the then celebrated Victor Noir, and he was promptly arrested by the police and lodged in Mazas Prison. He never recovered his right reason. Nearly forty years later I had a curious confirmation of the character borne by my old commander in his early days. Lord Roberts said to me one day, ' You were in the 69th Regiment. You must have known my old schoolfellow ——.' 'Yes, sir , he was my captain for ten years.' 'When I went to school at Clifton,' continued the commander-in-chief, ' he was the best boy in the school. The headmaster said to me when I went there, "Follow the example set by ——. I might talk a long time to you, but I could not say more. Do as he does." '

When I returned to Ireland I found that my father's health had grown worse. Two months later he passed quietly away, and we laid him in the old churchyard of Killardrigh, by the banks of the river and at the foot of the Galtee mountain, both of which he had lived beside and had loved all his long life.

The ruined church at Killardrigh was said to have been named after a high king of Ireland, an ' Ard Righ,' who met his death in the seventh century while bathing in the waters of the Suir. If the story be true, then a second king among men was laid in that lone graveyard in March 1870.

I had now to return to my regiment in Canada. No ' Look-outs ' there, and no outlooks anywhere else. Regimental promotion had begun, but it was not for me : the steps were all by purchase. I made a last attempt on the Horse Guards, and was kindly informed by a very choleric old Peninsular Military Secretary, who had a terrible reputation for vocabular vehemence to old officers (but whom on this and other occasions I found particularly gracious to young ones), that I had not a ghost of a chance. Then I sailed for America.

CHAPTER VIII

It was not quite correct to say that I had no military outlook at this time. There was a remote chance that a disturbance which had arisen on the banks of the Red River, in Manitoba, might develop into some occasion of active service. The newspapers had already announced that regular troops would be sent from Canada to Winnipeg in the coming summer. The commander of the little expedition, Colonel Wolseley, had been named. I had met him once or twice in Montreal, but only in the sense in which a subaltern without any record can meet a colonel who has a very distinguished one. I sat next him at an inspection dinner one evening, and when, in his capacity as Chief of the Quartermaster-General's Department in Canada, he had called for specimen sketches from regimental officers in order to select men for the Survey Service in Upper Canada, I had sent in two drawings, the very indifferent artistic quality of which I had endeavoured to compensate for by the geographical and historical associations I had connected with them. One was a plan of the cantonment in Tonghoo in Burmah, the other of the field of Waterloo ; neither had succeeded. I was not among the selected surveyors. This, however, did not prevent my sending a cable message from Ireland when I saw that Colonel Wolseley was named commander of the expedition to the Red River. Among the many vices which the ocean cable has introduced into the world, it has at least one virtue—the absent can sometimes be almost right. On this occasion my long shot hit its mark, and although I did not know that I had struck the target at Ottawa, I followed the shot as soon as possible. The longer the range the more likely is it that somebody may rub out the hit before

112

you can get to the marking butt. This, indeed, had almost happened. Everybody wanted to get on this expedition, which, small as it was in numbers, had such an immense ' beyond ' in it, a beyond into which steam power did not enter, where there were no roads, where there were still real live Indians and great silent lakes, vast woods and rushing rivers, and, more than these, boats and canoes in which brains would be at the helm, skill at the prow, and youth and muscle working at the oars.

Travelling via New York, I reached Toronto just in time to find Colonel Wolseley still there He was to start for Lake Superior the following day , all the staff officers had been appointed ; there was ' no berth vacant,' he said. I suggested one · that of an Intelligence officer who, travelling through the United States, might perhaps be able to get to the column in some part of the last three hundred of the six hundred miles lying between Lake Superior and the Red River. He caught at the idea, directed me to proceed to Montreal at once, and see General Lindsay there, adding that he would write that night to him

At this time Colonel Wolseley was in the prime of manhood, somewhat under middle height, of well-knit, well-proportioned figure ; handsome, clean-cut features, a broad and lofty forehead over which brown chestnut hair closely curled ; exceedingly sharp, penetrating blue eyes, from one of which the bursting of a shell in the trenches at Sebastopol had extinguished sight without in the least lessening the fire that shot through it from what was the best and most brilliant brain I ever met in the British army He was possessed of a courage equal to his brain power. It could be neither daunted nor subdued. His body had been mauled and smashed many times. In Burmah a gingall bullet fired within thirty yards of him had torn his thigh into shreds ; in the Crimea a shell had smashed his face, and blinded an eye , but no man who rode beside Wolseley in the thirty years of active life in which I afterwards knew him could ever have imagined that either in his grip of a horse or his glance at a man on a battlefield, he had only half the strength and the sight with which he had started in life. I never knew him tired, no matter what might be the fatigue he underwent. I never knew his eye deceived.

no matter how short might be the look it gave at a man or a plan.

I went at once to Montreal, saw that fine soldier, General Lindsay, then commanding in Canada, and found him favourable to my proposed appointment, the final sanction for which rested with the civil authorities at Ottawa. Meanwhile I was to await the answer at Montreal.

But before it came a strange little event happened. While we were all looking out fifteen hundred miles away to the north-west, a little flame of service sprang up, close at our doors, fifty miles south from Montreal. All through the 24th May telegrams were arriving at the headquarters office from places on the Canadian frontier, and over the boundary line, from Huntingdon and Hinchinbrook on our side, and from Malone and Potsdam Junction on the other side, announcing the arrival of bodies of armed men at, or near, the frontier. Of course, the numbers given varied, but the fact of the gatherings could not be doubted. The news came from our own people near the frontier, and from men in the Fenian ranks on the other side, among the latter being a man who years later, under the name of Major le Caron, became well known in London at the time of the Pigott Conspiracy.

The Military Secretary, Colonel Earle (afterwards killed at Kirbekan in the Soudan), sent for me. ' We have ordered your regiment up from Quebec. It will arrive here by train to-morrow ; you will join it at the railway station, and proceed with it to the frontier near Huntingdon.' He showed me the telegraphic messages received from that quarter. I wired at once to my colonel in Quebec that I would meet him at the railway next day with a horse ; then I went to a well-known keeper of a livery stable. He had a good saddle-horse—' the Doctor ' by name, a big chestnut animal. I secured this war-horse for as many days as might be needed, and was then ready for any eventuality Later in the day I received a telegram from the colonel appointing me Intelligence officer to the column, which was to consist of the 69th Regiment, and a corps of Canadian militia, whose headquarters were in the town of Huntingdon, in the neighbourhood of the menaced points.

When the train carrying the 69th Regiment arrived at the

Montreal station, I was there to meet it. It was pleasant to meet old friends again, for I had been nine months away in Europe, and there was much news to hear and to tell. I got ' the Doctor ' into a waggon ; and the train moved on, after a short delay, for Lake St. Francis, on the north shore of which it deposited us, bag and baggage. A couple of steamboats were here in waiting to ferry us across to the south shore of that beautiful lake, and from there the march to Huntingdon began. I got ' the Doctor ' off the boat at once, and rode on in advance to Huntingdon to gather the latest information at that place. The distance was about eight miles, the last two before Huntingdon was reached being over a ' corduroy ' road through a bad swamp. It was dusk when I got to Huntingdon. In the little square of the town I found the militia regiment drawn up, ready to march back to Lake St. Francis. The staff officer attached to the regiment and the colonel of militia had decided upon this retrograde movement in consequence of reports which had reached them of the enemy's movements at Hinchinbrook on the Trout River some six or eight miles south, and adjacent to the American frontier. I had arrived at an opportune moment, for a few minutes later the regiment would have abandoned Huntingdon and begun its retreat on Lake St. Francis.

I had known the staff officer at Hythe six years earlier. He was very much my senior in rank and service ; but I knew that to give up the town of Huntingdon would be a fatal mistake, even had there been no regular troops advancing to support that position. However, I had to proceed cautiously. I was only a subaltern ; the staff officer was a major, and he had already seen service. I asked him to come with me a little distance from the parade where we could not be overheard. I first got from him the information which had decided him to retire. It was generally a continuation of the news I had heard from the Military Secretary in Montreal on the previous day. I find in an old notebook some of these messages :—

' To MacEachern, Huntingdon.

' " Fenians got large reinforcements last night, field-guns and ammunition, provisions plentiful, expect fight Wednesday." Another message reported " Seven hundred well-armed men are at hand."

Another from Malone reported "150 Fenians here, they leave for Trout River." Another from Potsdam stated that "two companies Cavalry and three car-loads of men had arrived there from Rome, no fight before Saturday." Another from South Hinchinbrook said : "Telegraph operator just said 'good-bye.' Fenians close at hand, expect to cross frontier to-day."'

These reports from different places on the frontier showed that Huntingdon was the point aimed at whenever the concentration near the frontier was sufficient to justify a movement over the line , but it was easy to see also that there was not likely to be any advance in force for some hours; and in any case it was now night, the 69th would be up in a few hours, and here MacEachern and his merry men must remain. It was urged that the position at Huntingdon was not a good one, that the Seafield swamp, with only one practicable 'corduroy' road through it, lay immediately in rear of the little town, and that the supply of provisions at hand would only suffice for a few hours' consumption. These facts were all true, so far as rule ran ; but when you put your foot into that ready-made boot it is well to have elastic sides to it.

The regiment was dismissed to their tents, and an hour or two later the 69th marched into Huntingdon. Before I turned in for the night a big bearded man came to me 'I have two or three chaps here,' he said, 'and we have horses ; we would like to ride with you to-morrow to the line, if you 're gwyne that way.' I liked the look of the man and his chums, and without telling him where I was 'gwyne' to, I said I would meet them there in the market-place at daybreak, three hours later.

A cold mist lay on the land as we rode out of Huntingdon at four next morning, taking the main road south. I had the old scout and four younger men as companions. After a couple of miles we lessened the pace, and began to examine roads that led to right or left. It was about six o clock when we got to Hinchinbrook. It was only a cross-roads with three or four frame houses ; the mist had lifted, the sun was out, and one could see well on either side. The post-office and telegraph were closed ; a man came out of one of the houses, and for a moment eyed us suspiciously , but the scout soon made matters straight, and we got the news, such as it was. There was a

camp of Americans just over the border ; a few of their scouts
had been here the evening before.   The border line was a mile
and a half farther on.

I sent one of the men back with this information, sent two
more along the right and left roads, and then rode on with the
old scout to the front.   We trotted, but kept on the grass
border of the road.   The country was as green and fresh as the
end of May could make it ; apple-trees were in blossom, and
a strip of deep forest on the right was all in leaf.   Trout River
lay at a little distance to the left ; about three-quarters of a
mile farther on a large hop field crossed the road ; the hops
were already well up the poles, affording good cover the height
of a man.   We went cautiously through this cover, and still
more quietly as we approached the boundary line.   There was
a bend in the road before it got to the frontier, and a skirting
of wood at the bend, then a straight bit which ran direct to the
line.   The road was quite empty for five or six hundred yards
forward.   We rode on to the line   It was marked by a square
stone set in the earth ; two or three houses stood in trees just
beyond the boundary on the American side.   An early-rising
inhabitant or two were on foot here, but no information was
to be gleaned from them.

Of course, I would not cross the line, and still I did not like
to go back from it without any news, so I waited with the scout,
looking up the road which ran straight on American territory
for nearly a mile.   Suddenly a body of men marching in
columns of fours began to wheel out from a cross-road about
five hundred yards forward, on the right side.   They came
straight for the line, arms at the slope, and the sun bright on
the 'unbrowned' barrels of their rifles.   I made them out
roughly to be about two or three hundred.   Their appearance
seemed to put thought and tongue into one of the early inhabitants.   'Them 's the boys,' he said.   'I guess you chaps
had better go back now.'   The head of the column was coming
along at a brisk pace.   We took the hint and cantered back
along the road we had come until we got to the bend I have
mentioned ; there we pulled up under cover of the trees and
waited.   Thinking that the advancing 'boys' might have
halted on the line and not entered our territory, I turned my
horse and walked him round the bend whence I could see

the road to the frontier   There was no mistake. The 'boys' had come along, and were within three hundred yards of me, well within our ground. They shouted something, and I saw the rifles of the leading fours coming down to the 'ready.' I wheeled 'the Doctor' on his tracks and galloped round the bend, a few bullets going wide through the trees as I went. We rode back to Hinchinbrook, and awaited there the arrival of our column. It soon arrived. I showed the colonel the ground ; there were no men on the near side of the hop field, but as I had seen them almost up to that cover, they must be there. The river would be on their right, the forest on their left ; a front of half a mile lay between the two flanks. We went forward as soon as this was explained, the 69th along the road and in the fields on either side of it, the militia battalion in support, some in the wood. My old company, No. 10, led the advance. A new captain had it : he had purchased his company over my head, but we were old and tried friends ; besides, I was a free-lance now, and could ride where I liked, so I liked the old soldiers of No. 10, nearly every man of whom I knew intimately.

As we turned into the straight road leading to the hop field, I could see that the 'snake' fences on either side near the hops had been taken down and the timbers made into an obstacle across the road ; behind this fence a picket of about a dozen men stood with rifles in their hands, and to the right and left one could catch the glint of barrels here and there in the green leaves of the hops. We on the road were about the same number as the picket behind the obstacle. It was an interesting situation   The road ran quite straight between the two parties. We were without cover on it ; the other side had partial cover behind the thick timber fence. All the would-be combatants, save myself, were on foot ; the chestnut 'Doctor' offered a good target in the bright sunshine, which was in our faces. I wondered, indeed, why the enemy did not give us a volley at three hundred yards, low down the straight road ; they must have hit something. 'Mansfield,' I said to my friend, 'don't stand on ceremony, but give these fellows a volley at once.' The Sniders were already loaded, and off they went in six seconds. There was a lot of powder smoke in those days, and plenty of scattered shooting followed this opening, and we all ran forward, loading and fixing bayonets as we went. When we reached the wooden obstacle not a man was behind it, and we raced through it, firing and cheering. In a few minutes we were again at the boundary line : the battle (!) of Trout River was over. We had no one killed or wounded ; the enemy lost one man, it was said, and Colonel MacEachern's braves had come upon an old Fenian lying in a hole in the forest. Some United States troops appeared next day to police their frontier, and send the scattered bands of raiders back to their several cities. I had some long rides with the scout to the west of Trout River, where other bands of raiders had been reported, but they, too, had vanished ; and then we marched back to Montreal. I said good-bye to the scout with real regret ; he was a splendid fellow. A short time afterwards he sent me a letter with his photograph, which I still have. He signed the letter, 'Yours until Death, The Scout.' In the photograph he is depicted in baggy civilian Canadian clothes, with many pockets ; he has a large bushy beard and a big, broad-brimmed, brown straw hat. In his right hand he holds a large cavalry sword, in his left a pipe ; the butt of a revolver is visible out of one of his many pockets. I hope I may meet him in the next world. What splendid men I have met along the thin track of my path in life ! I should have liked to listen to the scout telling of these three or four days' rough-riding in after years. Once only did I meet any one who knew of Trout River. It was in a haircutter's shop near the Haymarket. After the manner of his profession the barber was extremely communicative. He had had a brother in the 69th Regiment, but he had suffered so much in Canada in the war there that he was never any good again   ' What war was it ? ' I asked. ' The war of Trout River,' he answered ; and then the details followed. ' The men had no food. they lay for days and days in the forest, until they had to eat their blankets.' I laughed so much that he suspended his operations to stare at my reflection in the glass   There are many ways of writing history.

I went to Quebec with my regiment, and waited for the reply to the letter sent to Ottawa. It came on 7th June, and on the 8th I began a long journey into the West.

There was one old friend to whom I had to wish good-bye,

however, before starting—Private Henry Connors of the 69th Regiment. Before leaving Fermoy ten years earlier, Recruit Henry Connors had been confided specially to my care by an old couple who had come from Cork to see their son ere the draft sailed for Burmah. From that time forward Private Connors had been my servant. No more faithful heart ever beat in body of man or master. He had always been delicate with lung trouble, and he was now dying in the regimental hospital in Quebec. He died while I was in the West, and when I came back I put a small stone over his nameless grave in the military graveyard which was then outside the walls on the historic Plains of Abraham The dust of many other good soldiers must have been there I had cut on the stone his name and regiment, and underneath :—

HIS MASTER'S FRIEND

HIS FRIEND'S SERVANT

It wasn't much, but it was true, and the meaning of the words had memories in them that went through many distant lands. It would be blasphemy to doubt of heaven while such souls are found on earth.

I have told the story of the next ten months of my life in another book,[1] and I shall pass over that interval now, though there were many things omitted from the old narrative which might be of interest to readers of to-day, for the things seen then, or their kind, are no more to be looked at by the eye of man We know that the old dodo wasn't thought much of when he was found flopping and flapping about, four hundred years ago ; in fact, his early discoverers called him the ' Silly ' How people would flock to see him if he were on view in the Zoological Gardens to-day ! Every egg would be worth a thousand guineas. But I have a long road in front, and I must get along it before the light fails.

At the time of the Red River Expedition it took three months to get from Quebec to the Rocky Mountains. It took me more than two months to return by dog-sled over the snow from the Rocky Mountain House of the Hudson Bay Company to Winnipeg alone. You can do the distance from

---

[1] *The Great Lone Land* (E B.)

Quebec to the mountains now in three days. I left Quebec in June, and reached the mountains in December, but there were many side journeys made by canoe and horse and stage-coach in the interval.

On the return journey to Canada it required a whole fort-night to get from Winnipeg to St Paul's, Minnesota. You can do it now in fifteen hours. And yet that is the least part of the change which these forty years have wrought Winni-peg, now a huge city, was then a village of thirty houses and perhaps a hundred and fifty inhabitants A dozen cities have sprung into existence where buffalo roamed and Indians warred in that day. Railways traverse the land in all directions, and the output of grain to Europe is enormous. I open the report which I wrote when I got back to Fort Garry, by desire of that admirable man, Mr. Adams Archibald, Manitoba's first governor, and this is what I find in the concluding paragraph of that lengthy document :—

'These, Sir, are the views which I have formed upon the whole question of the existing state of affairs in the Saskatchewan. They result from the thought and experience of many long days of travel through a large portion of the region to which they have reference If I were asked from what point of view I have looked upon the question, I would answer: From that point which sees a vast country lying, as it were, silently awaiting the approach of the immense wave of human life which rolls unceasingly from Europe to America. Far off as lie the regions of the Saskatchewan from the Atlantic seaboard on which that wave is thrown, remote as are the fertile glades which fringe the eastern slopes of the Rocky Mountains, still that wave of human life is destined to reach these beautiful solitudes and to convert the wild luxuriance of their now useless vegetation into all the requirements of civilised existence.

'And if it be matter of desire that across this immense continent —resting upon the two greatest oceans of the world—a powerful nation should arise, with the strength and the manhood which race, climate, and tradition would assign to it; a nation which would look with no evil eye upon the old Mother-land from whence it sprang; a nation which, having no bitter memories to recall, would have no idle prejudices to perpetuate, then surely it is worthy of all toil of hand and brain on the part of those who to-day rule, that this great link in the chain of such a future nationality should no longer remain undeveloped, a prey to the conflicts of savage races, at once the garden and the wilderness of the Central Continent.

'W. F. BUTLER,

'Lieutenant, 69th Regt.

'MANITOBA, 10th March 1871'

This report handed in, I started for Canada in horse-sleds over the snow. It was slow work, not more than twenty miles each day   I had as fellow-travellers a gentleman and his secretary, who had been sent from the Colonial Office in London to Winnipeg to report upon matters there, and an archdeacon, on his way to England to collect funds for the Church Mission in the new province of Manitoba.   We slept each night in the cabin of some Red River half-breed settler, laying our blankets on the floor in a row, the archdeacon usually having the centre. One night, near Pembina, the archdeacon sprang from his couch shouting, ' They are putting guns through the window ; they are going to fire ! '   A crash of breaking glass seemed to confirm his alarm.   I caught at the supposed gun barrel.   It was the tail of a cow.   The animal had been rubbing the hind part of her person against the small window frame, and her tail had broken the window and our sleep together.

I reached Ottawa, travelling via the United States, in about three weeks.   My report had been received.   It was the wish of Governor Archibald that I should return to the North-West, officially charged to take in hand the opening up of that vast region, carrying into practical effect the principles of Indian settlement, the establishment of a police, and the foundation of Government stations which I had advocated in my report.

I saw the Canadian ministers, Sir John MacDonald, Sir George Cartier, Mr. Joseph Howe, Sir Francis Hincks.   They were highly complimentary, said nice things about the three thousand miles' travel in the wilderness, most of it through snow and ice, and with the thermometer hovering somewhere about the zero of Fahrenheit, hemmed and hawed when it came to Governor Archibald's recommendation as to the commandantship of the North-West, and laid particular stress upon the letter they were writing to the Colonial and the War Offices in London on the subject of my services to Canada generally.

At that time I took the world very much without questioning its men or motives. Each of these excellent colonial ministers had wives, sons, and daughters. An army officer who married a minister's daughter might perchance have been a fit and proper person to introduce the benefits of civilisation to the Blackfeet Indians on the Western prairies, but if he elected to remain in single cussedness in Canada he was pretty certain to find himself a black sheep among the ministerial flock of aspirants for place, no matter what might have been the value of his individual services.

I found myself almost alone in Canada : the army, with the exception of one battalion, had been withdrawn ; my own 69th were in Bermuda. The military leave, which had been granted to me for the purpose of going out to the Rocky Mountains on a civil expedition when the Red River Expedition was over, had not yet expired   I determined to go to England.

Three weeks later I was in London. I received a similar charming reception at the Colonial Office from the minister of the day. Another letter expressive of official approbation was written, this time to the Secretary of State for War, in relation to my services in North America , and feeling certain that I had now run the elusive quarry, Success, to his last haunt, I presented myself once again at the door of the institution in Pall Mall, which, perhaps more than any other of its kind in the capital of the Empire, might fitly inscribe over its portals the best known words of the *Inferno*.

The moment was not propitious. The union under the same roof of the office of the Commander-in-Chief with that of the Secretary of State had just been effected. The dual wheels of administration were not running smoothly, and my unfortunate case seemed to be a little bit of grit between them. I must pay the memory of His Royal Highness the Commander-in-Chief the justice of saying that he did his best with Mr. Cardwell to obtain for me an unattached company. I had now twelve years' service. I had been five or six times purchased over by officers, most of whom were many years junior to me. I was told by all those heads of departments, military and civil, that I had done the State some service. The reward asked for, a half-pay company, did not seem to be a very large act of recognition ; nevertheless, the reply came curt and chilling, ' Mr. Cardwell could not sanction the promotion of Lieutenant

Butler to an unattached company, an appointment which, if now given, would confer purchase rights.' Truly, reason is sometimes a two-edged weapon. I who, had there been no purchase system, must have been a captain two years ago, must now, because they were abolishing the system, suffer a further loss of two years before the coveted and acknowledged step in rank could be given to me. I had, in fact, fallen between two stools. The book of the Red River reward was closed six months earlier ; the other book could not be opened until purchase was abolished !

Suddenly one morning the *Times* announced that Paris was in flames.

The news of war between France and Germany first reached us on the Winnipeg River in the preceding August, and at intervals the remote theatre of our little expedition had caught the echoes of these colossal combats in North-Eastern France and the investment of Paris. Then as I got farther away from all sources of information, and the winter deepened over the wilderness, complete silence had ensued , but on 20th February, when I returned to Fort Garry, I find one entry, ' Heard Capitulation of Paris.' From that day interest seemed gone. Now it woke again.

The gentleman who had been my recent companion from Fort Garry to Ottawa was at the Foreign Office. I went at once there and told him what I wanted—a passport for Paris as soon as possible. ' You know Voltaire's saying,' he answered, ' " Tigers and Monkeys " ? You will find the " tiger " fit on now I would not go if I were you.' I pressed my request, got the passport, and that evening took the mail-train from Charing Cross to Dover.

Daylight comes early in the end of May. The opening of the carriage door at Abbeville roused me from sleep ; a soldier with a *pickelhaube* on his head was in the carriage , a Prussian guard was on the station platform ; passports were scrutinised and passengers compared with them, and then we went on again. It was yet quite early when we reached St. Denis, the extreme point to which the train ran More Prussian guards and soldiers everywhere. No use in asking ; there we must remain. The État-Major would not be open until eight o'clock. Another man who had come from London forgathered with me at the station, and we sought breakfast together. Then came the État-Major. My companion spoke French with facility ; he was of the Law, and the ways of the Army were utterly unknown to him. Between us we made an excellent unit for dealing with a state of siege.

We were ushered in before a big bearded man, a Bavarian staff officer of high rank My companion spoke ; I prompted. The commandant was very civil and very firm. Into Paris we could not go, but we were free to ascend to the top of the abbey tower of St. Denis, and see Paris from that lofty standpoint We got passes for the abbey, and went to it. From the place in front we could hear the boom of heavy guns in the direction of Paris, but the church hid the view to the south. We were soon at the top of the tower. One scarcely noticed eight or ten officers who were already on the leads, so wonderful was the panorama that burst upon us. All Paris lay there, from Mont Valérien on the west to Vincennes on the east, and all Paris apparently burning A great pall of black smoke hung high over the centre of the city, fed and supported by eight tall pillars of flame and smoke, which rose straight through the calm sunlit atmosphere of a May morning. From the rounded summit of Montmartre on our right front a battery of heavy guns was firing steadily across the middle distance in the direction of the Buttes de Chaumont, Belleville, and Père la Chaise on our left as we looked due south. From another point on that left front, apparently the Parc des Buttes de Chaumont, a battery of the Communist army was replying to the guns on Montmartre. The shells were making great arcs, the trail of their flight made visible by the smoke of the fuses.

Under the curves of this cannonade the domes and towers of the northern half of Paris were visible, and some even to the south of the river The fires seemed to be in the centre of the city, in the region of St. Eustache, the Tuileries and Louvre, and the Hôtel de Ville.

From the Prussian officers on the tower we could get but little information. The Versaillais troops had entered Paris on its western side three or four days earlier ; there had been heavy firing all that time, and the progress from west to east had been slow but steady. They were now at Montmartre on one side, and beyond the Pantheon on the other. The 'Reds' had retired to the north-east extremities of the city, and they appeared to be making a last stand from La Villette to Père la Chaise. Fires had been raging for three days and nights ; many great monuments had been destroyed.

What a strange sight this was ! Assuredly St Denis in all its history from the days of Dagobert had never seen its equal. German officers watching the bombardment of Paris by France, smoking, spitting, and laughing as they watched !

One had now time to look to other points of the great circle that lay around this lofty tower. There underneath to the north was the battered fort of La Briche, which had suffered so much from the Prussian batteries beyond ; two or three miles to the east was the village of Le Bourget, the scene of terrible fighting a couple of months earlier. The old abbey where we stood had many scars and wounds to show. Shells fired high over La Briche from two Prussian siege batteries had met here before they went to earth ; the roof was pierced in several places , the tower on which we stood had been hit ; and a shell had taken the head from the big stone statue of St. Denis on the centre of the high roof.

We descended the long flights of steps to the great square beneath the pavement of which lie in a common grave all the dust of old royal France. Were the Germans on the tower above, and the scene upon which they stolidly looked, the punishments for that outrage of seventy-eight years earlier ? It seemed to us that we had been looking at the death of France.

There was nothing more to be done in St. Denis. Could we get by any means to Versailles ? Yes, an omnibus ran there daily, but one must have a pass to go by it. We went again to the État-Major, got the pass after another inspection of passports, mounted the roof of the omnibus, and waited for the start. It was not yet midday. All that long afternoon we trundled along a roundabout way to Versailles, keeping between two great loops of the Seine, and finally crossing that river on a ferry-boat near Bougival. At this place we passed from the German to the French lines. All the bridges had been broken ; the fields looked dishevelled and the houses tattered, for the big guns on Valérien had often reached them during the winter just over.

It was interesting to note, along the twelve or fifteen miles of our journey, the facility which this river of many windings had given the Germans for investing Paris on her western side. Break the bridges, watch well, and sit tight on the farther bank of the river—nothing more was necessary there, from St. Denis on the north to Bougival on the south.

We reached Versailles at dusk. My companion knew a compatriot, the correspondent of a leading London journal. We made out his inn and found him playing at billiards. ' You have not the smallest chance,' he said, ' of getting into Paris , awful work is going on there. The strictest watch is kept to prevent strangers entering at the Point du Jour, the only gate now open ; a special pass signed by the general is necessary. Half Paris is burning, and news has just come that the Archbishop and some forty priests have been shot by the Communists.' He directed us to where we could find sofas for the night, and with that we had to be satisfied. Nevertheless, I determined to have a try for Paris next morning.

The Versailles omnibus was like an ant whose road is cut ; the ant runs as far as the cut and back again. The bus was doing this at Versailles, running to the Point du Jour, and then coming back again. I got on the top of this conveyance next morning. My quondam companion did not come. We reached the Versailles end of the Point du Jour in the forenoon ; the bus stopped ; I took up my knapsack and began to cross the bridge. There was a guard at the farther end. The sentinels stopped me. An officer appeared , I presented my passport. He read it, turned it upside down, shook his head, and went back to his room. I put my knapsack down, and sat upon it with my back to the battlement. I thought that by this show of resigned acceptation to military authority I might thaw the military mind, but it had no effect. Presently a portly person came from the other, or Paris, side of the bridge. His passes were examined ; the omnibus was preparing to start back for Versailles, and he was going there. I took up my bag and ascended the vehicle with reluctance. Presently I addressed the portly man in the worst French. He replied in the best English. We forgathered. We found a link in a mutual knowledge of a distinguished Frenchman of that time who had resided in Ireland for many years—

Monsieur le Comte de Jarnac. M. D'Arcy (for that was my companion's name) was an Orleanist whose normal residence was in London. He possessed many sources of information, and seemed to be able to go where he pleased. He had now been in Paris for some days, and he was going to Versailles for one night. One confidence led to another. He thought he would be able to obtain a pass for me to enter Paris the following day ; meanwhile there was no place in Versailles where he could get a lodging for the night. I thought my landlady of the previous evening could manage this for him. We dined together in a café at Versailles, and then we walked out to see the great avenue leading to Paris. The evening was as glorious as May in its last week could make it. The three great avenues which lead from the open space in front of the palace were thronged with people. All kinds of rumours were afloat. The 'Reds' still held Villette and the Buttes de Chaumont, but the cordon of the Versailles army was being drawn closer around them ; great numbers of Communist prisoners and many cannon and mitrailleuses had been taken ; the loss of life was enormous ; the destruction of property was still greater.

Presently we could see movement and commotion going on far down the broad avenue towards Paris. Troops were advancing up the roadway between the elm-trees ; a wave of shouting and gesticulation accompanied them. The head of the column was soon abreast of where we stood—cavalry horses and men lean and hungry-looking ; faces grimed and greasy ; uniforms dust-covered and worn. Behind these came a great straggling band of Communist prisoners, men, women, and children, ragged, fierce, powder-marked, streaming with perspiration ; such people as I had never seen before, and have never seen since ; faces at the last gasp of exhaustion ; faces that looked scornfully at the howling mob of bourgeois, that shouting, racing crowd which ran under the elms on either side and ran out of the cafés, throwing vile epithets over the heads of the soldiers. At the end of this dismal column came the carts with the wounded. In one of these there sat, bolt upright, a woman in the prime of life ; her black hair hung loose upon her shoulders, her olive face had a gash across one cheek from which the blood was still flowing, her hands were tied behind her back ; two or three wounded men lay at her feet helplessly stricken, but had there been a thousand dead or dying around her it would not have mattered. It was her face that held the eye. I have never forgotten the face and figure of that proud, defiant, handsome woman. The cart passed with the rest, but I followed it with my eyes while it was in sight, and ere it passed into distance I saw the figure against the background of the great château as the terrible cortège filed away into the open space before the palace. There it all was, grouped, set, framed, and told as never pen could write it, nor picture paint it. Two hundred years of French history were there : the great King, the shameless Court, the wreck of France. And so, until after sunset, the stream flowed on · the dirty, ill-horsed dragoons, the cowardly crowd along the side-walks, the struggling, shambling masses marching in the roadway. Every phase of human age and misery was there : white-haired men of seventy, desperado boys of sixteen, old battered women, young girls clinging on the arms of wild-looking youths—all tired, hungry, blood-stained—this time the defeated ones in the everlasting strife between rich and poor, marching into the twilight. In a pocket-book of that time I find these scenes outlined in a few short sentences which end with the words : ' What hope ? What hope ? ' Then overleaf I read this · ' Everywhere around this scene was the beauty of the summer, the scent of leaf and flower ; the horse chestnuts and elms were rippling with the music of May, the air was filled with the song and chirp of birds.'

That was the eternal answer to my question. If I did not hear it then, I know it now.

I

CHAPTER IX

My new-found friend, M. D'Arcy, was as good as his word. Next day I attended with him at the État-Major in the palace and passed the scrutiny. We set out again on the omnibus for the Point du Jour. One incident occurred on the road, besides the passage of captured guns and prisoners, now familiar to me since the preceding evening. It was the coming of a strong body of cavalry, escorting a carriage in which sat a short man with round, owl-eyed spectacles and a general officer in undress uniform. We drew up to let this cavalcade go by, and I had a good look at the two men in the carriage. They were Monsieur Thiers and Marshal MacMahon—the chief of the newly formed Republic and the commander-in-chief of the French army. The fighting phase of the war of France against the Commune was clearly over.

When we passed the barrier at the enceinte of Paris, a long road lay before us to our destination in the Rue Vivienne. I carried my knapsack. My companion was already domiciled in the Hôtel des Étrangers, for which we were bound. There were no horses or carriages and very few pedestrians to be seen ; patrols, mounted and on foot, were about. We struck the Seine somewhere near Auteuil, and followed the right bank of the stream for a long distance. Looking up the river towards the north of Paris one still saw a bank of smoke, but it was nothing like what it had been two days before from St. Denis. It was dusk when we reached the Place de la Concorde ; a long May twilight had light still left to show at least some of the devastation that had here been wrought by fire and shell. The great offices of State that flanked the Place on its north side were all in ruins, roofless, and black with smoke ; masses

130

of charred and burnt papers covered the paved floor of the
Place, and were blowing in the breeze ; a strong smell of burnt
stuff filled the air ; the palace of the Corps Législatif and the
buildings on the Quai d'Orsay were black and roofless.   Looking
to the left up the Rue Castiglione one saw no column above
the Place Vendôme.   But the strangest sight was the Tuileries.
Nothing remained of that great historic pile but the bare, gaunt
walls, through the glassless windows of which the glow of
floors and rafters still burning below cast a deep red glare ;
the effect in the twilight was like that of lighted candles
set within a colossal skull.   I do not remember having seen a
single human being in that huge scene of destruction around
the Place de la Concorde.

At every entrance along the Rue de Rivoli great barricades
of stone and timber were standing.   The silence of death was
here.   Not a single lamp was lighted.   Twilight seemed to be
closing over an enormous graveyard in which even the tombs
were ruined.   Just seventeen months earlier I had looked at
this scene glittering in myriad jets of gas.   A turn of the thumb
and forefinger can put out a good deal of gas.

We turned into the gardens of the Palais Royal, and here
at last there was life.   It was now quite dark, but two battalions of regular soldiers were encamped in the gardens, and
their supper fires were still smouldering.

There was one old woman in the Hôtel des Étrangers, who
let us in after some debate, and got us some cold salt beef for
supper.

I could not enter into the details of the next week, although
it was a very wonderful week.   The days were gloriously fine ;
I was quick of foot and could go for many hours together
without tiring.   I explored the great city in every direction, and
I saw many scenes that are not likely to be seen again in our
time.   Morning after morning I started out early, ate and
drank somewhere, and got back at nightfall to the Rue
Vivienne   Troops were pouring into Paris, and the hunt for
Communists was in full swing ; the barricades were disappearing ; horses began to show in the thoroughfares again.   One
could follow the routes of the Versailles troops along both sides
of the river up to Belleville, and tell by the shell marks
and bullet holes the places where the fiercest resistance had

been made. A great stand had taken place in front of the Hôtel de Ville and along the line of the Boulevard Sébastopol. Great numbers of dead had been hastily buried in the square near the tower of St. Jacques, and the warm May sun was making the air smell badly. Another stand had been made at the Place de la Bastille. Ammunition seemed literally to have been poured along the streets in the vicinity of this spot : a tin hat suspended over the door of a hatter's shop had six bullets in it. At the corner of the Rue Castex and the Rue St. Antoine every wall, door, and window was pitted. The column of July had a dozen cannon-shots through its base.

The Hôtel de Ville was a scene of the greatest destruction I had ever beheld ; everything in it or near it was smashed to atoms—the great clock, the wonderful staircase, the statues, the bronze railings, the equestrian figures of Liberté, Egalité, and Fraternité—all was broken, charred, and brayed into bits.

I went on to Père Lachaise. Here the last stand had been made among the tombs, and it was here that the heavy shell fire I had watched from the tower of St. Denis had wrought the greatest havoc. Of the great and noble soldiers whose graves or monuments are in Père Lachaise—Ney, MacDonald, Suchet, Masséna, Kellermann, Foy, Lavalette, and Labédoyère —nothing was stirred or injured ; but some at least of the stock-jobber and capitalist fraternity—that dynasty which seems to have succeeded to the thrones vacated by the old despots—had not been so fortunate. The gorgeously vulgar mausoleum of Casimir Perrier had been shot into with bullets, and the tomb of the Duc de Morny had apparently served as an eating-table for the ' Red ' soldiers, for there were broken loaves of bread and ends of wine bottles on it.

In the Place de la Concorde the Egyptian obelisk had escaped a rain of shells fired from a Versailles battery at the Arc de Triomphe, but the statue of Lille was shattered to pieces, its head and bust lying on the ground. The winged horses at the main entrance to the Tuileries Gardens were wingless, the marble balustrades were knocked about, and the trees and asphalt paths and floorings rent and torn with shells.

To me the pity of it all centred in the column of Austerlitz, and its statue lying prone in the dust and litter of the Place

Vendôme   The Prussian shot from the siege batteries of Chatillon and Meudon had spared the dome of the Invalides, but Frenchmen had been found base enough to pull down in cold blood the bronze pillar made from the cannon of Austerlitz, with the statue of the Great Conqueror on its summit.   That sight hardened my heart to the scenes I was now to witness. These were the hunting out of those wretched people, all through the north and north-east of Paris.   By this time the prisoners taken by the Prussians in the war had all returned to France, and it was easy for the new Government to obtain soldiers ; but they were soldiers upon whose faces it was not difficult to read the story of the defeat and demoralisation of that war.   They had been prisoners, they had been marched away from disastrous fields of defeat and surrender, huddled together in tens of thousands, just as they were now huddling their own brothers and cousins into the camps at Satory and Versailles.

One saw soldiers everywhere — idle, undisciplined, dirty. Few among them seemed to care for themselves, or for any one else.   There was no pride about them, no apparent sense or knowledge of the things they were looking at on every side. The moral rivets of their individual bodies and souls seemed to be as loose as were the social and political screws of the body politic in the collective fabric of the State.   The marines and sailors were of quite a different type : one saw in them a look and demeanour alert and serious : they seemed to know what had happened.

Paris was now locked up more securely than ever.   People returning to their homes from the country were allowed to enter ; people wanting to leave Paris for the country could not go out.   The prisons were all full, and over and over again one saw repeated in smaller groups the scenes I had witnessed at Versailles on that second evening there.

I went one day to the prison of La Roquette.   It was there that the Archbishop of Paris and some forty priests had been shot in cold blood by the Communists.   M. D'Arcy was with me on this occasion, and we were passed in at once.   We were shown into a small courtyard of the prison by a young naval lieutenant, who coolly explained to us the processes of the trial and execution of Communists.   ' We strip their right shoulders,' he said. ' If the skin of the neck and shoulder shows the dark mark produced by the kick of the chassepot rifle the court pronounces the single word " *classe* "; if there is no mark of discoloration on the shoulder the president says " *passe*," and the man is released. Those to whom " *classe* " is said are shot. One hundred and fifty were shot at daybreak this morning in this courtyard.' There was ghastly proof around that the man spoke truly. The courtyard was paved with round stones, and one had to step from stone to stone to avoid the blood that filled the interstices between them. A horrible smell, as of a shambles, filled the yard. Along the wall where the condemned men had stood the high-growing dock and marshmallow weeds had their heads all cut off, and the wall was pitted with innumerable holes by bullets. It was a battalion of Breton sailors who were employed on this duty.

In a room of the prison the officer showed us the hand and ring of the murdered archbishop. Probably these ghastly relics were kept there in order to nerve the Breton sailors to their terrible work.

In another courtyard stood a great pile of rifles, knapsacks, and accoutrements, all made for fighting the Prussians. This was the end.

I had seen enough of Paris in her agony, and would have been glad to shut my eyes upon her sufferings ; but to leave the city was now much more difficult than to enter it had been a week ago. The thought that had been growing in my mind above every other thought in those days and amid those scenes was the hopelessness of all this social world of our so-called civilisation. Was this all that we had been able to do for the people, for the men who had nothing, for those poor whom we were always to have with us ? Nations fought themselves into victory on one side and the other, dynasties rose and disappeared, religions ebbed and flowed ; but in this war there was no cessation, no equilibrium, no end. The have's and the have-not's were always face to face, ready to shoot down or to rush in. Often before my mind at this time came that scene in the Elysée on the morning of the 22nd June 1815, four days after Waterloo, when Napoleon, hearing the shouts of the populace of the faubourgs calling upon him to dissolve the Chamber of Deputies and proclaim himself Dictator, exclaimed

bitterly, ' Poor people ! they alone stand by me in the hour
of my reverses, yet I have not loaded them with riches or
honours. I leave them poor, as I found them ' How many
since that day have had their chance of doing something for
these submerged millions, and have done nothing ! And yet
now, when I look back upon it all, over the almost forty
years gone since I saw the fall of the Commune, it seems that
only on one road, humanly speaking, lies the hope of redemption for them. It is outlined in another utterance of the
Great Conqueror, recorded as spoken on that same day of his
abdication.

'You come from the village of Gonesse ? ' said Napoleon
to the boy page who had brought him a cup of coffee. ' No,
sire, from Pierrefitte.' ' Where your parents have a cottage
and some acres of land ? ' ' Yes, sire.' ' That is the only
true happiness.' Yes, and it is the only true wealth, of men
and of nations. Man under modern dispensations has been
graciously permitted by his masters to go back to the land
only after he is dead : I think if they would permit him to do
so during his life, and allow him that ' cottage and some acres
of land,' things would not be so bad in our world. Did not a
son of Cain build the first city ?

I got permission to leave Paris. Trains ran from the Gare
du Nord again. In the carriage with me were two English
surgeons who had been doing ambulance work in those final days
of the Commune. One, afterwards a well-known man, related
some incidents which had come under his notice in these last
fights. An old woman was found crouching under an upturned
cart behind a barricade ; the troops advanced thinking the
barricade had been abandoned by everybody ; the old woman
shot with a revolver the first soldier who approached her. ' I
have had three sons killed in this fighting,' she said, ' and I
swore that I would kill one enemy. You may shoot me now.'
They did so.

I went to Ireland, and began at once to write a book on those
great lone spaces of the earth which I had quitted only a few
weeks earlier. It seemed so strange that there should be
these vast, vacant lands, while here the city-pent millions were
murdering each other with such ferocity, and I longed, too, to
get back to the wilds again. In the army there seemed to be

no chance for me. When my leave of absence expired, I was
ordered to join the dépôt of my regiment, then at Chatham.
I went there in the end of 1871. The men in authority were
exceedingly kind, work was light, and I was able to devote
several hours every day to my manuscript. It grew rapidly.
In that little dingy red-brick subaltern's quarter on the old
terrace in the ' Phonghee ' barracks at Chatham I lived again
in the wilds. What an infinite blessing is the mystery of
memory ! No possession or instinct belonging to man can
touch that single gift—to look back, to remember, to be young
when you are old, to see the dead, to paint a picture upon a
prison wall, to have ways to escape, to be free—all this out of
Memory. Surely this was ' the breath of life ' breathed into
the brain of man when God gave him ' a living soul.' And yet
there are people who say they cannot see the soul !

While I was thus far away in memory in the lone spaces an
unexpected piece of good fortune happened. Horatio Nelson
Case had ' struck oil.' A syndicate had been formed in Canada
for the development of Petrolia, and our plot of forest-land
was wanted by it. Case was adamantine. He would only
take six thousand pounds for our lot. He got it. I telegraphed to my officer-partner in Bermuda to proceed at once
on leave to Canada to be present at the division of profits.
He could not, or would not go. The profit available appeared
to be a simple sum—five thousand two hundred pounds to be
halved, and halved again. But in business of this kind there
is nothing simple ; it is always compound. I had calculated
my share of one thousand three hundred pounds, but somehow
or other it worked out a good deal less. It always does. Any-
how the conclusion of the ' bear ' transaction, begun in the
Brooke Swamp three years earlier, left me with a clear thousand pounds. Had it come a year or two earlier I would
undoubtedly have purchased a company in the 69th Regiment,
and might have eventually blossomed into a retired major.
So, my dear young friend, if you meet with a check in life or
a disappointment in your profession, as in three cases out of
four you are bound to do, remember an old soldier's advice, ,
' Go on again.' Repack your knapsack if necessary, but
whatever articles you throw out of it, don't unload that imaginary baton of field-marshal. It costs nothing to carry, it has

no value to anybody except yourself ; but neither has the apple of your eye.

In the middle of April 1872 I was gazetted to an unattached (half-pay) company in the army. I had finished my book, and sent the MS. to a publisher, and was immensely pleased when he was good enough to accept it. I was now free to go where I chose, and I chose the wilds again. I left my postal address at the War Office, ' Carlton House, Saskatchewan.' I have an idea that the name ' Carlton ' in the address induced the clerk in the War Office who had to deal with the postal addresses of officers to refrain from raising any objection to the remainder of the domiciliary location ; or it may have been that the head of his department, with a wider geographical knowledge, had said to his subordinate when the paper was presented to him, ' Not far off enough ' In any case, no objection was raised. Carlton House was at that time nine hundred miles from the nearest railway station, but it was the point of distribution for the winter packet dog-post, which left Fort Garry just before Christmas ; and wherever I might be in the territories of the Hudson Bay Company, letters would find me some time. Then I started for New York.

I set out with no fixed plan of travel. I wanted to go beyond where I had been before, and the ' beyond ' that lay to the north of the Saskatchewan Valley was a very big place. You could get a round two thousand miles in it in almost any direction north of an east and west line running through Fort Carlton.

I had a general idea of getting into the basin of the Mackenzie River, descending that great stream nearly to its mouth, then going into the valley of the Yukon, ' and so on and so on,' as my Levantine interpreter used to say on the Nile, twelve years later, when he had exhausted the one hundred and twenty-five English one-syllable words which were his entire linguistic stock-in-trade, and the possession of which enabled him to draw the pay and allowances of a major in the British army.

In the few months I had spent in Chatham I was in the habit of visiting the library of the Royal Geographical Society. It was the time when Livingstone had not been heard of for years ; an expedition was being organised by the Society to look for him   I offered my services, was not accepted, and, true to the old habit of ' going on again,' I set out shortly after in the opposite direction to Lake Bangweolo (where the great missionary-explorer had been last heard of), with the result that, just one year later, I found myself at Lake Athabasca, twelve hundred miles north-west of Fort Garry, with the prospect of another twelve hundred miles up the valley of the Peace River to the Pacific coast at Vancouver. The narrative of that journey has been written long ago.[1]

Before striking north from Fort Carlton I had spent three months in a hut at the ' forks ' of the Saskatchewan, in company with a brother officer of my regiment, and trusted friend, Captain Mansfield. Mansfield had left the 69th Regiment, tired of serving without seeing service. We had a plan that, after tasting again the wild life of the prairies, we would settle in some part of the Saskatchewan Valley, and begin ranching life there with a herd of cattle driven from the States. Had we carried this intention into effect, our ranch would have been the first of its kind in the Canadian North-West. At that time I think I may say with truth that I stood almost alone in my belief that this vast region had a great future before it. Among all the officers of the Hudson Bay Company I did not know one who believed in the potentialities of the land in which they had spent their lives. Furs it had, and minerals it might have, but for the grain or food products of the earth, they did not think anything of it. Even at Winnipeg at this time so slight were the expectations that the place would become the site of a large city that I was offered, in the month of August 1872, sixteen hundred acres of land, where the town stands to-day, for sixteen hundred pounds. This offer was pressed upon me by an old army pensioner, Mulligan by name, who had gradually bought up for a mere trifle the grants of land given to private soldiers in the 6th Regiment some twenty years earlier. Dissatisfied with the trend of public opinion after the Riel Rebellion of 1870, he was desirous of leaving the place for ever. For myself, I am not sorry that I stuck to the army ship. The best and the worst that can be said of it is that it is a poor profession : I

[1] *The Wild North Land.* (E B)

hope it will long remain so. 'I look around on every side,' wrote Carlyle, 'and I see one honest man in the community. He is the drill sergeant.' Well, I will not go so far as that ; but this I can say, that if the soldier be honest it is because he is poor, and if he is poor it is because he is honest. He is unfit for business, they tell me, and I agree with those who say so. You will usually find that when the soldier has tried his hand at business he has made a fool of himself, and has lost his little money. He believes in others, that is the mistake he makes in business ; he thinks that a man's word spoken should have as much weight as when it is written across a penny postage stamp, and he finds out, generally too late, that it hasn't. Even when the soldier tries to be a rogue, he usually makes a mess of it He is like a trooper in the 11th Hussars at Canterbury, who once complained to his general that whenever there was a row in the town he was invariably caught by the police, because of the cherry-coloured breeches he was compelled to wear : 'them darker-coloured overall chaps get off,' but he, the red-breeched one, was sure to be nailed in the end, no matter how many corners he got round in the run home to barracks. In no part of the Empire does the soldier make such a fool of himself as inside of Temple Bar. East of that historic boundary he is a child ; there was no necessity for the City Fathers to stipulate that soldiers should unfix bayonets whenever they came within the city precincts : they disarm themselves when they go there. There were only two soldiers in history who did well in the city of London : one was Oliver Cromwell, the other was George Monk. They both plundered it.

I think I may add to this digression by putting down a little incident which happened in the Crimean War, but of which I only became aware two years ago. On the night preceding the attack on the Redan on the 18th June 1855, a party of officers of the Fourth Division, who were detailed for the assault, were playing cards in a tent on the heights before Sebastopol. The 'fall in' was to go at 2 A.M., and there was no use in lying down that night. Before the card-party broke up accounts were settled A cousin of mine—a captain in the 57th Regiment—received from a captain in the 17th Foot, named Croker, an I O U for a considerable sum of money, which he, Croker, had lost to my relative. A few hours later Croker was killed at the Redan. There had only been a half-hour's interval between the 'fall out' for the game of cards and the 'fall in' for the great game of war, so of course my cousin tore up the I O U, and thought no more about the transaction. A couple of months later he received a letter from the army agents, Cox & Co., in London, informing him that they had received on the day of his death an advice from the late Captain Croker directing the sum of £—— to be placed to the account of Captain Butler in their hands. So much has been said and written in recent years against the old army and the old regimental system that I give this little incident as a trifling tribute to both.

During the autumn and winter of 1872, and the first half of 1873, I had movement, sport, travel, and adventure sufficient to satisfy the longings of anybody. I was at that time boiling with the spirit of movement, and distance alone sufficed to lend enchantment to my prospect of travel. The scene could not be too remote, nor the theatre too lonely. The things I did not want to see or know of were trains and steamboats ; the canoe or the prairie pony in summer, the snow-shoe and dog-sled in winter, one's own feet and legs at all times —these were good enough for passing over the surface of God's wonderful world. I was a fair shot, and even where the Hudson Bay Company's posts were some hundred miles apart, and Indian camps were few and far between, the gun and the baited fish-hook could still provide dinner and supper; and for bed, old Mother Earth gave it, and the pine brush made mattress and pillow. I have often thought that the reply of the once potent Indian chief, Black Hawk, to the American commissioner who offered him a chair to sit on at a conference on the Upper Mississippi eighty years ago, held in it the whole secret and soul of the wilderness. 'Thank you,' said the Indian chief, as he seated himself on the ground, 'the Earth is my mother, and on her bosom I can rest myself' You can never know that mother until you go and live with her in the wilderness ; it is only there that she takes you on her lap and whispers to you her secret things. It is only when you join the ranks of the wild things that they will accept you as one of themselves and will cease to look at you as a stranger.

Fancy a place where there are no drains, no coal smoke, no factory chimneys; where you cannot speak ill of your neighbour, nor envy him, nor tell him the simplest form of lie, nor be bored by him—that last, the greatest of all the earthly beatitudes! And the strange part of it is that if you have once tasted well of the wild fruit, you have got an antidote for ever against being bored. My friends sometimes say to me, 'How can you listen so patiently to that terrible old bore, General Pounce?' or, 'I saw you to-day in the morning-room with that stupid old Major de Trop, and you seemed to be hanging on every word he said.' At which I smile, but say nothing, for it would destroy my happiness if the secret were known. As he ripples along, I launch my canoe on the stream of his story, merely on the sound of it, and I sail away into the lone spaces. It is the Athabasca, the river of the meadows, the Souris River, the river that echoes, that I am on again. He, poor fellow, hasn't the slightest suspicion of what I am doing. He never asks me a question. He wants none of my thoughts, and he gets none. He only wants something to speak at, and I give him that generously. Then, when he is quite tired, he goes away, and I go to the writing-table and scribble down some doggerel such as this :—

> 'If a bore had seen what one swallow saw
> Or could read from a rook his Mayday caw
> Or could riddle aright one wild-bee's hum,
> No bore he would be—but he might be dumb.'

But then we would have changed places, and I might have been the bore.

At last, in the middle of 1873, I got out through that great tangle of mountains, lake, and rushing river which forms the northern portion of British Columbia, and with one dog, the untiring 'Cerf volant,' for companion, reached the ways of civilised travel and the Pacific Ocean. In the very centre of this tangle of mountains and rapids I had struck a small camp of gold-miners at a place called Germanson, on the Ominica River, a large tributary stream which joins the Peace River west of the Rocky Mountains. To get to this spot we had been working for twenty days in a 'dug-out' canoe against the flooded stream of the Ominica. We were a party of four. The steersman was a little Frenchman from Belfort, Jacques Pardonnet by name, a man of extraordinary knowledge and pluck, qualities to which was mainly due under Providence our escape from many perils of rock and rapid, whirlpool and ice-floe, for we had launched our 'dug-out' on the Upper Peace River before the ice had been cleared from the current.

As we drew near Germanson, Jacques began to speak at the camp fire in the evening of an English captain who was at the mining camp the previous year He called him by a name that had been familiar to me at Fermoy fourteen years earlier : if he had known the officer's Christian name identification would have been assured, for the first name had been Napoleon ; but he knew only the captain's surname. On entering Germanson the first person I came upon was the very man.

It was the end of August when I got back to Canada proper, the Canada of the St. Lawrence River. I was fairly puzzled what next to do. The long trail through the north and west by the Athabasca and Peace River to the Pacific had eaten a big hole into the round thousand won out of the day in Brooke Swamp three years earlier. To tell the truth, it is a very wide step from the real wilderness to that state of semi-civilised savagery which is the life of the frontier settler, those first and second stages in the evolution of the ranch and the wheatfield from the primæval prairie and the pine forest. When the wild man and the buffalo disappear from the stage, the next comer, whether man or beast, doesn't show to advantage. Even the old white hunter, the trapper, the 'Leather-Stocking' of the immortal Fenimore Cooper, has to fold up his camping-kit, shoulder his rifle, and move off into lonelier lands or deeper forests. He cannot stand it. As it was in 'the old Colonial days' of America, so was it forty years ago. When I first went to the Platte River in 1867 a few 'Leather-Stockings' were still to be found at the forts of the United States troops ; and foremost among that small, lessening band was the celebrated Bridger, the grizzled veteran of the great days of Captain Bonneville, Fitzpatrick, and Sublette. One day a newcomer from the east, seeing this old veteran Bridger standing silent at Laramie, thought to open conversation by asking if it was not a long time since he had come out west. The old hunter did not seem to have heard his questioner, and the remark was repeated. Then Bridger took his pipe from his mouth, and gravely answered as he pointed towards Pike's Peak in the west: 'Young man, do you see that thar peak?' 'Yes.' 'Well, when I came out to these prairies that thar peak was a hole in the ground.' He then went on smoking again.

One evening when I was in this undecided frame of mind as to where I would go and what I would next do, I opened a paper in an hotel at Ottawa, and read in the cablegram from England the announcement that an expedition was being prepared for the West Coast of Africa. Sir Garnet Wolseley was to command. His staff would consist of many officers who had served under him on the Red River expedition. No troops were to be sent until after the general and his officers had reached the West Coast. It was expected that this campaign would be over by March. Sir Garnet and his friends were to sail from England on the 8th September. That was all. It was now the 30th August. I read the message carefully a second time, took in the situation, went to the telegraph-office, and sent a message to Sir Garnet Wolseley in London that I was coming. Then looking up the steamer sailings I found that there was a steamer leaving New York on the 3rd September. The telegrams of the next day brought further particulars. The well-known unhealthiness of the West Coast of Africa generally, and of the Gold Coast in particular, was the reason assigned for the extraordinary fact that no troops were being sent with the general and his staff to the new seat of war. It was hoped that the native negro levies would suffice. If, after the general had arrived at Cape Coast Castle, it was found that the natives would not fight the soldiers of the King of Ashanti, then white troops would be sent from England, and an advance made upon Coomassie.

It is the most precious privilege of youth not to question anything. What did it matter if the Gold Coast had been the White Man's Grave ever since Columbus had been there? One never dreamt of asking whether a climate was good or bad. A missionary who would stop to inquire if his predecessor had disagreed with the cannibal king who had eaten him would be as ridiculous as the young soldier who troubled his head as to the precise points of disagreement between his constitution and the climate of the country to which he was bound. It is the business of the young soldier to agree with his climate even when it disagrees with him.

Even the quickest of steamships went slowly in those days compared with the ocean fliers of to-day. The *Russia* took ten days to get to Liverpool, and I missed the start of Sir Garnet and his staff from the same port by eight hours.

I remember little of the voyage save a small personal incident in it which was a pleasant surprise to me. I had left England seventeen months earlier, while my little book of travel was still in the printer's hands. Its subsequent fortunes were therefore scarcely known to me, for I had been buried in the wilds during the greater part of the interval. One evening, when I was sitting in the smoking-room of the steamer, a man observed to another passenger, ' I hear the author of *The Great Lone Land* is on board the steamer.' As I had the manuscript of another book of northern travel in my bag, nearly completed, the chance remark was doubly pleasant to me. Perhaps I should find some balance in the Army bankers' hands to my credit, and perhaps, too, the publishers of my first literary venture would be favourably disposed to try a second one.

When I reached London from America, I found a message from Sir Garnet Wolseley directing me to follow him to the Gold Coast, and I received official information from the War Office that my passage would be provided in a West African steamer, sailing on the 30th September. So on the last day of September I left England again in the steamer *Benin* bound for Cape Coast Castle. A terrible-smelling craft was the old *Benin*. Fever seemed to have established itself securely amid her close, ill-kept decks. A couple of voyages earlier, eleven men had died out of her small crew, a steward and two cabin servants being among them. On this voyage of ours the captain and some half-dozen others were to go. Like every other sea-captain I had ever sailed with, this commander of the *Benin*, Captain Stone, was a splendid fellow. ' I hope to be back again by Christmas,' he said, ' and to spend the holidays with my wife at home in Dublin.' He never came back. A

month later he was in a hammock-shroud under the waters
somewhere in the steaming Bight of Benin.

'Remember, remember the Bight of Benin ,
Few come out, though many go in '

So ran the old sailor's song of our grandfathers' days, when
Tom Cringle kept his log and Captain Marryat wrote his sea-
stories. They tell me things are better there to-day. Perhaps.

The *Benin* touched at many places on the coast—Sierra
Leone, Palmas, Liberia, Jack-Jack, and Monrovia. A little
while before, a strange thing had happened at the last-named
place All these ships trading to West Africa carried in round
holes near the scuppers on the deck two rows of roundshot,
six or nine pounders , these were not for hostile use, they were
kept for a funereal purpose—that of sinking the poor dead men
deep in the Bight of Benin, by being fastened to the foot of
the hammock-shroud. But one day when the vessel was
steaming into Monrovia, and the signal gun had been duly
loaded with powder for the blank shot which was to wake up
the government and postal officials of that place, a wag on
board quietly dropped one of these roundshots into the carron-
ade on the top of the powder. Presently, bang ! went the alarm
gun, and then a round black object was observed hurling itself
through the air in the direction of the wooden pier whereon
the sable officials were already drawn up in state to greet the
English steamer. The shot struck the pier, sending woodwork
flying in all directions ; the officials fled, the President of the
Republic of Liberia leading, the Postmaster-General, a very
old negro, bringing up the rear I never heard how the matter
ended.

The *Benin* reached Cape Coast Castle early on the 22nd
October. A surf-boat came out with an officer for mails. He
offered to put me on shore. As we paddled in through the
heavy surf, which is ever rolling in three great lines of foam
against the shores of tropical Africa, I asked the officer his
name. It was the same as that of ' the captain,' formerly of
Fermoy, whom I had left at the Ominica gold-mine in British
Columbia four months earlier. ' Any relation in America ? '
' A brother somewhere in the wilds of whom I have not heard
for years, if he is still alive,' he answered. ' He was alive four

K

months ago,' I replied; 'and what is more, he gave me a message for his brother in the service, should I chance to fall in with him.' I had come almost straight from that distant spot. The first man I met at the end of the fifteen thousand miles was the brother of the last man I had seen in Ominica.

CHAPTER X

As steam bends the stoutest blackthorn wood, so the hot, moist climate of the Gold Coast bends and makes limp the stoutest human body.

This melting work begins even before the coast is reached. No sooner has the ship turned eastward from the Atlantic into the 'Bights' than an immediate change becomes perceptible in the atmosphere; an oppressive, damp, steamy air is breathed; the body streams with perspiration of a clammy, weakening kind; the very sap of strength is bleeding at every pore. There is no fury about the heat Compared with the range of the thermometer in the Soudan, or even in India, the heat on the coast or in the forest behind it is nothing; but it is incessant, unvarying, and its quality of excessive dampness is the killing factor in it The sapping process goes on night and day: a peculiar damp, leaden look is on the skin. As poor Prince Henry of Battenberg wrote of the climate twenty years later, 'the damp heat is indescribable, so also is the effect it produces. Even if you sit quiet without moving, perspiration streams off your body day and night. The air reeks with malaria and poison. . . What would not one give for a few whiffs of pure air without these dreadful miasmas that hang about one like ghosts ! ' But on the day of arrival all this had yet to be learnt ; and I stepped ashore from the surf-boat, and went up the wretched street that led from the old Slave Castle to Government House with as light a step as though I were still in the Black Cañon of the far-away Ominica.

The general and his staff were assembling for breakfast. It was pleasant to meet old friends of Red River days again —Redvers Buller, Huyshe, McCalmont. Baker Russell was down with fever, and McNeill with wounds. New men were there too : Brackenbury, Maurice, Lanyon. Evelyn Wood was at Elmina. Hume was making a road towards Coomassie. It was the habit in later years to call these men, and a few others, ' The Wolseley Gang.' I see in the dictionary that the word is derived from the Danish, and that it means, in its primitive sense, ' to go,' but I don't think that was the meaning its users attached to it. I see, too, that its modern signification is sometimes ' a number of persons associated for a certain purpose, usually a bad one.' I look back now over nigh forty years, and I don't think there was any bad purpose individually or collectively in that little group of men. I accept with pleasure the Danish definition of the word, ' to go.' We, for I was a humble member, certainly did go : some dropped on the road early, and others fell out later ; a few struggled on to the end. They rest in many places : one at Prah-su, another under Majuba, another in the middle of the Desert of Bayuda, another at Spion Kop, another under the sea near St. Helena, another in the sands at Tel-el-Kebir, another in the veldt at Magersfontein. Poor old ' Gang ' ! They kept going as long as they could go, and now they are nearly all gone. May they rest in peace !

It would have been difficult to match the military situation which was now existing in and around Cape Coast Castle. A general and some thirty or forty officers of various abilities had landed on the most pestilential shore in the world for the avowed object of driving back a horde of forty thousand splendidly disciplined African savages, who had invaded British territory. All the hopes founded upon the idea that the native races who lived under our protection in the forest lying between the sea and the River Prah—Fantis, Assims, Abras, and others—would rally under English leadership to do battle against their hereditary enemies, the Ashantis, had proved entirely fallacious. Palaver had followed palaver, the chiefs and kinglets were profuse in promise, feeble in performance, and cowardly in action. Nothing could induce them to tackle the Ashanti enemy. If men wanted to study the effect, good and evil, upon man brought up with discipline and without it, here on this coast was to be found the best field for such an inquiry. On one side of the Prah River lived a people possessing to an extraordinary degree a high military spirit, on the other a people as cowardly as could be found anywhere on earth. Both were of the same race : in ancestry, colour, size, language, and feature they were identical. A hundred years earlier they had been one kingdom : what had happened to make this extraordinary change in character and habit ?

I think it would be correct to say that beyond the Prah the old African idea of a cruel but effective system of despotic authority had been maintained ; and that to the south of that little river of forty yards span the blessings of trade and commerce had steadily sapped the moral strength and physical courage of the ' protected ' tribes.

An American writer has said that if you put a chain round the neck of a slave, the other end of the chain will fasten itself round your own neck. Perhaps that was what had happened here. This coast had been for two hundred and more years the greatest slave preserve in the world. All these castles dotted along the surf-beaten shore at ten or twelve mile intervals were the prisons where, in the days of the slave-trade, millions of wretched negroes had been immured, waiting the arrival of slave-ships from Bristol or Liverpool to load the human cargo for West Indian or American ports. It would not be too much to say that from each of these prison-castles to some West Indian port, a cable of slave skeletons must be lying at the bottom of the ocean In that terrible trade the protected tribes of the coast were the prime brokers. They bought from the black interior kingdoms of Dahomey and Ashanti, and they sold to the white merchant traders of Europe ; slaves, rum, and gunpowder were the chief items in the bills of lading. The gunpowder went to the interior, the rum was drunk on the coast, the slaves, or those who survived among them, went to America. If two in ten lived through the horrors of the middle passage the trade paid. John Wesley knew what he was talking about when he said of that hellish traffic that it was ' the sum of all human villanies ', and yet there never was one man in the world to whom it was possible to know even half of the villanies concentrated in that single phrase—the slave-trade.

After a week on the coast, one began to know the way of

things fairly well. This coast had ways of its own that no other coast known to me possessed. Our forty special-service officers and their motley groups of natives were distributed between the seaports of Elmina and Cape Coast Castle, and in certain positions a few miles inland, chiefly along the forest track leading towards the River Prah. The great forest did not come right down to the seashore ; there was an interval of bush some six or eight miles deep before the real trees began. In this deep real forest lay the Ashanti army spread out along a circle of crooms or villages distant from the sea about twelve miles. Little was known about the numbers of this army : it had originally been forty or fifty thousand men, but many forms of disease were said to have thinned its ranks since it had crossed the Prah six months earlier. Still less was known as to the intentions of its commander, Amonquatier by name. The spies sent out by us brought back no trustworthy information ; they were as cautious and as cowardly as were their chiefs and kinglets. At last some tangible news reached us from this mysterious Ashanti camp at Mampon. It was brought by a fugitive slave woman direct from the Ashanti headquarters ; and the story told by the runaway had so many little bits of domestic detail and family intrigue woven into it that the more important facts of Ashanti movement and intentions seemed to derive confirmation from the lighter parts of the woman's tale.

The Ashanti army in the forest around Mampon was breaking up, and was falling back to the Prah River under orders from the King of Ashanti. The sick and wounded had already moved ; the main army would soon follow, but first it would take Abra Crampa, a town lying some twelve miles from Cape Coast Castle, near the forest track to the River Prah. This news, confirmed by reports from this road of Ashanti scouting parties having appeared in the vicinity, put us all in action at Cape Coast Castle. If we only had the soldiers, what an opportunity was now offered of destroying the retreating army of Ashantis ! It was moving across our front at the slow rate of progression which alone was possible in this dense forest ; but we had only a few West Indian soldiers with which to strike it ; arms, ammunition, forty officers brimming over with energy and action, and no men. During the follow-

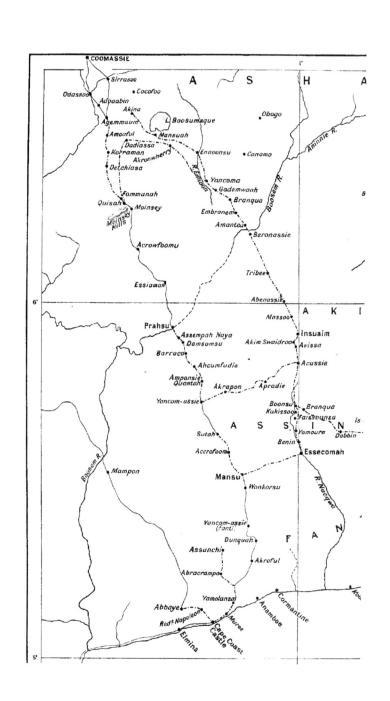

ing week some of this band of forty officers started off in as many directions. As for myself, I had in me all the power and go of the frozen lands I had quitted a few months earlier. It seemed impossible that one could not still cover the old American distances. Of course the conditions were as opposite as those which lie between the coldest ice and the hottest sun ; but youth takes small heed of such differences or measurements. Between the night of 25th October and that of the 29th, I covered some seventy miles of forest and swamps, in a temperature a good deal higher than that of the tropical hothouse at Kew. In these four or five days I had seen and sampled the forest, the crooms, the kings, their armies, and their method of fighting. A page description [1] of the 29th October will suffice to tell the story of many days and places :

'At daybreak the whole force was to move to Dunguah from Abra Crampa to attack the wing of the Ashanti army near that place. The King of Abra's warriors led. A lieutenant of the Royal Navy was attached to this tribe by dint of extraordinary exertions he got his crowd into some order, and cleared the village two hours after the appointed time. They were supposed to number five hundred men : I stood by the pathway and counted them as they passed ; they numbered one hundred and forty of all ranks. The procession moved in this order : six scouts, the king, two blunderbus-men, one carrying a very large horse-pistol, fifty men with long flint-guns, two drummers with skull drums, two men with powder barrels, a standard-bearer with an old flag, Pollard, R.N., sixty or seventy more men, a large negro with an entirely flat nose, and a small crimson smoking-cap for uniform (he was called the Field-Marshal, and the title was not given in any derisive sense). We got to Assanchi by noon. The day was fearfully hot ; the sun streamed down upon the forest, drawing from the darkest depths of tangled creeper and massive tree-trunk a steam of dense, exhausting atmosphere As we emerged into the overgrown plantain-gardens around the village of Assanchi, a couple of shots were fired on the left, and an Abra scout limped in with his legs cut by " slugs." The wildest confusion now ensued among the Abras, and it was only by actually laying hands upon them and by placing them in the required positions facing the enemy that any order or plan could be evolved. While we were at this work another volley announced a new foe in the bush on our left. Then came shots and shouts from the thick plantain-

[1] From *Akim-foo, the History of a Failure.* (E B)

leaves, and running thither I came upon six or eight men struggling in the dense brushwood, some on the ground and some on their legs In the centre of the mass there was a short, stout savage with his hair twisted into spiral spikes which stood straight out from his head. He was fighting for his life , and so strong was he that he was able in his twistings to move the three or four men who had him down. A couple of other Abras were striking him on the back of his head with the butts of their long " Dane " guns ; but they were unable to stop his writhings. At the edge of the group stood a tall Houssa soldier with a long knife in hand, ready for an opening which would enable him to draw it across the throat of the Ashanti. He was so intent on watching his opportunity that he did not see me. Just as I came up the unfortunate underdog man heaved himself up a bit from the ground, and the movement seemed to give the Houssa the chance he was looking for. He leant forward to get a better draw for his knife across the man's neck ; but as he did so I caught him full on the ear with my fist, and over he went, knife and all, into the bushes At the same instant the Ashanti rose, and seeing a white man close to him he threw himself forward, caught hold of my hand, and was safe. He was the first full-blooded Ashanti taken, and I was very glad to have him because I was doing Intelligence work at this time for Redvers Buller, who was down with fever, and we badly wanted solid information from our enemies. But what was of more importance was that Sir Garnet Wolseley was in need of some trusty messenger to send to the King of Ashanti in Coomassie, and this prisoner would be just the emissary to send there. But before I could get him safe from the crush, we were all very near coming to grief, for a fresh body of Houssas, belonging to Baker Russell's regiment, came upon the scene, and hearing a row going on in the bushes, they levelled half a dozen rifles upon us, intent upon observing the great rule of African warfare, which is to fire first and then look to see what was fired at afterwards. Fortunately for us Baker Russell was near this party. he saw the situation, and the muzzles of the Houssa Sniders were thrown up at his terrific word of command. By this time the marines and sailors in rear were thoroughly exhausted ; the day was swelteringly hot, the path was deep in mud and water, and the narrow track was only wide enough to allow men in single file to move along it. Many strong men went down that day, some of them did not get up again. The record of the day's work would be incomplete if it did not finish as it began with the army of the King of Abra under the command of

Lieutenant Pollard, R.N.   It was directed to feel its way to the main road at Donguah.   It fell in towards evening with an Ashanti camp : panic immediately ensued ; the one hundred and forty Abras, the Field-Marshal, the drums, and the horse-pistol man ran in various directions through the forest.   Pollard discharged the six barrels of his revolver at his vanishing army, and found himself alone in the great forest.   He was thoroughly exhausted, and night was coming on   After a time six or eight of his army crept back through the bush, got him on their shoulders and carried him by a by-path to Akroful on the main road.'

I have dwelt upon this day's work because it grouped into it many incidents and experiences peculiar to West African warfare.   One saw then the utter hopelessness of the original idea upon which the expedition had been based—that our debased and degenerate protected tribes could be able to fight the army of the King of Ashanti.   One understood, too, something at least of what this coast climate meant to a European, in the waste of strength and the deadly sap of health and energy.   Even without exertion, the strength of the body seemed to be hourly melting out of the system.   It was now the end of October.   Two entire months must elapse before white troops could arrive on the coast from England.   Would we last over that interval ?   Of all the strange things in life human hope is the strangest.   No matter how dark it may be on this side of the hill, the other side generally gets the credit of sunshine   If life is really a vale of tears, there are bursts of laughter coming through the sobs from some imaginary upper glen.

Work in a new region now opened for me   In a kingdom called Akim, some hundred or hundred and fifty miles northeast from Cape Coast Castle, there reigned two kings—Cobina Fuah and Coffee Ahencora, both of whom were supposed to be of better fighting quality than the sable monarchs dwelling near the coast.

A commission to these Akim sovereigns was duly given to me, and I was directed to proceed ' in one of Her Majesty's men-of-war to Accra, as a special Commissioner to the king and queen and chiefs of that district, in order to raise the whole of the fighting men in Western Akim for the purpose of closing in Amonquatier's army as it is endeavouring to re-cross the river Prah into Ashanti. . . . It is impossible,' went on the words of the Commission, ' to give you more precise instructions, and there is nothing to add further than that the major-general relies upon your zeal and discretion, and on your knowledge of barbarous people, to carry out quickly the objects of this most important mission which has been confided to you.'

My Commission bore date 2nd November, and by the evening of the 3rd I had got together a dozen Snyder rifles, two Union Jacks, a few servants, ammunition, a bag of a hundred gold pieces, some Australian tinned meats, and a lot of proclamations and addresses to black kings and queens in general, but particularly to the potentates reigning in the regions lying behind the coast at Accra. By dint of hard labour everything was ready for embarkation, and I got on board the gunboat *Decoy* late in the afternoon. Steam was already up, and we were soon rolling along to the eastward, pitching and tossing from one side to the other in those gigantic waves which never cease to roll, night and day, against the shores of tropic Africa. We rocked all night in the cradle of the deep, and at daybreak were off Accra. Another big slave castle was here, and the huge bastions of yet another prison could be seen three miles deeper in the Bight, at Christianburg. The last glimpse seen of the shore after sunset on the previous evening had been of slave castles ; the first sight in the morning was of slave castles ; and round that fatal coast-line, between the feverish forest and the yellow sand, they stand, now lonely and untenanted, with rusty gates and empty vaults, the mouldering monuments of two centuries of a gigantic injustice.

I got on shore as quickly as possible, for the night had been one of sleepless torment. Here at Accra the debasement of the negro seemed to be even greater than at Cape Coast Castle. A great ' Custom ' was going on to celebrate the movement of Captain Glover's native force from Accra to Addah, at the mouth of the Volta. ' Dashes ' of rum and gunpowder had been plentiful for days earlier, and the result was to be seen in men lying on their backs along the foul sea-front, firing guns into the air, turning head over heels, and firing as they turned, and uttering a strange mixture of Coast-English curses and invocations to some forest fetich for fortune in their coming campaign.

All that day and the next day I spent in Accra, endeavouring to evolve out of this hideous scene of naked and unabashed negro animalism the semblance of a sober convoy for my inland journey to Akim. Night came, but no convoy. The gun-firing might have been less than on the first day; but the drunkenness did not appear to have diminished. I had, however, the satisfaction on the first day of making the acquaintance of one of the most remarkable among the many remarkable persons to whose efforts are due the establishment of our Empire in Africa—Captain Glover, R.N. He had spent many years on the shores of the Bight of Benin. To him more than to any other man belongs by right the merit of being the first to discover the value of the trade which lay at the back of this equatorial coast forest, behind the kingdoms of Ashanti, Dahomey, and Benin. Forty years from the present time, Glover, as governor and maker of Lagos, had already foreseen the possibilities of forming a British possession which would embrace the countries of the Niger from its source to the sea. He was before his time. That great region has now many claimants for its possession, and it is still a matter of doubt in what direction its trade will eventually seek its outlet.

On the evening of the 5th November I got away from Accra with a very motley crowd of carriers, the greater part of whom were still under the influence of the ' Custom.' I have not space to tell in any detail of the march from Accra to the Akim Prah.   On the second day I had marched my men into a state of semi-sobriety ; but new difficulties arose. My kings, Fuah and Ahencora, had heard of the largesse distributed by Captain Glover at Accra, and they had both set out from Akim to share in these wonderful ' dashes,' which, no doubt, rumour had magnified to them.   Two days from Accra I met King Fuah moving in all the pomp of negro buffoonery towards the coast. It was a repetition of Pollard's army, with variations — sword and pipe bearers, horn blowers, umbrella men, skull mace-bearers, litter-carriers, three of the king's wives, bodyguards, and at last King Fuah himself. We had been exchanging messengers for three days : he beseeching me to await his arrival at Accra , I sending emissaries to tell him that he must return to his own country, whither I was coming , that he was turning his back upon the Ashanti enemy ;

that there were only old women left at Accra, and that it was in
his own kingdom of Akim that I would bestow upon him the
gifts, arms, and ' dashes,' which I was commissioned to give
him by the general-in-chief at Cape Coast Castle. All to no purpose. So now we met at a place called Edoocfoo, three marches
from Accra. I was in no frame of mind to brook delay in
opening this palaver. I told King Fuah exactly the state of
affairs : Captain Glover was not the commander of this expedition, neither was he the head dispenser or ' dash '-giver of all
the good things of negro life ; I read and explained Sir Garnet
Wolseley's letter ; I told Cobina of Akim the exact position
of affairs, now that the Ashantis, broken and disheartened, were
retreating on the Prah, offering to him the precious opportunity
of striking them in flank and destroying them, if he would now
return with me to his kingdom, get out his fighting men, and
move with me against his ancient enemy, at whose hands he
had suffered so many injuries in this and other wars. All was
useless. To Accra he must go, for it was there that fetish
should be done, and ' Custom ' carried out. I tried many
things with this obstinate Akim. I ' dashed ' him six Snyder
rifles, ammunition, wine, as an earnest of what things would
be his if he did as the English general wished him to do. I
tried first to work on his greed, then on his greediness, and
finally upon his sense of shame. He had had a good name in
Cape Coast Castle, would he add to it by coming back with
me, or destroy it by running away to Accra where there were
only women and cowards left ? ' Tell him,' I said to the
interpreter, ' that I can never go back : I must go forward.
If he returns with me now he will become the greatest king
that ever reigned in Akim ; if he goes on to the coast he will
cover himself with disgrace and his name will be a byword.'
No use. To Accra he must go. So we parted.

Weary beyond words, I set my face to the north, and plodded
on to the next miserable croom. This was West Coast war ;
these were the poor, down-trodden people we had come to
give our lives for. I positively laughed as the full absurdity
of the position forced itself upon me. In the evening I reached
a town called Koniako, where dwelt an old chief named
Quassiquadaddie, in whose house I stopped the night. It
was clean and comfortable, with walls neatly plastered, and a

good four-posted bed in an inner room—the best habitation I saw on the coast outside the towns. Quassiquadaddie did the honours admirably, and, what was of more importance, he was full of valuable information of route and distance. Another day's march brought me to Eniacroom, where my second king, Coffee Ahencora, was awaiting me. He too was bound for ' Custom ' to Accra, but my messengers had stopped him. After another long palaver I succeeded in effecting a change of purpose, largely due to my being able to pit his prospects if he went back to the Prah with me against those of his rival monarch Fuah who had disregarded my wishes and continued his course to the coast. But he would do nothing in a hurry, and in this matter of getting a slap at the Ashantis before they crossed the Prah, hurry was the whole essence of the problem. I was marching two, perhaps three, miles to their one.

Here at Eniacroom I had to wait two whole days while this second king was making up his mind, with the aid of a score of counsellors, as to what he would do. The heat was intense all this time. The women of the town came to stare at me in great numbers : all day while light lasted they flocked round my hut, looked through windows, round corners, and along the tops of mud walls   Although the feeling of being constantly stared at is not a pleasant one, there were circumstances in this case which made it less irksome than it might have been. With the exception of the very young girls and the old women, the majority of the ladies had babies with them ; these they carried seated astride on a sort of bustle held to the small of the back by a thin piece of cotton cloth. The manner in which these little black babies kept looking round their mothers' backs, and groping with tiny fingers for the maternal bosom in front, was very comical ; and one marvelled at the exceeding patience with which the mother bore the constant importunities of her offspring. But patience is the everlasting lesson of Africa. ' What patience is required in this African travel ! ' I find myself writing on this day, 11th November. The king came to see me frequently. He would return with me to his town, Akim-Swaidroo ; but he had to settle a dispute with a neighbouring chief on the way : would I act as arbitrator in the matter ? What was it about ?

About a goat. The oath of friendship which this chief had sworn to him had not been sealed by the killing of a goat : the omission of this sacrificial rite was the cause of the dispute. What was my opinion ? I replied that the matter was of such importance as to render its postponement until after the termination of the war imperative. This view did not seem to suit the king or his council ; and they all began a laboured exposition of the question at issue, ending by again urging that I would use my influence to bring the recalcitrant chief to a sense of his transgression. While still adhering to the necessity of postponing the case, I indulged in some observations upon goats in general ; I further remarked that they were perfectly distinct and different from sheep, and this being the case, I thought that mutual concessions would best advance the interest of all parties. When the interpreter had got these profound opinions into their Akim equivalents, I was astonished to observe an expression of agreement on the faces of the king and his counsellors. They uttered a kind of prolonged ' Hah,' which I read as a sort of ' I told you so.' They would start, they said, to-morrow. Night came at last to end the visits and the begging, and to hide the black faces at windows and doorways, corners and chinks ; and I lay down to sleep with the prospect of a start next morning. But there was one thing the night could not hide : that these past twenty days of toil had told terribly on my health and strength. The desire for food had grown less and less ; a lassitude never felt before had come upon me ; sleep brought with it no sense of rest or refreshment.

At last I got away from Eniacroom. The king and his retainers were also on the road. The march was only one of eight miles, but it taxed all my strength to accomplish it. The path was deep in mud, and the hammock could not make way among the crowded and tangled trees, so I went on on foot. A raging thirst consumed me, and whenever we reached running water I had to drink deeply. What, I asked myself, was this strange, dry feeling ? Only some passing ailment, I thought : I will walk faster and shake it off. We were now in a forest of prodigiously large trees, matted underneath with tendrils and creeping plants. Those giant trees seemed as endless pillars on an endless road. I reached another croom,

and sat down in a porch while a hut was being prepared. The
dry heat of the skin grew drier , the thirst became more
incessant ; then came a pain that seemed to be everywhere
at once—the dull, dead, sick pain of African fever.

Hitherto I have written in detail of the Ashanti War of
1873 through the first three or four weeks of my personal
experience of it.   I have done so because I wished to put before
the reader a picture of life with the real negro at home.   I
thought also that the narrative might be of use as showing
these little wars, which have been so frequent in our history
during the past fifty or sixty years, in comparison with the big
wars of earlier days, the wars which Othello thought ' made
ambition virtue.'   These old wars seem to me to bear the same
relation to our modern wars—opium wars, colonial wars, which
might fitly be called ' sutlers' ' wars—as the glory of an old
English cathedral of Plantagenet times compares with the
meanness of houses and shops that are grouped around its base.

This Ashanti War of 1873-74 has been forgotten long ago.
Pestilence killed ten men for every one knocked over by a
bullet. Now, when more than thirty years have passed, I
look back on all the toil and sweat and sickness of that time,
and the picture I see is a sad but splendid one—men, the best
I ever met with in my long service, toiling on, despite of fever
and dysentery, over narrow forest paths ; some of them worn
to skeletons, all with drawn, haggard features ; down with
fever one day, staggering along the dark path the next day ;
eating wretched food ; fighting, urging, wrestling with recalcitrant carriers ; streaming with perspiration at all times ; yet
always putting a good face upon the worst ills that fortune
sent them.

And, fixed as that picture of the human factor, I see another
memory—that great, gloomy forest ; these endless arches of
colossal cotton trees, under which two other growths of forest
flourish, the lower one a mass of tangled and twisted ever-
greens, the middle one hung with spiral creepers like huge
serpents hundreds of feet in length. Below all there is the
hot, wet earth emitting foul odours from its black mud-holes,
and many pools of slime-covered water. There is dense fog in
the early mornings—a 'thick smoke' the natives called it—fierce
sun on the lofty tree-tops at midday ; but only in fretted

patches can the hot rays reach the ground through these great trees, of which the trunks run up one hundred feet without a branch, and then spread forth for another hundred feet into massive limbs, every one sufficient to make a forest tree. Evening. A splash of water upon all the land ; rain pours upon the big leaves in ceaseless torrents, and the roll of thunder crashes loud and long over the echoing forest depths. So closely does the forest hem in the crooms that if one could walk along its upper surface, one would look right down into the little clusters of mud and wattle huts which form the village homes.

In this forest and in these crooms I now spent three very long months, the longest I ever remember. During November, December, and January I marched about nine hundred miles— every day with a little more difficulty. Not a week went by but my bout of fever came. Sometimes it would last two days, sometimes only a night ; but always one rose from the wretched bed on the earthen floor a little weaker and thinner, until at last the bones seemed all that was left of the body. Long before the campaign was over I was able to join the ends of thumb and forefinger and run the loop thus made from wrist to elbow, and from elbow to shoulder, without having to open the circlet. The body wasted in a similar proportion. How I was able to walk was often a subject of wonder to me. A year earlier I had been doing twenty and thirty mile marches daily on snow-shoes, with dogs, along the frozen Peace River ; and as then I had attributed hardiness in the cold largely to the fact that I had bathed in the open sea during a previous winter, so now I believed I was able to walk this tropic forest, notwithstanding a state of extreme emaciation, because that fifteen hundred mile tramp in the snow had habituated my legs to marching.

Of this fever, which began, as I have said, on the march from Eniacroom to Dobbin, I must say something. I can never forget that first attack. For three days and nights I lay in the corner of a very small hut on a door with two logs of wood under it and a blanket spread over it. I drank incessantly, and was always thirsty. The fingers seemed to be lighted candle ends ; the throat was parched ; the mouth was filled with an odious taste ; every bone and joint ached ; the head reeled with a sickness worse than that of a rough sea , when sleep came, it brought terrible visions, so that one would say on waking, ' I must not go to sleep again ' I had, of course, no doctor, and but one or two medicines I swallowed large doses of quinine—twenty grains at a time. When the night grew still, and the incessant noises of the negroes' daily village life ceased, loathsome things came out from the mud walls and thatched roof and prowled about my room. A large black rat ran several times across my door-bed as I lay tossing upon it in sleepless pain.

On the morning succeeding the third night of this misery some lightening of the fever must have come : I was in a profuse perspiration, terribly weak, but could breathe more freely. The idea of escape from this foul sick-room came to me. If I could only get out of this horrible place I should be better , and if I did not get better, the big forest would be a fitter place to die in than this hateful hole There was not a soul to speak to ; the candle, stuck in a bottle, had died out ; the night was wearing towards daybreak ; that strange little animal of the sloth species, which gives out a series of terrible shrieks as the dawn is drawing near on the Coast, was already sending his dismal howls through the forest. I got off the bed and staggered to the hut window. Day was breaking ; the croom and the forest were wrapped in fog, but, above, the stars could be seen. I was horribly weak, for no food had passed my lips during three days. The cool air seemed to revive me, and I felt that I must tear myself out of the grasp of this fever. I called my servant ; he roused the hammock men ; for the first time they were ready, and I was carried out of the still sleeping village before daylight had fully come. For ten days following this day the routine was the same . night usually brought a return of the fever—more quinine, more perspiration, in the morning less fever and less strength.

King Ahencora, finding that I had left Dobbin and was making for his capital of Swaidroo, set out at once after me When I reached Swaidroo I was scarcely able to stand , but my brain was clear enough to realise that this so-called city of a strong king was just like a score of other crooms through which I had passed , that the Akims were exactly as all the other tribes—Assins, Denkeras, Arbias,

Accras, and Agoouahs had been—a hopeless lot of craven beggars.

I must run quickly through the crowded events of the next three months. After twenty days of travel, palavers, toil, and fever I reached the Prah at Prahsu with a following of one chief, three scouts, and twenty-six Akim soldiers. This was the total muster which had rallied to my call ! My first king was still doing fetish at Accra ; my second monarch had reported himself very lame that morning from a place twenty miles to the rear.

The last six miles of the paths to the Prah presented a very gruesome appearance ; dead bodies lay along it in advanced stages of decomposition ; the stench was horrible ; and everything betokened the stricken state in which the Ashanti army had crossed the sacred river, the banks of which I was the first white man to reach.

The first phase of the war was now over ; the next would open with the invasion of Ashanti when the British troops had arrived at the Coast.

The plan of invasion was as follows :—the entire English force was to move along the main road to Prahsu, cross the river, and advance straight upon Coomassie. I was again instructed to visit Akim, collect as many men as I could gather in that kingdom, cross the Prah at a place some thirty miles higher up stream, and invade Ashanti on my own account. Thirty miles still farther to my right, Captain Glover was to lead all the Volta natives he could collect together, with nine hundred or a thousand disciplined Houssas, into Ashanti. The date for this simultaneous crossing of the frontier was fixed for the 15th January. I did not get back to West Akim until the 23rd December, so that I had three weeks in which to prepare, collect, organise, arm, and equip this new expedition. It would be impossible now to go over again these three weeks' work. It will suffice to say that I reached the Prah at a place called Beronassic on 13th January, to find a following of about one hundred Akims, and with a pulse beating at about the same figure. A bad night of fever followed the long, hot march over a rugged track, filled in many places with stagnant water, and crossed by roots of trees laid bare by rain torrents. Again came the old routine of the night, now so familiar—the wakeful hours, the sickness, the wet fog, the daylight, the lightening of the fever. As I lay in the languor of the next day, messages came from Fuah and Ahencora, from Darco and other chiefs, all secretly delighted that the white man was down again ; and that three other English officers, who had just arrived from the main road to assist in this new expedition, were also lying, some ten miles back on the road I had come, prostrate with fever. 'Surely I will delay the crossing of the Prah,' they urge 'No, the orders are the 15th.' On the 15th I was able to move again, and I set out for the Prah—three miles I found an advanced guard of some fifty Akims on the near bank of the river. 'Move your men across,' I said to the chief in command, 'and make camp on the Ashanti shore.' 'They could not cross,' he said, 'they were too few, the Ashanti fetish held the river ; they must wait until more men had come up.' 'Then we shall cross alone,' I said. 'It is the day named by the English general : his orders must be obeyed' Two of the three sick officers had arrived that morning We rested a while in the Akim camp, then I told the policemen to carry a few loads down to the edge of the ford. There was a ridge of sand in the centre of the river, and beyond it the current ran deep and strong. We waded to the sand island, then divesting ourselves of clothes, we took the deeper water. In the centre it rose to our lips ; then we just touched bottom, caught the outlying branches of a fallen tree, and climbing through them, got to the farther shore. It was midday. Not a sound stirred in the great forest The Akims stood in groups on the south shore gazing at the white man's doings. The sight was certainly a curious one three white men and six native policemen carrying baggage had invaded Ashanti.

CHAPTER XI

As these days now come back in recollection, I could easily write a volume about them. Their strangeness has grown stranger to me. It is all thirty-five years ago, and a thousand other scenes have crossed the looking-glass since then, and yet in that infinite wonder, the mirror of memory, I seem to see it all to-day perhaps even in truer perspective than I was able to see it in then.

Looking back now upon that big forest, with its days of disappointment, its nights of sickness, its toilings under those gloomy green arches, the endless vistas of that gigantic labyrinth of trees, the horrible brain-pictures that grew in the long, dark hours when the brain still saw after the eyes closed, I can perceive things that I did not discern then. I see much that was good and human in these poor black savages—true and faithful service, patience, honesty, strange childlike acceptation, doglike fidelity. These traits were common among them, the lower ranks possessing a hundred times more of them than the upper ones. After all, we were expecting too much from these Coast negroes. Firstly, we expected they would accept as truth everything we told them; but why should they? For three or four hundred years the white man had robbed, tricked, and enslaved them; had dragged them in hundreds of thousands from their homes, crowded them into foul ships, lied to them, lashed them, cheated them in trade. What reason was there now that they should think honest, truthful men had all at once come amongst them, whose words they were to believe at the first sound? I once asked the best and most truthful negro I met on the Coast this question, ' When a white man speaks to a black one, what does the black man

think of what he is told ?   Does he believe it ? ' ' No,' was
the prompt reply, ' he thinks every word the white man says
is a lie ' Secondly, we expected to find among them the
habits of punctuality, obedience to command, order, and even
discipline, which we had been accustomed to find at home ;
but surely this was wrong. It was our drink, our trade, our
greed, which had hopelessly demoralised the native African.
We wrung our wealth out of his sweat ; we drugged him with
our drink ; we shot him with our guns ; we sold him powder
and lead, so that he might shoot and enslave his fellow-black.
These castles along his Coast were the monuments of our
savage injustice to him.

Thirdly, we were wrathful with the tribes of the Coast
because they did not at once turn out and fight the Ashanti at
our bidding   In this, too, we were looking for more than we
had a right to expect. When the Ashantis had come down
upon the tribes six months earlier, the help we had been
able to give these tribes against their enemies was of the feeblest
sort. In that invasion they had suffered almost everything that
they could suffer ; thousands had been killed, all the villages
had been destroyed, the fetish trees cut down. ' The wayside,' says one very accurate writer,[1] ' was littered with corpses,
with the dying, with women bringing forth children.' All the
tribes knew this, even those whom the tide of devastation had
not reached   Why then should they have rushed at our bidding again into a fray which had already proved so disastrous
to them ? It is a peculiarity with many of our people that
they do not know how much they do not know   There is
nothing in a land before they came there. History began when
the first English traders arrived   Before that event there was a
blank   The erection of Smith's shop marks the year one. This
method of thinking is not confined to traders. I remember a
very high civil authority at the War Office once remarking to
a military officer whose business it was to take daily to him a
map showing the progress of our troops in war against the
Zulus, ' Dear me ! what a lot of geography these wars teach
one.' It is a little late to begin the acquisition of that knowledge when the fighting has begun. But we must finish our
story.

[1] Winwood Reade

Little by little, in the days following our unique passage of the Prah, I succeeded in getting an increasing number of Akims over the river and inducing them to go forward with me into Ashanti. By 22nd January we were at Yancoma, a place about twenty miles across the frontier. No enemy had been seen, but traces of scouts were here met with. From this place two paths led towards Coomassie : we followed that which went by Ennoonsu to Akim and Cocofoo. It seems a marvel to me now how we got the Akims along. Their numbers had increased to over one thousand, and more men were coming in. Many of the men and a few of the chiefs were of good stuff and spirit, but the kings and leading men were in a state of fear that was often comical to look at. It was this element of comicality in the black man which was the saving clause in all the long chapter of fever, fiasco, and apparently fruitless effort which had by this time reduced my body to the condition of a walking skeleton. I was certainly the one officer on the Coast who had dwelt wholly and entirely among the natives. For three months I had literally lived alone with them ; the ways of their daily lives had become familiar to me. As the body of the African is almost destitute of clothing, so is his mind an open one ; he has few concealments, physical or mental. You think, perhaps, that only in civilised communities is the study of human nature possible, but it is not so. Africa is the real bed-rock school of that study. Civilisation, even at its best, has often to curb itself in order to keep its clothes on. The African has not to write a novel when he wants to take them off. The negroes say that Adam and Eve and their children were all black, and that Cain only turned white through fear after he had killed Abel and when he found that he could not hide the dead body of his brother. I do not pretend to decide the question, but it is significant that the black man to-day does not build cities, nor, if he can help it, does he like to live in them. I have an idea that he will exist on the earth a very long time.

We got to the Ennoon River, had a skirmish there on 25th January, in which the enemy was routed and some heads taken by the Akims. After another delay there of two days I managed to get the kings, lords, and commons of Akim, now numbering fourteen hundred men, forward on another day's march in the direction of the city of Cocofoo, one of the sacred spots of Ashanti situated near the Lake Boosumaque, from the waters of which the King of Ashanti obtained fish for his palace. We were now well into the old kingdom of Ashanti. Only one among the four officers (Brabazon), who had joined me three weeks earlier, was fit for service on this day ; two of the others were prostrate with fever ; the fourth, MacGregor, was just able to stagger along the track. Two hours' march brought the advanced guard under Brabazon in contact with the enemy at a village called Akina, situated on the top of a steep hill and more than one thousand feet above sea-level. Here there was another skirmish , we had two Akims killed, but their heads were not taken. The Ashantis retreated, and the village was ours. It really seemed that Fortune had at last declared for us. I had now to close up the ranks of my extraordinary army, fortify this commanding position, and boil up the spirits of my kings for a further advance upon the enemy.

On the early morning of the 28th January a party of Ashantis stole into our camp along a bypath, fired at and wounded some Akims who were lying asleep near a fire, and got away unmolested. We had taken in Akina a very sacred fetish stool belonging to the chief of the town , the night raid was said to have had for its object the recovery of this venerated relic.

I spent the 30th January urging upon the kings the necessity of making another forward move. We must now be very near to the main line of advance, probably only a few miles from it. On the preceding day one of our scouting parties had entered the town of Mansuah at Lake Boosumaque, which they found deserted. They brought back news that the Ashantis were in a camp at Cocofoo, a few miles to the north of Mansuah, and that the King of Ashanti, Coffee Kerrikerri, was with them. They added that there was another large camp of the enemy at Amoaful, on the main road west of Akina. This news of the scouts filled my kings with fear. One of them, Darco of Accassee, chattered with terror as he urged in palaver the dangers they were in. I had just received a despatch from Sir Garnet Wolseley, dated Fommanah, 25th January, a hurried postscript to which announced that the King of Ashanti had acceded to all the demands of the major-general, and that in view of his submission a speedy termination of hostilities was probable. When I communicated this news to my kings they one and all declared that the King of Ashanti was a liar, that he meant to fight, and that his people were determined to do so. In this view they were right. The acceptation of Sir Garnet's terms of peace was only a pretence to gain time. Subsequent events proved that the news brought by my scouts from Mansuah was quite correct. Ten thousand Ashantis were at Cocofoo between Akina and Coomassie.

On the afternoon of the 30th January the entire force of Akims on and around the hill at Akina suddenly began to move out of their camps back along the road we had come from the Ennoon River. The kings had given me no warning of this intention : my campaign in Ashanti was at an end.

A fortnight later I reached the Coast. On the march down I met the then Captain Redvers Buller, Head of the Intelligence Department, and from him I heard the other side of the story. During the two days spent in Coomassie he had collected a mass of Ashanti information.

' Ten thousand Ashantis were gathered at Cocofoo in front of you,' he said ; ' they were not at Amoaful. The presence of your force at Akina until the evening of the 30th kept them from being on our flank the next day.'

So, after all, my Akim venture had been of some service to the campaign. There would be little gained by attempting to after-cast either what might have been if this Cocofoo army of ten thousand had been present with the other ten thousand which fought so stiffly at Amoaful on 31st January ; or again, what might have happened if they had fallen upon my fifteen hundred or two thousand Akims at Akina ; or again, what would have come to pass if I had succeeded in inducing my kings to make another forward move on that 31st. Of all the might-have-beens, those in war are the most futile.

In Sir Garnet Wolseley's despatch to the Secretary of State, written on the evening of the day upon which he left Coomassie, this sentence occurs :—

'So far as the interests of the expedition under my orders are concerned, Captain Butler has not failed, but most successfully achieved the very object which I had in view in detaching him for the work he so cheerfully and skilfully undertook. He has effected a most important diversion in favour of the main body, and has

detained before him all the forces of one of the most powerful
Ashanti Chiefs.'

Although I got down to the sea the wreck of a wreck, I
imagined that all my troubles were past, and that I should
only have to get on the deck of a transport and lie down to
rest for twenty days. That was not to be.

Three or four days after I reached Cape Coast Castle a virulent
fever, compared to which the other intermittent fever I had
suffered had been as nothing, suddenly burst upon me like a
thief in the night, and the pent-up poison of the long toil
broke out in overwhelming illness. I possess no record of the
next two or three months, and only a very dim recollection
of the earlier half of that period. I was embarked on board
an old and indifferent steamship which was told off for the
conveyance of sick and wounded from the Coast. Twenty-six
officers, mostly suffering from fever and dysentery, had to be
put in hammocks below the main-deck The accommodation
for sick people was very bad The heat was intense; most of the
attendants were themselves either sick or convalescent Something happened on the third or fourth night after sailing, the
exact particulars of which I cannot recall; but I remember
leaving my swinging cot below, climbing to the open deck,
and being there in the night air with very scanty covering for
some time Then there was a crash, and I remember striking
some hard substance with my head as I fell upon the deck.
How long I remained lying unconscious on that wet deck I do
not know; but all at once consciousness returned, and with it
a numbed sort of fear I remember getting down the steps
of the ladder as best I could, and regaining my cot. Next
morning the doctor found me in the highest fever. It would
not be possible to speak or write of the next ten days' suffering.
Sleep left me—nothing was able to bring it back. At last
death was supposed to have come one morning. I dimly
remember people gathered about the cot, and one good comrade
asking in my ear for my last wishes. I remember, too, suddenly
declaring that I died a Catholic. Then there is a blank, but
not altogether, for I can recollect that after the usual final
settlings of face and limbs had been made—the eyes closed,
and the sheet drawn over the laid-out figure—there was a

curious indistinct idea in my brain that it was not as people supposed ; that I was still conscious, and even that I was being carried by invisible hands, or being floated on towards a great cloud-veil, the passing through which it seemed was to be the final passage out of life. There was no sensation of bodily pain. How long I lay in this condition I don't know, but I remember men coming again about the cot, lifting the sheet, and touching me and talking to each other. Then I thought, ' These men are about to prepare my body for the sea ' ; and as in these hot latitudes the time between death and burial in the ocean was a very short one, I felt the extreme horror of the situation, and longed to be able to make some sign or movement by which they might know that I was not really dead. Next I heard one of the men who was moving my limbs suddenly say to his comrade, ' I don't think he's dead.' It was ' Bill,' or ' Tom,' or ' Jack,' but I have forgotten which name it was. The other man replied, ' Dead ? you something or other, why, I saw him die at eight o'clock this morning.' Then there was some more arm lifting or moving, and the man who had first spoken went on, ' Well, I don't think he's dead ; anyway, I 'll go for the doctor.' Then more people came about the swinging cot ; something was done, and I awoke or became actively conscious again.

For many days after this coming back I lay hovering on the brink—a shuttlecock between life and death. One day I had a narrow escape. I jumped from the cot suddenly in raging delirium, and rushed along the main-deck, looking for any exit that might promise escape. I sprang into the first open door ; it was the cook's galley. Men caught hold of me ; the skeleton had the strength of six sound men. I could not be got out of the place until an old acquaintance came. Then I went quietly back with him. After that I was put into a closed cabin, and special men were told off to watch day and night. As we slowly sailed into cooler latitudes the fever of the brain grew less ; and at Madeira a Portuguese clergyman came off to the tossing ship, bad sailor though he was, to bring to the ' ruckle of bones ' the final ministrations of that Faith, the tinkle of whose Mass-bell—more continuous and far-reaching even than the loud drum beat of England which the American imagined circling the earth and keeping company

with the hours—carries its morning message of mercy to the
sinners of the world.

I lay for two months in Netley Hospital, and at last, when
the summer was half over, was declared fit for the outer world
again.   Of course, I missed all the rejoicings, the feastings, and
the field days that followed the return to England of the
victorious general and his little army, but I was not forgotten
at Netley by queen or country   Her Majesty came to my
bedside and spoke some very gracious words to me, among
them being a message of peculiar thought and kindliness.
'When Sir Garnet Wolseley rode up to my carriage at the
Windsor Review, the Duke of Cambridge whispered to me,
"If you wish to please Sir Garnet, the first question should be
an inquiry for Captain Butler." '

In the Ashanti Gazette I was promoted to a majority in the
army, and made a Companion of the Bath. It now only
remained to get into the Bath-chair to which I had also been
appointed, by the excellent doctor at Netley. And here I
desire to say a word about a body of gentlemen-servants of
the State with whom a long active life made me familiar—the
medical officers of the army. I have known them in many
lands, and under the varying conditions inevitable to military
life. I never knew them to fail   There is no finer sight in
war than the figure of a military surgeon kneeling beside a
wounded man just behind the fighting line. Shots may come,
and shots may go, but the surgeon goes on at his work, quietly,
coolly, and with hand as steady and dexterous, and gaze as
concentrated on his business, as though the scene were
the operating-room in a London hospital.

Until the close of my work in Akim I had no doctor with
me ; then one was sent at the time the three officers, Brabazon,
Paget, and MacGregor, joined my column. The doctor, Lowe,
was a big breezy sort of man, who on his arrival laughed at
malaria. 'It is only a convenient professional expression,'
he said. A day or two later he was 'down with fever' at
Yancoma, and for the rest of my short campaign I had him
carried in a hammock.

At long last I got away from Netley. I made for the west
coast of Ireland, to regain, if possible, the health and strength
which seemed to have been hopelessly lost on the west coast

of Africa. I was still able to move only a few yards on my feet, so I drove as much as I could. The outside car, the great cliffs of Clare, and the heathery glens of Kerry—these were now my doctors. In three weeks I was feeling a different man, though still very weak. At last I came to a little seaside hotel where a few fisher and shooting folk formed the company.

One day in late September some of them asked me to go into a neighbouring bog to look for something. I went with them. A snipe got up in front of me ; the effort to get the gun to the shoulder caused me to stagger, but there was a bank close by, and I leant against it while aiming. Bang ! the snipe was down. I was well.

I was loth to leave these wonderful scenes which had given me back life's most precious gift, and, learning to walk, I tarried off and on among the Kerry hills, shooting and writing.

One day in February 1875 a telegram came from Sir Garnet Wolseley in London :—

'Come at once, and be ready to start with me for South Africa on Thursday.'

My book on Akim-land [1] was all but finished. I put up the MS., packed my things, and was in London the next day.

Then I heard what the telegram meant. Sir Garnet Wolseley was going to Natal in a joint civil and military capacity— Governor and High Commissioner. He had asked four of his old Ashanti staff to go with him. I was one of them. Five days later we sailed from Dartmouth for Cape Town and Durban. The voyage was then of nearly twice the duration that it is to-day, and we had full time to study the work to be done, as our vessel steamed slowly southwards, skirting these same jaws of Benin, which, just a year ago, had all but closed their bite upon me. One day, while steaming through this steaming sea, something went wrong with the machinery, and we stopped for a few hours to set it right. A large number of sharks gathered about the ship. The water was very clear, and with the sun straight overhead it was possible to see down through its unruffled surface to a great depth. The sailing voyage to India fifteen years before had taught me something of a shark's ways in these waters, for we had lain becalmed in

---

[1] *Akim-foo, the History of a Failure.* (E. B.)

them for many days. I crumpled a newspaper together and dropped it over the stern. A huge shark came swimming upward towards the white floating object. I had a rifle laid on it; as he snapped, I fired. The bullet hit him fair in the head; he turned a complete somersault out of the water and lay dead as a stone on the surface, then the great body began to sink slowly, belly upwards It was curious to watch it fathoms and fathoms below, the glare of the tropic sun striking on the snow-white body as on a looking-glass 'I have sailed the sea for thirty years,' said our captain, 'but that is the first shark I ever saw shot dead.'

All the members of this new mission had been former comrades on the Coast with me. Colonel Pomeroy Colley, whose extraordinary vigour and energy a few months earlier had saved the transport service from collapse on the Gold Coast, was the only officer among our group who had had previous service in South Africa. Major Henry Brackenbury [1] had also distinguished himself in the late campaign as military secretary to Sir Garnet Wolseley; and Captain Lord Gifford, V.C., had a name which was then a household word in the service and out of it for the cool and determined courage with which he explored with a small band of native scouts the labyrinths of the forest in front of the Ashanti enemy. A new colonial secretary for Natal, Mr. Napier Broome, was also of our party. He had been a recent leader-writer on the staff of the *Times*

We made a merry party. Our chief was of that rare make of men in whom the thing we call 'command' in the army is so much an essential item of their nature that one has no more thought of questioning it than one would think of asking a bird why he flew, or a river why it flowed. Wolseley was the only man I met in the army on whom command sat so easily and fitly that neither he nor the men he commanded had ever to think about it And it was this fact of command by right that made his companionship as easy to others as his leadership was easy to himself. It was such a delight to meet a general of a type entirely different from anything of the kind I had ever seen before in our army, that the chief regret I had, on this my third turn of service with him, was that I was less

[1] Now Sir Henry.

likely to be of use to him now than I had been in Canada or Ashanti.

The poison of the bite of the Gold Coast was not yet all out of my veins, and Natal in March was said to have still a fervid sun above it.

We reached Cape Town on 17th March, had a few days there, and then went on in a splendid frigate, the *Raleigh*, to Durban. This vessel had just been launched, the first and last of her type, meant for steam and wind, with great engines and large masts—a combination which our own experience was shortly to prove useless. Sir Garnet carried a letter from the Admiralty directing the admiral at Simon's Town to detach a ship from the flying squadron for his transport to Natal, and the *Raleigh* was placed at his service. After a dinner on board Admiral Randolph's flagship we rowed to the *Raleigh*, and were received by Captain Tryon on his quarter-deck. His name will be long associated with one of the most tragic chapters in modern naval history. In weighing anchor immediately afterwards something went wrong in the operation of catting the anchor, and, as the sea was rising before a south-easterly wind, the huge mass of the anchor swinging just at the water-line was considered dangerous, and there was a good deal of hauling work before it could be secured. Captain Tryon came into the deck cabin where we were assembled, to explain what had happened. The trouble was complicated because a rock known as 'the Roman' was only a short distance off, on the lee side, so that if the ship went ahead the anchor would swing against her bows, and if she didn't go ahead the wind might take us on 'the Roman' rock. Wolseley was seated on the table. 'My dear captain,' he said, 'on the deck of a British ship-of-war I always feel that I am on the safest spot in the world.' When morning came we had cleared False Bay and were steering in the teeth of a violent south-easter. Tryon was a veritable Triton, a powerfully built man, with a large strong face and a deep voice. He spared nothing on this occasion to make the few days we were on his ship pleasant to us. The *Raleigh* burned nearly three hundred tons of coal in twenty-four hours ; but in the face of the south-easter she made slow progress, and her captain and officers were not a little put out when, in the middle of the driving mist of the first day's storm, we saw our old friend the *Walmer Castle* steaming slowly past us, burning some thirty tons in the same period. But the gale went down the next day, and then canvas had its chance, and took it splendidly. With every stitch set on the huge masts, the ship sped along the coasts of Kaffraria for four hundred miles, and on 29th March the sight of a canvas-clouded frigate coming up to the roadstead at Durban was the first intimation the people of Natal had of Sir Garnet's advent among them

Then began some six months of most varied and interesting work. The central object of the mission was to induce the Government and people of Natal to alter their Constitution, giving to the Crown larger powers in the nomination of members to the Legislative Council, the object being to prevent the recurrence of certain repressive measures against the natives which the Secretary of State considered had been hostile to the spirit as well as to the letter of English law.

The part which fell to my lot in the programme of work was a varied one. I was nominated Protector of Indian Immigrants, a position which gave me a seat on the Council and also in the Legislative Assembly of the colony

I had to report on the land system existing in Natal, with a view to the introduction of British colonists, to study native questions, and take part in the debates when the Legislative Council was in session. Meanwhile a season of social hospitalities was begun on the most lavish scale. Dinner parties at Government House were of nightly occurrence. Dances were constantly taking place. Within a fortnight the ladies were all on the new governor's side. It could not well have been otherwise. Who could resist the fascination of this young general, in whom an extraordinary capacity for labour of the most serious kind was combined with a buoyancy of spirit and natural kindness of character seldom found united in the same individual ?

Of course, 'the attempt to tamper with the Constitution,' as it was called by a section of Natal society, gave rise to considerable opposition ; and when the Legislative Council met, very lively discussions took place in that small assembly at which ambitious Hampdens and journalistic Vanes were present. But the whole thing was in truth a teacup tempest.

The eternal African native was the sole reality in it, and all the talking, and the travelling that was to follow the talking, got Natal no nearer to the solution of that immense human problem.

The longer I have watched the workings of the great and the little representative and deliberative assemblies of the world, the more I have been disposed to think of the dog on the deck of a canal boat, who imagines he is pulling the load because he stands barking at the old horse that is dragging it. But perhaps if that dog did not think he was doing all this work, he might be biting some of the people at the other end of the boat.

The Natal Constitution Bill passed by a very small majority, and then came a time of intense interest to me personally. We started up country to visit, first, the locations from which the tribes of Langalabalele and Putili Zulus had been recently ejected, at the foot of the Drakensberg Mountains ; then the line of the Tugela River and the Ladysmith and Newcastle districts ; and, finally, I was to be detached on a mission to President Brand in Bloemfontein, the Kimberley Diamond Fields, and Basutoland. If, a quarter of a century later, it was to fall to my lot to hold a high civil and military position in South Africa on my own account and to endeavour to tell the governing powers of England of the size, weight, and substance of certain forces and quantities in the problem with which they would then have to deal, I owe it largely, if not wholly, to the mission I was now about to undertake, that many warning words written and spoken by me under circumstances of no little difficulty and complexity in that later time, were at least found fairly accurate when all the account was closed.

We set out in mid-June for the Drakensberg, with saddle-horses and waggons. The weather was perfect, the scenery not to be surpassed. Tower-topped mountains, ten and twelve thousand feet in height, snow-crowned and purple, rose as Natal's western boundary wall. Along the feet of these we travelled, each night camp measured from the last night's one by the ' trek ' of the oxen—sometimes ten miles, sometimes five, for there were many drifts to be crossed and hours were often lost at some of them. But with our horses to let us rove in front or on the flanks of the transport waggons, the shortest day's trek often gave us the longest day of sport or rambling. June is South Africa's mid-winter, a season of brilliant sunshine and clear frosty nights ; sunrises of great silent beauty, with snow-white mists rising from unseen river beds, and climbing slowly up the mountain's eastern face, thinning and dissolving as they ascend ; evenings of still more perfect lustre when the sun has gone down behind the many domes and turrets of the Drakensberg, and the western sky above the serrated snow is one vast green and saffron afterglow. These were pleasant days.

We struck the Tugela in the centre of the great angle which half encloses it for some miles after it has come down in three great jumps from the top of the Drakensberg , then we jour-neyed past scenes which, twenty-five years later, were to loom large in our history to Ladysmith, and up to Newcastle, a tiny village of a dozen houses. From this place Sir Garnet Wolseley followed the Tugela Valley, and I began my journey through the Orange Free State to Kimberley.

At that time no land on earth seemed to lie in greater peace and surer prospect of its continuance ; but, strangely enough, I find in a pocket notebook I then carried a quotation which must have expressed some foreboding in my mind, other-wise it would scarcely have found entry there .—

'Thus far their (the white men's) course has been marked with blood, and with blood must it be traced to its termination either in their own destruction or in that of thousands of the population of Southern Africa.'

From Newcastle in a long day's ride I ascended the Drakens-berg by the Ingogo Valley and Botha Pass, thence by post-cart from Harrismith and Bethlehem and Winburg to Bloemfontein. This was a five days' journey. Above the berg the land was all a great rolling plain of veldt, unmarked, unfenced, with enormous herds of blesbok, springbok, and other antelopes grazing or galloping over it, the cart path a thin ribbon of lighter colour winding away through a brown waste, over which blew a wind of the keenest and most invigorating freshness. At intervals, on either side of the road-ribbon, table-topped hills rose near and far, breaking the dull monotony of the lower level, until the straight lines of their summits became merged into a distant horizon.

M

At Bloemfontein I presented my letters of introduction to President Brand, and during the following days I had many interviews with that remarkable man. Bloemfontein was then only a large village, but on market-day the place was crowded with men in well-horsed Cape carts, or large waggons drawn by many oxen—a fine, manly, heavy-bearded, and broad-shouldered race of men, and with women with large fair faces, big figures, and light brown hair. Babies were very numerous.

I passed on to Kimberley, travelling in a four-horsed post-cart which left Bloemfontein shortly before sunset. A little Bushman driver and two half-Hottentot, half-Bushman girls were the only other occupants of the vehicle.

A strange green porcelain-coloured sunset tinged half the western sky and presaged some weather turmoil from the west, into which we were rapidly driving, and a wild storm broke upon us before we were many hours out. First, blinding dust, then a deluge of rain, which soon turned into blinding snow, and thunder and lightning such as I had not seen even on the Gold Coast. The lightning was everywhere at once, so rapidly did the vivid flashes follow one another, and simultaneously with them came the burst and crash of the discharges. We were moving through an atmosphere so charged with electric currents that, looking up, I saw for the first and last time in my life a curious phenomenon—a bluish light like that of a tall thin candle flame extending some inches from the top of the long whip handle which the driver had in his hand. The post-cart owner in Bloemfontein had provided a large sheepskin ' karrosse ' for my use, but I could not allow the two wretched Bushman girls in the back of the cart to lie cowering in the wet snow, and the karrosse made them less miserable.

At four in the morning we reached the village of Boshoff, the rain still falling in torrents. Next day Kimberley was reached in baking sunshine. At that time Kimberley (or Colesberg) was a strange place. It had just concluded a small rebellion on its own account—had risen against its English governor and his colonial secretary, established a provisional government, rescued a recalcitrant storekeeper from the hands of three constables, and done several other free and independent things. No Dutchmen or Boers took part in this movement, which had its origin in some Government order permitting the black men to work as diamond diggers for themselves. The approach of six companies of British soldiers marching from Cape Town had caused a general stampede of the four chief standard-bearers of liberty—an Englishman, a German, an Irishman, and a Natal colonist—across the border, and things had resumed their normal condition of good-fellowship.

I found the British battalion (the 24th Regiment) encamped at Barkley, on the Vaal River, north of Kimberley. It was this battalion, with nearly all the officers who were now present at Barkley, which was totally destroyed by the Zulus at Isandula four years later.

Many interesting characters had gathered in Kimberley at this time Eton and Harrow men , old army officers ; young adventurous spirits from the Cape Colony ; East End and German Jews in great abundance—all these were to be found. The late Mr Rhodes was there, but I did not meet him. The town consisted of corrugated iron and canvas, the streets were deep in mud and empty bottles, and ten or twelve thousand negroes were at work in Colesberg pit, which was twelve acres in size and two hundred feet in depth. Every grade and shade in life was represented here. There was a university man who gave readings in the Town Hall, and his rendering of Tennyson's 'May Queen' so deeply affected a huge Cornish miner at the back of the audience that he ejaculated in a deep voice at the end of the words 'For I 'm to be Queen of the May, Mother ' : 'And so am I ! ' He was a large, bearded man, and he appeared so thoroughly in earnest in the matter that the reading could not be continued.

I got back to Bloemfontein on 23rd July, through a country where thousands of sheep had been killed by the snow-storm ; and after many more conversations with President Brand, in which twenty-five years of the previous history of that part of South Africa were reviewed, I set out for Basutoland, intending to enter Natal by a pass over the Drakensberg near the great Tugela Waterfall. We camped at Thabanchu the first night, where the old chief of the Barralongs, Moroko, ninety years of age, still dwelt, and reached Maseru early the next day.

The commissioner here, Colonel Griffiths, had seen much colonial service ; and, like Colonel Southey at Kimberley, he had gone through campaigns in Kaffraria under Sir Harry

Smith. We rode together over the remarkable table mountain called the Berea, where the paramount Chief Moshesh had defeated a column of British troops in the war of 1852 ; then, having bought a couple of Basuto ponies for the ride to Natal, I set out on the 4th August for the head of the Caledon River. Unfortunately, one of the ponies came down under me on some flat rocks as we were nearing a French Protestant mission station at the advanced posts. The cap of my knee was deeply cut ; but the excellent wife of the missionary dressed the wounds, and I went on the next morning towards Leribe, a ride of over forty miles, where dwelt the Basuto chief Moloppo, the son of Moshesh, the owner of fifty wives, and reputed to be full of craft and cunning. The agent at Leribe was Major Bell, an old Cape Corps soldier, who had fought under Harry Smith at Boomplatz in 1849. The next day's ride from Leribe was through scenery of a very wild and striking character. We were bound for the kraal of Letsika, still higher up the Caledon. I had with me two Basuto policemen, with whom I could not exchange a word ; but we got on well by signs, and when one has been in the habit of living with any one African race, it is easy to be at home with another. The root ideas and tokens are the same everywhere ; so is the food.

Our path lay through a gorge in the mountains, at the bottom of which the river ran in deep curves. The sun could not reach the bottom of this glen, which was bounded on either side by steep precipitous cliffs of sandstone rock, ending above in turrets and spires. The path wound in zigzags up to a ledge, upon which stood the kraal of Letsika.

Lower down on the level ground we had met a Basuto, galloping for all he knew on a grey pony, coming towards us. The policemen called to him to stop, but as he had no bit, and only a rope at one side of the pony's mouth, he could only pull up by circling his steed round and round us until the animal came to a stand for want of a smaller circle space. They had heard I was coming, and he was riding to the nearest store, ten miles, for some English food, coffee, sugar, etc. They had killed a kid in the kraal. How like all these people were to old Bible folk ! It was we who were different. We got to the kraal with tired horses. Letsika was a good-looking young man, and his young wife did her household work well. They had evacuated their circular Basuto hut, which was swept and ready. The kid was cooked and eaten ; then Letsika and his wife came and sat on the clay bench that ran round the wall. They had a Basuto Bible, printed in English letters ; I had a story of Bret Harte's.

To Letsika's astonishment, I read, letter by letter, his Bible, my pronunciation evoking frequent laughter ; and to my own astonishment Madame Letsika spelt out Bret Harte in the same manner, the French clergyman's wife having taught her at the mission school.

As night closed, the literary entertainment was continued by the light of a fibre wick floating in the grease of the fatted kid.

Next day we continued the ascent, along dizzy ledges round which the ponies crept with wonderful sure-footedness, ascending often by steps cut in the rock. I should have been glad to dismount at these places, but as the native guides kept their saddles, I did the same. No horse in the world can beat a Basuto pony in mountain climbing.

On our left we had the Roode Berg, and on our right the Mont Aux Sources began to show its turret tops. This is the highest mountain south of the Zambesi, and from its sides the largest rivers of the Transvaal, Natal, and the Cape Colony shed their waters.

In the afternoon a violent storm came sweeping after us up the Caledon ; its coming was preceded by a loud howling noise lower down the valley. I was riding in front, the two Basutos some distance behind ; they called out something to me, but I did not understand, and before there was time to do anything the wind was on us. It struck so hard that my pony was blown off the path, fortunately landing on a slope two or three feet lower down. After this experience we all dismounted at the bad places. We reached the source of the Caledon, then mounted the steep divide on which snow was lying, but the gale was sweeping the ridge so furiously that we could not stand before it. Below, on the farther side, lay Witzie's Hoek, where dwelt Paulus Moperi, a cousin of old Moshesh's. Paulus had been to London in early years, and he did not appear to have been unduly astonished at anything he had seen there. I once asked an educated negro on the

Gold Coast what his people thought of Englishmen. ' Half a fetish, half a fool,' was the answer ; ' a fetish because they do things we can't do, and a fool because they come out here to do them.'

From Moperi's kraal I crossed the Drakensberg by a rough bridle path into Natal, and in a long day's ride reached the Tugela presidency, where my damaged knee was again dressed.

Another ride of fifty miles took me from the presidency to the valley of Colenso, by reaches of river and spurs of mountain to which another quarter of a century would bring celebrity.

On 12th August I reached Maritzburg.

CHAPTER XII

I FOUND all the members of our mission reassembled in Government House, Maritzburg, after their various travels. Reports had now to be written embodying the impressions formed upon the different subjects of reference—native affairs, land tenures, Crown lands, and the possible trend of affairs in the Dutch states beyond our borders

A notable visitor had joined Sir Garnet Wolseley's party in the person of Mr. James Anthony Froude. My friend, General Sir Henry Brackenbury, in a recent volume of recollections, referring to Mr Froude's presence at this time, has said that 'Butler got more into his (Mr Froude's) confidence and intimacy in a day than he (Colonel Brackenbury) had done in six months, in the woes of Ireland they had a subject of deep common interest to both.' My recollections of that pleasant intercourse and of those social gatherings round the general's table in old Government House, at the foot of the slope that led up to Fort Napier and the Zwart Kop, are not quite General Brackenbury's   He is not fair to himself.   I think that if Mr Froude honoured me with a larger share of his conversation than that which he gave to my companions, it was because being Irish and Catholic I presented, perhaps, a wider target for his shots than they did.   In his own way he had a deep and fervid affection for Ireland. His heart was set in Kerry, and I have an idea that it was by the lessons he had learned in the study of Tudor and Stuart times in that part of Ireland that his views of the Dutch question in South Africa had been coloured and even moulded. He liked, too, to try little bits of religious or political badinage upon me.   I remember his asking me in a large company if J

183

had gone when at Madeira to see the Portuguese statue of the
'Winking Virgin,' which was said to be there.   I said that I
had not, and gave as my reason that I had seen so many
winking ladies in England that the sight had ceased to have
novelty for me.   It was afterwards that we became friends.
At this time Mr. Froude was terminating a quasi-political
mission to South Africa, undertaken at the request of Lord
Carnarvon, in the interests of the Confederation of all the
States and Colonies.   What a strange retrospect those thirty-
four years present to-day !   How eager we were at our
writings, our proposals, our plans for colonisation, for native
government, better land division and tenures, extensions of
railways and telegraphs, and half a dozen other matters—so
hopeful about it all.   And how exceedingly droll it must all
have seemed to the little cherub up aloft, who, no doubt, saw
the thirty years then coming as we saw the thirty years that
had gone.

At the time of this mission of ours South Africa had enjoyed
profound peace for a quarter of a century.   Two weak battalions
of infantry sufficed to give it garrison.   Old racial issues were
disappearing ;   that best form of race-amalgamation was
steadily progressing—intermarriage.   Then began, first at
Kimberley, and later in the other mining centres, the introduction of the new element, the preaching of the religion of
' the top Dog and the under Dog ' ;   the bounder suddenly let
loose in the ' Illimitable,' to be followed by a quarter century
of strife and bloodshed, until to-day we are arrived at the
precise spot—Confederation—which Mr. Froude and a few
other people then strove for, and which was just as possible
and as attainable at that time as it has been found to be
to-day.   In the eye of the very young child and in that of
the old man there is the same strange look of surprise,
the wonder of what it is all about, and the question of ' What
it was all for.'   And doubtless so it will be to the end,
until we can all sit with the cherub and see both sides of the
swing.

Not the least interesting among the personalities met with
in this visit to South Africa was the then Mr. (Sir) Theophilus
Shepstone.   In the earlier days of my journey, while we were
still in that beautiful region in Natal lying at the foot of the

Drakensberg Mountains, that quiet land of the Putili and Langalabeleli tribes, I enjoyed many a day's companionship with Mr. Shepstone. He had begun to study human philosophy at the bed-rock. He had lived among the Zulus from his child-hood Half the philosophers of the world have to go down from the class before they can go up to the clouds. They are like plants nurtured in a hot-house, unable to stand in the open. Shepstone had been always in the open. With him the years had drawn out the telescope of life to its full focus ; he saw long distances, and, moreover, the hills on the horizon had other sides for him. He had the native habit of long silences ; then something would occur—the sight of a blesbok on a hill-top, a flower by the wayside, an outcrop of some coloured rock in a landslide—and the silent spring of thought would begin to flow in words. He would repeat some anecdote heard from an old Zulu chief a generation earlier, told in those quaint conceits of language which the wild men fashion so easily out of the winds, the waters, and wilderness in which they live. People wonder how men whom we call barbarous have so often in their lives a natural level of right and wrong, a sense of good and evil which we imagine belongs to our-selves and our civilisation only. They forget that in nature everything has a right and a wrong side, and that it is only in art you have to teach people on which side the shadow falls. I think that a day's ride in the company of that old white Zulu chief and statesman was worth a whole term in a University.

Shepstone made one mistake in his life ; but of that later.

Another friend met at that time in Natal was Dr. Colenso, a brave and devoted soldier fighting an uphill battle against the greeds and cruelties of man. He was not in touch with the majority of his fellow-colonists in those days, for causes which will be familiar to readers of Nathaniel Hawthorne fifty years ago, or of Olive Schreiner in our own time. When you cut down the forest or clear the brushwood in a new colony, the first crop that springs from the soil has many weeds in it. It is inevitable that it should be so ; perhaps it is even neces-sary. The man who doesn't know how much he doesn't know may have his uses in a new land, where there is plenty of space.

We left Natal early in September, and reached London a month later.

It was an interesting moment, the close of the year 1875. Mr. Disraeli, having then fairly settled his account with home politics in the previous eighteen months of office, was free to launch forth into foreign enterprises. Some great specialist of the brain had said that until his sixtieth year a man was himself, that from sixty to seventy he belonged to his family, and that from seventy onwards he was merged in his tribe. Disraeli was now in his seventy-first year. The Eastern instinct glowed strongly within him—how strongly only the Memoirs will tell ; but, looking back now, it is not difficult to see that signs were showing above the surface in November 1875 plainly indicating the whitherwards of coming events.

Shortly after our arrival in England I attended a levée held in the old Horse Guards by the Duke of Cambridge. His Royal Highness was kind and gracious, said some nice things about bygone service, and a week or two later I was agreeably surprised to receive a letter from his military secretary asking if I would accept the position of deputy assistant quartermaster-general at headquarters. I replied in the affirmative ; and before I could be gazetted to the appointment another letter came from another high official asking if I felt disposed to proceed first on a mission to trans-Caspian Persia for the purpose of reporting upon the Russian movements along the Attrek Valley in the direction of Merv, afterwards taking up the post at headquarters. All my natural inclinations lay in the direction of Persia as against Pall Mall, and I replied accepting the mission to Merv ; but the proposal fell through owing to the refusal of the Foreign Office to sanction the necessary expenditure, and shortly before the year closed I joined the staff at the War Office.

It was a marked change of scene, from the extremity of the circumference where my service had hitherto led me, to the exact centre of the system.

And a highly centred system it was at that time, far more than it is at present. A corporal and a file of men could not move from Glasgow to Edinburgh except with the sanction and under the sign-manual of the headquarters in London. ' I am glad to hear that you are going to the War Office,' wrote

a general of the widest experience to me. 'You will at least
see there the extraordinary system under which our army is
administered, and you will also be able to form a judgment upon
the stability of the human pillars which support the edifice of
administration.' The thing that soon became clear to me,
holding even a subordinate position in that great congeries
of confusion then known as the War Office, was the hopelessness
of any attempt to simplify or improve matters in any way.
A vast wheel was going round, and all men, big and little, were
pinned upon it, each one bound to eat a certain set ration of
paper every day of his life   It was not the subject so much
as the paper that mattered.   In the months following my
appointment I saw a great deal of Major Redvers Buller,
who held an appointment similar to mine in the adjutant-
general's office, then presided over by Sir Richard Airey.
My own office had for its head Sir Charles Ellice, and
later on Sir Daniel Lysons.   Many other officers whose names
became known to army fame in subsequent years held positions
at this time on the headquarters staff—Colonel T D. Baker,
Colonel Robert Hume, Colonel, afterwards Sir, Charles Wilson,
Sir Patrick MacDougall. Captain Herbert Stuart, Sir John
Ardagh, and others.   I would speak in particular of Colonel
Robert Hume, R.E.   He was an exceptionally brilliant officer,
mixing wit and work in a rare combination.   Like most of
the young and ambitious soldiers of the time, his economic
resources were not large, and he had a hard struggle, as the
real head of the Intelligence Department, to work his official
position and maintain a large family.

When the long-expected war between Russia and Turkey
began, the work that fell to his lot in briefing or coaching the
ministers responsible for the conduct of foreign affairs was
very great.   He died of a slow fever about the time of the
occupation of Cyprus.   He had distinguished himself during
the Ashanti War as the engineer-in-chief of the expedition,
and no doubt his constitution had suffered on the Coast.   But
I knew something of his family affairs at the time, and I believe
that a life of the largest value to the State was lost, not because
of the labour it was doing in the public service, but because
of financial anxieties and worries at home

At the moment when Colonel Hume was finding brains

and knowledge, geographical and other, for ministers and statesmen whose names figured large in the European congresses that preceded and followed the Russo-Turkish War, he frequently sat late into the night at home working a sewing-machine to keep his children in clothes !   What a lot of splendid human steel I have seen cast on the scrap-heap in my time, in the fulness of its strength and usefulness, through the selfish stupidity of a system which never seemed to know the worth of any human material it had to deal with !

The mass of old and confused buildings in Pall Mall in which the administration of the army was then carried on was quite typical of the confused work itself.   Six or seven houses had been selected, and thrown into intercommunication by means of three-step doorways and devious stairways.   All grades of London houses had thus been brought together—from the fine rooms of a ducal residence, where one saw walls and ceilings with medallions by Angelica Kauffmann and Italian mantelpieces of the finest sculpture, to the mean-looking lobbies and by-rooms of what had been once a silk-mercer's establishment.   The old sailor proverb about the island of St. Helena—that you had the choice of breaking your heart going up, or your neck coming down—had in a small way its parallel in the Pall Mall makeshift building with its many stairs ; and it was typical also of the misfortunes attending upon the house that is divided against itself that for fully forty years the department of State which most vitally affected the existence of the Empire was attempted to be carried on in a hole-and-corner collection of buildings, most of the rooms of which were as unhealthy to the administrators as they were unsuitable for the administration.

The division existing between the civil and military sides in the War Office was as lasting a source of trouble to the men who went into the houses as it was an active agent in producing faults in the work that came out from it.   Men spent the greater part of their time in official hours in writing ' minutes ' from one dingy room to another across these dusty passages and dark corridors.   The clerk who could write the sharpest minute in the most illegible handwriting was a valuable reinforcement to his particular side, and he had never to be at a loss in finding opportunity for discharging his ' minute ' guns into the ranks of some opponent.   Plenty of fighting could be had all round.   The strangest part of it was that nobody ever seemed to think *why* it was wrong, or to question the foundation upon which the system rested—a foundation which was entirely wrong in principle, and was therefore as certain to work out as wrong in practice as though it had been a piece of architecture set on false foundations and built upon faulty measurements. In my time I knew in that old building half a score of Secretaries of State.   It was almost pathetic to see each of these men in turn begin in hope and end in failure.   Those among them who made the fewest mistakes were those who tried the fewest changes   bad as the old machine was, it went better with oil and leisure than it did with grit and energy.   It was like a man whose constitution is thoroughly unsound, but who, neverthe- less, can sometimes reach old age, if he does not play pranks, or imagine himself either a young man or a strong man.

To understand the truth about our military administration you must go a long way back in history—in fact, to Oliver Cromwell.   One fact alone in the history of the last seventy years should give pause to all military reformers.   It is this, that at the end of every war waged by us in that period we have come to a unanimous agreement that we were totally unprepared for the war when we entered upon it ; and yet if you go back to the beginning of each of these wars you will also find that when we began them we were perfectly certain we were ready, down to the traditional last button.

London in the middle 'seventies was a gay place of residence. Much of the gold which the Franco-German War had poured into it four years earlier was still there ; men and women, horses and dogs, even the sparrows, looked fat, sleek, and jolly ; only the poor were still thin.   I look back to a host of friends, kind, hospitable souls, chief among them on the army side being Sir Garnet Wolseley, Redvers Buller, Evelyn Wood, R. Owen Jones, Robert Hume, Henry Brackenbury, T. D Baker, Lord Gifford, John Ardagh, Cecil Russell, Baker Russell

Everybody was eagerly watching the war-cloud in the Near East, speculating where the cloud would burst , little un- noticed parties of selected officers were going out to look at the scenery of islands in the Levant, or seek for snipe along the

Suez Canal, or ride through Asia Minor for the sport of the thing. Everybody knew that something was coming. The names of places well known in old war days — Gallipoli, Sebastopol, Constantinople, Varna, the Dardanelles—came again into constant conversation. More distant names also entered into the imaginary map of the theatre of coming war which we were so frequently constructing—Kizil, Arvat, Cabul, Candahar, the Oxus, Merv.

It is all thirty years ago, and two-thirds of the map-makers are dead. The world has known many wars since then, and, as usual, it was the utterly unexpected thing that happened in the end. Wherever you went in London in the later 'seventies, you saw numbers of little yellow-faced men, with dark, shifty eyes, and a peculiar expression of half pain and half pleasure upon their Mongolian features. No one took them at all seriously as a possible factor in war or statesmanship. It was true that they wore hats and trousers, but did not they also eat rice ? If any one at those pleasant club dinners had even hinted at the possibility of these little yellow men meeting and beating the armies and navies of the great white Czar, he would have been treated as an undiluted lunatic. These little men were then busy learning in London the lesson of how Asia was to whip Europe. Nothing so fraught with momentous results to the world had happened for thirteen hundred years.

There was one little club dinner at this time which was by far the most interesting I had ever sat down to, and which left on my memory recollections not to be effaced in life. In the winter of 1876 Major Robert Owen Jones asked me to meet an old friend and brother officer of his, Colonel Charles Gordon, at the time a passing visitor in London from the Egyptian Soudan. Of course, the name of Chinese Gordon was familiar to every soldier in the service, but, as usual, men accepted the sobriquet without troubling themselves much about the deeds that had won it ; indeed, some years later, I met an officer who believed that ' Chinese Gordon ' was a Chinaman born and bred.

The day of the dinner came ; there were only mine host, Gordon, and myself. We met in the hall of the club, and I was introduced to a man of middle age, rather under middle height, of figure lithe, active, and well-knit, and with a face

which still lives in my memory, not because it had any marked
peculiarity in its profile or full-face, but because of something
indefinable in the expression of the eyes   On the ocean one
is able at a glance to discern the difference between the
surface that has the depth of the Atlantic under it, and that
other surface which has the mud of the English Channel only
a few fathoms below it.   A depth like that of ocean was
within Gordon's eyes.   I never saw thought expressed so
clearly in any other man's.   Above these windows of his soul
rose a fine broad brow, over which a mass of curly brown hair
was now beginning to show streaks of grey.

We sat down to dinner ; there was the little restraint natural
to men meeting for the first time, but that soon wore off, and
before the dinner was half over conversation was in full flow.
It was the best and cheeriest talk I ever listened to   Gordon's
voice was as clear and vibrant as the note of an old Burmese
bell, which has a great deal of gold in its metal.   We adjourned
to the smoking-room, and there the stream of thought and
anecdote flowed on even better than before.   In turn came
the Nile, the desert, the Khedive Ismail (from whom Gordon
had that day received a letter begging him to return to Egypt),
the fever of the lake regions, and how there was a new prophy-
lactic for it called Werburgh's tincture, the efficacy of which
was such that ' it would make a sack of sawdust sweat '   Then
he would change to the Lower Danube and its races , the
Russian, the Bulgarian, the old Turk, Sebastopol.   He spoke
in low but very distinct tones, and his voice, varying with its
subject, carried to the ear a sense of pleasure in the sound
similar to that which the sight of his features, lit with the light
of a very ardent soul, gave to the listener's eye   I never heard
human voice nor looked into any man's eye and found similar
tone and glance there, nor did I ever meet a man who had
equal facility for putting into words the thoughts that were
in his brain.   You had never to ask an explanation ; the thing,
whatever it might be, was at once said and done.   That night
was the only one in my club life in which I saw the man with
the bull's-eye lantern come to say the hour of closing had
come and gone.   We were alone in the big smoking-room,
but I had not been aware of it.   I met two men in my
life who possessed this charm of conversation, Sir Garnet

Wolseley and Charles Gordon, but in Gordon the gift was the greater.

A few months after this time the war-cloud broke along the Lower Danube and in Asia Minor, and the spring and summer of 1877—the year that saw my marriage—were full of rumours and preparations. At first it seemed that the Russian march upon Constantinople would meet with feeble opposition ; then came Plevna, the fierce fighting in the Balkans, the taking of Adrianople, and the forward march of the Russians upon the Bosphorus. The excitement reached its highest point in London, but it was of a very frothy nature, the music-hall god ' Jingo ' playing a very conspicuous part in it.

All these wars and rumours of wars kept the staff in Pall Mall chained to their desks, but as the great war seemed to draw nearer to us, or we to it, the lesser war of which I have already spoken between the rival sides in the War Office grew less. ' The reserves were called out, and, despite of all the vaticinations and prophecies of failure and desertion, the reservists turned up almost to a man.

Notwithstanding the journalists and the Jingoes, an impression began early to pervade the War Office that there would be no war. The letters of that time which have since seen the light show that this idea was also prevalent in India. Lord Lytton gauged the position very accurately when he wrote to a friend, upon hearing that a mob had broken Mr. Gladstone's windows, ' I don't think the great heart of the English people is likely to do more than break windows just at present.' Had he known, however, as I came to know later, the personalities and the means employed to smash these few panes of glass in Harley Street, he would not have confused the breakers even with a London mob, still less with the mass of the English people.

By a strange coincidence, I happened to meet Mr. Gladstone in the Opera Arcade on the day his windows were broken by a few blackguards who had been specially hired for the business. The dark, piercing eyes had an unusual flash in them. A shower of rain was falling at the time, and the great leader had stopped a moment in the shelter of the arcade. He had no umbrella. I had one, and as I was at the door of my club, I offered it to him. The expression of his face softened instantly, and he thanked me in most courteous terms, but said the shower was a passing one and that he did not need any protection from it.

The pretence of a war was kept up until the Congress met in Berlin in the middle of 1878, and then the bubble burst. The whole business had been quietly arranged weeks earlier between the high contracting parties.

Amidst the knowledge of facts gathered in these years at the War Office few impressed me more strongly than the power possessed by the civil side of stultifying any attempt which military officers might make to better the position, or improve the efficiency, of the men in the ranks. An officer in the 60th Rifles, whom I had known in Canada, had invented a very complete and highly sensible set of military equipment, belts, knapsack, and other accoutrements, which was very much lighter and easier to put on, take off, or carry than the existing equipment.

This officer had spent his little all in bringing the new patterns to perfection. Committees and Boards had reported most favourably upon them. Soldiers upon whom they were tried, on guard and on the march, had declared them to be lighter, easier to manipulate and to wear than the old heavy, hard things our infantry soldiers had so long been condemned to carry. Nevertheless, no progress could be made in getting this new equipment taken into general use, and time after time the unfortunate designer and patentee used to appear at the War Office, only to meet with the same negative opposition. On one occasion his feelings of disappointment so overcame him that he quite broke down. I then found where lay the source of this dead-weight opposition. It was in the man who held the contract for the old man-killing stuff. I use the term 'man-killing' with reason. Many a time, when going the round of some military hospital, as I have already related, I have asked an old soldier what he was suffering from. 'Them pains, sir,' would be the answer; and 'them pains' were ascribed, nine times out of ten, to the wearing for twenty-four consecutive hours of 'them belts.'

In the knowledge that I was thus able to gain of the power possessed by the army contractor began a lifelong effort to expose the evils of the contract system as it was practised and

N

sustained by our army administrators ; but it was only towards the close of a long military career that I was able to deal it one good crushing blow, and though my own knuckles suffered, through the action of a few men in high positions who suddenly stood up on the side of the contractors, I never grudged the temporary annoyance their interference caused me.

In the sudden mania for acquisition which Lord Beaconsfield inaugurated in 1875-76, certain measures were begun in South Africa and in India which soon produced their various fruits of friction and strife. In September 1876 it was decided that the Transvaal was to be annexed. I don't think the full story of that event is known to many people now living, and it is sometimes of interest and always useful that events from which very great issues came should be traced to their fountain-heads.

I had returned from a flying visit to America in September 1876 to find my old friend and companion, Mr. Theophilus Shepstone, in London. He had been summoned home from Natal for the purpose of conferring with Lord Carnarvon, for whom the recent failure to bring about the confederation of the South African States had produced new conceptions of policy and new advisers of procedure. When I met Mr. Shepstone he entertained no thought of a speedy return to South Africa, and I looked forward to the opportunity of meeting him frequently in London during the autumn, and having many more of those conversations and discussions upon South African questions the interest of which I have already alluded to in this chapter. He had arranged to dine with me on a certain evening, but on the day of the evening on which we were to meet I received a telegram from him telling me that it had been suddenly decided he was to return immediately to Natal, and that, as he was sailing next day, our dinner could not come off. A day or two later a battalion of infantry, then in Ireland, was ordered to prepare for early embarkation for the Cape of Good Hope. Knowing what I knew of the drift of things generally at this time, I put both these sudden orders together without any difficulty. The next question that arose was as to the port to which the transport taking out the infantry battalion should proceed in South Africa. There were four ports possible—Cape Town,

Port Elizabeth, East London, and Durban. No decision would be given on this point. Meantime the troops were on board, and the ship was ready to sail. I went to the Colonial Office to point out the necessity of a speedy decision, in order to save demurrage, etc. Still no decision could be arrived at. I then suggested that the transport should sail, and call for orders at St. Vincent, and the thing that struck me as strangest in the matter was that the officials with whom I was dealing were at that time unaware that there was a cable to St. Vincent by means of which it would be possible to leave the matter of destination still an open one for nine or ten more days

My proposal was finally sanctioned, and the transport sailed about a fortnight or three weeks after the departure of Mr. Shepstone for Natal.

A curious thing now happened. Both the mail steamer carrying Mr. Shepstone and the transport steamer carrying the reinforcements were wrecked on the South African coast, forty or fifty miles from Cape Town. Thus the annexation of the Transvaal, decided upon early in September 1876, was ✓ delayed by untoward events some months Mr Shepstone was finally able to proceed to the Transvaal in December 1876.

Sir Bartle Frere went out as High Commissioner in March 1877, and the annexation of the Transvaal was a declared and accomplished fact on the 12th April in the same year.

These little movements, unknown and unnoticed at the moment of their occurrence, were in reality the spring-heads of the stream of events destined to plunge South Africa into a state of intermittent war for twenty-six years, and to cost Great Britain a sum of not less than three hundred millions of money ; and to-day, after all the blood spilt and the treasure spent, we are pretty much ' as we were ' in South Africa.

The new policy soon began to bear fruit. Kaffraria had been annexed by stroke of pen, and the Kaffirs responded by stroke of assegai. Troops were sent from England ; the recalcitrant natives were soon hunted out of their patches of bush and forest near King William's Town, and the troops were then sent northwards to Natal for purposes the scope of which the Government at home knew very little about. It soon transpired that it was the intention of Sir Bartle Frere to break the power of the Zulus beyond the northern boundary of Natal. The time seemed to him to be opportune. Natal, which up to this period had only seven companies of infantry to its garrison, had now seven battalions within its limits. The Lieutenant-Governor of Natal, a man of exceptional sense and foresight, did not want war, but his views were set aside. A ' Bill of Indictment,' as it was called, was prepared against the Zulu king, Cetewayo. The usual toll of cattle was demanded from him, and, before time was allowed for the collection of the animals, four separate columns of invasion entered Zululand. From the right column to the left there was a distance of about two hundred miles. It was to be the usual picnic expedition. ' There will be no fighting,' people said in Natal. ' The Zulus are too good-natured. It will only be a walk over.'

It was in the month of November 1878 that a staff officer of high position at the Cape came to my office in Pall Mall, and in a few words sketched the situation then existing in South Africa. ' There was absolute peace in Zululand,' he said. ' The difficulty was to poke Cetewayo up to the fighting point.' When I heard of the movement in four separate and far-apart columns, I said to my friend : ' It may fare roughly for one of the pokers ; we are giving Cetewayo the tongs.'

In the last days of the year I left England to spend a few weeks with Sir Garnet Wolseley in Cyprus. We had occupied the island five months earlier : the newspapers were still full of the recent acquisition, the visit promised many points of interest, and it gave more than the promise. During three or four weeks I traversed the island in every direction, from Nicosia to Kyrenia on the north coast to the top of snow-clad Troados in the west, and to Famagusta in the extreme east. I had been a stranger to the East since leaving Burmah and India fifteen years earlier. All the young life of America and the black life of Africa had since been my companions, but here in Cyprus it was the East again, the East with the Turk added on : the ragged squalor, the breast of the earth dried up and desolate, the old glory of Greek, Roman, Norman, and Venetian civilisation lying in dust and ashes under a thing that was itself a dying force in the world.

On 23rd January I set out with Sir Garnet Wolseley and three of his staff from Nicosia to Mount Olympus, to find a site for a summer camping-ground in the pine woods on the south shoulder of the mountain, five thousand feet above sea-level. Day had just broken. As we rode along the track leading to Peristerona, the conversation ran entirely upon the war which was then opening in Afghanistan. What bad fortune it was that the chief and so many of his staff officers should be hidden away in this dead island of the Levant, when so much of stirring moment in the outer military world was about to open. 'I have put my hand to the Cypriote plough and must hold it until the furrow is finished,' was the chief's summing up. But, at the moment when we were cantering along the track that early morning, the remnants of Lord Chelmsford's main column of invasion were moving out of the wrecked camps at Isandula in Zululand, and the commotion which was to follow this disaster was destined to move us all to South Africa a few months later. For myself I was to go there almost at once. I returned to England via Trieste, where the news of the massacre at Isandula reached me. I telegraphed the quartermaster-general offering my services for South Africa, and two days later, 15th February, was in London Two regiments of cavalry, several batteries of artillery, and eight battalions of infantry were immediately put in orders for Natal, and on the 28th February I sailed from Southampton in the ss. *Egypt*, bound for the same destination.

CHAPTER XIII

I was again in Natal. Three and a half years had passed since I had left the colony in profound peace : it was now seething in strife. Of the four original columns of invasion, the principal one had been cut in pieces at Isandula ; the action of the remainder had been paralysed. That next the coast had entrenched itself at Etchowe ; all its transport had been taken by the Zulus. The northern column, under Colonel Wood and Major Redvers Buller, had been alone able to move out of its fortified position at Kambula ; but the mounted portion of the force had just suffered very severely at a place named Zlobane in Northern Zululand, and, although the columns had been able to defeat the attack of a Zulu ' impi ' on the day following the disaster at Zlobane, it was no longer a mobile entity. News of these events reached us at Cape Town, and when we got to Durban Lord Chelmsford had just succeeded in effecting the relief of the garrison at Etchowe which had been brought back within Natal. So that, of the original plan of campaign, there only remained Colonel Wood's column upon the soil of Zululand.

The state of confusion existing within Natal could scarcely be exaggerated. To the extreme of over-confidence which had, indeed, been the primary factor in the disaster of Isandula, had succeeded the dread of a Zulu invasion. You will usually find that the term ' picnic ' at the rising of the curtain upon one of these little wars is readily changed to ' panic ' before the conclusion of the first act. The reinforcements now pouring into Natal reassured public opinion, which had grown over-excited at the report of a native Natal woman living in Zululand, who had come down to the Musinga Drift to tell her father what the Zulu soldiers were saying to Cetewayo : ' The

English are now afraid to meet us in the open , they are lying behind stone walls. Let us raid into Natal.' No doubt it would have been possible for detached parties of Zulus to carry into effect this idea, had their king been inclined to accede to the wishes of his soldiers , but he would not sanction it. All through this time he never abandoned his old belief that he was the friend of the English, and their ally against the Dutch ; and he clung to the promises made him by the Government of Natal through Mr. Shepstone at the time of his coronation, all of which were now forgotten. ' Ah, Shepstone ! ' he is said to have frequently exclaimed at this time, ' why have you grown tired of carrying me on your back ? '

The staff billet to which I was appointed was that of assistant adjutant-general under the general commanding the base and lines of communication—Major-General Sir Henry Clifford, V.C. Of him I shall say at once that among all the generals I have been brought into contact with, none possessed a personality more lovable, none had a higher courage, a larger sense of public duty, or a greater aptitude for untiring toil. The endless labours of his office during the ten months in Natal that were now beginning broke down the health and sapped the great physical strength of an exceptionally strong man ; and he returned from South Africa, a year later, only to die.

For some weeks after landing, he and I worked together in a stifling little office in Durban, the corrugated iron roof of which in the semi-tropical climate of the coast made the temperature almost insupportable in the afternoons. After a while, General Clifford moved to Maritzburg, and I was alone in the Durban office. It was a strange life at first. I lived, worked, ate, and slept in that office. For weeks there was no respite from work. Troops were pouring in and moving on up country ; demands for every article in the long catalogue of modern war equipment for transport—remounts, medical stores, camp equipment, clothing, ammunition, and fifty other things—were incessant.

War brings all the fantastic idiosyncrasies of human nature to the surface. Men will rob and pillage and rape and burn in war who would have lived very passable and decent lives in peace. Many of them think that it is part of the business ;

and, of course, the meaner and more sordid the war is, the more that part of the programme becomes possible.

I have seen, even at a peaceful railway station in England, a plethoric captain of Volunteers, proceeding to his summer camp in uniform, begin to leer and ogle at the passing female sex generally, who, had he been in his usual dress and at his daily business vocations, would have been the picture of decorous provincial family respectability.

Our work at the base of operations was largely added to by the shipwreck at Cape Agulhas of a transport carrying a vast amount of army stores—saddles, boots, harness, and other things. These had to be replaced, as far as they possibly could, by local purchase ; and the merchants of Durban and Maritzburg soon amassed fortunes by selling their indifferent wares at fancy prices. Part of my work was to sanction those purchases : they covered everything from anchors to needles. Of course we were robbed right and left, despite our work of day and night. Sometimes I caught the thief ; but oftener he escaped scot-free. Nature blessed me with a good memory, and I could recollect fairly well the description, at least, of the articles the purchase of which I had previously sanctioned : so, when the passing of the bills came, I was able, generally speaking, to remember whether I had approved the purchase in the first instance, or not.

One night I was going through these monotonous files, when my eye fell upon an entry—' One water-cart, £25.' I was morally certain that I had not given sanction for the buying of this article. The official was ordered to produce it. It was not to be found in any of our numerous storehouses ; and at last, after searching inquiries, it was discovered that no such article had been bought ; that the nearest approach to it had been a water-can, price 5s., and that an ingenious understrapper in the Ordnance Office had changed the words ' watercan ' into ' water-cart,' and made the 5s. in the figure column into £25. This, however, was the merest trifle in the account of our losses. We had sent men out to buy horses in every direction. One unfortunate man was purchasing animals in the Orange Free State : he had forded a ' drift ' easily in the morning, made many purchases in the day, and came to the drift again in the evening. Rain was falling ; the water was running breast deep , his horse missed his footing ; rider and horse were carried into deep water, and the man was drowned. When his body was recovered, it was found to have on it a leather belt full of gold pieces, more than three hundred in number. These represented exactly ten per cent. on the purchases of horseflesh made that day. It was their weight that had caused him to sink like a stone.

Shortly after landing, I visited Maritzburg on business. The troops were now moving up country. Lord Chelmsford was also going forward. I met, in the little Government House in Maritzburg so well known to me three years earlier, the Prince Imperial, at this time a visitor with the Governor, Sir Henry Bulwer. We had a long conversation : he had many questions to ask about the Zulus, the up country for which he was about to start, the climate, horses, arms, equipment, everything. ' Although he was an artillery officer,' he said, ' he preferred to be as he was now, attached to the staff. He might thus be able to get in closer touch of the Zulu enemy than if he remained with a battery of artillery.' Within one month of the day upon which we thus spoke, this splendid young soldier—handsome, active, brave to a fault, the very soul of chivalrous honour, and yet withal of a singular grace and gentleness—fell fighting, deserted and left alone by his escort, one against twenty of this same Zulu enemy. The manner in which this news came to us in Durban was singular. I had a single Zulu to look after my few wants in the office which was now my home. Every morning he entered the room, set the bath on the floor, and went out as silently as he had come in ; but on the morning of 3rd June he spoke a few words : ' A big "inkoos " had been killed.' Later that day or the next came the details of that wretched tragedy in which so many things besides life had been lost.

Ten days later, the body of the Prince Imperial was brought to Durban to be embarked on board a ship-of-war for England. I think that the scene as the funeral cortège wound down the Berea Hill towards Durban was the saddest but the most impressive sight I had ever witnessed. It was the sunset hour ; the eastern slope of the Berea was in shadow, but the town beneath, the ships in the roadstead, and the deep blue Indian Ocean beyond the white line of shore were all in dazzling light.

The regiments that had gone up country had left their bands on the coast, and, one after the other, these took up the great March of the Dead, until the twilight, moving eastward towards the sea, seemed to be marching with us as we went. Night had all but closed when we carried the coffin into the little Catholic church at the base of the Berea Hill.

I could not get any money from the State or from the Colony, but the people of Durban readily answered my appeal ; and, though we had only twenty-four hours' notice, the church was entirely hung in black cloth, violets were in profusion, and many wax lights stood around the violet-covered bier upon which the coffin lay. A few French nuns prayed by the dead, relieving each other at intervals through the night. As the cortège, followed by the mourners, came slowly down the hill, I heard from the groom who led the prince's charger the particulars of the final scene—so far as it had been possible to put them together at that time, for none save the Zulu enemy had witnessed the last desperate struggle. But the servant had seen his master's body, and that bore a tribute to the dead man's courage more eloquent than had thousands acclaimed the last struggle, not for life—that was hopeless —but for honour. There were twenty-six assegai wounds, all in front of the body ; the high riding-boots were found filled with blood—so long and so firmly had the boy stood under the rain of spears ; for though there were eighteen or twenty Zulus facing that single figure, they dared not close with him while he stood. The scene of the fight was a long, shallow, sloping valley between hills ; a Zulu kraal was close at hand, with patches of mealies around it ; then came a donga, with grass growing high in places near it, and a spot of bare ground by the edge of the donga (a dry watercourse) where the body was found lying. Some of the Zulus carried guns : they had stolen up through the mealie gardens and fired a volley at the party, who were in the act of mounting their horses. The captain of the escort galloped away, followed by his men in a general stampede. The prince must have been still dis- mounted when they ran, for his grey charger was found with the holster cover torn off, as though the prince had caught it in the act of mounting. The horse was restive at mounting at all times ; and in the confusion of the shots and the galloping

away of the escort, it would have been more difficult than ever
to gain the saddle. But the groom was certain that if the
holster flap had been of good leather the prince would have
been able to mount, for he was of extraordinary activity in
all matters of the riding-school, and could vault from the
ground on to the back of any horse. The man's statement of
opinion found corroboration in an incident which occurred a
month before this time. It was thus described in one of the
Natal newspapers :—

' As time rolls on, the death of the Prince Imperial loses none of
its melancholy significance, and no doubt many an incident of his
brief stay here will, sooner or later, come to light. One in particular
may be mentioned When at the Royal Hotel, the prince asked Mr.
Doig to show him his horses. At the Crown stables there was a
wild young horse which had just thrown one of the stable hands.
The prince, without the aid of stirrups, vaulted into the saddle,
and although the horse bolted away and made every endeavour to
throw him, he brought him safely back to the stable, and dropped
from the saddle with a most extreme nonchalance. The horse has
since thrown another rider and broken his leg.'

The next morning we all assembled again at the little church,
where an old French priest said a requiem Mass. Then we
carried the coffin to the hearse, and the long procession passed
through the town to the wharf at the Point, two miles distant,
with the same solemn parade as on the previous evening. At
the wharf the coffin was handed over to the naval authorities,
and taken to the flagship in the outer roadstead.

In her strangely sad history South Africa has seen many
sad sights, but none so sad as this one.

I am writing to-day thirty years after that terrible tragedy
occurred. Three years ago I visited the scene where it
happened ; walked the ground by the fatal dongas, and stood
by the cross which Queen Victoria caused to be erected on the
spot where the body was found the day following the death
of the prince. Nothing has changed in the valley of the
Ityotyozi A few Zulu kraals are there still ; the dry dongas
may have worn a little deeper ; but the long yellow grass is
waving there, and the mealie patches ; and the big dark slate-
coloured hills slope up on west and south, and the deep dry

channel of the Ityotyozi curves away toward the north-cast, the highest tributary of the White Umvolosi River.

No man will ever pierce the 'Might have been' of history. Fourteen years after the death of the Prince Imperial, I met in the Mediterranean a distinguished admiral in the French navy, and we spoke of that day in Zululand. 'If the Prince were alive to-day,' he said, 'he would without any doubt be Emperor of the French. The French people would have hailed him as their chief'

I have spoken of the chaos which reigned in Natal following up the disaster at Isandula. To that chaos, to that general scramble of direction, to the absence of any real thinking or governing power running through all the army staff machinery of the time must, in the first and leading sense, be attributed the death of the Prince Imperial As usual in our history, the men who were first at fault got off, and the unhappy subordinate actor in the tragedy was immolated. There was no excuse for the conduct of the captain of the escort and his miserable scratch following of six makeshift troopers ; but neither was there any excuse for the general in command of the army, nor the staff officers whose duty it was to see that this young French prince, a volunteer to us in this war and engaged in doing our duty for the moment, should not be allowed to go out into an enemy's country without full and proper escort, and under the eye and command of an old and experienced mounted officer. What were these people thinking of when they allowed that wretched party to go nine or ten miles from camp straight into a land full of armed and lurking enemies ? Four months before this time, an entire British regiment and four or five hundred other troops, artillery and cavalry, had been assegaied to a man at a place within a day's easy riding distance of, and twenty miles nearer to our frontier than, this valley of the Prince Imperial's death.

It was afterwards said by way of excuse that the prince was brave to rashness, and that it was his reckless daring which led to his death What an excuse ! making the fault of those who were responsible for the escort and its leadership only more glaringly apparent. It is all a horrible black night of disaster, with a solitary star of one man's glorious courage shining through it.

When they came to look over the poor boy's papers, they found among them a written prayer; these sentences were in it :—

'My God, I give Thee my heart; but give me faith. To pray is the longing of my soul. I pray not that Thou shouldst take away the obstacles on my path; but that Thou mayst permit me to overcome them. I pray not that Thou shouldst disarm my enemies; but that Thou shouldst aid me to conquer myself. . . . If Thou only givest on this earth a certain sum of joy, take, O God, my share and bestow it on the most worthy. . . . If thou seekest vengeance upon man, strike me. Misfortune is converted into happiness by the sweet thought that those whom we love are happy; and happiness is poisoned by the bitter thought that, while I rejoice, those whom I love a thousand times better than myself are suffering. For me, O God, no more happiness: take it from my path. If I forget those who are no more I shall be forgotten in my turn; and how sad is the thought which makes one say, "Time effaces all"! . . . O my God, show me ever where my duty lies, and give me strength to accomplish it. . . . Grant, O God, that my heart may be penetrated with the conviction that those whom I love, and who are dead, shall see all my actions; that my life shall be worthy of their witness, and my innermost thoughts shall never make them blush.'

Reading these sentences, one seems to lift a corner of the veil that hangs between man and the Face of the Inscrutable. Happily for those who have to work in war, there is still time left for thinking.

A few days after the close of this sad chapter, the telegrams from England via St. Vincent announced that Sir Garnet Wolseley was coming out to relieve Lord Chelmsford of his command. 'The cloud of misfortune seems ever to overhang this miserable and luckless war,' thus wrote Archibald Forbes, from Camp Itelezi Hill on the night of Whitsunday. It was true. But there was more than misfortune in all that had happened: things were done that read to-day as beyond possibility of credence. The advance into Zululand was made in two columns—one entering by Landmann's Drift over the Buffalo River; the other by the coast-road from Durban over the Tugela to Port Durnford. This latter force, consisting of two brigades of British infantry and cavalry and artillery, had now been creeping slowly forward, with many halts between the creeps, for about six weeks. It was now halted at Port Durnford. Of certain officers many stories were current, and numerous were the epigrams and lampoons which the Natal newspapers indulged in at the time.

A letter written by a staff officer of high place early in July speaks of a general ' moving, at a time when transport is above all things precious, with a waggon fitted as a movable hen-house, with coops and places for hens to lay so that he may always be sure of his fresh eggs for breakfast. He dresses or did dress (I fancy Sir Garnet has altered matters) in the most absurd costume, with a sombrero hat and a long pheasant's feather, and an imitation puggaree tied in what he considers a picturesque and artistic carelessness on one side. He telegraphed to —— for six milch cows among other supplies ; but ——, while meeting all his other demands, telegraphed back, " Must draw the line at milch cows." ' Describing the appearance of the streets in Durban, the same writer says : ' The streets are full of all sorts of military and naval types ; the wonderful number of straps and dodges that some of them have about them is a sight, and every one seems to try how many odds and ends he can carry about him. Y—— is said to beat every one ; a man describing him to me said, " He only wanted a few candles stuck about him to make a Christmas tree ! " ' These descriptions are in no way exaggerated. They might, indeed, be amplified and yet be within the truth. What is there in the air or soil of Africa which seems to unlevel the heads of so many newcomers in that part of the world ? Truly, a master-spirit was wanted here.

Sir Garnet Wolseley reached Durban on the 28th June. He landed early ; rode round the camps, hospitals, and storehouses ; had breakfast, and started by train for Botha's Hill and Maritzburg, where he was sworn in. He was back in Durban the next day ; went on board a man-of-war, and sailed for Port Durnford—intending to land there, pick up the Coast Column, and move with it at once towards the King's Kraal at Ulundi But now South Africa came into play. The violence of the surf made landing impossible at Durnford ; Sir Garnet and his staff were obliged to return to Durban. I had horses and waggonettes ready for them, and they left for

Port Durnford by land. Through these various contretemps six days had been lost. Meanwhile, on 4th July the action at Ulundi was fought, and the Zulu War was practically over.

It was full time ; it had lasted eight months, and was costing one million pounds each month. A war with the Zulus, if properly planned and carried out, meant from its beginning what it was found to mean at its end—just thirty minutes' fighting. The arms of an enemy, and his methods of using them, are the chief factors which should dictate to a general the disposal of his forces, and his fighting tactics. The Zulus were armed with assegais ; they did not fight at night ; they charged home in dense masses in open daylight ; they had neither artillery nor cavalry. Eight good infantry battalions, two regiments of light cavalry, three field batteries, and three hundred native Basuto scouts would have been amply sufficient to do in seven weeks what at least twice that number of men, guns, and horses succeeded in accomplishing, after defeats and disasters, in the same number of months.

As I look back over forty-seven years of service, the thing that astonishes me most is the entire absence of the thinking faculty in nine out of ten of the higher-grade officers with whom I was associated. What obtained at Aldershot was made the rule throughout the world—from Greenland's icy mountains to India's coral strand. It was not Cæsar, most imaginative of tacticians, who was the teacher it was his so-called camp over the Long Valley, with the Basingstoke Canal at the end of it, and the site for the luncheon beyond that again, which set the lesson of the tactical application of the three arms, and often gave the key to victory. I knew of one very successful leader at Aldershot who regulated the movements of his brigade by the direction which the refreshment carts took in the commencement of the fray. They were supposed to be under a sort of hypnotic inspiration from the mind of the garrison sergeant-major as to the point at which victory would declare itself, and the battle would terminate at 1.30 P.M.

While the new commander-in-chief in Zululand had now to proceed with the final phases of the capture of Cetewayo, and the settlement of Zululand, we at the Base and on the Line of Communications had to prepare and carry out the embarkation of more than half the army, and quite two-thirds of its late generals and their staff.

Some of the battalions and batteries had been a long time up country, and very large arrears of pay were due to them, as well as to the very numerous irregular corps which had been recruited for service after the disaster at Isandula. It would be difficult to imagine anything more irregular than the majority of the rank and file of these latter bodies : the Turkish title, Bashibazouk, seems alone suited in its sound adequately to describe them. Their regimental titles were also suggestive in many instances of the general trend and direction of their discipline and methods—Sham-buckers' Horse, Raafs' Rangers, the Buffalo Border Guards, etc., etc.

To pay off, disarm, and embark those worthies was a work requiring some little tact and method on the part of the officers who had to deal with them under their respective heads. These various units of raffish swashbucklers now came to the port of embarkation to be paid their reckonings and to pay them again into innumerable public-houses of Durban. I devised many plans by which the evil might be lessened. Sometimes I put a pay officer and his paysheet, with a good guard of regulars, on board a transport in the outer anchorage, and informed the men that they would only be paid on board ship. Another plan was to encamp the corps six or eight miles out of Durban, in the vicinity of a railway station, by means of which they could be fed and supplied from the port. The scenes which were daily taking place were often of a very ludicrous description. A battalion of infantry, to whom some five or six thousand pounds had to be paid, would reach the wharf for embarkation, having been made the recipients on the march through Durban of a public luncheon and innumerable quantities of large water melons— the latter a most innocuous fruit on any ordinary occasion, but somewhat embarrassing when presented to a man after a hearty meal and many libations *en route*. I had prepared, however, for the dangers of the embarkation from the wharf in the large flat boats, and a dozen steady men with boathooks stood ready to gaff the men who fell into the water—a precaution which bore fruit in more senses than one, for many of the men deemed it a point of honour to hold on by their water melons even when they were in the sea. The acme of confusion was, however, reached on the occasion when some eighteen hundred 'details,' prisoners, 'insanes,' sick, and absentees from previous embarkations had to be put upon a troopship in the outer anchorage.

At the last moment a train had arrived from Maritzburg with six 'insanes' for shipment to England. The transport was still in the roadstead, so a boat was sent out to her. The corporal in charge had just time to run up the gangway with his charge ; the anchor was already up. On reaching the quarterdeck, crowded with eighteen hundred men, the six 'insanes' saw their chance, and while the corporal was handing his papers to the staff officer on board they adroitly dispersed themselves among the miscellaneous crowd of men thronging the decks. Identification was entirely impossible in that mixed crowd : the corporal had to get back to his escort in the boat as quickly as possible, and the big troopship moved off to shake her motley collection of men into that subsidence which only grows more complete as the sea grows more restless. But the hour came when the staff officer asked the sergeant of the guard, ' Where are the six insanes ? ' No man on board could say where ; and soon the rumour passed from deck to deck that there were six madmen at large among the troops. Every man began to take a strange interest in his neighbour. ' And who is thy neighbour ? ' asks the catechism. ' Mankind of every description ' is the answer, so far as I can recollect it over the lapse of years. But surely that reverend and estimable namesake of mine, when he penned that question and answer, can never have contemplated a contingency such as this crowded troopship, with twenty different corps represented in its human freight, and at least two unknown madmen at large upon every deck ! And yet never could there have been a time when men regarded their neighbour with more lively interest. A council of the leading authorities on ship-board was rapidly assembled, and a course of action decided upon. Practically it came to this, that the whole mass of military was placed under observation ; a select corps of observers was organised, and the work began. Any man who was sitting apart in the anticipatory stages, or after effects, of sea-sickness found himself walked round and suspiciously regarded ; at frequent intervals a man would be tapped on the shoulder and told to come before the doctor. When the vessel reached Cape Town there were twenty-six men under observation, and it was afterwards found that not one of the six 'insanes' was among them. A curious thing now happened : after a while, some sergeant or corporal, more observant than his comrades, remarked that there were certain men in the crowd who were ready on all occasions to lend a hand in running in the suspected ones, first to the doctor and afterwards to the 'observation' hold. The eagerness and alacrity of these few men attracted first praise and then suspicion. There was an expression of self-satisfaction on their features which was peculiar to them alone among those whose duty it was to discover the missing madmen. Then their off moments were watched, with the result that when the ship reached St. Helena the 'observation' hold was cleared of its former inmates and the six insanes were duly installed therein.

At last the weary work of sweeping up the wreckage of a war which was unusually fertile in shipwrecks drew to an end. A crowd of contractors flocked to the base to batten upon the expected spoil when the time for selling surplus stores came. Enormous accumulations of food, forage, and all the other paraphernalia of war had to be got rid of. At first high prices were obtained ; then the usual rings were formed. We had some thousands of tons of food-stuffs to sell, and the dealers saw their chance : they would only give first one shilling, and then sixpence, for a heavy sack of Indian corn. I had two large transports sailing with troops, the cargo decks of which were empty. 'All right, gentlemen ; we will put these two thousand odd tons of excellent food-stuffs on board these empty vessels and send them to London.' Then the counter-attack began. The dealers worked hard to prevent this move ; the departments were also hostile to my proposal. It had not been done before ; it would complicate departmental accounts ; it was a new departure, etc., etc. 'But is it not common-sense ? ' I said. 'These innumerable sacks of food, for which we can get sixpence here, will sell in London for ten or twenty times that figure. We are already paying enormous prices for the freightage of these ships ; it will cost us nothing to send all this food to England.' This and a lot more I urged. At last sanction was given, and I saw the enormous stacks of supplies vanish into the empty ships, the cargoes to fetch in London even more than I had anticipated.

This war against the Zulus in 1879 was, in fact, a small undress rehearsal for that other war which was to be fought in South Africa twenty years later.   But new men had in the interval come upon the scene ; the older ones who still remained above ground were set aside , and every error made in 1879-1880—in strategy, tactics, foresight, administration, transport, remounts, supplies, multiplied by the power of twenty or perhaps thirty—was repeated in 1899 and 1900   Four million pounds were thrown away in the war of 1879 , at least one hundred millions were flung to the winds in that of 1899 and the two following years.

> ' It 's a way we have in our Army,
> It 's a way we have in our Navy,
> It 's a way we have in Pall Mall '

How often in my small sphere I have laboured hard to save fifty or a hundred thousand pounds, making thereby enemies for myself in every direction among contractors, clerks, and officials in general, only to find in the end that there was some colossal noodle above me whose signature had the power of flinging ten times my savings into the melting-pot of waste, inefficiency, and ineptitude. ' I go to Paris to find my enemies there,' said Marshal Vendôme to Prince Eugène, as they parted somewhere in the ' Cockpit ' during the War of the Spanish Succession. ' And I to Vienna, where mine await me,' replied the prince. It is a very old story ; it is certain to grow older.

While Durban was the scene of the closing phases of the Zulu campaign, robberies and burglaries became unusually prevalent, as many of the Government stores had to be kept in large marquees, into which ingress was easily obtained at night.   To check these robberies, a non-commissioned officer of the Ordnance Department was put in the large marquee at nightfall, with orders to fire at any interloper he might chance to find there. Unfortunately for the plan, a drunken old conductor, who had come down from the front, had gone quietly into the marquee earlier in the afternoon for the purpose of sleeping off his potations among the piles of blankets within. He was in a profound slumber when the watch was set, and he remained in it for hours after ; but at length, towards midnight, he awoke and began to stir himself. Bang ! went a revolver some little distance from his resting-place ; then another shot, and another. ' Holy Moses ! ' he shouted, ' are the Zulus on us again ? ' This was, I think, the very last of the scares in the Zulu War. They had lasted without intermission from January to July. The shadow of a cloud in the moonlight moving over the side of a hill was sometimes enough to set the rifles going in one of the laagers of the invading force, or even to cause fire to be opened from the ramparts of one of the forts on the line of communication. It was always the advance of a Zulu ' Impi ' that was conjured up in somebody's excited imagination. On one occasion, when many thousand rounds of ammunition were fired off, the ' Impi ' came on again and again, only to wither away before this *feu d'enfer*, which went on for many hours. When day dawned, a single dead cow was discovered lying upon the field of battle.

Early in January 1880 all the work was over, and I was able to leave Durban for England. I had an interview with Sir Bartle Frere at Cape Town. He seemed feeble and broken, but his eye had still the old look in it. He spoke much about the war, and I gathered from his conversation that matters had not been going well between him and the Home Government. ' But,' he said, ' what other course could I have pursued ? My military advisers told me that they had an ample force for the invasion of Zululand ; that they were ready and pre- pared in every respect. I was bound to believe their reports. I had no means of knowing otherwise, nor had I any right to think they did not know what they were speaking about.' Of course, that was quite true ; but it was a dangerous time to begin a war in South Africa when already there was war beyond the Indian frontier in Afghanistan. At the time Sir Bartle Frere was speaking thus, Sir Frederick Roberts had been sent up near Kabul. That city was again in the hands of the enemy, and the relief of the English garrison had still to be effected. That Afghanistan had been in Sir Bartle Frere's mind at the time he was urging on the destruction of the Zulu power is extremely probable, for I find in my notebook this reference :—

'At the beginning of the Zulu War —— (Lord Chelmsford's chief adviser) is said to have remarked that they would march through Zululand and then go on to Afghanistan.'

But more interesting even than my visit to Sir Bartle Frere was a visit to Cetewayo in the castle at Cape Town   Previous to my leaving Natal I had received a letter from Major Ruscombe Poole (the officer who had charge of Cetewayo) asking me, if possible, to bring some few bundles of green rushes from Zululand when I was coming to Cape Town, in order that one of the king's wives might make some mats, on which the king could sleep. (He was unable to sleep in an English bed.) I sent into Zululand, through Mr. Grant, a true friend of the Zulus, and I soon had three large bundles of green rushes to take with me to Cape Town.   The first thing I did on arrival was to get the bundles on to the top of a four-wheeled cab and drive to the castle.   Everything leaving the docks was subject to duty ; but as rushes were not in the taxable cata- logue, the gatekeeper had to let me through free.   I was soon in the room wherein the unfortunate Cetewayo was kept.   He was delighted to get this little bit of his beloved Zululand in his dreary four-walled prison.   It was the same as putting a bit of green sod into the cage of a lark ; only the unfortunate Zulu king wept when he saw these reminders of his old home, and he said to the interpreter as he shook my hand, 'Say to him that he has brought sleep to me : now I can rest at night.'

I reached England in the middle of February 1880.   The Government of Lord Beaconsfield was on its last legs : every thing had gone wrong with it ; all the castles in the East had crumbled, and in the South things were no better.   Shere Ali, it is true, was dead beyond the Oxus River, Cetewayo was a prisoner in the castle at Cape Town , but other spectres were rising above the frontiers of both countries.   Sir Bartle Frere had asked me to see Ministers when I got home, but they were already in the throes of dissolution.   Thinking that some one in colonial authority might wish to see me, I put down a few recent impressions upon the general trend of affairs in South Africa which read fairly accurate to-day :—

'The state of Dutch feeling in the old Colony (Cape Colony) is being affected by the condition of the affairs in the New (the Transvaal). The one-sidedness of whites and natives is increasing; emigration is the only cure.'

On the voyage from the Cape the steamer touched at St. Helena. It was close to sunset when the anchor was down. 'How long can you give me, captain ? ' I asked. 'Two hours,' he replied. I was off to shore at once. I found a small black boy with a small pony at the landing-place. Away we went through the single-streeted town, and up the steep mountain path—the black imp holding on by his pony's tail as the ascent steepened. I knew the road, for I had been over it sixteen years earlier. It was dusk when we gained the zigzags on the track above the ' Briars ' ; then came the bit of level curving track by the alarm post, and then the well-remembered side path to the left dipping down steeply to the head of Rupert's Valley. There in the dusk was the silent tomb again ; the dark cypress trees, the old Norfolk Island pines, the broken willow, the iron railings, the big white flagstone in the centre of the railed space—all the lonely encompassing lava hills merging into the gathering gloom of night ; and only a yellow streak of afterglow, still lying above the western rocks, to make the profound depths of this valley seem more measureless.

I was back on board the *Nubian* ere the two hours had expired. The time at the grave had been short ; but it did not matter : twenty-six years later I was to be there again, a dweller for days together on the ridge of Longwood above the tomb.

CHAPTER XIV

LORD BEACONSFIELD resigned office after the General Election of March, and Mr. Gladstone came into power in April 1880. In the new administration the Marquis of Ripon was appointed Viceroy of India, Colonel Charles Gordon going with him as private secretary.   Lord Ripon had, quite unknown to me, proposed my name for that position, but Mr. Gladstone had not approved the selection.   He considered that a Catholic viceroy in India was sufficiently experimental without further endangering the position by the appointment of another of the same creed to a subordinate but still influential post.   So, in place of proceeding to our great Eastern dependency ' in a position of considerable power and influence and full of very interesting though very hard work,' as its last holder, Colonel Colley, had described it, I was sent as chief staff officer to Devonport, having been previously promoted lieutenant-colonel in the army for services in Natal.

Military life in England can never be ' magnificent,' still less, of course, is it likely to be ' war.'   In India it can be both. As private secretary to the viceroy I should have received between three and four thousand pounds a year ; as assistant adjutant-general of the Western District I received six hundred pounds.   Service in England, however, possesses the saving grace of having a large measure of humour attached to it ; nothing makes for humour more than make-believe.   An army, the officers of which are dressed for the benefit of the London tailor, and the soldiers of which are administered largely in the interests of the War Office clerk, must of necessity afford situations replete with humour ; but the laughter they evoke has to be paid for by somebody in the end.

Before the year 1880 closed, war had broken out again in South Africa and Afghanistan. Up to the middle of the year the prospect, people said, was entirely peaceful. The leading authority in Eastern affairs—Sir Henry Rawlinson—had publicly declared that the outlook on the side of Candahar was eminently tranquil. The Transvaal administrator—Sir Owen Lanyon—repeatedly asserted that no apprehension need be entertained in that country. Suddenly, as though he had come in a balloon, Ayub Khan descended into the valley of the Helmund. With equal rapidity the Boers concentrated at Heidelberg, and declared the Transvaal a Republic. In midsummer Burrowes was 'annihilated' at Maiwand. In December, Anstruther, moving with the headquarters of the 94th Regiment from Heidelberg to Pretoria, was destroyed at Brunker's Spruit. Then in rapid succession came disasters at Laing's Nek, Igogo, and finally at Majuba, where poor Colley fell. Before the defeat of the late Government he had been transferred from the private secretaryship in India to the position of lieutenant-governor of Natal. In the months following my return from Natal to England I had seen a good deal of him in London, and I was present at the banquet given to him by the Colonial Office in May on the eve of his departure for Natal. How full of felicitations and of hope were the speeches of everybody that evening ! Particularly optimistic was the speech of Lord Kimberley, the Secretary of State. A new South Africa was about to arise out of the mists and vapours of the past, they said, as indeed we shall find them saying seventeen years later when another 'Proconsul' was about to depart for the same destination. All make-believe again. When will our governors realise that, of all the foundations possible for building empire upon, this of make-believe is the very worst ?

I was in London when the news of Majuba arrived there. On the evening of Sunday, 26th February, a telegram had been received at the War Office from Colley announcing the occupation by him that morning of a commanding position overlooking the Boer camp, and completely commanding the ridge of Laing's Nek. The Boers were preparing to trek from their camp. I had seen a copy of this message late on Sunday evening. At breakfast next morning the full report of the

disaster, which had followed immediately upon the despatch
of this message, was in all the London papers. I went to the
War Office. None of the higher officials were there. Sir
Garnet Wolseley was then residing some twenty miles from
London. I knew that he would pass through Trafalgar
Square, and I waited there until he came. Then I walked to
the War Office with him. Colley was, I think, the dearest
friend he had in the army ; certainly he was the one in whom
he trusted the most thoroughly. He felt his loss deeply. It
was a very busy day in the Office ; reinforcements were under
orders immediately, the Duke arrived early. There were
councils and consultations. Before the afternoon had come
everything was arranged. Sir Frederick Roberts was to go
out in command. Sir Garnet Wolseley must remain at the
War Office as quartermaster-general. The command of the line
of communications had been offered to Colonel T. D. Baker,
who was abroad at the moment. In the event of his refusal, Sir F. Roberts asked if I would accept the position. Of
course I said ' Yes,' but Baker took the post ; and, as is known
to everybody, the Peace of O'Neill's Farm was made before
the commander, his staff, or the reinforcements arrived in
South Africa.

For more than a year now the work in the Western District
was of the usual staff type common to home service. I have
spoken of the humorous contrasts by which it was sometimes
enlivened. An Easter Monday Volunteer Review at Portsmouth or Dover, or a Grand Field Day at Aldershot, not un-
frequently provided the incidents which caused these pleasant
interludes in what must have been otherwise a period of a
somewhat monotonous character.

The army in its higher ranks still swore, not perhaps as
lustily as it did of old in Flanders, but still a good deal more
than was good for it, or for those who had to listen to it.
There was once a general commanding at Aldershot whose
reply to a royal personage, on an occasion when the display
of forcible language was more than usually emphatic, struck
me as being exceptionally neat and appropriate. He had been
the recipient during the operations of a good deal of strong
language, and at the final ' pow-wow ' some allusion was made
to those fireworks of the tongue. ' I don't mind being called

a d—— fool,' he said, ' if it pleases your Royal Highness to call me so ; but I do mind being called a d—— fool before your Royal Highness's other d—— fools,' and he swept his hand towards the large and brilliant staff grouped behind the commander-in-chief.

The troubles in South Africa and Afghanistan had scarcely subsided ere things began to threaten in the valley of the Nile. When a ' question,' as it is called, suddenly seems to approach solution, or to demand some active treatment, the general public (who up to this point have been kept entirely in the dark in relation to it) are suddenly deluged with information about it, but it is always information of a single type and pattern. The Egyptian question, which began to assume light in 1881, was a striking example of this rule. It had been slowly maturing in the minds of certain politicians for several years. As early as the winter of 1875-76, three military officers had been sent to Egypt to report upon frontiers and possibilities. The movement of Russian armies in Bulgaria and Asia Minor two years later postponed action ; then came the deposition of Ismail Pasha in 1879 ; the succession of Tewfik as Khedive ; the budding of a National party in Egypt in 1880-81, and the subsequent intrigues of Jews and Gentiles, Turks, Arabs, Greeks, and Syrians ; of all those extraordinary, astute human units grouped under the name of Levantines, whose greeds, lusts, and various financial activities have played such a promi- nent part in shaping the flow of the history of the last forty years.

In such watching of the world's forces as I have been able to give through thirty of those years, I have been struck by a general course of action which has pervaded most, if not all, of those various movements. I would describe it thus. The faddist appears first upon the scene. He is, generally speaking, an honest and sincere man, quick to catch impressions, eager to tell about them, of an overweening vanity, an un- balanced ambition, and a facility for putting thought into speech or writing far beyond his power of putting thought into sense or action. This man is consumed by a wish to do something. He would canalise the plain of Esdraelon, flood the valley of the Jordan with the waters of the Mediterranean, run a railway from the Euphrates to the Himalayas, repeople

Palestine with the children of Israel, supplant Christianity by Buddhism, or Buddhism by Confucianism ; in a word, he is a little of a genius and a good deal of a madman with a purpose ; the mass of madmen have no purpose. The second man to appear on the scene is the politician. He sees in this idea something which he may be able to turn to his own purpose—a new frontier, an outlet for trade ; a bigger vote at the polls, a higher place in a cabinet. Then comes the great financier, the man of many millions, the controller of vast enterprises. He is really the final factor in all this business. When he takes sides, throws his weight into the scale, the matter has passed into the region of practical politics, and the old nebulous proposition has become the supremely important question of the hour.

I know of no more illuminating work published in recent times than the *Secret History of the English Occupation of Egypt*, by Mr. Wilfrid Scawen Blunt. In the pages of that book the devious ways of diplomacy are made clear : the genius, the politician, the young diplomatic attaché, the Foreign Office official move to and fro before our eyes ; and, at last, we find the financier whipping the whole pack together and letting loose the dogs of war.

It is not a very high or ennobling level from which to begin the business of war. Compared with most of the old causes of conflict which our fathers knew of, it is decidedly below the average standard of dynastic jealousies, the rivalries of States, the great social or political questions, such as underlay the Civil War in America—even of the old loves of men and women. These were all subjects likely to call from war the thing which Shakespeare considered made ambition virtue.

But the soldier of to-day has to be content with what he can get, and the gift war-horse which the Stock Exchange is now able to bestow upon him must not be examined too severely in the mouth.

On 11th July the forts at Alexandria were bombarded by the British fleet, with the result that the forts were destroyed and a large portion of the town was reduced to ruins. The huge shells flew wide and high, some of them reaching Lake Mariout, two miles inland. The Egyptian army retreated from the city during the night following the bombardment, and the rearguard, with numerous bands of Arabs, fired and plundered a large portion of the European and Levantine quarters of the city.

The bombardment of Alexandria was a strategic and tactical error of the first magnitude. It was known in London that Alexandria could not be made a base for the conquest of the Delta in August. Ismailia, on the Suez Canal, was always recognised as the true base from which to deliver a rapid blow, the object of which would be the capture of Cairo. The possession of Alexandria was no more essential to the campaign than the possession of Smyrna or the Piræus would have been. The longer the Egyptian army could have been induced to remain at Alexandria, the better it would have been for us.

By forcing Arabi Pasha to withdraw his troops behind Kafr-Dowr, we enabled him to mask Alexandria with a small force and use the bulk of his troops in the desert at Tel-el-Kebir. But space forbids that I should delay over the political and strategic aspects of the war in Egypt, and I must pass to the relation of my own personal experience in that short campaign of 1882.

It is not impossible that the English Cabinet believed, when they gave a half-reluctant consent to the bombardment of Alexandria, that the destruction of the forts would be followed by the collapse of the National movement, but, as has happened so often in our military history, the exact opposite of the expected occurred. The determination of the Egyptians to resist intervention in their internal affairs received fresh strength and purpose from the spectacle of destruction wrought by the British fleet in what was an entirely one-sided conflict, and in the month following the bombardment it became abundantly clear that if the National movement in Egypt was to be overturned, an army of invasion must be sent into the Delta.

This army was hastily got together in the latter part of July, and it left the United Kingdom in the first half of August. It had not undergone any preliminary organisation or preparatory training in brigade or division ; the regimental battalion had sufficed for all preparatory work, and the larger units of military command, together with their generals, staffs, and transport, were to be put together at the port or place of disembarkation, after the expeditionary force had landed in Egypt.

Of these generals and their staffs there was an extraordinarily large number, a number out of all proportion to the strength of the fighting men. There were, I think, some eighteen general officers to twelve thousand bayonets. On taking the three arms—infantry, cavalry, and artillery—together, there was a general to every nine hundred men. At first sight this plethora of the highest rank might seem of small account, but in reality in war it was certain to prove a serious injury. Even in a campaign of exceptional activity, the days of actual fighting must bear small relation to the days when there is no external fighting. When there is no external fighting going on, internal squabbles are apt to show themselves in camp or on the march. Staffs are also belligerently disposed on these occasions. The feathers of the domestic cock have for many years been used to distinguish general and staff officers in the British army. 'Fine feathers make fine birds' is an old saying, and why should not the plumage of the rooster, fluttering gaily in the cocked hat of generals and staff officers, have some effect upon the heads of the men who are called ' the brains of the army ' ?

I cannot delay over these domestic differences. In spite of them the flow of action, under the inspiring touch of the commander-in-chief, moved steadily forward from the base at Ismailia to the big grey, gravelly desert that lay in front of the Egyptian lines of Tel-el-Kebir. There were minor actions fought at El Magfar and Kassassin before this point had been gained on the Sweet Water Canal, which ran from the Delta to the Suez Canal at Lake Timsah, and of these minor actions, that which took place at El Magfar on 24th August was the most important. Three days earlier the advanced portion of the army began to land at Ismailia. All through the 22nd and 23rd, horse, foot, and artillery were got on shore, and an hour before daybreak on the 24th they pushed out into the desert along the Sweet Water Canal, the waters of which had been shrinking with ominous rapidity throughout the previous day and night. The canal had, in fact, been dammed at Magfar, ten miles forward in the direction of Cairo, and the railway had been broken at the same place.

Sir Garnet Wolseley, dissatisfied with the reports he received from his Intelligence Department, had determined to ride forward with a few mounted troops, in order to see for himself what was in his front. He took a few staff officers with him, of whom I was one. Two Horse Artillery guns and a couple of infantry battalions were to follow the mounted men. I have never forgotten that first morning out from Ismailia. Here, as day broke, was the desert at last, the first sight I had ever had of it. There is nothing like it in all the world—only sand, the sand of the hour-glass, but made infinite by space, just as a tumbler of sea water becomes infinite in the ocean. Sand, drifted into motionless waves, heaped in ridges, scooped into valleys, flattened, blown up into curious cones and long yellow banks, the tops of which the winds have cut into fretted patterns as it blew over them. And all so silent, so withered, and yet so fresh ; so soft, so beautiful, and yet so terrible.

The reconnaissance was to be a morning ride ten or twelve miles forward, then back ; haversack food, and water from the canal, the bank of which the left of the advancing column was to keep in touch with. This canal, which made life possible at Ismailia, Suez, and Port Said, made a sharp angle in its course not far from Ismailia. The advancing troops followed the two sides of this angle. I and another officer of the staff struck straight from Ismailia into the desert, so as to cut the angle on a shorter line than that on which the troops moved. We were some three or four miles out when the sound of cannon shot came booming over the desert from the direction of our left front. The sun was now high above the horizon, and the mirage was showing distorted water patches and inverted bushes on many sides, but it was easy to steer towards the cannon sound.

We had cleared the soft sand hillocks that surrounded Ismailia, and the surface of the desert was now good going. In twenty minutes we were in the little oasis of Abu Suez, close to the railway and canal, where the hard desert was mixed with patches of soft clay, on which mimosa scrub and weeds grew. Here we found the commander-in-chief, a squadron or two of Household Cavalry, and a company of mounted infantry. A mile or two in rear a battalion of infantry, one of Marine Artillery, and two Horse Artillery guns were coming in clouds of dust along the railway track from

Nefishi. From where we stood, the desert for three thousand yards rose gradually to Tel-el-Mahouta, where some lofty mounds of sand and broken pottery still marked what is supposed to have been the spot at which Pharaoh decreed that the Israelites should make bricks without straw. These mounds ended the forward view; they were now black with figures, while to the right and left of them a long, open line of Arab camel-men and horsemen stretched along the skyline far into the desert on either flank.

It was a very striking scene: the morning sun shone full in their faces; musket barrel and spear head flashed and glittered along the desert ridge, while behind it the heads of many more men and camels showed above the ridge, and beyond them again straight columns of black railway smoke were rising into the still, clear air of the desert, showing that the resources of civilisation had also been called into request by the Egyptian enemy, and that his infantry were being hurried up from the direction where lay Tel-el-Kebir to make head against our further advance. These smoke columns really changed the plan and purpose of the morning's work. The reconnaissance became a fixed movement. The commander-in-chief was here, and here he would stay. He had in the ground immediately around him a favourable position for fighting an advance-guard action which would give six or eight hours for bringing up reinforcements. Away went an A.D.C. back to Ismailia to hurry up the Guards Brigade and what odds and ends of the three arms had disembarked. It was now nine o'clock, and the sun was rapidly making his presence felt. Not a breath of wind stirred. Adye would take an hour and a half to reach Ismailia, the troops another hour and a half to turn out. The march through the sand in this burning sun would take three, four, or five hours; say seven hours must elapse before anything of consequence could arrive.

The opening moves on the Egyptian side were well done. A single gun placed at the Mahouta mounds opened the ball with a shell so well aimed that after it had passed a couple of feet exactly over the commander-in-chief's head, as he stood with his staff on the top of a sand hillock, it burst among the leaders of an artillery team just arrived upon the field. Half an hour later five additional Egyptian

guns are in action on this ridge, their shells falling freely
among the sand hillocks and ground folds where our nine
hundred foot soldiers are partially concealed from Egyptian
sight. The mounted men are out nearly a mile to the north
on the gravel ridges, keeping in check a flanking movement
which the Egyptian is making in that direction threatening
to overlap our right. Altogether, it makes a very interesting
little battle picture, to the scenic effect of which are added
other qualities of doubt, expectation, chance, and calculation,
the presence of which makes a battle by far the most
exciting and enthralling of all life's possibilities to its mortals.
What has Arabi got behind the desert ridge ? That is the first
point. By ten o'clock he has shown six guns on the ridge ;
their practice is now so good that between ten and ten-fifteen
o'clock he has burst eight shells on and close around the hillock
where our two Horse Artillery guns are hard at work trying to
reply to these heavy odds. At twelve o'clock six more guns
are pushed over the ridge crest on our extreme right, enfilading
our first position and partly taking it in reverse. Behind those
new guns we can see at times men moving in formed bodies to
our right. About noon A.D.C. Adye is back from Ismailia :
the Guards Brigade was to move at one o'clock. The Duke of
Cornwall's Regiment from Nefishi was a mile or two in rear ;
two Gatlings and a party of sailors from the *Orion* were at hand.
Meanwhile, the heat had become simply outrageous, the sun
stood straight overhead, the yellow sand glowed like hot coals ;
not a breath of air stirred over these hot hillocks.

It was a curious situation. What if the Egyptian puts another
ten or twelve thousand men and a couple of brisk batteries on
our flank? He has a railway to the foot of this ridge ; our railway line has been broken in two or three places between us and
Ismailia. It is all soft, hot sand for our men, who are just off
ship board. But the Egyptian would not come on ; he kept
playing at long bowls with his twelve guns, and as the afternoon
wore on his chances grew less. The Duke of Cornwall's
Regiment arrived at one o'clock. At four came some squadrons
of dragoons, and at six the Guards and four Horse Artillery
guns reached the field. Better than any or all of these came
the sunset hour, the cool breeze from the north, and a few carts
with food of some sort. Speaking for myself, the last reinforce-

ment was the most welcome. I had started from Ismailia at
5 A.M., with a cup of coffee and a biscuit in the inner man, and
a tiny tin of ' Liebig ' on the outer one, for we were to have been
back in Ismailia for breakfast These, with a slice of water-
melon, had kept me going for thirteen hours under a sun and
in an atmosphere the strength and fervour of which it would not
be easy to describe. The thing that struck me most throughout
that long day and dwelt longest in my memory was the bearing
of our chief. The enemy's guns might multiply from over the
ridge in front and to our right flank, the shells drop faster
and closer upon our ten or fifteen hundred men, the sun might
glow stronger overhead—it didn't matter ; cool and cheery,
with a kind word for every one who approached him, an eye for
everything that happened on front or flank, or amongst us, he
personified more than any man I had ever seen the best type of
the soldier

I remember a little incident that happened during that
afternoon when the Egyptians were pushing their left attack
with greater ardour, and their fire had compelled our cavalry
on the right to retire from the position they had first occupied directly on our right flank. Ordering his horse to be
brought up, the commander-in-chief mounted, and telling me
to accompany him, he rode in the direction of the cavalry, who
were then about a mile distant in the desert, where they were
drawing a good many of the enemy's shells upon them. When
we had got about half-way across the intervening space, and
the Egyptians, spotting us, had begun to favour us with some
shots, the commander-in-chief pulled up, saying, ' I cannot stand
the pain of this leg of mine any longer, the —— London boot-
maker has made the leg of my right boot so tight that when I
was dragging it on in the dark this morning the riding breeches
got so wedged and crumpled upon the calf of the leg that its
pressure has been intolerable for some time past. Can you get
it right for me ? ' We dismounted, I made him sit on the
sand, got the boot off, cut a slit in the leather, and we went on
again. I thought it strange at first that he had not required
this little service of me while we were still among the troops in
the sand hillocks, instead of waiting until we were out in the
barest part of the desert and quite visible to the enemy on two
sides ; but then it occurred to me that had this boot pulling-off

P

been performed in the midst of the men, who were by no means too happily situated under the conditions then existing, there might easily have spread the idea that the commander-in-chief was down, and that the surgeons were preparing to cut his leg off ; and so he had kept the pain to himself for hours rather than ease it under the eyes of his soldiers.

We soon reached the cavalry. The two squadrons were kept moving slowly on the desert in open column in order to distract the aim of the enemy's gun-layers. A shell had just dropped into them and killed a horse. Its rider was on his feet in a moment, calling out, ' Three cheers for the first charger in the Life Guards killed since Waterloo ! '

An hour later the first of the reinforcements arrived upon the field. The relay was specially welcome to the two Horse Artillery guns, which had fired off two hundred and thirty rounds that day. There were other targets now for the dozen Egyptian guns to fire at ; but the army of Arabi had lost its chance, one that was not likely to occur again in this short campaign.

' The Chief ' [1] returned to Ismailia at sunset. I was left to see the reinforcements in and the bivouac arranged, then I rode back along the canal under a brilliant moon. It was nine o'clock when I reached Ismailia. It had been a long day, more than sixteen hours of saddle, sun, and sand, fourteen of them on little except canal water. In six hours we were to be off again to Magfar. It was not likely that the twelve Egyptian guns which had kept firing at us until after sundown would have got far away from Magfar at daylight next morning ; there would, therefore, be every chance of getting some of them by a rapid advance of all our mounted troops at daybreak.

I got a shakedown on the office floor for a few hours ; and we were again clear of Ismailia at 3.30 A.M. on the 25th August, floundering through the deep sand in the dark. We reached the scene of yesterday's fight as day broke. The troops, now swollen to a division, had left their bivouac, and were formed up on the desert facing Mahouta, the cavalry and artillery on the right, the infantry near the canal, the whole in attack formation.

We were soon on the top of the ridge from which the Egyptian

---

[1] The name they called Sir Garnet by.—E. B.

guns had pounded us on the previous day. A long stretch of desert opened at the farther side towards Kassassin, ten miles forward.   The sun was now well up and the mists were drawing off from the desert ; several trains were moving along the railway in the valley to our left front ; clouds of dust forward showed that artillery was retiring before us   A rapid survey of the scene sufficed.   The Chief called me to him. ' Gallop to Drury Lowe,' he said ; ' tell him to take all his cavalry and Horse Artillery forward, and *coûte que coûte* capture one or more of those trains   An engine would be worth a lot of money to me now.' I galloped off without waiting for the order to be written, and soon overhauled the cavalry, which were moving along the gravelly desert in advance, under a dropping shell fire from some Egyptian guns on lower ground near the railway. I delivered my order to General Drury Lowe ; the cavalry went forward at the best pace they could ; but the horses, all just off shipboard, were already showing the severe strain of the last twenty-four hours in sand and sun.   Five hours later the railway station at Mahsamah was captured by General Lowe ; the Egyptian camp, with seven guns and large stock of ammunition and rifles, was taken ; many railway trucks with camp equipment and provision also fell into our hands, but the engines got away.

I cannot delay over the next fifteen days' work.   It was hot and hard on all ranks, for the very success which had attended these opening moves in the campaign had imposed upon men and animals exceptional difficulties.   Twenty miles of the canal were in our possession up to the lock at Kassassin, its weakest spot, but it required no small strain upon troops and transport to keep the force necessary to hold that important point supplied with food and forage over these twenty miles of shifting sands, when the canal was dammed and the railway interrupted.   When these obstacles and interruptions had been surmounted, and two or three engines were at length running on the railway, the concentration of troops was swiftly accomplished, and on the evening of 12th September the Army Corps was in position at Kassassin, six miles distant from the Egyptian lines at Tel-el-Kebir.

One had been kept so busy during these preparatory days that there was little time to give to matters of policy or politics outside the actual labour.   It was only on an occasional evening that one could get away for a ride in the twilight over the sand hills outside Ismailia. It was a strange sight to see on those occasions more than one hundred large ocean-going steamers' lying packed together within the compass of Lake Timsah, their lights at night being visible over the desert for long distances. It often occurred to me to wonder why no attempt was made by the Egyptians to move a light column with a few guns from Salahiyeh, only eighteen miles distant to the north-west, over a good hard desert, and fire twenty or thirty shells among those steamers packed like herrings in a barrel. There was a Pasha with some eighteen thousand men and ten or twenty guns lying at the end of the railway at Salahiyeh. What was that Pasha about all this time ? One evening in the first week of September I happened to be out along the Sweet Water Canal at the north end of Ismailia. At a point where the desert approached the canal a small group of Arabs and camels were squatting on the ground under the trees ; there was no mistake about these men and their animals— children of the desert, all of them. The sheik was a tall and handsome man of the Howawak tribe. Presently a few men of rank in tarbooshes came along in the twilight and passed out into the desert mounted on those camels. The centre of that little group of Egyptian officials was Sultan Pasha. They disappeared in the direction of Salahiyeh. I need not have troubled my head about the general, the eighteen thousand men, and the ten or twenty guns at that place, nor did I after that night. We will go on to Tel-el-Kebir.

The night of 12th September fell dark upon the desert ; there was no moon. Stars were bright overhead, but when one looked along the desert surface all things were wrapped in a deep grey gloom impossible for the eye to pierce. All through the afternoon the staff had been busy writing copies of the orders of the commander-in-chief, and striking off small plans showing roughly the formation in which the troops were to move from the positions they were to occupy in the desert lying north-west of the lock at Kassassin and about one and a half miles distant from it. Things went on as usual in the camp during the day and evening, but when darkness had fully closed in the troops moved out from their camps into the desert, leaving their fires burning. The *point d'appui* was a mound known as the

'Ninth Hill' on the level, gravelly ridges north of the canal and railway. At this spot a line of Engineer telegraph posts had been erected, running due west for a thousand yards. This line was designed to give a marching point for the directing column to move along when it first started. When the end of that line of posts was reached, the direction would be by the stars alone. The formation adopted for the movement of the Army Corps across the six miles of open desert extending from Ninth Hill to the lines of Tel-el-Kebir was at once simple and yet closely calculated—simple, in order to meet the conditions imposed by a moonless night ; thoroughly thought out, because the formation in which the Army Corps started must be that in which it would engage the enemy when he was found, as it was hoped. There could be no manœuvring, no afterthought, no rectification after these seventeen thousand five hundred officers and men with their sixty or seventy guns had been launched out into the night from the plateau of Ninth Hill, a gigantic bolt of flesh, steel, and iron shot westward into the darkness.

The march and the attack were made in two lines. The first line, of eight infantry battalions, moved in two distinct bodies, separated from each other by an interval of twelve hundred yards. Both of these bodies marched in lines of half-battalion columns. The second line, moving a thousand yards behind the first, was in a similar formation to the first line, but continuity between its brigades was maintained by a line of forty-two field guns, which filled the twelve hundred yards from the right of one brigade to the left of the other. On the extreme right of this infantry and artillery formation marched General Drury Lowe's Cavalry Division, with two batteries of Horse Artillery—twelve guns , while on the extreme left, and in the lower ground of the canal and railway, moved the Naval Brigade and the Indian Division. The entire front of the formation measured from north to south seventy-four hundred yards; its depth from east to west was about two thousand yards. From the desert at Ninth Hill to the lines of Tel-el-Kebir was all but four miles in a direct line. The surface undulated slightly, but maintained a general uniform level of from a hundred and ten feet to a hundred and thirty feet above the sea. It was throughout hard enough to make movement easy, and yet sufficiently soft to make it almost noiseless. We were all in position by eleven o'clock, lying in the desert near Ninth Hill as silent as the stars that seemed the only living things in view.

About half-past one the march began due west. We went slowly forward for less than an hour, then halted and lay down. It was a sort of trial mile to test the working of the scheme, the steering of the great mass, and its discipline. All had worked smoothly, there was no noise, no confusion, everything had gone mysteriously well, as a clock works as regularly in the night as in the daylight.

During this halt I was lying on the sand near the commander-in-chief (he had told me to ride beside him that night) ; the staff were scattered on the desert close by. I held the reins of my horse twisted round my arm, for the drowsy hours had come. We had been at work all day, and it was easy to drop off to sleep on this cool, dusky sand bed. I had a second charger, ridden by a groom, following in rear. I had told the man to keep a tight hold of this horse at any halt on the march, for the animal had a nasty temper, and a way of his own on all occasions. I tried all I could to keep awake during the halt, but could not succeed ; the blinking stars above, the vast, dusky desert around, which already seemed as though it had swallowed our host, the deep silence that prevailed, all tended to produce a state of semi-consciousness or partial oblivion. All at once I felt something moving close to me. I was wide awake instantly. Two horses were there beside me, the one fastened to my arm, the other standing beside him, saddled, and with the reins trailing on the ground. It was my second horse. The servant who was in charge of him, sleeping a hundred yards behind, had let my horse go, and the animal, more intelligent than the man, had picked his way through sleeping men and horses until he got to his old stable companion, with whom he stood quietly—all his temper tamed, and his rough manners softened by the strange desert night-world in which he found himself. About three o'clock we began to move forward again. (My groom had come up to seek me in consternation.) The night was now darker than ever ; the stars by which we had heretofore moved had gone below the western desert, but the Pole-star was always there. By it we were able to find new

lights on which to steer west. For more than an hour now
the march went on in absolute silence, except for one strange
occurrence. Suddenly to our right front a peal of wild and
hilarious laughter rang out in this deep stillness. It ceased
almost as abruptly as it had arisen. One expected that some
alarm might have followed this weird, unwonted outburst, but
the void was all still again. It afterwards transpired that a man
in one of the Highland regiments of the leading brigade of the
Second Division had carried a bottle of very strong rum with
him, and his repeated application to this source for sustain-
ment during the march had ended in a hysterical paroxysm.
Fortunately, we were at the time more than a mile away from
the enemy's position.

During the next hour the strain of things grew. I rode on
the left of the commander-in-chief. He had given the leading
of the staff group to me. As one by one some guide-star
dropped into the mists that lay deep upon the horizon, another
star higher in the heavens had to be taken for direction, and
that at times became obscured or dimmed by some passing
cloud, but at no time was the Pole-star, over my right shoulder,
and the star in front, upon which I had laid my horse's ears,
hidden at the same moment. Sir Garnet Wolseley had in his
possession a very fine repeater watch given to him by the late
Lord Airey. By striking this watch he knew the exact moment
of the night, and as the minutes between four and five o'clock
began to strike longer numbers, they seemed to draw into
tighter twist all the strands of our expectations. And yet, as
I can see it now, what did it matter to this old desert and to
these older stars ? '_Our_ guides,' we thought them. Ours !
Had not Moses led his Israelites here three thousand years ago ?
Had not Napoleon marched the best soldiers known to the world
over these sands and under the same stars ? Countless Pharaohs
had driven their chariots across these brown ridges ; and one
day did there not come along this route into Egypt a man
leading an ass on which a woman rode, bearing in her arms a
Babe, who was to be a wider conqueror than they all ? What
did our little night-march matter in that catalogue or context ?
Perhaps the poor hysterical Scottish soldier, whose weird laugh
broke so rudely upon the desert silence an hour before, knew as
much about it as the best of us !

It was about half-past four when the commander-in-chief told me to ride in the direction of Sir Archibald Alison's Highland Brigade and tell him to move forward as rapidly as possible, as the entrenchments must now be close before us, and the daylight could not be far off behind us. I took ground towards the right front, and soon struck full upon the Highland Brigade. It was a moment of very considerable danger and confusion to that body of men. An order to halt for a few moments had been given by the brigadier a little while earlier. This order passing from the centre to the flanks did not reach the outer companies for some moments; thus, when the centre companies halted, the outer ones still continued moving, though keeping the touch, as it was called, inwards. The result was that the flank battalions wheeled inwards and lay down in a kind of half-circle. When the word to advance was again given in a low voice, they moved to their respective fronts and came nearly face to face with each other. A terrible catastrophe might easily have happened in the case of raw and inexperienced troops ; but discipline was good, and the brigade was reformed in line by the efforts of the brigadier and his officers. I stayed with Sir A. Alison until everything was straight, gave him the message to push on with all possible despatch, and then turned to find my chief. I had counted my horse's steps in coming to the Highland Brigade, and calculating that the commander-in-chief would have continued to move to his former front, I steered a course south-west, as I had before come north-west. Captain Maurice had accompanied me to the Highland Brigade. When we got to a spot which I reckoned to be in the track of the commander-in-chief's route I pulled up, and dismounted in order to see better towards the east. Presently a few heads appeared against the horizon. We were straight on the staff track.

I reported what had happened, but that the brigade was now in full march forward. There could be little doubt that we were now not far from the enemy's works, but, so far as sight and sound went, they might as well have been a hundred miles away. At no time during this dark night had the stillness of the desert space been more profound or the darkness deeper. This desert seemed still to have kept embalmed in its sands one of the old plagues of Egypt.

The commander-in-chief decided to dismount at this spot and await developments. In the next twenty minutes I could hear the repeater repeating its minutes frequently, ' Four, forty, forty-five, fifty ' ; all was still dead silence. Looking eastward, I thought that the dawn was already showing in the horizon, but it was a dawn such as I had never noticed in the eastern heavens before. A large shaft of pale light, shaped like a sheaf of corn, and of the colour of pale gold, was visible, shot straight up from the horizon some twenty degrees into the heavens. It appeared to be rising from where the sun would be, due east. I called the attention of the commander-in-chief to this strange foreglow of the coming day, and he too believed it to be the approaching dawn. It was in reality the Great Comet of 1882, which had not been visible before, as the comet was actually going round the sun at that time, and was lost in the sun's rays   It had got round now, and its long tail, whisked before it, had become suddenly visible to the naked eye, while the head was still lost in the solar rays.

We mounted and rode on. We had only proceeded a short distance when the all-pervading silence was broken by a single shot to our right front ; then came two or three more shots, and then a thunderous roll of musketry, mixed with heavy gun fire, swelling from our right front far along the western desert on either side. When this great volume of fire first broke out all was still dark ; five minutes later, in that short dawn, the eye was able to distinguish objects on the desert within a quarter of a mile ; in ten minutes the landscape and the line were all revealed to us. To our left front a large earthwork was sending shells on three sides. We were at first too close to it for damage , but it soon found our range—about a thousand yards—and shells began to fall about us. This earthwork, the largest of any in the enemy's defences, was an isolated redoubt standing at least a thousand yards in front of the main line of entrenchments. The record of the night-march, with particular reference to this isolated and advanced sentinel battery, is a very curious one. Had the march of the Highland Brigade of the Eleventh Division been made along a due east and west line from Ninth Hill, some portion of the left of the brigade must undoubtedly have struck the work. I am not sure that the centre of the line would not have come full against it. It would be impossible to say what the ultimate effect upon the fortunes of the day would have been, but it is safe to say that the loss to the assailants must have been out of all proportion larger than it actually was. I shall not here discuss this question, but press on to the end.

As daylight broadened things took better shape. We could see that the large work immediately on our left front stood at a considerable distance in advance of the main line of works : from this main line a body of cavalry was coming out in rear of the advanced redoubt. Our big group of staff had been ordered to scatter at this time, so as not to draw too concentrated a fire from this redoubt. The commander-in-chief still kept me by him. I called his attention to the movement of the enemy's cavalry. ' Order the squadron of the 19th Hussars to meet them,' he said. It was not in sight. I galloped back to meet it, and they went forward at a canter in column of troops, passing within three hundred yards of the eight-gun redoubt, and offering a splendid target to it. The redoubt fired four or five shots as the squadron passed it, but neither man nor horse was hit. When I rejoined the commander-in-chief the firing of musketry and artillery was in full swing, but the flashes from the big guns were dying out in the increasing daylight. We galloped to the right front, and soon struck the main line of works. The desert was here dotted over with wounded men, chiefly of the Highland Light Infantry ; the old colonel of the Duke of Cornwall's was down with a bullet through his jaws. Farther to our right, our line of forty-two guns had broken into columns, and the leading batteries had already entered the enemy's line. Galloping through the gaps they had made in the parapet, we were soon inside the works. The detached fort had continued to follow our course with shells ; it was now the only unsilenced redoubt in the enemy's line. Inside the works, the desert was strewn with dead Egyptians, dead horses and camels. The sun was now well above the horizon. To the right one could see the First Division moving quickly in regular formation across the desert. Portions of the Second Division were still in our front, descending the slopes towards the railway station of Tel-el-Kebir, and to our left, where the desert sloped to the railway and canal, the wrecks of Arabi's late army were strewn in all directions   Down the slopes, through the camps, over the railway, and across the canal, the white-clad fugitives were flying south and west in dots, in dozens, in hundreds. Desultory firing was going on everywhere, but actual fighting had ceased thirty-five minutes after the first gun was fired.

It was about 6.20 A M when we reached the canal bridge at Tel-el-Kebir. Beyond the canal lay the Wady Tumilat, a narrow sheet of green lying between two glaring deserts. Two or three hundred Highlanders, a squadron of cavalry, and some odds and ends of mounted corps had just arrived. The first thing to be done was to stop the shooting which was going on at everything and often at nothing   The seamy side of a battle was here painfully apparent ; anything seemed to be good enough to let off a rifle at. Dead and wounded men, horses, and camels were on all sides. Some of the wounded had got down to the edge of the water to quench their thirst ; others were on the higher banks, unable to get down. Many of our officers dismounted and carried water to these unfortunates, but the men were not all similarly disposed. I heard an officer ask a man who was filling his canteen at the canal to give a drink of water to a gasping Egyptian cavalry soldier who was lying supporting himself against the battlement of the bridge. ' I wadna wet his lips,' was the indignant reply. Close by, in the midst of her dead and dying fellow-countrymen, a woman attached to the Egyptian camp was washing her infant at the canal, concentrating her attention on the child as though to steady her thoughts , and many of the wounded Egyptians had managed, as they lay, to cover their heads with pieces of paper to try and keep off the flies and the scorching sun.

When the orders for the movement of the cavalry and Indian Division to Cairo and Zagazig were issued by the commander-in-chief on the bridge at Tel-el-Kebir, and these two bodies had started on their respective roads, I took up my quarters at the lock-keeper's hut on the south side of the bridge, had something to eat, and then started on a fresh horse to go back over the battlefield.

The saying that ' dead men tell no tales ' has the lie given to it on every battlefield , this one was no exception. I directed my course to the part of the field and the entrenchments across which the Second Division had come. Vast numbers of Egyptian dead cumbered the ground from immediately behind the parapet where the Highland Brigade entered to quite a mile within the works in the direction of the bridge. This portion of the position had an inner double line of works extending obliquely along it, facing north, and it was among these lines and gun emplacements that the dead lay thickest. They were often in groups of fifteen and twenty, heaped together within the angles of small works into which they appeared to have crowded ; the main line of entrenchments had also great numbers of dead behind it. The ground showed everywhere the complete nature of the surprise which had overtaken the enemy. Arms, accoutrements, uniforms, the cotton clothes of the fellaheen, boxes of cartridges and food —a general debris of everything lay exposed upon the desert. Of wounded there were very few to be seen ; too many successive waves of armed men had crossed this portion of the field. The sun was now a flaming fireball overhead. I had been at work for fully twenty consecutive hours. When I returned to the lock-keeper's hut at the bridge, things had not improved in the Wady Tumilat. Several men had managed to get across the canal, and the people in the hamlets had been robbed and ill-treated by these blackguards. This is part of the performance of the lower sort of the soldier-mind : to them war means plunder. It has always done so, and it will always do so. Indeed, it may be truly said that the instinct of plunder in some shape or form is the strongest passion among men. That it comes out in war is only justifying the old proverb that the ruling passion grows strong in death ; death had been very plentifully exhibited that morning over these three miles of desert from the Egyptian lines to the bridge at Tel-el-Kebir.

In this respect I do not imagine that the instincts of man have changed much since Moses marched this way three or four thousand years ago. If anybody should be disposed to doubt this opinion, I would ask him to read the *Life of Sir Neville Chamberlain* at pages 143-150 of that remarkable work. Sir Neville Chamberlain knew the realities of war as few men knew them in our time, and when he raised his voice in a vain protest against the whole horde of financial civilian-warriors who were howling to let loose hell upon the women and children of the Dutch republics some ten years ago, he knew what he was speaking about.

Somebody said of the Egyptian War of 1882 that it was 'the Counter-march of Moses.' Since that time poor Moses has had rather a surfeit of wars, and perhaps to-day he is not so ready to embark upon them in a general 'damn the consequences' sort of spirit.

There is one thing which I should like to put on record regarding this battle of Tel-el-Kebir. Complete surprise though it was to the Egyptian soldiers behind their entrenchments, they nevertheless fought with the greatest determination against overwhelming odds. Not a moment was given them to awake, form up, prepare, or move into position. The assault fell upon them as a thunderbolt might fall upon a man asleep. The leaders in whom they could trust were, like themselves, fellaheen ; few among them knew anything of war, its arts, manœuvres, or necessities ; they were betrayed on every side, yet they fought stoutly wherever ten or twenty or fifty of them could get together in the works, in the angles of the lines, and in the open desert between the lines. The heaps of dead lying with and across their rifles facing the up-coming sun bore eloquent testimony to that final resolve of these poor fellows. Peace be to them, lying under these big mounds on the lone desert—ten thousand, it is said. No word should soldier utter against them ; let that be left to the money-changers. They died the good death. Dust to dust. They did not desert the desert, and Egypt will not forget them.

CHAPTER XV

ALL resistance in Egypt ceased at Tel-el-Kebir on 13th September. Cairo was surrendered on the 14th to a small force of cavalry, and on the 15th Sir Garnet Wolseley, His Royal Highness the Duke of Connaught, the staff, and a battalion of the Guards reached the capital at 10 A.M. Redvers Buller and a sapper private drove the engine of the train that carried us to Benha. The scene in the streets near the railway station was a curious one. Several Pashas and officials were on the platform, and we waited some time at the station for some formality or other. Buller said to me, ' Let 's get a cab and drive to the Abdin Palace, where we are to live : I am very hungry.' We did so, and in a quarter of an hour we were at the palace. There was only an old Nubian ' bowab' in the place. Not many Arabs were to be seen in the streets, and most of them took little notice of us, though some scowled, and the irrepressible Arab boy hissed vigorously at us as we passed. The Abdin Palace looked the most enchanting place of rest and coolness I had ever seen. What a change to those lofty halls and broad staircases, cool corridors, gilded ceilings, and crystal chandeliers from the blinding heat, the foul dust, and the innumerable flies of the desert ! But all such things without food are of little use to hungry men, so we got into our cab again and told the driver to go to an hotel. The first two or three we tried were barred and bolted, and silent as the grave. At last we struck one in which there was a ' bowab,' and after a good deal of talk between him and the interpreter he consented to open the door. Yes, there was food in the house, he said, and he would cook some breakfast for us. In half an hour he had an excellent omelette and a bit of meat served up, and he confided to the interpreter that he knew where the key of the cellar was, though that door was also sealed. Most excellent Nubian! Down we went to the cellar, took one bottle of claret from an old dusty, cobwebby bin, resealed and locked the door, put up a paper over the lock saying what had been done, and, having duly signed it, sat down to breakfast We were in a hurry, as there was plenty of work to be done at the palace, so we ate our food and drank our wine without delay, and went out again to the cab. So far, all had gone well in the cool house, but once in the sun things went very differently. My head had begun to swim ; the carriage seemed to be always turning a very sharp corner ; my companion was looking at me with a strange look on his face. 'Old chap,' he said, ' I think we had better take a turn through the city before we go back to the palace.' I quite agreed. At that moment I would not have met the commander-in-chief for a good deal. We drove about the half-deserted streets for half an hour, and the effects of this wonderful old heady wine, suddenly swallowed, went off almost as quickly as they had come.

Cairo was at this time a wonderful place. It can never be again as it then was. Moses in Levantine form had not yet come back. What pictures they were, those streets of old Cairo! It was my duty to hunt out all the tents I could find in the storehouses of the citadel for the use of our troops, as all the camp equipage was still at Kassassin. Arabi's late officials, although they were all coffee, cigarette, and obsequious courtesy, were in no hurry to show me the extent of their stores and camp equipage, but I kept at them for two days, until I had dug out sufficient for our immediate wants. The filth and vermin in the permanent barracks everywhere made it perfectly impossible to put European troops into them. At this work I managed to see a great deal of the outer side of Cairene life, and to get several glimpses into the inner scenes too. I had to take over, with Herbert Stewart, the old palace at Abbassiyeh, and as the harem of the late Pasha of the blood was still located in that building, the work was a protracted one ; for the ladies had to be removed from room to room before we were allowed to enter the apartments, and thus we were playing a sort of hide-and-seek with them through the palace.

In a short time our men were comfortably provided for, chiefly in tents on Gezireh Island, and then we had time to do a little sightseeing in Cairo and its vicinity. Wonderful sights some of them were. I got up one morning very early in order to see the comet, which had now become visible at that early hour. From the roof of the Abdin Palace one could see the whole city and the land from Mokattim to the Pyramids. Before day came, the Great Comet stood above where the sun would rise. It resembled a vast wheat-sheaf of light, or a flaming broom sent to sweep the stars out from the threshold of the sun. The city slept in the shadows. Then, one by one, from a hundred minarets rose the cry of the muezzin—the weirdest wail of man to God that can be heard over the world. Then as the light grew stronger the old domes of forgotten sultans and Mameluke chiefs could be distinguished rising above the city buildings to the east and south, and looking westward across the palm groves that fringed the great river one saw the Pyramids changing from grey to rose-pink in the growing light—vast and clear-carved as though they had been finished yesterday, and had not saluted the sunrise over Mokattim for twice three thousand years. 'If you make the canal from Suez to the Mediterranean you will bring the English into Egypt,' said Mehemet Ali in his old age, as he sat in the window of his little palace in the citadel looking out upon that wondrous scene below. Well, they made the Suez Canal, and the English came into Egypt by it, and their bugles were now sounding réveillé from camp and quarters in the city ; nevertheless, somehow these giant sentinels standing erect in the desert, who began their watch six thousand years ago, seemed as they reddened in the sunrise to be even smiling at the thought that this new invader of the Nile Valley was to be the last they were to look at.

Nothing in the world has lasted as Egypt has lasted. They will tell you that the tombs and temples of the Nile have defied the tooth of time because of the air, the sand, and the sun of Egypt ; but far more wonderful has been the lasting of the Egyptian people amid the mud, the yellow water, and the lentil gardens of the land. A thousand invaders have swept this Delta. Egypt has rubbed them all out one after the other. What was the secret ? A Turkish officer gave me the only clue to it I ever got. ' When a man of my regiment,' he said, ' comes and asks me to be allowed to marry, I ask him, " Whom

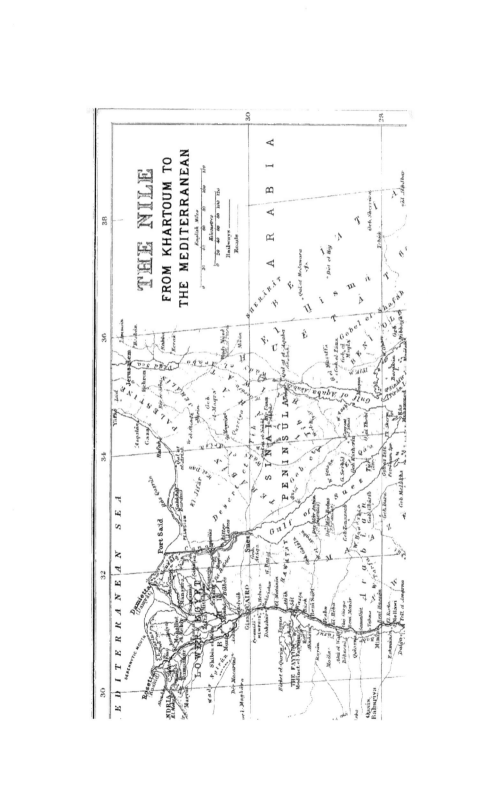

do you want to marry ? " and he generally replies, " I want
to marry a Nubian or a negro " ; and when I ask the reason,
he says, " Because then my children will be Turks ; whereas,
if I marry an Egyptian girl, the children will be Egyptians." '

You look in vain in Egypt to-day for any distinctive feature
or figure of Turk, Circassian, Mameluke, or Greek , all are
Egyptian, and, strangest part of it all, are Egyptian in the
face and form of the type which you find graven on tombs and
temples that were built many thousand years ago   How has
this result been arrived at ?   I think it can only be explained
by the simplicity and the uniformity of the elements out of
which the bodies of the children of Egypt have been built—
Nile mud and Nile water, fashioned and fertilised into Nile
food, through the agency of the Nile sun.

On the 18th September it was thought necessary to move
Arabi Pasha from Abbassiyeh to the Abdin   The most
truculent among the old Circassian and Syrian officers in the
service of the Khedive soon after this entered Cairo, and their
enmity to Arabi was so bitter that his life was in danger at
their hands.   A very base and cowardly attack and outrage
was made upon him one night in his prison.   There were
circumstances connected with the secret history of the constitutional party in relation to the ex-Khedive Ismail and
the present one, Tewfik, which made the assassination of Arabi
Pasha quite a possible contingency.   ' Dead men tell no tales '
—nor would even a dead ' Pasha of three tails.'   The next
plan was to get Arabi tried by a court-martial composed of
Circassian and other officers of this class, and sentenced to
death as an Egyptian in rebellion against his country and its
ruler.   There was a very real danger that this course might be
followed.   The bondholder would not be strenuously opposed
to it, and his representatives, who were then in the ascendant
in Cairo, made no pretence that this course would not have
been thoroughly in keeping with their wishes.   A number of our
own officers were also in favour of it, but there were others
who thought otherwise   I remember being at the Abdin when
Arabi was removed thither from Abbassiyeh.   A large group
of officers had gathered in the verandah of the building to see
Arabi arrive.   He was brought under escort in a carriage.
He alighted, and began to ascend the steps as one tired and

Q

weary. When he saw the group of officers he pulled himself together, drew himself up, and saluted us with dignity. I noticed that only one officer besides myself returned the prisoner's salute ; that one was General Drury Lowe. I was in good company.

A week later Khedive Tewfik was brought into Cairo under the protection of our troops, and for several days after his arrival the fate of Arabi hung in the balance.

It is now made pretty clear, by the publication of papers and private correspondence of that day, not only that the putting to death of Arabi under the shelter of Khedivial authority was an idea perfectly agreeable to persons in very high ministerial positions in England, but that its frustration was largely due to the devoted efforts made by Mr. Blunt and a few other friends of justice at the time in London.

Of course, I could know nothing of all this in Cairo. I was immersed at the time in the details of my official work with the troops. Sickness of a grave character had broken out among the army, and changes of camp sites, hospital arrangements, etc., occupied all my time. But in the evening at our mess I heard the fate of Arabi frequently discussed, and it was easy to see that the tide of opinion was flowing strongly against the prisoner.

It was announced one evening that the chief of the staff, Sir John Adye, would leave for England next morning to resume his duties at the War Office. A thought struck me. I had known Sir John many years ; I knew him to be a straight and honourable soldier, and a personal friend of Mr. Gladstone. It had become quite clear to me by this time that the larger part of the information which had been transmitted to England from Egypt during the past six months bearing upon this National movement had been either grossly exaggerated or was absolutely false and misleading. Many of the men who were engaged in transmitting this information were profound haters of the ministry then in power, and particularly of their chief, Mr. Gladstone, and to some of them the idea of making that statesman an accessory before the fact to the judicial assassination of Arabi was possessed of a sort of subtle and refined satisfaction. It is curious to mark now in the pages of Mr. Blunt's extraordinary book the accuracy with which,

in my own small sphere, I had gauged the situation. When I
got to my room in the Abdın Palace that night I sat down and
wrote a letter to Sır John Adye, which I intended to hand to
him next morning at the Cairo railway station when he was
starting for England. I began —

'Nothing but a very strong belief in the necessity of doing what I
can to avert what I believe would be a national crıme makes me
now write to you upon a subject far removed from the sphere of
military duty which has hitherto given me a claim as an officer of
your staff to communicate with you. I write to urge you to telegraph from Alexandrıa to England to stop the execution of Arabi
Pasha (should the Court which ıs sıttıng, or about to sıt, condemn
him to death) until you have arrıved ın England and are ın a position
to place before the Government a full vıew of the Egyptıan questıon
as it will then have taken ıts place ın your mind, ın just and true
proportıon

'You may ask why I, holding a subordinate position on the staff
of this expedıtion, should thus take up a question removed from the
class of work I have hitherto done in this campaign. I would, ın
the first place, poınt out that lenıency toward men who have been
in rebellıon has seldom been thrown away ın history : the wounds
inflıcted ın war, no matter how deep they may be, soon heal compared
to those which are left ın the memory of a people by the work of the
scaffold.'

Then I instanced the great war of the South against the
North in America, where, after four years of tremendous
fighting, only one life had been taken on the scaffold, and that
one the lıfe of a man who had starved to death and cruelly
maltreated thousands of Northern soldiers.

'If we go further back in history, can any one say that the
execution of Ney and Labédoyère made the Bourbon throne more
secure, or gave the Settlement of Vıenna a longer lease of existence ? Dıd St. Helena ensure the continuance of the restored
dynasty ? Had there been no St. Helena, there might have been
no Second Empıre. But let us look at this matter from another
poınt of view. In what light will history regard the execution of
Arabi ? It will be written that we, a great and powerful Empire,
vanquished this man and then surrendered our prisoner to the
vengeance of weak, and therefore cruel, rulers. The voice of the
civilised world will be against us. Legal téchnicalities and petty
quibbles will be forgotten, and history will record a strong verdıct

of condemnation against us. It is the same all along the line. It will be useless to say the act was not ours, we cannot get rid of our responsibility that way : the world will not accept the transfer.

'There is another point and I have done. It is perhaps a selfish point. Will the execution, as a traitor, of the man against whom all our immense preparations have recently been made—the seas covered with our ships, the desert with our men—will the execution of the object of all this preparation, effort, power, as a felon, redound to our own proper pride, or to " the pomp and circumstance " of our profession ? It strikes me that in condemning Arabi to the scaffold we cut down the measure of our own achievement to a very low point. Another thing I can foresee. If Arabi's execution should be carried out, many of the men who are now foremost in calling for it will be the first to turn round and fling the stone of reproach at the English statesman whom they hate with far greater intensity of feeling than that which they bear to their Egyptian prisoner, and they will not fail to pursue Mr. Gladstone to his grave with the cry of blood-guiltiness.

'I must apologise for the length to which this letter has run. I can only excuse it by pleading the never-failing kindness and courtesy I have received from you whenever my duties as your staff officer brought me into contact with you.'

I have taken this letter from a rough draft in an old pocket-book in which I find it most indifferently pencilled. I sat up all night writing and copying it out, and when all was finished it was time to go to the railway station to see the old chief of the staff off on his journey.

I handed the letter to him on the platform. I thought there was a look in his eye as I gave him the document as though he imagined it was some matter of personal promotion or reward about which I was troubling him, and I just said, 'Not about myself, sir.' I never heard again what happened, but the trend of events soon satisfied me that the executioners were not to have it all their own quick way at once. At the time my letter was written (at the end of September), the execution of Arabi by order of the Khedivial court-martial had been virtually settled, as we now know. On 27th September it was announced that the court was to be named *instanter*. The correspondent of the *Times* in Egypt reported that ' the Khedive, Sherif and Riaz Pashas all insist strongly on the absolute necessity of the capital punishment of the prime offenders, an opinion from which there are few, if any, dissentients.' That this court would then have been a packed tribunal of the very worst description was just as certain as that the sun would rise on the Mokattim side of Cairo the next morning. All the passions were now in entire possession of the Egyptian vantage points : the Levantine jackal, the Khedivial eunuch, the bloodthirsty Circassian, the Greek money-lender, the many representatives of Dame Quickly's old and highly endowed profession—these were now flocking into Egypt in thousands. With them were coming the former advisers of the English Foreign Office, whose persistently erroneous counsels had, as we now know, produced the crisis which had just been closed by the slaughter at Tel-el-Kebir. Behind these various persons and professions this unfortunate fellah, Arabi, had ranged against him the entire tribe of the Levites and High Priests of Finance, foreign and Egyptian, from the heads of the great Jewish banking-houses in Europe to the humble ' schroff ' money-changers at the street corners of Alexandria.

With all these powerful interests, schemes, monopolies, policies, and professions in league against his life, the chances of the late leader of the National party might well seem hopeless ; and so they would have been had not breathing time been given. Whatever may have been Mr. Gladstone's earlier prepossessions against Arabi and the National party, his better angel prevailed, and it was decreed that a full and open trial should be accorded him. That was sufficient to ensure his ultimate safety. Neither Turk, Jew, Infidel, nor imaginary Christian could face the publication in court of the secret papers of which Arabi's counsel were now in possession. These papers, cleverly hidden from the Khedive's police by the wife of the prisoner, saved the situation. Arabi owed his life, under Providence, to the splendid pluck and generous purse of Mr. Wilfrid Blunt ; and, looking back upon it all to-day, I am not sure that the memory of Mr. Gladstone is not still more deeply indebted to the same gentleman.

Many days of that time live in my memory, but one has particular place in it The commander-in-chief gave a huge picnic at the Pyramids of Sakkara, the site of ancient Memphis. We went by steamer to Beddreshin on the top of the Nile flood. More than one hundred Arab donkeys were collected under the palms on the west shore. These were quickly mounted, and away we went for Sakkara. Nearly all the higher officers of the expedition were there—Sir Garnet Wolseley, the Duke of Connaught, Generals Willis, Graham, Alison, and some ninety others of various degrees and qualities, several civilians being among them. To most of the party the Egyptian donkey was still a strange riding animal. If you tried to ride as in an English saddle, discomfort was inevitable ; the stirrups were not fixed, and if you leaned more to one side than the other the sliding stirrup leather went in the same direction, and a fall in the sand was the result. If you sat well back, almost over the donkey's tail, and threw your legs well out in front, you soon found a balance which seemed to fit into the animal's short gallop. Prominent among our uniformed party rode Colonel Valentine Baker Pasha, who, for some reason known only to himself, had come to the picnic in a fashionable London frock-coat, a tall black silk hat, and the rest of his costume in due keeping. All went calmly and quietly on the outward journey. We saw all the wonderful sights ; the house of Tei, that mar-vellous interior wherein all the industries, the duties, the domestic life, and the amusements of the oldest civilisation in the world are graven and coloured in characters as clear and vivid as though they had been done yesterday. Then we dived down through the sand of the desert into that vast rock warren of the Serapeum, which the genius of the great French Egyptologist first revealed to our modern world. The wonder of it all was endless as one looked at these vast sarcophagi of polished syenite. How did these old people get all the seventy solid single-stoned tons of granite or porphyry into huge side niches which open from the vast rock gallery under the desert ? Greater even than the wonder was the prodigious foolishness of the whole thing. All for dead bulls ! Stifled with the heat, the candle smoke, and the smell of bats of this subterranean bull warren, we got up at last into the desert air, and were soon at work upon the scores of good things which Cook had provided for our refreshment by order of the commander-in-chief. More tombs, more pyramids, more stone carvings, more hieroglyphics, more sarcophagi, and at last we were off again on donkey-back for the Nile. Then the fun began. The donkey boys prodded the animals behind, some of the younger guests raced their donkeys at full speed in front, the burly figure of Baker Pasha seemed to become the central point in the human stream that poured over the desert sand, and then along the top of a great embankment built to retain the waters of the inundation. What with the heat of the sun and the stifling atmosphere of the many sepulchral chambers and galleries visited, all our clothing had become bedraggled and saturated ; but if this was the case with khaki and dust-coloured homespun, how fared it with the black frock-coat, tall silk hat, and fashionable nether gear of our Piccadilly-clad Pasha ? Words could not paint that picture . the silk hat was bent and broken by frequent contact with the roof of rock cavern and tomb chamber ; the frock-coat looked as though several policemen had been tussling with its owner ; the legs of the fashionably cut trousers had worked up under the exigencies of the donkey saddle until the ankles were where the knees ought to have been. There was no stopping :—

> ' With hark and whoop and wild halloo
> No rest *Ben Ram'se's* echoes knew.'

And thus we reached the steamer at Beddreshin satiated with sarcophagi, and with a thirst for tea such as only the dust of six thousand years of mummy powder could give us.

I left Egypt at the end of October with feelings of keen regret. There was nothing to make one imagine at that moment that events would soon arise in the valley of the Nile which would call one back to that region. The Egyptian chapter seemed closed, and I was sorry to quit a land in which the ends of time seemed to be always touching each other ; the oldest relics of man's pride and power lying prone in the dust, the latest efforts of his endless husbandry blooming fresh and fair over all the garden of the Delta More interesting to me than the tomb or temple of the dead past in the desert was the endless picture of the life of the fellah in the soft green level of his homeland ; his fields of grain in their many stages between seed and stubble, his plots of onions, sweet-smelling beans, deep green clover, cotton, and flowering flax ; the brown canal banks, where the cattle, goats, donkeys, and camels stood in the shade of the acacia-trees in the hot hours, munching the stalk of sugar-canes, or nibbling the golden ' tibbin ' ; the big blue buffaloes, with their horns and noses just showing above the yellow water ; and the date palms rustling in the cool north wind round some old marabout's tomb, whose little dome shows very white over the green fields ; and under the glorious sunshine the great flocks of white pigeons skimming over villages, the strange 'paddy' birds standing in the inundated fields ; above all, man, woman, and child at work everywhere, sowing, reaping, weeding, working the water wheel in winter, and in summer, when the Nile is pouring down its flooded waters, opening the little watercourses from one field to another with their feet to let the saving flood flow on its way.

To-day it is the same as it was in that far-off time of the Exodus, when Moses told his people that ' The land whither thou goest in to possess it, is not as the land of Egypt from whence ye came out, where thou sowedst the seed, and wateredst it with thy foot as a garden of herbs ; But the land whither ye go to possess it is a land of hills and valleys, and drinketh water of the rain of heaven.'

This short war had at least been the means of teaching me a few great lessons which were of use later on. I saw and learnt a good deal of the machinery by which the thing can be done to-day, the turn given to the wheel which sets ' public opinion,' as it is called, into one channel or the other. I thought the war was ended, but I was wrong. Doubtless the Great Comet, as I saw it that morning flaming over Mokattim, knew more about what was coming than any of us :—

'Comets importing change of times and states,
Brandish your fiery tresses in the sky,
And with them scourge the bad revolting stars.'

Quite so ; but which had been the bad, revolting star in this Egyptian business ? That one, ' Canopus,' famous night-jewel of the southern desert ; or that other one of the northern heavens, ' Arcturus,' which had guided us to overwhelm the sleeping fellaheen host at Tel-el-Kebir ? The Egyptian peasant in revolt against his plunderers, or an English Liberal Government in revolt against Liberalism ?

Some day, perhaps, Egypt will help us to answer the question. She has ever played a strange part in the destiny of empires. The late Lord Salisbury came to the conclusion towards the close of his life that we had an unfortunate facility for ' backing the wrong horse.' I think we have had an equal knack of generally hanging the wrong man

When the army of Egypt returned to England it was the recipient of a good deal of public and private adulation and reward, which lasted through the winter and into the summer of the next year.[1] Then things assumed their old shapes again.

One day, in the late summer of 1883, I received a letter from a syndicate of company promoters in the city of London asking me if I would undertake a journey to the north of the Saskatchewan River, in order to investigate and report upon a large tract of land in that region, about the agricultural capabilities of which they were desirous of obtaining trust-worthy information previous to the formation of a joint-stock company for its future development. It was added that Lord Dunraven had been also approached in the matter, and that he was willing to undertake the journey provided I was also agreeable to it. Of course, I accepted. I forget what the emolument was to be—one hundred pounds, and out-of-pocket expenses, I think ; but that didn't matter. I would have given more than I could then afford to give merely to see again the great prairies and the pine forests of my earlier days.

The season of the year, the autumn, didn't much matter. Indeed, nothing matters when your heart is in a matter.

After several delays I left Liverpool on the 6th October in a brand-new steamer, the *Oregon.* She was the latest vessel then off the stocks, and she was expected to break the record of that time, which she did, getting into New York on the evening of the 14th. Ship, ship's company, passengers, and ocean were at their best. Every human item seemed to be represented in the two hundred passengers. Beauty and the Beast could be studied close at hand   The charm of the one lies in its great contrast to the ugliness of the other, but we ought not to say the ' Beast,' for there are very few beasts that are ugly ; it is the mass of ugly people in the world that makes us worship beauty when we see it.

It was interesting to look at America again after an absence

---

[1] I was honoured by being appointed extra A D C to the Queen

of ten or a dozen years. The sharpening process seemed to be still going on among the population. Is it destined to continue until the original Caucasian has been fined down to vanishing point ? At the moment it seemed to me that the Irish and the German stock were having the reproduction business all to themselves, but the African black was beating them both.

I got away up the Hudson Valley the next day. Commercial enterprise was so far unable to spoil the glories of the sunset skies and their reflection on the broad river, but it had seized on every rock and headland on the shores to defile and deface them with hideous advertisements of pills, purgatives, and pick-me-ups ; even the moonlight was sought as an illuminator for these horrible concoctions. One asked oneself who were the men and women who swallowed these things ; and were the ' Castoria Bitters ' and the various Capsicums, the names of which were written in five-feet letters on the grand old rocks, the real grindstones upon which the sharpening or attenuating process of the American human family was going on ?

Dawn found us in Vermont. A great round moon, now safe from the desecration of the city advertisement, was going down in fleecy folds of vapour beyond Lake Champlain ; the big woods were glowing in their autumn tints as the sun came up, mixing his bright, new golden coinage with the molten moon-beams in the west. White frost was on the ground, and there was ice on the little pools already. There was no time to lose if the Saskatchewan River was to be crossed free of ice. I hurried on north, for the objective point was a station called Troy, on the Canadian Pacific Railway, from whence a stage waggon ran once a week to Prince Albert, on the North Saskatchewan. If I missed that weekly stage, then there could be no chance of getting to my destination before the winter had shut up the land from human observation. How easily can our best-laid plans be jeopardised ! At Milwaukee, on the 19th October, the train stopped for dinner. After the meal, by a stupid mistake I got into what seemed to be the last carriage in the St. Paul's train. A moment later I saw the carriage in front move slowly away from the one in which I sat. The northern train was moving so very slowly that I thought I could catch it running, for we were still in Milwaukee city. I

Photogravure by Annan & Sons Glasgow, from a photograph by Heath, Plymouth.

Lieutenant Colonel W. F. Butler, C.B.
Taken in 1883 as Queen's A.D.C.

was out and after the train in a second, going all I could, and neither gaining on it nor losing. I had a large overcoat on, and but for that I think I should have caught it up. All at once there came a break in the track on which I was running, caused by a switch block in the rails ; over that I jumped, and as I lighted at the far side of the obstacle, bang went something in the calf of my leg. I stopped, dead lame ; away steamed the express, with all my baggage, and all my hopes of getting to the Saskatchewan for another fortnight. Suddenly I heard behind me the roar and whistle of an engine. I looked back and saw a single locomotive coming on my line of rails at a rapid pace. As it approached I noticed that the driver was leaning out to one side of his engine and shouting at me, but as I had already hobbled out of his track I didn't know what he wanted of me. Then I saw him slowing down, and I guessed what he was at. He pulled up suddenly. ' Jump on, stranger ! ' he shouted. I caught hold of the rail of his engine, and lifted myself by it to the driver's platform. He gave one glance to see that I was safely on, then he seemed to let her head go, and away we went forward. By this time the St. Paul's express, still going slowly, for there were numerous street crossings on the line, was a quarter of a mile ahead. Holding on all I knew, for I was now quite out of breath, I gave one look at my good friend. He was a big strong man, with a great round face and a lot of hair round it. His eyes were steadily fixed on the rails ahead, the train in front, and the crossing-places ; both his hands were on the stops and goes of his engine, and he was able to check his speed or let go as he pleased. When we got clear of the streets he let out full speed, and was soon within a hundred yards of the express, which so far had seemed to take no notice of us, and I began to fear that my good friend would give up the stern chase in disgust. But I heard him growling something about ' going to St Paul before he 'd stop ', and I was completely reassured, for there was a light in the big eye that was nearest to me that told me it had now become altogether a personal question between him and the express.

As though to bring matters to a climax, he now let out his engine to a full gallop, and I thought he was going to ram the train in front, for he would run up quite close to it, and then suddenly rein in his charger. All the time he was making a wonderful amount of steam whistling. At last the express caved in and pulled up ; then only did my friend relax his stern silence. He helped me to get down from his engine. I flung a five-dollar note on to the floor of his locomotive, told him he was the best friend I had ever met in the world, and then hobbled to the last carriage of the express, and scrambled on its platform. As I did so I saw that the driver had quitted his engine and followed me. He put the five-dollar bill on the platform, saying, ' Thank you, stranger, but it wasn't for that I did it,' and went straight back to his engine. In another second we were steaming north. I then saw that the number of his engine was 218. When we got to St. Paul next morning I wired to the stationmaster, Milwaukee, asking the name of the driver of 218 engine ; the reply came that the name was Bill Macauley. It was worth a sprung leg just to have met such a man. The passengers were very kind. They had been watching the race with interest, and one of them, seeing me so lame, brought out a bottle of ' Pond's Extract.' According to its label this compound cured every pain and ailment of man, woman, and child ; that it relieved the great pain I was then in is certain, and, though lameness lasted for many days, it gradually wore way. Of my good friend I shall have more to say later.

I got to Troy station, three hundred miles west of Winnipeg, and found there an old friend waiting for me—another Mr. Macauley, this one an old officer of the Hudson Bay Company, with whom I had spent some days at Dunvegan, on the Peace River, thirteen years earlier. The stage was not to leave Troy for a few hours, and my friend had his two-horse buggy at the station to drive me some two miles to his fort at Qu'appelle, which the stage would pass some time later in the day. I have not forgotten the beauty of that drive across the rolling prairies from the railway to Qu'appelle, in which one was brought all at once face to face with the old-remembered glories of space, silence, and sunset ; with the extraordinary clearness of the prairie atmosphere, through which the blue line of horizon lay clear-cut fifty miles away ; the intense blue of the long, winding lakes ; the copses of yellow cotton-wood ; the oak thickets, now crimson in the Fall, and the curious, white sandstone cliffs to the north of the lakes, the echo at the foot of which had made the early French fur hunters give its sweet-sounding name to the place two hundred years earlier.

My joy at finding myself once more in a lone land of silent beauty was, unfortunately, of short duration, for when, three or four hours later, the stage stopped at the Hudson Bay fort, I saw at a glance that I should have as companions through the three hundred miles to Prince Albert three or four of as rough specimens of the first-fruits of Canadian settlement as could possibly be met with in the Great West.

That evening the stage stopped at a lone hut named O'Brien's. The stage manager or owner was of the party, as the trip was a sort of pioneer undertaking to bring the Saskatchewan into touch with the new civilisation of the Pacific railroad. This new civilisation appeared to be terribly anxious to begin its labours, and of its apostles it might be said that they were hard at work swearing themselves into office through the whole three hundred miles that still intervened between the railway and the savagery of the Saskatchewan. As there were no Indians or half-breeds or wild animals in this region, the inanimate things of hill, wood, water, and plain received their full baptism of fire at the hands or tongues of the new-comers ; the driver scattered imprecations on everything ; the lumberman smoked so incessantly that his benedictions could only take form in occasional words jerked out between whiffs of tobacco smoke, but they were strong words when they did come. Of wit, even of a coarse kind, of humour of any kind, there was none among these men , it was all the dull, heavy, cursing, spitting, eructating, and smoking kind of savagery. In O'Brien's hut that evening I thought with regret of the old days in some Indian or half-breed camp, where, if the floor-space and the head-room were no larger, the study of human character and habit was infinitely more interesting When the time for lying down came I took my roll of bedding outside, and had a capital night's rest in the open prairie in a tempera-ture of only twelve degrees below freezing-point. I was up at 5 A M., and had the satisfaction of making the lazy civilisers get up too. The driver was inclined to be aggressively impre-catory, but I effectively silenced him by saying that if he would kindly show me where he kept his oats, I should be glad to feed his horses for him every morning at five o'clock. This offer seemed completely to change his mental attitude towards me, and I found, too, that whatever might be the prevailing tone of his conversation with men, he was uniformly kind and thoughtful about his animals.

On the 28th October we reached the South Saskatchewan, at the same spot where I had lost my little black riding horse through the ice just thirteen years earlier. It was strange to look again at this and at other old scenes of camp and adventure in those times of former travel. Many of the old things of that time had gone for ever into the Silences. There was not a buffalo to be seen from Winnipeg to the Mountains ; most of the Indian prairie tribes were broken up, and the wild men who had followed the great herds and lived on them were now scattered into a few isolated and remote reserves, destined soon to disappear altogether from the land.

One thing was still here unchanged : it was the twilight. Before that hour came the stage had reached its stopping-place, and I was able to get away from its atmosphere to some neighbouring hill, or by the edge of some lakelet, where one could look again at some of the old sights, the great red sun going slowly down over the immense landscape, and leaving the western sky a vast half dome of rose-tipped wavelets from horizon to zenith. Scarce a sound but the splash of a wild duck on the placid lake, scarce a movement but the motion of a musquash swimming in the rainbow-coloured water, his head forming the beak of a bird-of-paradise, whose gorgeous wings and body plumage were the widening ripples that followed after.

In the last days of October I reached the land north of the North Saskatchewan, which it was the object of my journey to see, and at a point fifty miles north of the river I turned back again to the south. I found that the million acres, which were to become the property of the syndicate destined to exploit them, formed an oblong block of territory lying to the south and west of the sub-Arctic forest which roughly bordered it on two sides. The Saskatchewan made the southern boundary, and a range of low hills, called the 'Thickwood Hills,' the western. The land was of good quality, suitable for cultivation or grazing. It had water and timber, and it lay between two thousand to two thousand five hundred feet above sea-level. The trail of the fur traders to the north lay directly through it. In favourable years good wheat was grown on it, but summer frosts as early as the 20th August had often injured the grain. On the whole, looking to the great distance which intervened between this region and the railways, I could not recommend that it should be made the basis of a joint-stock company, the capital of which was to be one to two million dollars. That was the nature of the report which I submitted when I returned to London. But of this more anon; I have still to get back there in this narrative.

In the Indian reservation I found my old acquaintance, Mistawassis, the Cree chief of my former visit. Once a man of fame and influence over the prairies, he was now reduced to a very miserable condition. His story, told in his own way, put the whole question, as Indian story always did, in short and true language.

'In the old days,' he said, 'before the Canadians came, we had food and clothes. At times, it is true, the snow caught our people on the plains and we froze, or at times the buffalo were few out on the prairies and we wanted food, but that was only at times; now we are always in want of food, our clothes are full of holes, and the winter winds come through them, to find our bodies thin for want of food   I can go back for fifty years, but no time like this time can I find. Our men and women put on rags over rags, but it is only hole over hole; we cannot get warm. I once had plenty of horses, but they are gone one by one to buy food. Most of the men who came to this reserve with me are already dead, and only six years have gone since we came here. They (the Government) were to have put glass windows in our huts, but only the frames without glass came. Our oxen have died dragging flour here from Prince Albert.'

Times had indeed changed with poor old Mistawassis since I had seen him in 1870. He was then the owner of seventy horses, his buffalo robes were numerous; he had hundreds of bags of pemmican wherewith to trade with the Company for tea and sugar. Alas for the Red Man! it was the same here on this North Saskatchewan as it had been on the Assineboine, the Red River, the Mississippi, the Missouri, and a hundred

other rivers big and little over this Great West ; and yet it
was not one hundred years since the ' Blackbird,' chief of the
Minatarries, five hundred miles south, had asked that he might
be buried on the top of a hill overlooking the Missouri, so that
he might be able to see his white brother the trader passing
in his trading boats up and down the river.

I got back to the North Saskatchewan on 2nd November.
The ice was now forming rapidly, and it would soon set in the
broad channel, but we got over in the ' scow ' to Carlton with
only a wetting. The question was now how to get back to
the railway. I hated the idea of the stage again. The prospect of another five days' ' boarding and bunking ' with the
' civilisers ' was too much for me. The land north of the
Saskatchewan was still safe ; I would keep to it, follow the old
trail by Fort Pitt to Edmonton, and then make my way to
Calgary, which at this time was the end of the railway east of
the Rocky Mountains. It was a good six hundred miles, and
the winter was fast setting in ; but I had been over the road
thirteen years before, and some old friends in the Hudson
Bay Company were still alive along it. Preliminaries were
soon arranged through another old companion in travel,[1] and
on the same afternoon I recrossed the river to the north shore,
saw the ' scow ' hauled up for the last time that year, and with
old Dreever, a cousin of the man who had been my guide in the
early part of the night, thirteen years ago, when we eluded the
search of Riel and Company at old Fort Garry, I turned my
head westward for Edmonton. We had an American buckboard and three horses, all Dreever's property.

We camped that night by some large willows between two
frozen ponds. When twilight came, and the wind blew in
gusts through the willows from far off, and I saw the horses
feeding on the ridge against the afterglow, I felt a silent joy
such as I had not known this time in its fulness. Here at last
was the lonely land still untouched. ' When we drew up the
scow,' I wrote that night, ' we cut the painter of " civilisation,"
but the savagery lies at the south side of the river.'

For ten or twelve days we drove at a trot through a rolling
land of mixed wood and grass, the latter now yellow like ripe
corn, and growing in places three and four feet high. The

[1] Mr. Clarke, Hudson Bay Company.

camping-places were good, with ample store of dry timber for fuel. ' What a delight it is to be making a camp once more with an honest man,' I find myself writing on the second evening out. On the 3rd and 4th November there were beautiful displays of the aurora before daybreak : veils of radiance flung across the stars , great showers of red and yellow light pulsating and quivering from the northern horizon to the zenith. The dawn would sometimes break in the east in strange, deceptive mixings of earth and clouds. I would have forgotten where earth and sky had met in the east when day closed on the previous evening, and throwing back the blankets next morning, I would see what seemed to be an immense lake stretching far south-east to north-east, having its farther shore clearly defined with bays, inlets, and islands in it, the nearer shore only a short distance from our camp. The distant shore seemed to rise into mountains, with snow on their summits, and stars above them. As dawn brightened the reflections in the lake began to change in colour from grey silver to molten copper, and then as the sun drew nearer the horizon the whole phantasm of lake, mountain, and stars melted into the realities of the daylight.

Dreever, the driver, like all the good men of mixed parentage in the North-West, had in his nature the best instincts of the wilderness. He possessed the power also of telling its stories with a quaint choice of words which, though few and simple, showed his genius for reproducing the scene he wished to describe, with great and touching fidelity One morning we sighted the ' Swan Lake,' a sheet of blue open water lying to the right. In the previous summer a French priest had come there with six or seven Cree Indians to hunt moulting geese and ducks, for the lake was a great haunt of wild birds. They made a small ' dug-out ' *bateau*, and went out into the lake ; a gale came on, the *bateau* overturned. The priest swam well, and, one by one, he brought the Indians to the overturned boat, to which they clung ; but they were not able to retain their holds, and, one after the other, they were washed off by the high-running waves. A child, his especial favourite, was thus washed away three times, and was as often rescued and brought to the drifting boat again At last he too was swept off and lost. Then the priest said, ' Why should I live ? ' All those

R

who had come out with him in the boat were gone, and he it
was who had made them come, so he went too.   There, where
the white strip of sand showed between the two lakes, the
boat and the bodies were drifted in by the winds, and the
priest and the Indians were buried there.

We reached Fort Pitt long after dark on the evening of the
6th. We found here a strange mixture of the old and the
new peoples ; the new represented by a Canadian police officer
who was a son of Charles Dickens, and the old having as its
champion the chief, Big Bear, who was supposed to be kept
in awe by some ten or twelve of Mr. Dickens's police stationed
at Fort Pitt. Mr. Dickens bore a striking resemblance to his
illustrious father. He struck me as having a keen sense of
humour. He had a habit of laughing, a soft, musical, thought-
inspired laughter, which was quite peculiar to him, and which
I think he may have contracted from the Indians, in whom
I had occasionally noticed it, the result, perhaps, of long-
continued silent watching and thinking upon animals, birds,
and the ways of men and women in the wilderness.

Ruskin has somewhere said that he didn't want to hear
theological discussions or sermons about the possibility of
miracles as long as he could see the sun rise and set. The
Red Indian and the white sick man represent, perhaps, the two
classes of men who most frequently see the sun rise, and the
other world is not far off to many of these people.

Big Bear, who was supposed to be under the peculiar
supervision of Mr. Dickens's police, had persistently refused
to go upon a reservation. ' Why should I go into one place ? '
he used to ask the Hudson Bay officer and Mr. Dickens. ' Do
I not see all the Indians who go into one place die off faster
than ever they died by the guns and knives of the Blackfeet ?
Are they not all starving ? ' They would tell him then that he
was old, and that that was the reason why the Canadian
Government, wished him to be easy and comfortable on a
reserve. To which Big Bear would reply, ' It is true that I
am old, but I have fed myself for seventy years. I can still
hunt and feed myself, and I will stay in the open country till
I die ; then, when I am dead, you can put me into some one
place if you like.' I heard here the same story I had been told
all along the trail from the Touchwood Hills to Fort Pitt, a

distance of seven hundred miles as I had travelled. 'The Canadian newcomers were so rude and overbearing in their attitude to the older people of those regions that there was every prospect the latter would rise in rebellion and try to clear the new people out.' Hudson Bay men and old residents were unanimous in holding this opinion

They were right. Within two years from that time the rebellion occurred. It was easily suppressed. It was the last flicker of the old life. Henceforth there would be no prairies, no Indians, no moccasins, no old stories told by camp fires; only barbed wire, the grain 'elevator,' the machine-made boot, and the two-cent newspaper.

We reached Edmonton late on the night of the 12th November in a driving snow-storm. The winter was now well in, and for the last three mornings the thermometer had been below zero at daybreak.

CHAPTER XVI

THROUGHOUT the five hundred miles covered since I had crossed to the north shore of the Saskatchewan at Carlton, the land, with the exception of the establishment of Mr. Dickens's small police party at Fort Pitt, was exactly as I had left it thirteen years before.

At the Hudson Bay forts some ' old-timers ' had gathered—old French Canadian or Scottish servants of the Company, who had lived all their lives in the great wilderness, and now wished to die in it.   These old people had their memories for company, and wonderful memories they were.   Most, if not all of them, had seen ghosts at some time in their lives.   It might have been when they were lying in camp, storm-bound, by the shores of the distant Lake Athabasca ; it might have been during some awful tramp of forty days and nights from Engewa to Esquimaux Bay in Labrador ; it might have been during a stay, all alone, of a month in midwinter at La Pierre House on the Upper Yukon, when the other white man had died, and there had been no means of communicating the news of his death to the next nearest white man, who lived three hundred miles away on the Mackenzie River ; but ghosts the old men had seen some time or other in those long years.   If the younger men hadn't themselves seen ghosts, they had heard their fathers or grandfathers talk of them often enough over the log fire in the winter evening.   Years before in Red River I had heard a quaint story of old Prudens and the wild goose—a goose story, not a ghost story.   One day in early spring, when the wild geese were passing high over the prairies to their breeding grounds in the Arctic, old Prudens in his farmyard on the Red River saw

a 'wavy' detach itself from the flock overhead, and, flying
downwards, alight in the middle of his own domestic geese in
the yard.   Orders were given that the newcomer was not to be
disturbed in any way.   The 'wavy' dwelt with his domestic
brethren in plenty all that summer , but when autumn came
the wail of the wild geese was heard again descending from the
V-shaped flocks that now were passing south to the swamp-
lands of the Mississippi.   The call was more than the visitor
could resist ; for one morning he spread his wings and, soaring
aloft, rejoined his wild friends flying southwards.   But, when
spring returned, so too came the 'wavy' to take up his summer
station once more with the domestic cousins in the farmyard.
For half a dozen autumns and springs this curious visit was
repeated, until at last a springtime came but no 'wavy' came
with it to gladden the eyes of old Prudens.   When the last
flock had passed over, the old man said sorrowfully . 'He hasn't
come back : I shall die this winter.'   And die he did, said the
story.

At Fort Victoria on this journey I met a young Mr. Prudens.
I asked him about his grandfather and the wild goose.   Yes,
he had heard the story often told by the old people, he said,
perhaps it was only foolish talk ; but Dreever, my driver, didn't
think so.   He liked these old stories better than the new ones
which had already come into the Saskatchewan in the form of
the ten-cent American novel—the *Dime Illustrated*.   'These
novels,' he once said to me, 'they don't do a man any good ;
he only loses his sleep by them '   I didn't know about that, but
I do know that I have learned more of the secret of life from
the stories of the Red Man, the old French fur-hunter, and the
old soldier, than ever I gathered from the pages of all the
up-to-date and sitting-up-at-night novels that were ever
written.

Despite the snowstorm and a temperature below zero at
Edmonton, I found that ' a boom ' had just passed over that
old Indian trading station ; and in this boom my recent
acquaintance, Johnny Prudens, had had a part.   Prudens had
a farm near the fort.   The Edmonton ' boom ' had been
started several hundreds of miles away, at Winnipeg, and
Edmonton knew nothing about it.   Suddenly a telegram
arrived offering thirty thousand dollars for Prudens' farm.

Prudens was away fur-trading at Lac La Biche. What is to be done ? A messenger cannot be got at less than two hundred dollars who will go in search of Prudens. Meanwhile, the telegraph operator sees his way to a deal on his own account. He and another partner start out to meet Prudens, and offer him six thousand dollars for his farm. Prudens sells, knowing nothing of the thirty thousand dollar limit. Then there is a long delay before the deeds of sale can be prepared and the money raised. At last this is effected, and all the parties concerned go to Winnipeg to settle matters and pay the purchase money. But by this time spring has come, and the boom has subsided, the necessary dollars cannot be obtained ; the operator has to put his recently acquired farm up for sale by auction—the reserve price being fifteen thousand dollars ; the audience burst into guffaws of laughter. Then twelve thousand dollars are tried ; no answer. Finally a purchaser is found at eight thousand dollars, less expenses. What Prudens eventually got out of the transaction was not stated ; but the operator was glad to get back to his telegraph station the owner of a new buckboard. At Edmonton I was on the borderland again. Calgary, my rail destination, was only two hundred miles to the south ; and boom and counter boom would henceforth form the staples of all conversation. How often I was to hear the boom story repeated ; the first fixing of the new city site ; the plans made out of square, corner lots, and marketplaces , the names given : ' Rapid City,' ' Humboldt City,' ' Manchester City,' ' White Mud City,' etc., etc. Then I would hear the story of the man who went in a buckboard to see for himself the destined centre of civilisation and progress which had already arisen, it was said, in the wilderness ; how this man got on the stump of a tree in the centre of ' Manchester City,' and by springing on the stump had shaken the ' muskeg ' and quagmire swamp for two hundred yards all round his footing , how another man had taken his old German wife with him to prospect ' Rapid City,' a site somewhere on the South Saskatchewan ; and how, when daylight had revealed the whole sad spectacle to the old lady, she had burst into a torrent of reproaches against her spouse, finishing up with imprecations upon the head of Horace Greely, whose well-known advice to the young men to ' go West ' had been the origin of all her losses and disappointments. ' If I meet that old ——, I 'll give him hell,' she would say.

I left Edmonton on the 14th November, travelling by horse-sled due south. The snow was about eight inches deep, and we sped along at a good pace over the same trail as that which I had followed when going to the Rocky Mountain House in 1870. Curiously enough, I had as driver the same excellent half-breed who had been then my companion—Johnny Rowland—and, to make the coincidence stranger, we met on the trail Paul Foyale, who had also been with me on that occasion. On the night of the 15th we reached the crossing place at Battle River, where a Cree Indian, responding to the incoming civilisation, had built himself a tiny hut of wood and mud on the bank above the river. Coyote, the owner of the hut, was away hunting, but his family, represented by a very old grandmother, a wife and some children, were present. There was also a baby, four days old, who, the old lady informed me, was her sixtieth descendant then living Except in the Egyptian Mummy Museum at Boulak I had not seen a human face so deeply wrinkled, nor hands so scraggy, nor nose so prominent ; yet the hair was still jet black as it hung down in wisps on either side of the gaunt cheeks. The baby's mother was at household work ; and the old grandmother was alternately engaged in holding the baby, and expelling a small black puppy dog, whose work in the world was to roll over everything on the floor —threatening even to precipitate himself into the frying-pan wherein our supper was being prepared.

We started from Coyote's at daylight, and soon ran into lighter snow, for a ' Chinnook wind ' was blowing, and when we reached the Wolf creek the ground was so bare that the sleigh made bad progress. Next morning, the snow being quite gone, we packed our things on a loose horse, hid the sleigh in a thicket, hung up the harness in a tree, and set out riding the other two horses for the Red Deer River. Rowland rode bareback ; I had a saddle borrowed from the Coyote family. It proved an instrument of surpassing discomfort. Of Mexican origin, it had undergone many changes at the Coyotes' hands. What-ever had been capable of decay in it had gone, and only the hard bone framework remained. It was so small that one had to sit as much on the cantle as in the saddle. It was only a question of time as to how long the agony could be borne. After three hours of inexpressible pain, we reached the banks of the Blindman's River, found a cart there, and with its aid got on to the Red Deer River at dusk. 'I have found a new instrument of human torture,' I wrote that night in my diary, ' in case civilisation reverts to the ancient practice — the Coyote saddle.' Two days later I reached the railway at Calgary, having passed on the second day from the mixed wooded and plain country into a region entirely devoid of tree or bush—a region which was one vast sea of short gray grass. These last two days were of easy locomotion, thanks to the kindness of a Canadian gentleman named Beattie, who had recently settled within the wooded region lying north of the treeless waste.

Crossing the Bow River at sunset, Mr. Beattie's waggon narrowly escaped an accident. Ice was running in the river, making it difficult for the four horses to keep their footing in the strong current. One of the leaders fell and could not get his legs again ; so it was necessary to cut him clear of the harness. This was done by a smart young fellow going out over the backs of the wheelers, but he too had to get into the water, and he was chilled to the marrow when we hauled him again into the waggon.

It was dusk by the time we got across the Bow River, and drew up at the Calgary House in what was then a small village. The first thing was to get a drink of spirits for the half-drowned man , but, unfortunately, in Calgary the sale of all intoxicants was a crime punishable with heavy penalties. I took the hotel-keeper aside and told him the case was an extreme one, and the youth might easily die of cold and wet. We arranged a compromise ; the hotel man would serve up tea all round for our party, but in one cup he would put surreptitiously a glass of the forbidden liquor. Not a word was to be said, for there were police spies about, and discovery would be fatal to the hotel. Half a dozen cups of tea soon came in on a tray. No one said anything ; there was a profound silence as the tray went round. I never knew exactly what happened, but the only certain thing about the transaction was that the slip between the cup that held the whisky and the lip for which it was intended was complete. The half-drowned youth got only the drink that cheered ; but who among our party received the inebriating part of the beverage never transpired.

I left Calgary next morning by train for Winnipeg. For three hours before sunset on the previous evening the Rocky Mountains had been in sight to the west, and to the south one could see over the level waste the smoke of railway locomotives rising in tall, black columns above the clear prairie horizon.

That the difficulty in the case of the stimulant for the half-frozen youth the previous evening had not been imaginary, a look into the next carriage in our train showed. Two men of the mounted police were there in irons on their way to prison. Except for the irons, no one could have imagined that they were prisoners ; the freest and easiest familiarity prevailed between them, their escort, and the other passengers. They were 'in' for having given information to certain liquor-sellers that a police raid was being organised against them, and that fact may have been accountable for the exhilarating effect which the handcuffs appeared to exercise upon them. Anyway they were jollity itself, and it was only the escorting constables who looked sad and depressed

At midnight the train reached Medicine Hat. While daylight lasted not a tree or twig had broken the long monotony of the waste ; even the grass had disappeared, and great dunes of sand showed at intervals along the railway line, wind-blown ridges mixed with patches of snow. But all day long the wonderful snowy peaks showed well above the prairie rim, and when I looked my last towards the west over a vast expanse of snow-covered plain, they still rose in an orange gloaming as grand and lonely as when I had first set eyes upon them in the days when the red man and the buffalo were almost the sole denizens of this mighty waste.

As there was a delay of a couple of hours at Medicine Hat, I entered a small wooden saloon oyster bar in search of food and warmth, for it was miserably cold. A man came in shortly after   I have heard a good deal of hard swearing in my day, but never anything that approached the prodigious blasphemy of that Medicine Hat man. He particularly swore against some place near Medicine Hat which he had left that day, where the temperature was, he averred, with many imprecations directed against anything from a thermometer to an oyster tin, exactly one hundred and ten degrees below zero. If you were disposed to doubt or question the accuracy of that reading of the thermometer, the alternative was like that which Cromwell gave his Irish prisoners, only that Connaught was left out.

I got to Winnipeg on 22nd November, and left it on the 25th. Our passage from a prohibition country into one of free drinks was curiously coincident with what at first appeared to me to betoken a tendency towards tooth-washing in the travelling community such as I had not before met with in the west. The tumbler on the washstand of the sleeping car was in constant requisition. After a time, when at last I found it in its proper place in the dressing-room, there was a strong spirituous aroma about it which suggested the possibility of its having been put to other uses than tooth-washing.

At Milwaukee I took advantage of a halt to look up my good friend Bill Macauley at the station dépôt. I soon found engine 218. Bill was burnishing his steed. I introduced myself to him ' Was you the man,' he said, ' that telegraphed the superintendent to ask my name ? ' ' Yes. What happened ? ' ' Wall, he came along one morning, and ses he : " Bill, what game have you been up to ? " " Why, Boss ? " ses I. " Cause," ses he, " there's a chap up in St. Paul's wiring down to know the name of the driver of your engine, and saying he's mightily obliged to you. What for ? " I told him it must be the man I found lame on the track, and that I just picked him up on my engine and caught the express for him. " Well, Bill," ses he, " you mustn't do that again, Bill." ' Then Bill told me that he was from Belfast ; came out as a boy, was doing well, liked to give a hand to anybody that needed it, and never gave a thought to it again. So we parted.

I reached London shortly before Christmas. Serious news had been received from the Soudan. The profound stupor which had fallen upon the peoples of the Nile valley one year earlier had suddenly been broken by an ominous occurrence. Hicks Pasha, an Anglo-Indian officer, with some six or eight English officers and ten thousand native soldiers and followers (chiefly men of Arabi's old army, who had been sent in chains to the Soudan in the winter of 1882) had been destroyed on the march from the Upper Nile to Kordofan by a Nubian

Mohammedan Mahdī at the head of revolting tribes who had flocked to his standard from all parts of the Soudan. This was probably the last portion of the Empire from which news of trouble was anticipated. Everybody had been talking so much of the love borne to us by the peoples of the Nile valley that we really had come to think that Tel-el-Kebir had closed the Egyptian question once and for all, and there was nothing more to be done but to send half a dozen Englishmen into the heart of the Soudan to ensure its easy occupation. The conquest of Arabi had given the god Jingo a new start, and some among his votaries were even disposed to regard John Bull as his prophet—a profitable prophet, grateful and comforting to everybody ; London, a modern Memphis, erecting statues to its specially selected Bulls, and setting up the Golden Calf for universal worship Nevertheless, at this particular moment, Christmas 1883, the inner councils of London presented a strange picture of weakness and indecision.

The question of what had to be done in the Soudan could have been decided in six hours by the same number of experienced officers assembled at a round table. Whether the Soudan was to be abandoned or retained required action in either case. If the garrisons were to be withdrawn, the roads for retreat must be kept open at any cost. If the revolt of the Mahdi was to be suppressed, an army must be sent to do it, and whichever course was to be followed, no time must be lost. The tide of revolt was rapidly rising in the Soudan, and the main lines of retreat or of advance were certain to have their communications interrupted by the increasing volume of the revolt.

But if there was indecision in the governing mind in London, the perplexity and weakness of the administrative powers in Cairo were ten times more pronounced. At this very moment, the 19th December, they were sending from Cairo to Suakim on the Red Sea a wretched force of three thousand six hundred nondescript men with six guns, under Baker Pasha (whom we last met at the tombs of the Bulls). The composition of this absurd expedition, and the commission given to its commander, are to-day accurate measures by which judgment can be formed upon the foresight and ability of the English administration then in power in Cairo.

Baker Pasha was 'to have supreme civil and military command in all parts of the Soudan which might be reached by his forces.' He was commissioned 'to pacify the country between Suakim and Berber (two hundred and forty miles); but was only to resort to force after all other means of conciliation had failed.' It will be sufficient to say that, three days after landing, he advanced three miles from the shore with his three thousand men; met a body of 'about twelve hundred' Arabs, armed with swords and spears, his forces were almost entirely annihilated in a few minutes, leaving in the hands of the Henandoa Arabs three thousand rifles, six cannon, all their baggage, ammunition, and clothing. An eyewitness thus described the scene: 'Cavalry, infantry, mules, camels, falling baggage and dying men, crushed into a struggling, surging mass. The Egyptians were shrieking madly, hardly attempting to run away, but trying to shelter themselves one behind another' Baker Pasha and his officers did what they could to stay the rout; then they galloped for the shore

Even this disaster does not appear to have awakened the governing minds in Cairo and London to a sense of the real situation in the Soudan. That is the curse which invariably attends upon the fool's paradise of 'Make-believe.' I went frequently to London in these days, but saw nowhere any sign of preparation nor heard any rumours showing that there was the slightest realisation of the true state of matters existing in the Soudan. On 18th January 1884, General Gordon, as everybody knows, was despatched at one day's notice to Khartoum, with one other officer, his mission being to bring away the garrisons and to establish settled government in the Soudan. Seven weeks had then passed since the news of Hicks' disaster had been received. Could human fatuity have reached a deeper point? A week after Gordon's departure, I received at Devonport a summons to attend the War Office. I made sure the order meant something for the Nile, and I was never more disappointed than when I found it was only a confidential civil mission to the Government of Canada, the land I had just returned from. I made it a rule of life to take any service that was offered, and never to ask for anything except active service. In the present instance, it happened that the mission to Canada which I was now asked to undertake had been accepted by Colonel Stewart of the 11th Hussars, but his sudden departure with General Gordon for Khartoum made it necessary to get another officer for Canada, and I had been selected for the service. I sailed from Liverpool the first week in February, had a fifteen day voyage of exceptional severity even for that season of the year, and in the course of the following six weeks saw a good deal of the Canadian administration. Lord Lansdowne was then the governor-general, newly arrived, and the veteran Sir John Macdonald the premier of the Dominion. Early in April I was back in London, and it was possible to take up Soudan affairs again.

There was little change in the situation. Unparalleled vacillation of purpose had continued to mark the whole conduct of affairs ; telegrams were flying between Cairo and London ; expeditions were sent to the Red Sea littoral, only to be recalled after a lot of useless slaughter had occurred. It is difficult to go back now after these twenty-five long years are gone, and to read again the official records and diaries of that time, the real truth of which still remains untold and unacknowledged. What was the meaning of all this beating of the air, these masses of useless verbiage, these opinions and counter-opinions, these short marchings out and marchings back again, in which eight long months were wholly wasted at a time when every hour of every day was precious to us ? Let us see whether now, with the experience of the intervening years, and the recollections of my personal share in the work of the months following my return from Canada, I can put together some tangible theory of that fatal interval. Three salient factors have to be dealt with in the matter—the man Gordon, the men who held in their hands his fate, and the physical, military, and economic situation of Khartoum at the time.

Readers of General Gordon's life will remember that he spent the greater part of the year 1883 in Palestine, where he was engaged in visiting the sites identified with the history of the Old and New Testaments. How little his mind concerned itself with the affairs of Egypt those who have read the voluminous letters written by him from Palestine, and published by his sister, Miss Gordon, will not need to be reminded ; but to the agents and servants of the Egyptian bondholders the presence in Palestine of their great antagonist could only appear as a menace to their designs upon Egypt.

So far for the man Gordon. Let us turn to the actual position at Khartoum immediately after Gordon arrived there. From the first day of his arrival, the strategic position was almost a hopeless one. From one end of the Soudan to the other the Mahdi was triumphant. All the garrisons, which it was the particular mission of Gordon to relieve and withdraw, were sealed up within their dozen towns, hundreds of miles apart, unable to hold any communication with each other or with Khartoum : even this place was menaced. Weeks before Gordon reached Khartoum, despairing messages had been received from it in Cairo along the thin thread of the telegraph, which was now the sole frail link that remained between Egypt and the Soudan. Dongola was doubtful ; Suakim on the Red Sea was menaced. The line Khartoum—Berber—Abu Hamad —Korosko—Assouan formed the only route by which communication was possible, and formed a route, too, along which it was easy to maintain communication. It would not have cost England or Egypt twenty thousand pounds to make that road as secure against the Mahdi as was the remainder of the line from Assouan to Cairo. Only two places on the six hundred miles between Korosko and Khartoum required looking to : Berber, two hundred miles north of Khartoum, and Abu Hamad, three hundred and thirty-seven miles from it. From Abu Hamad to Korosko the desert was Egypt's. I do not think that in the whole range of modern military history another such example of stupidity can be found to equal the omission on the part of the governing authorities in Cairo to secure the route Korosko to Khartoum after General Gordon had passed along it to his destination At whose door that responsibility should rest I have still no means of deciding ; but when I read again, after the lapse of more than twenty years, the voluminous despatches and telegrams which cover the momentous months between January and May 1884, all the old wonder I used to experience at that terrible omission comes back, and I ask myself afresh what were all these ministers, agents, generals, sirdars, and high functionaries in Cairo dreaming of when they allowed that single door of relief and communication to be closed upon the man we had sent so glibly to his fate ? It

was so easy to keep the door open ; two thousand men
sent to Berber via Korosko and Abu Hamad would have
sufficed. Berber was only a three-weeks' journey from Cairo
via Korosko , it would have cost twenty thousand pounds.
From the day Gordon passed Abu Hamad on his way to
Khartoum, until the fall of Berber sealed his fate, there elapsed
a period of about sixty days. During that interval the
various military and civil authorities in Cairo were exercising
their minds in planning costly expeditions to Suakim, which
were as remote from the possibility of reaching Berber, under
the conditions then existing between that place and Suakim,
as they were from effecting the occupation of Timbuctoo.
Nay, they were even rendering the problem of communicating
with Khartoum by any road increasingly difficult on every side.

Writing in his celebrated Khartoum journal on 22nd September 1884, Gordon has entered remarkable words. He quotes
the Mudir of Dongola's observation to him in March that the
authorities in Cairo seemed desirous of ' riveting the tomb-
stone over Khartoum.' And again, four days later, he writes
on 26th September : ' It is a curious fact that any effort to
relieve the garrisons is contemporaneous with the expiration
of the period stated in March regarding the time they could
hold out, viz. six months. There are some ugly suspicious
circumstances all the way through.' Undoubtedly there were,
but I have never been able, then or now, when five-and-twenty
years have gone, to say where the ugly suspicious circumstances
ended, and the dense stupidities began. My own personal
reading now of the events of the time is, that there was only
one man then in authority to whom the fate of Charles Gordon
in Khartoum was a real, tangible, ever-present anxiety—that
man was Lord Wolseley. With him I had many interviews
after my return in April 1884 from my second visit to Canada,
and we discussed at length the various routes by which Khartoum could be reached by troops. By men who knew what
had been done on the Red River Expedition in 1870, the
practicability of ascending the Nile in boats such as those used
to reach Fort Garry could not be doubted ; but we were only
a small band against the many military competitors in Cairo
who now came forward with proposals for expeditions on their
own account to the Soudan.

What struck one most about these proposals was the fact that the main point in the problem was almost invariably left out of the calculation—time. It would have been possible to get into the Soudan from any part of the coast of Africa if time had been of no importance ; but how was the relief of Gordon to be accomplished by an English force in the interval of the few months still remaining to the garrison of Khartoum before starvation would compel it to surrender ? The cruel part of the proceeding was that this war of the *ways* enabled the Government of the day to postpone the *means* by which alone relief could be effected. Through May, June, and July the talk of relief went on, but not one effort was made to give money.

At last, late on the 4th August, I received a telegram from Lord Wolseley, who was then the adjutant-general of the War Office. It merely said : ' I want to see you here to-morrow.' Of course, I guessed what it meant. The Nile route had been selected for the attempt to reach Khartoum. Next morning I was in Pall Mall, but only to find that the final word had not been spoken by the Government. Even at this eleventh hour all that could be said was : ' We have it in contemplation to despatch a strong brigade of British troops to or towards Dongola by the Nile route. Proceed at once to find four hundred boats similar to those used in the Red River Expedition. If you cannot find such boats, you will have to build them.'

Another officer, a comrade of the Red River, Colonel Alleyne, R.A., was joined with me in this belated search. A bundle of papers was handed to us, but the purport of these we knew only too well, and a hansom cab was more to our purpose than all the tons of writing at the moment on the tables of the War Office. We laid our plans on the 5th, and by the evening of the 6th August two things were clear : not in England could be found four hundred new, sound boats fit for the work they would have to do ; build them we must. In the bundle of War Office papers handed to us was one in which the Admiralty had declared that the construction of four hundred boats would take from two to three months. I had been too long as a fly on the great wheel of English officialism not to know something about the limits of time or cost given by our great spending departments in cases such as this. The difference between private and public enterprise in England in all these matters can be measured by the difference between an express train and a parliamentary one. With only the aid of a hansom cab, we found that some Lambeth boatbuilders would build boats for us within four weeks from the date on which they got the order. If there was one boatbuilder on the Lambeth wharves who would give us five boats in four weeks, surely all England could supply the remaining three hundred and ninety-five in the same period.

The next things to decide were the shape, size, and weight of the boat. This we did at Portsmouth on the 7th August. We got together in the dockyard the load the boat would have to carry—biscuit, preserved meat, groceries, tent, arms, ammunition sufficient for twelve men during one hundred days. We put the load with twelve men into a man-of-war gig in the basin, found that load was too heavy for the boat, and the boat too heavy for the work we wanted ; and then and there we laid the lines of our new, ideal Nile ' whaler.' She was to be thirty feet in length, six feet six inches in beam, two feet three inches in depth ; to weigh, with fittings complete, about one thousand pounds. I have told the story of these boats in the *Campaign of the Cataracts*, and must now press on to the long road we have before us. It will be enough to say that, before any official sanction could be given to spend a five-pound note on this work, we had designs, specifications, dimensions, all finished ; a trial boat actually being built at Portsmouth in one week ; cargo ' found,' as the *Official History of the Soudan Campaign* says, ' to answer admirably ' , and, by the evening of the 11th August, we were satisfied that, once the Government sanction was given, we could, by ' touching the button,' set forty-seven boatbuilding firms at work from Peterhead round the English coast to Liverpool.

At last, late in the afternoon of 12th August, a war official came to the temporary office in which I was working to summon me to the office of a high parliamentary Government official. I found there several heads of the contract and finance departments.

The parliamentary official began by observing that he understood I had been charged with inquiries and arrangements as

s

to boatbuilding on an extensive scale. I answered that that was so ; that our work of design, preparation, and inquiries had for some days been finished ; and that we only awaited the word ' go ' to proceed to immediate action. Then there came a slight pause, broken by the high official asking in a doubtful tone if I really thought those four hundred boats could be built and shipped from England in the time he had seen stated in a paper of mine—one month ? I answered that I had not much doubt of the general correctness of that estimate Then came another little pause, followed by the official's writing a few words upon a half-sheet of notepaper, which he handed to me. I read, ' Colonel Butler, you may proceed with the construction of four hundred boats.' That was good, but his next spoken words were better . ' Gentlemen,' he said, turning to the representatives of the departments of finance, contracts, and control, ' I have assembled you here to tell you that Colonel Butler has a blank cheque for the building and equipment of these boats, and his decisions as to expenditure are not to be questioned.'

I bowed and retired. That evening forty-seven telegrams to forty-seven boatbuilders went out. The Nile Expedition had begun. But what a cloud hung over it ! Turn it in one's mind in any way, the problem came back to the same point— the 12th of August ! How easy it would all have been had this decision been given two months earlier !

The whole tone and temper of the Government came out in the despatch which was sent at this time to Egypt by the Secretary of State for War. There are passages in that document which literally take one's breath away when we read them to-day. This :

' Her Majesty's Government are not at present convinced that it will be impossible for General Gordon, acting on the instructions he has received, to secure the withdrawal from Khartoum, either by the employment of force or of pacific means, of the Egyptian garrison, and of such of the inhabitants as may desire to leave.'

And this :

' Her Majesty's Government are of opinion that the time has arrived when some further measures for obtaining accurate information as to his (Gordon's) position, and, if necessary, for rendering him assistance, should be adopted.'

And this :

' Her Majesty's Government have therefore come to the conclusion that the best mode in which they can place themselves in a
position to undertake the relief of General Gordon, should the
necessity arise, would be by the provision of means by which such
an expedition could be despatched to Dongola, and, as circumstances
at the time may render expedient, to Berber and Khartoum.'

And this ·

' This movement could, in the opinion of the Government, scarcely
fail in the first instance to afford the means of obtaining full and
accurate information as to the position and intentions of General
Gordon, and it is probable that such a demonstration would in itself
be sufficient to strengthen his position, and to secure the co-operation
of the tribes which have not joined the movement of the Mahdi,
to such an extent as to enable General Gordon to secure the principal
object of his mission.'

I think the despatch from which these passages are taken
stands absolutely without a parallel in history ; the force of
fiction, make-believe, and pretence could go no further.   One
can realise, too, from this despatch the forces that were against
us in the expedition now beginning.   The permanent Government, that is to say, the vast army of under-secretaries,
assistant under-secretaries, chief clerks and their assistants,
were opposed to us.   The temporary Government, *i.e.* the
ministers of the time, were at best lukewarm in support of this
half still-born child of theirs.   Perhaps of both it might have
been said that they were more passive than active in their
attitude towards us, but even that means much where the
balance between failure and success is in even pause of poise.
The London press were strongly against us, but, worse than
all, British Cairo, civil and military, were to a man against
us.   Every general who had his own pet plan for going to
Khartoum had the same reasons for not liking our methods
of going there as the French marshals in Spain had for looking with no friendly eye upon each other's operations in the
Peninsula.

As for the attitude of the civil Government, the point need
not be laboured ; the telegrams exchanged between Khartoum
and Cairo tell their own story.

From the 12th August, when official sanction was given, the work of boat preparation went on night and day ; and so well did the contractors keep their appointed times that, within the time specified in my original promise, the whole four hundred boats were delivered, put on board of eleven ships, and the ships had actually sailed for Egypt. Nearly one hundred boats were clear out of England twenty-seven days after the orders to build them had gone out. Four thousand tons of food had gone forward to Egypt in the same time

I reached Cairo early on 25th September, and went straight to the Boulak railway station to see some sixty of our boats pass by on the railway waggons to Assiout. That morning one hundred of them passed the station, not a boat damaged or a plank stirred They were due to arrive at Assiout next night. So far we were a full week ahead of our estimate of time, but now came a check from a quarter least expected. *On the preceding night the Egyptian army officials had sent eighty waggons loaded with beans, lentils, and butter from Cairo along this route to Assiout, thereby blocking all access of our boats to the Nile for three whole days.* When I reached Assiout on 1st October the block had just ceased. I had been hoarding the days gained as a miser hoards gold, and now half my gains had gone through this action of the Egyptian army. I went to the telegraph office and wired the chief of the staff at Wady Halfa :—

'Three days lost through action of E.A. officials Would it not be better to send the Egyptian army back to the beans and lentils, than to send the beans and lentils forward to the Egyptian army ? '

I got to Assouan at daylight on 7th October. At noon thirty-two of our boats arrived there ; that evening we anchored them at the foot of the First Cataract, and next morning the ascent of the cataract began It was to be the first important test of the planks of the boats to overcome a Nile rapid The prophecies of failure had been many. It will suffice to say that, when evening came, thirty-two boats were at the head of the cataract anchored opposite Philae, not one having suffered the smallest injury in the ascent Then on to Wadi Halfa. The boats were now arriving hand over hand, and on 18th October one hundred and thirty of them were at the foot of the Second Cataract. Here, again, the plan was marred by that worst of all combinations—the men who won't see and the men who don't see. They were in high place, and I was powerless against their ruling. At this point that ruling was destined eventually to kill the expedition. The order was given that the English boats, now numbering one hundred and thirty, were to remain idly at anchor at the foot of the Second Cataract, while some sixty or seventy heavy native craft were to have the right-of-way through the Bab-el-Kebir (the Big Gate of the Cataract). *This decision cost us a loss of ten days.* We had, in fact, been doing too well up to this point It was but seven weeks since these boats had their keels laid in England, and here we had over one hundred of them one thousand miles up the Nile, and the remainder were coming on in quick succession. The Second Cataract of the Nile has lived in my memory since October 1884 as a spot in the world where I suffered mental torture of the acutest kind—that which results from seeing terrible disaster ahead and being powerless to prevent it. The essence of the problem which this expedition had to solve was a simple one. We cannot afford to lose one hour ; we are two months too late at this work ; it is a race against famine ; there is still a certain margin of time left ; in what manner can that narrow balance be best used ? What is the earliest date at which a brigade of British infantry can be assembled at Korti on the Nile, ready to march across the two hundred miles of Bayuda desert to the Nile again at Metemmeh, a place within one hundred miles of Khartoum ? Korti was distant from the Second Cataract three hundred and thirty miles. The first hundred of these miles held eight cataracts or rapids, all of them combined forming, in the opinion of Commander Hamill, the same amount of obstruction to navigation as the Second Cataract offered in its total of nine miles. There were thus three hundred and ten to three hundred and twenty miles of good water, and nearly twenty of cataract and rapid between the two places. Now there was no difficulty whatever in taking our boats, light, in fifteen days from the head of the Second Cataract to Korti. I did the journey myself in that time travelling light. If we allowed double time, or, say, even thirty-five days, for boats carrying their full loads of one hundred days' food for the men, it was quite possible to have placed at Korti a daily average of two hundred British soldiers in twenty boats, each boat having on arrival at Korti sixty-five days' food and three hundred rounds of ammunition per man. To replace at Korti the thirty-five days' food eaten out on the upward journey, it was only necessary to have added four extra boats to every unit of twenty boats. These four extras would have returned empty from Korti, their surplus cargoes enabling the two hundred men to have their food completed for one hundred days onward. This simple plan would have resulted in assembling at Korti, by a date which I shall presently deal with, five thousand men ready to march across the one hundred and eight miles to Metemmeh.

Now, remember that we had one hundred and thirty of our 'whalers' at Wady Halfa, below the Second Cataract, on 18th October, fifty of them on 14th October. It took three days to pass boats to the head of the Cataract. Had we been allowed to begin passing them up on the 18th October at the rate of even thirty a day (we did fifty a day easily later), we should undoubtedly have been able to have the first batch of twenty-four ready to embark their crews and supplies on the 23rd October. Thirty-five days later, viz. on the 27th November, this unit of twenty-four boats would have been at Korti ; every day after the 27th November would have seen two hundred men landed there, with one hundred days' food, ammunition, tents, etc., etc., complete. To collect five thousand men at Korti would have required twenty-five days from the 27th November, so that on the 22nd December the last of the force could have started from Korti to Metemmeh, the advanced portion of it, say three thousand men, having left that place fourteen days earlier, on the 8th December.

Fifteen days later, viz on the 23rd December, these three thousand men could have been at Metemmeh, within one hundred miles of Khartoum ; they would have met at Metemmeh Gordon's four steamers ; and the same journey which Sir Charles Wilson made one month later would have been accomplished with the advantages of a higher Nile level, Khartoum still held by Gordon, and the fact that another two thousand troops were marching from Korti to their aid.

Let us turn now to what this march across the desert would

have needed. That too was a simple matter. It would have required five thousand camels carrying the kits, food, water, blankets and ammunition for these five thousand men. Water for seven days only need have been carried, as at Gakdul the tanks and water-skins would have been refilled. Water, 100 lbs. ; food for thirty days, 90 lbs. ; ammunition (200 rounds), 10 lbs. ; kit, 20 lbs., leaving a good 150 lbs. available on each camel for reserves of food, hospital comforts, ammunition, etc. One camel-driver to every three camels.

This plan would have enabled some six hundred thousand pounds of food-stuffs to have been carried across with the infantry to the Nile at Metemmeh ; more than half the camels would have then been available to return to Gakdul and Korti to assist the carrying over of other supplies and the accumulation of reserves of all kinds at Metemmeh, which would be the new base for the forward movement on Khartoum by the left bank of the Nile.

This final advance would have had Gordon's four steamers to accompany it on the Nile. Omdurman was held by Gordon until the 15th January. Allowing ten days for this final advance upon Khartoum, and a halt of three to five days at Metemmeh for the arrival of the two thousand infantry there, the united column of five thousand men would have been before Omdurman on or about the 6th of January.

Of course it can never be known if the arrival of that force would have still saved Khartoum on that date. It fell to the Mahdi twenty days later, as we know ; but famine was then the chief if not the only cause of the disaster, and it had only become acute during the week previous to the fall.

A word as to this march across the desert. The Bayuda is not a desert in the sense of the deserts of Nubia and Egypt ; it has vegetation, and its surface is hard and, generally speaking, good for marching. The season of the year was most favourable, and, above all, in physique and strength the men were perfect ; the six weeks' pulling at the oar, tugging at the track-lines, and ' portaging ' had made them hard as nails and fit for any work. The passage of the Bayuda, with kits and baggage, etc., carried on camels, would have been child's play to such men. If the papers of that anxious time, between the 18th October and the 20th December 1884, are still preserved in the records of the War Office, there will be found in them many telegrams and memos from me urging those who had then the executive management of the expedition in their hands to the adoption of methods of loading, movement, and progress of our boats very different from those which had then been ordained and accepted.

Nevertheless, although we had lost by the end of October a full fortnight out of these precious days hitherto saved in the estimate of time given in London on 10th August, there was still time, as subsequent events proved, to have reached the Nile at Metemmeh as sketched above, if even on this first day of November other counsels had prevailed at Wady Halfa, and our boats had not had imposed upon them a load of over half a ton in weight more than that which they had been designed to carry. These extra twelve hundred pounds were destined to lose us another ten or a dozen days on the passage to Korti.

I must pass on from the thought of that horrible time. It was one long, unbroken nightmare to me.

CHAPTER XVII

Delays on the Nile. Success of the 'whalers' Letters Korti The Desert
column Fall of Khartoum. The River column Kirbekan. News of
Gordon's death.

LORD WOLSELEY left Wady Halfa for Dongola in the end of
October, in the hope, I think, that the confusion existing at
the former place would tend to diminish, through its com-
ponent parts being drawn off up the river after him, but this
result did not follow Things became more congested and
confused at Wady Halfa. No dominant mind, no far-seeing
eye remained there. The rival interests and ambitions in
staff and in command which had done so much harm in Cairo
during the six preceding months had now again an opportunity
of showing themselves, and I think that I am well within the
truth when I say that to this cause must be ascribed the loss
of another week, or perhaps ten days, in the steady and continuous flow of the troops up the river. Our boats came on
up the Second Cataract in ever-increasing numbers; by the
middle of November we had despatched one hundred and thirty
of them with thirteen hundred troops, and seventy more with
food and ammunition, for Dongola, and we had another two
hundred boats, fitted and made ready to the last pin, waiting
to embark at Gemai, at the head of the Second Cataract,
their two thousand more men. But these two thousand men
were still far down the river at and below Assouan. During
the seventeen days following the 6th November, only fifteen
weak companies of infantry were ready for embarkation at
Gemai

On 16th November Lord Wolseley came tearing down from
Dongola, doing his fifty miles a day on a camel I met him at
two in the morning at Gemai. What had happened ? Why
were not the troops moving up in greater numbers ? Why
were the companies that had already embarked not doing

quicker work in the ascent of the river ? These and other questions he asked me while the train at Gemai was halting, taking water. I could only speak of my own part in this great work. He was bound for Wady Halfa and would there see for himself. We had sent off two hundred boats ; we had two hundred more lying idle waiting for troops sixty yards from where we were talking. As for their progress, it was no wonder their work had been slow in the rapids ; they were carrying twenty-one days' more food than the load they had been designed and built to carry. I had protested that this load was excessive, but I could do no more I found at Halfa I had ceased to stand where I did from the first inception of the enterprise in London up to the day—the fatal day—that Lord Wolseley had left Halfa for Dongola.

Next morning, the 17th November, I started up river to hasten the boats in their ascent. In five days, working from dawn to dark, I reached Sarkamatto, at the head of the great Dal Cataract, over ninety miles of the worst water on the Nile, including the cataracts of Semneh, Ambigole, Tanjour, Akasha and Dal. These five days had revealed to me the physical causes of the slow ascent of our boats over these river obstacles, and in addition had laid bare a good deal of the moral obstructions to our progress. At all the stations on the banks where garrisons of the Egyptian army had been placed, with the exception of Semneh, the favourable or friendly mind was conspicuous by its absence. In the ranks of the Egyptian army our boat expedition had few friends, nor was this matter for much wonder when the history of the previous six months was taken into account. The Egyptian army of that time was, in its English officers, as strong in ambition as its rank and file were weak in striking power. From Sirdar to junior English subaltern, its officers were as the dogs of war straining on the leash. In the conflict of routes, the one by the Nile had been the peculiar perquisite of the Egyptian army, and portions of that force had been gradually moving up the Nile since December 1883 These units were now—November 1884—echeloned along the river at various points between the Second and Third Cataracts to the number of about three thousand men, and they had to be fed, camped, and generally supplied by the river route. It was for this supply service that the heavy native craft had been passed through the Second Cataract in the end of October, keeping back our English boats, and losing us, as I have said, a full fortnight of our precious time , and all for nothing, as the event proved, for almost the whole of this native craft to which right-of-way had been given became wrecks, either in the Second Cataract or in the succeeding rapids through which I had just passed. The shores of the Nile below Semneh were literally lined with these wrecks. The course that was pursued with regard to the Egyptian army seemed to me to be the worst of three possible alternatives first, they might have been withdrawn altogether to Lower Egypt, thereby relieving the strain of transport by thirty per cent. and leaving our road clear ; second, they might have been pushed on to Dongola, marching by the right bank of the Nile, and at Dongola they could have lived on that province ; and, third, they might be left, as they were left, between the Second and Third Cataracts, to lessen our supplies, block our way, and be all but useless to us in any way. The first course would have left the Egyptian army officers with a grievance, but it would have meant for us a clear road to our destination. The second course would have had the great advantage of making the Egyptian officers willing rivals in this enterprise ; the third and adopted course not only kept the grievance intact, but it added fully twenty per cent. to the innumerable difficulties which we had to face and overcome. There was yet another alternative possible : it was to have sent the Egyptian army to Suakim, and with three or four battalions of British troops from India, let it hammer away at the Dervishes under Osman Digna from that side, and endeavour to open the road to Berber. If it failed, no great harm would have been done ; if it succeeded, the gain to the general stock of the effort to save Gordon and Khartoum would have been very great.

At Dal on the 21st November I had realised that, under the existing conditions of affairs, the prospects of reaching Gordon in time had already become terribly doubtful. I wired back to Halfa a list of the things that seemed to me to demand the quickest measures of reform, and then I pushed on for the head of the Third Cataract, with the intention of getting into direct touch with Lord Wolseley, and laying my accumulated

knowledge before him. Workıng, as before, from early light
to dusk, I reached the head of the Third Cataract on the 27th
November, havıng averaged twenty miles a day, cataracts,
rapids, and all included. But the telegraph had beaten me,
notwithstanding all my haste. I was about to experience at
the head of the Third Cataract what was perhaps the cruellest
check of all my lıfe. I knew the whole thing now It was the
last hour ın the chances still left to us of savıng Gordon. This
was the 28th November. No boat save mine had yet passed
this Third Cataract. Why ? Because three weeks had been
thrown away in the starting of the boats ; because, even at
this eleventh hour, our boats were loaded up to their gunwales
and down to the water's edge with cargo largely in excess of
theır rightful loads ; because, as yet, the work was being done
under the benumbing ınfluence of all the doubt and distrust
in the possibility of our English boats overcoming the difficulties of this long rıver ascent, whıch the six months' fight
between the Army Councillors in Cairo had long since made
the common property of the officers and men of the rıval
armies in Egypt.

Instead of being taken at once as the sole means of reachıng
ın time, and with sufficient force, the destination for which we
were bound, our boats had been grudgingly accepted by the
various chiefs, staffs, and departments as things which had to
prove their fitness for the task before any one would believe
in them. Hence there had grown up the thousand queries
and the querulousness which, in an enterprise such as this
we were engaged upon, meant a lot of lost power in every
day's work and ın most men's individual efforts ; the horrible
' What is the use ? ' and ' Why ıs this last hour asked of us ? '
which knock off from every hour some moments and from the
day's work a few mıles. Oh, how I gnashed my teeth at this
apathy, as ın that upward journey of ten days, through cataract,
whirlpool, and rapid, I saw it, heard it, and felt it in heart
and soul ; at military station, on sandbank ; in the lifting of
a biscuit-box ; ın the halt or the start ; until at last, by the
sheer dumb proof which the boats were themselves giving of
their capacity to their captaıns and their crews, belief in them
grew stronger, and many ceased at length to doubt, ' crab,'
and grumble. But the moment of their admitted triumph

had not yet arrived, and already the sands in the hour-glass of possible success were running very, very low. I have said that I was beaten by the telegraph. It was in this way. I firmly believed that if I could get to Lord Wolseley for even one hour, I should have little difficulty in showing him the exact state of matters over all the two hundred and twenty miles between Dongola and Wady Halfa. I was not at that moment aware of the contents of the letter he had received at Wady Halfa on the 18th November from Gordon, dated Khartoum, 4th November, but I knew that Khartoum was hard pressed by foes without and want of food within, and I was as certain as man can be that with our boats, and in the food they carried, lay the only chance we had of arriving in time to save the town. There was no use in deploring the time already lost, but to get the last mile of distance for our boats out of every remaining day, and save the first and last glint of daylight for our work in the time that yet remained to us, did seem to me an object worth every risk that could be run to win it. It was in this effort that the telegraph beat me. It had been at work from Wady Halfa to Dongola. It was decreed that I was not to pass beyond the head of the Third Cataract ! I was not to see the commander-in-chief ! I must go back to Dal ! What I wrote that afternoon in my boat in the middle of the Nile, somewhere in the broad water below the isle of Argo, I could not now recall, but I remember that my pencil flew over the blank backs of some nine or ten large Egyptian telegraph forms, as no pen or pencil of mine ever went before or since. I handed the packet of tissue sheets to the messenger to give to Lord Wolseley in Dongola, and then turned down-stream with, I think, the heaviest heart and saddest brain I had ever known in my life

When evening came, I put into the village of Mochi and began to write again :—

' You have known me long enough to know that disregard of orders, much less disregard of *your* orders, is not my line of conduct, but I would have thought that there was enough in the past to show that when you set me a task it was best to let me work it in my own way. Had you tied me down six years ago on the Red River you would not have known at Fort Francis that the Winnipeg River was only a week's work for the expedition, and the men would

have been committed to the swamps of the north-west angle of the
Lake of the Woods as all the experts and others, save myself,
counselled and advised. Again, if you had not given me my own
head in Ashanti eleven years ago, you would have had ten thousand
more fighting men arrayed against you at a very critical moment
in the battle of Amoaful ; and, coming down to our work of yesterday and to-day, was it not through your letting me work this boat
idea from the beginning on my own lines that you have at the
present moment six hundred boats ready above the Second Cataract,
that I have one above the Third Cataract, and that there might
have been fifty above it to-day had the old order of time and despatch
of troops been adhered to ? and that all this had been done within
the limit of time, please remember, which the highest naval authorities in England had declared would be required for only building
the boats in England. I go back over the past and speak of the
present work now only because your words and actions to-day
have forced these recollections upon me. It had never entered
my head for a moment to remain more than a few hours in Dongola.
I should have gone down the river again in a very different position
and armed with a very different authority from that which I shall
now do ; not that I shall not use every effort, sparing myself in no
way to effect the more rapid movement up river ; but my words
will not be heard in the noise of the slap in the face I have been given
to-day, the sound of which will be grateful to many to whom I am
distasteful because I have been identified with this expedition by
ceaselessly furthering its interests. I freely admit that the ortho-
dox English staff officer would have stopped at Hafir to-day, to-
morrow, and the day after, eyeglass in eye and cigarette in mouth ;
but, on the other hand, he would have taken sixteen to eighteen
days to ascend the river from Sarras to Hafir, and when acting on
your orders to go back on the seventeenth or nineteenth day to
try and galvanise the slow moving mass of boats into quicker
work, his words would have had about as much effect upon Tommy
Atkins as his cigarette smoke would have had in dulling the
Egyptian sky. Unfortunately perhaps for me, these were not my
methods of work ; and I fear they never will be. I realised from
the first that we were dealing with a lot of unwilling horses at these
Nile fences, and that the only chance of getting them quickly over
the water-jumps was to give them a lead over.'

Then I set down again the many things that had tended
and were tending to delay us—the loads, greater than those
first intended, and double those carried on the Red River ,

the mistake of having *increased* the boat-loads and *decreased* the number of men per boat, thereby reducing the live motive-power and adding to the dead weight in every boat, and all this following upon a clear loss of ten to fifteen days in starting from the Second Cataract. But above all these things combined I put the moral factor, the impression engendered originally in the minds of the men by the long-continued abuse of the boat scheme, that they (the boats) were not able for the work. The men of these earlier days of boat-work were not keen at it. My notebooks of the time were full of instances of laziness .—

'The work,' I wrote, ' at its best was mechanically done : in its normal state it was lethargic ; at its worst it was unwilling, careless, and even worse. Heart there was none in it. There was neither insolence nor refusal, no positive insubordination ; simply a clogged, lethargic " hands-down" attitude that was even more hopeless than the most insubordinate refusal ; the word " alacrity " had no place in the day's business.'

I might multiply that extract by many others of a similar kind. This enterprise of ours was the grandest and the noblest work in war tried in my time. I felt all the enthusiasm of its splendid purpose, its colossal difficulties, its grand theatre, this wondrous old river, in every fibre of my being ; and in all the length of the chain at which we tugged from Cairo to Dongola, I knew there was only one man to whom I could appeal with the hope of being listened to at this last moment possible to our success. Well, it is all long buried in the dead past now. But for the last few days as I write I have been looking again into the old notebooks, wherein I find some of the letters and telegraph messages and orders blurred and blotted with the sweat and dust of many a bygone bivouac, and it comes back again with something of the sweet and the bitter which I then knew— for, despite failure and dashed hope, that old wonderful river, in the various phases of its own mysterious life, had become to me a strange solace, despite the savagery of its wild rocks and the whirling waters of its cataracts.

During the thirty days following the rebuff at Hafir, I went up and down the cataracts, hustling lagging boats, giving a lead through a rapid, getting an extra half-hour out of a bevy of boats, distributing copies of a general order to commanding officers, and often taking a hand on the tug-line to shame some loitering boat's-crew into better work.

In the dangerous reaches above the Second Cataract I had a few quiet spots selected, on island or mainland, into which we steered at dusk, tied up, lighted a fire of driftwood, had supper, and laid down blankets for the night. These are the memories of the Nile that still live with me, and it was these scenes that soon made me see, through the foredoom of our failure, how small it all was in comparison with this mighty desert of death and the stream of life that flowed through it. Mixed up with messages to Wady Halfa, boat orders, and letters to Dongola, I find bits such as this :—

' 14th Dec. Kaibar —Sent camel with letters to Dongola. Got away 8.30 Three hours' writing. Late sleepers and starters, the modern soldier and officer. The breed is falling off. Another rasping letter from ——. Fine breeze up long reach of river to the two big rocks. Freshness of wind off desert and fragrance of aromatic sand plants. Officers lose touch of their men as they rise in rank. It is the penalty they pay for promotion. Napoleon in 1815 was not the General Bonaparte of 1796. Camped near " sont " trees, beside old graves. Petrified wood. Granite boulders. Sadness of these Nubian Nile evenings—the wailing sounds of the water-wheel all through the night, the low moan of the wind through ragged thorn bushes and dry grass stalks. There is more true philosophy, as it is called, in the Lord's Prayer than in all the books ever written by man ; take it slowly word by word and weigh the words. With regard to this expedition, ask M——, or any other independent man who has worked this line of communications, as to what the feeling of the Naval and Egyptian (Army) officers is. Ambigol, Dal, latterly Absaret, Kaibar—all alike. Shot a wild goose. Camped on island in middle of Third Cataract. Stars. Roar of river.

' 14th Dec.—Up to top of Cataract. Hard pulling in rapids, but did it all by oars and sails. No tracking. To Abu Fatmeh at 8 30 A.M. Earle there Here all the swells are passing up to Korti. All going by camel, too precious to trust themselves in boats, apparently. I am to be the Moses of the expedition, not to enter the promised land.

' 15th Dec —Off down the Third Cataract again. These rapids are my treadmill. Big fish killed in shallow water ; Krooboys forced him on rock and Tom Williams stunned him with blow of axe on head — five feet in length and a hundred and twelve pounds in weight. Good eating to-night. Camped island below Cataract. Found my camel and Farag the driver on mainland He had been up to Dongola, down to Dal, and up again here in last ten days. Splendid fellow, black as night. Cold night. Crew tired.

'16th Dec.—Off to Kaibar on camel. Farag finds a donkey and comes as guide across desert. Donkey collapses, shutting up like a closing telescope Go on alone, through desert of rocks, four hours, then sight Nile and two big rocks. Three hours more to Kaibar. Many sails of boats visible on reach below Cataract. Thirty have passed Kaibar in last four days. Camel tired. Sleep on ground very soundly after long ride Wallets for pillow. Camel near me.

'17th Dec —In steam pinnace No 102 from Kaibar towards Hanneck through twenty or more boats all doing well Poor boats! Some of them look worn, pitched, patched, and tin-plated, yet going gaily in light wind and able to do more in the long run than any steam pinnace. Passed poor old Colonel ——, wounded at Tel-el-Kebir, full of pluck, teeth all gone, and helmet too. Got wood for pinnace on Isle Adwin. What work! Recalls West Coast days eleven years ago. Ran aground on sandbank going up west channel, in water up to middles, trying to shove her off. No go, sand silts up round us in strong current. After an hour boat still fast in mid-river. Natives come out. Watching play of sand in current, I see only chance is to get head of pinnace up-stream, sand has then no lee side to silt up on. We get head up-stream. I take helm, crew in water stamping on sand. Go ahead full speed Shove bow, keep sand shifting with feet. Scrape over bank into deep water. All jump in. Away up river to Zimmet Island, which we reach after dark. My boat comes down to meet me at Wood Station, and I get to Gibbs' Camp late Gibbs wrecked five times in thirty-nine days in nuggers between Sarras and Fatineh. Greeks at Dongola buy Hicks Pasha's treasure from Dervishes at four shillings the sovereign! This Greek is the man we are really fighting for. He will outstay us all.

'20th Dec.—Down river again to Kaibar. Struck rock in Shaban rapid, damaged, repair. Passed seventy-five boats going well, good wind. Found two Colonels on portage.

'22nd Dec.—Passed forty-six boats over Cataract. All day on portage. Arrived, Colonel of Gordon Highlanders and two boats, seventeen days from Gemai. That is what should be!

'23rd Dec.—Passed twenty boats over Cataract. Hot day. Old sheik of Cataract and his men and boys on rocks. Sheik gives them

one piastre a day. I keep his pay in arrear. He says he will strike.
I tell the interpreter to say to him my stick will do the same : three
shillings a boat too much to give the old rascal. Gesticulations,
shoutings, rocks. Work well done.

'24th —Writing telegrams. Peel, Wortley pass to Korti All
the others gone there. I am out in the cold with a vengeance.
Wrote letter in reply to Buller, who has gone on to Korti a week ago
on camel. Curious Christmas Eve.

'25th —And stranger Christmas Day. Naval Brigade passes
Kaibar fifteen days out from Sarras. At 2.30 I start up river again,
get a goose with a long-shot bullet at dusk, and have him for dinner
—a welcome change from Chicago "bully" beef. Moonlight in
the desert rocks. Stars, intense silence, no sound to-night of water-
wheel, man or beast, from the surrounding desert Are the shep-
herds keeping their night-watches, as of old, on the Judean hills ?
Outlines of those hills the same as these Stars, Canopus, Sirius
all here too. How the scene is brought before one ! '

It was at this time that an express reached me from Kaibar
reporting that a box of treasure, carried in a cartridge-box,
had been missed from a camel ammunition convoy four days
earlier farther down the river—eleven thousand pounds in
gold. The convoy was then at Kaibar. I sent back an order
directing the convoy, about one hundred and forty camels,
to proceed on its march next day across the desert to Abu
Fatmeh as usual, and I wrote privately to the officer in charge
telling him to halt his convoy some four miles out in the open
desert and to await my arrival , then I rode out to the spot
indicated. I found the convoy halted as directed. I formed
the men, soldiers and natives, in two lots, and told them that
a box of treasure was missing ; that it could not have been lost ,
that it must either have been stolen or be still with the column ;
and I offered twenty-five pounds reward to any man who would
step out and say where the box was. I told them further that
if no one would reveal the whereabouts of the treasure, I would
be obliged to institute a close search in saddles, bags, etc.,
and even to strip everybody to their skins I gave five minutes
for reflection, and then began the search. Everything was
opened out , the place was as bare as the palm of one's hand ;
the sun was brilliant above ; nothing was found—not one
golden sovereign could be seen in package, pocket, or saddle.
There was nothing more to be done, and after an hour spent

in this fruitless examination, I ordered the convoy to load up
and proceed south. I reported the loss, the box of golden
sovereigns was ' written off ' in the official phraseology, and in
due time the convoy reached Dongola, and proceeded with
the other camel transport across the Bayuda towards Metemmeh. The day of Abu Klea came , the square, inside of which
were the baggage and riding camels, was broken by the wild
rush of the Arab spearmen, and a desperate fight ensued within
the broken square itself, a fight in which the wedged mass
of camels alone saved the day. In the midst of the fiercest
fighting a cry arose for more cartridges ; boxes were hastily
opened, and out from one of these boxes rolled a mass of golden
sovereigns. The fighting was forgotten by the men who were
nearest to the scene, a wild scramble ensued, and in half a
minute the last piece of gold had been fobbed up. What had
originally happened was that the cartridge-box containing the
gold had got mixed up with the cases of ammunition, and as
the boxes had only some small private mark to indicate them,
the mistake was only discovered in the square at Abu Klea.

I spent the 26th December forcing up the rapids which
extend for several miles below the Third Cataract, and giving
help to the many boats which were now labouring over a
particularly difficult piece of water called Shaban. This
cataract was not marked upon our maps, but it had proved the
most dangerous of any in the whole river. Of the dozen
soldiers and *voyageurs* lost in the length of the five hundred
miles from Wady Halfa to Hebbeh, Shabah cost us three lives.
I had now run it up and down half a dozen times without
accident, but in this last trip on 26th December it all but
caught us, and in a way most unexpected.

We were forcing up a very bad ' gate ' between rocks, and
were doing well in very swift and apparently deep water,
when the stern-post suddenly touched a sunken rock, stopping
the way on the boat   Instantly the bow fell off to one side,
and the boat swung round at a tremendous pace, pivoting upon
the held stern-post. The passage was extremely narrow between the rocks ; if the bows touched the rock ever so slightly,
we were over in water running faster than any mill-race. The
bows whirled round clear. I don't think there were four
inches to spare. A week earlier we had run this passage, but

the river had fallen a foot in the interval, and that sunken tooth had got within biting distance of our kelson. It is such an incident as this which makes the cataract reaches of the Nile so difficult and dangerous.

I got to my island haven in the Third Cataract early on the 27th, and found there the following note from Colonel Frederick Maurice of Abu Fatmeh, addressed to me ' At top of Shaban Gate,' 25th December .—

' Received last night following telegram from Genl. Buller, Korti : '' If you can get at Butler, ask him to come here as soon as can.'' I have your camel ready for you, and if you decide to go by camel will make up a party for you somehow, but wait for you to decide numbers, etc. Christmas and New Year best wishes.'

I rode the camel to Fatmeh, the boat arrived later , we filled in with a hundred days' rations, and at 9.30 next morning we were off for Korti. By the evening of the 30th we had covered eighty miles of river ; then the north wind fell, and the oar and track-line had to be used. On New Year's Day Debbeh was passed, and at sunrise on 4th January I reached Korti.

1 have already told in detail the story of the Nile Expedition as it had impressed me as a subordinate actor in its strangely varied scenes [1] I regarded it then, and I still think of it, as the most remarkable attempt made in modern times to conquer in four months the difficulties of great distance, the absence of food supplies, and the opposition of a very brave and determined enemy, flushed by a long career of victory, and filled with a fanaticism as fierce as that which had carried the Arabian soldiers of the Prophet over half the Eastern and Western world twelve centuries earlier.

The Nubian village of Korti was a strange place in the first half of January 1885. One saw there on the high bank of the Nile an extraordinary mixture of the masses and the classes of English social life. The English boats were arriving in crowds daily, all carrying their five months' food supplies— three months for their own crews, and two months for the camel column which was to cross the Bayuda desert to Metemmeh. Truly had these wonderful little ' whalers '

[1] *The Campaign of the Cataracts.*

brought their own revenges along with them. Here, in the face of guardsmen and journalists, and officers and men of twenty different regimental corps, was written large in the vast verity of victuals—the only truth that appeals to all classes and creeds—the fact that by the means of these long-derided and abused boats, and by them alone, had this concentration of men, horses, and camels been possible at this Bayuda village fourteen hundred miles from Alexandria—all done within four and a half months from the date on which the long-delayed permission to build and equip these same boats had been grudgingly given to me in London.

I shall enter here extracts from two letters I had written from London to my wife in August 1884 .—

'*9th August*

' Here I am after four days of intense heat. I do think I have done in these four days four weeks of ordinary War Office work. But such vacillation you cannot imagine ! They are veering about like weathercocks It is terrible to have to serve such idiots. The heat is Egyptian . eighty-four degrees in the coolest room.'

And again .—

'*12th August.*

' A hasty line to report progress It would take long hours to tell you of the struggles of the past week One day we won, the next we lost, but to-day the opponents of my plan have caved in, and our four hundred boats are to be ordered. We have got two hundred already fixed, and hope to have the other two hundred settled in two days from now. I am to go out in charge of them in the end of September. This morning I got a letter from Lord —— by mounted messenger to go to breakfast with him at nine o'clock. We had a long fight all day with the " Fuzboi " (*i.e.* the Authorities), and at 4 P.M. we won In a week from this day the whole four hundred boats will be out.'

Just two months later, on the 17th October, I wrote thus from Korosko .—

' Here I am on my way to Wady Halfa, all going well so far as my particular business is concerned, but the outside work of transport and supply is by no means so flourishing. I do not hesitate to say that in the long seven hundred miles from here to Cairo, eight out of every ten of our own people are either actively or passively opposed to our expedition, ready to make the most instead of the least of difficulties, and to " crab " the project as much as they can. It is a most unfortunate state of things, but, in spite of all difficulties, I feel pretty certain of getting one hundred of our boats away from the Second Cataract by the 1st of November or sooner.'

Another snapshot letter, ten days later :—

' BAL-EL-KEBIR, 2ND CATARACT, 26th October.

' During the last three or four days my work has at times been more than exacting. I have had a hard battle, but as I write I am a winner all along the line. Briefly the position was this. The railway from Halfa to Sarras had quite broken down. In London it had been counted on for the carriage of our boats round the great Second Cataract. We were, therefore, face to face with the necessity of taking the boats through this Second Cataract, the worst obstacle on the river. I examined the cataract on the day following my arrival at Halfa, and saw the manner in which the naval people proposed to take our " whalers " up. I saw at once that they must smash the precious craft to atoms. They really did not know the first principles of rope-work in rapids. I protested, but to no avail, they were to have their way. Then I came out here, fifteen miles from Halfa, and determined to stop them when they had smashed the first boats. On the way out I heard of the loss of one, and the dangerous escapes of a few others. I wrote most strongly to Lord W. and to Buller, protesting. The camp of the sailors is six miles from here, and I found that they did not arrive at their work here until 9 A.M. No boat had yet passed the " Great Gate ", the one lost had been lost lower down the river. I determined to take a boat through the " Great Gate " with natives, on my own plan, before any of the sailors appeared on the scene. The telegram will probably have told you of my success. The boat was through by 7.45 A.M. safe and sound, and when the naval people arrived, they found the problem solved. Lord W. and Buller appeared later : then the navy tried their plan. We waited four hours on the locks At last the ponderous gear was set going, the boat narrowly escaped destruction three or four times, and nothing but her wonderful strength and buoyancy saved her Then all were convinced, and I was allowed to have my own way. But what a fight it has been ! I was deserted by all. Buller was dead against me. It was not a pleasant thing for them *to be obliged to eat their own words with their own eyes.* (Allow me the bull.) This is a wild spot I am camped on a point with rapids all around, the heat is a hundred degrees in my tent ; but I am very well, thank God, and yesterday was a

bright day in my life. What I prized most was the success of the
boats ; the one tried by the navy was put by their methods into the
worst whirlpool in the " Great Gate," and rode it through in
triumph. . . .'

One more snapshot letter from that distant time and I have
done :—

'KORTI, 12th *January* 1885

' I sent you a few words of cheer at Christmas by wire, but my
letters have been getting fewer. I really had not the heart to write
bad news. I had suffered so much from what I must always regard
as unjust treatment at the hands of my " best friends " that I could
only go on day after day working, and lying down each night with
the hope, which work done gives, that it would all come right in
the end Well, it has come, if not right, certainly better than it was.
The past cannot now be undone—those long weeks when I was denied
the most pressing wants. That is over, thank God, but the harm it
all caused to the boats cannot be set right. It is too long and too
painful a story to tell you now ; but sometime perhaps you will
hear it all. I had gone over my weary river reach between Kaibar
and the Third Cataract for the eighth time, when I got a telegram
calling me up here. I came like the wind, completing the *straight*
run from Sarras to Korti in eighteen days—the quickest passage
made by any boat. No 387 had covered above one thousand miles
of the Nile since I quitted Gemai on the 17th November. The
papers will have told you long ago what is being done here, but they
will not have told you that three-quarters and more of the supplies
for the Desert Camel Column has come from our " whalers." . . .
I have indeed had ample recompense for the thought and labour
given to these boats and to this expedition in the unspoken approval
of the officers and *men*. The latter know well enough who works
for them. . . . I have sent to Cox & Co. my pay and allowances
for last three months, only £160 or thereabouts. It is less pay, all
counted, than I got in Devonport, and I have a lower position on
the staff here than I had there. So much for what you thought
" my sincere friends " would do for me in the way of " local rank."
Still, I say to myself that " it is all right." War is the sum of all
human wrongdoing, and it also holds every other possible injustice
in it. Never mind, " cheer up." It will be all for the best in the
long run '

At Korti, in that first week of 1885, there was only one thing wanting—camels. Had two or three thousand additional camels been collected at Korti by Christmas Day 1884, a brigade of British troops might have easily reached Metemmeh on the 10th January, even as things then stood as regards men and supplies . and a second brigade have been following closely in their wake. But there is little to be gained out of ' might have beens ' by people who are fed and nurtured upon the false facts of doctored history.

When I reached Korti on 4th January, the advanced portion of the Desert Column had already left that place for Gakdul, a watering-place half-way on the road to Metemmeh, but the number of camels to mount and carry supplies, even for a force of two thousand fighting-men, was totally insufficient, and it was necessary to unload the camels at Gakdul, form a dépôt there, and bring the animals back again to Korti for another load of supplies. Thus the leading portion of the force left Korti on the 30th December, arrived at Gakdul after a forced march on the morning of the 2nd January, started again for Korti on the same evening, and reached that place at noon on the 5th January, having covered a total distance of one hundred and ninety-six miles in five days and twenty-one hours   This march sealed the fate of the Desert Column. The camel is a much enduring beast of burden, but one hundred and ninety-six miles in one hundred and forty-one consecutive hours was more than even he could bear. It was pitiable to see these poor beasts dragging themselves to the river on the 5th, 6th, and 7th, many of them falling dead at the water's edge as they tried to drink. The main body of the Desert Column finally left Korti on 8th January, reached Gakdul on the morning of the 12th, and at 2 P.M. on the 14th January started on the remaining ninety miles to Metemmeh. The camels were now completely done. As the *Official History* says, ' They had been marching for sixteen days almost without a rest on a short allowance of food, and with little water ' Every single camel had been doing, or trying to do, the work of two, perhaps of three animals   I need not delay over the remaining history of that unfortunate column. It fought splendidly at Abu Klea and Abu Cru, and reached the Nile on the night of 19th January. Gordon's four steamers, which had been lying there since September, came into touch with the column on the afternoon of the 21st. The 22nd was spent in making a naval reconnaissance down the river to Shendy, which town was heavily shelled. The 23rd was taken up with the naval business of carrying out repairs to the steamers, and at 3 P.M. on that day, Captain Lord C. Beresford, R.N., reported to Sir Charles Wilson that the vessels were ready to proceed At 8 A.M. the next day, the 24th January, two steamers, *Bordein* and *Telahawiyah*, left Gubat for Khartoum All the rest is too well known. On the 28th the steamers came into sight of Khartoum at 11 A.M., and, steaming slowly forward under a heavy fire from several points, realised about 2 P.M. that the city was in the hands of the Mahdi. As they were returning down-stream the news of the fall of Khartoum two days earlier reached them. Our great Nile Expedition had ended in failure.

Meanwhile, at Korti, the despatch of the infantry column destined to proceed to Berber in boats by the river had gone forward unceasingly, and on the 16th January I left Korti, having by that date seen two hundred and seventeen boats repaired, stored with a hundred days' supplies, and sent forward to Hamdab at the foot of the Fourth Cataract, about fifty miles up-stream from Korti. In the dozen days spent on the river shore at Korti many people came to look at our work, and exchange a word with me, too many of them a last word— Herbert Stewart, Primrose, Burnaby, Wilson, Piggott and De Lisle, Dickson, Swaine, Grove, Talbot, Pirie, Peel, Brocklehurst, Wardrop, Rhodes, M'Calmont, Barrow, Alleyne, Adye, Stuart-Wortley, Fitzgerald, Colborne, Martin, Sandwith, Blundell, Wauchope, Boyd, O'Neal; and there would also come along this high bank to have a word about the boats the special correspondents attached to the Expedition: Williams, Cameron, St. Leger, Herbert, Colborne, Bennett-Burleigh, Melton Prior, and another who was something of many things, one of the most dauntless mortals I ever met in life. Many of these men left their bones in the Soudan; some rose to high place in their profession, but the story of the end of the one whom I have last mentioned, is so strange that I must tell it here

I first met him in California in 1873, on my way from British Columbia to the West Coast of Africa. We next met in the Cataract of Dal, where I found him attempting to work up the Nile in a tiny steam launch which held himself, a stoker, and one other person. He was wrecked shortly after, but got up with the Naval Brigade, made the desert march, and was present with Lord Charles Beresford in his action at Wad Habeshi above Metemmeh on the 3rd February. On his way up the Nile he had indulged in the then, and now, fashionable tourist pursuit of tomb-rifling and mummy-lifting; and he had become possessed of a really first-class mummy, which, still wrapped in its cerecloths, had been duly packed and sent to England. When the Nile Expedition closed, he went to Somaliland, and, somewhere in the foothills of Abyssinia, was finally killed by an elephant, and was buried on a small island in a river flowing from Abyssinia southwards. The mummy got at Luxor eventually reached London. The correspondent's friends, anxious to get their brother's remains to England, sent out a man with orders to proceed to the spot where he had been buried and bring the remains home. This man reached the river, together with the Somali hunters who had accompanied the deceased on his hunting expedition the previous year, but no trace could be found of the little island on which the grave was made ; a great flood had descended from the Abyssinian mountains, and the torrent had swept the island before it, leaving no trace of grave or island. Now comes the moral. The mummy was in due time unwound in London, and the experts in Egyptology set to work to decipher the writings on the wrappings Truly were they spirit rappings! There, in characters about which there was no cavilling on the part of the experts, were written a varied series of curses upon the man who would attempt to disturb the long repose of the mummified dead. 'May he,' ran the invocations, ' be abandoned by the gods. May wild beasts destroy his life on earth, and after his death may the floods of the avenging rivers root up his bones, and scatter his dust to the winds of heaven.'

The only other verification of the curse of a mummy that I have met with is one still more striking. It will be found recorded in a well-known work on Syria and Palestine, *The Land and the Book*, by Thomson, an American missionary in Syria. He tells us that some time in the 'fifties of the last century, the hidden tomb of an old Phœnician king was discovered at Sidon. The lid of the sarcophagus bore a long

inscription in Phœnician characters. It was found to be a
continuous adjuration to 'Every royal person and to every
man not to open my sepulchre . . . nor to take away the
sarcophagus of my funeral couch, nor to transfer me with my
funeral couch upon the couch of another.' Then comes the
sentence : for ' the holy gods . . . shall cut off that royal
person and that man who has opened my couch or who has
abstracted this sarcophagus, and so also the posterity of that
royal person . . . whoever he be, nor shall his root be planted
downward nor his fruit spring upward . . . because I am to
be pitied, snatched away before my time like a flowing river.'
The missionary Thomson (he is writing in the late 'fifties) then
goes on to say : ' These imprecations will scarcely be visited
upon Louis Napoleon, or the officers of the French corvette,
La Sérieuse, on board of which the sarcophagus was carried
to France.' Had he waited another dozen years or so he might
perhaps have omitted that final sentence.

I make this digression because I have always objected to
the ghoulish desire on the part of so many of our people to rifle
tombs in Egypt, a practice which, in spite of regulations, has
obtained extensively in recent years. I have myself been the
recipient of an official order to embark eighteen large cases of
tomb ' finds ' as ' regimental baggage ' at Alexandria.

I can tell only in brief the fortunes of the River Column,
which left the foot of the Fourth Cataract on the 24th January
1885, in two hundred and seventeen of our boats, carrying
twenty-four thousand men, fully provisioned for three months.
Of the river and the country before us nothing was known
beyond the fact that the former, for a distance of over one
hundred miles, was regarded as being hopelessly impracticable
for boats of any description, and that the shores consisted of
rocks piled together in such confused masses as to render
the passage of horses and camels along them impossible for
long distances. ' You will get your boats over the cataracts
between Wady Halfa and Dongola,' a traveller in these regions
said to me in London in September, ' but you will never get
them over the cataracts of the Monassir country.' It was
this country of the Monassir that now lay in our front, and, to
add to its natural embarrassments of land and water, the whole
of the Monassir tribe and that of the Robatab, with Arabs

from Berber, had elected to try their strength against us in the worst part of the route, a long defile known as the Shukook Pass.

From the 24th January to the 10th February we worked away at these rocks and cataracts harder than ever, but with the difference that the Toilers of the River had to be protected from hostile attack along the shores. To me fell this duty, and I was now riding the rocks on an Arab pony, as before I had been breasting the rapids in a boat. But, though moving on the shore, I had still charge of the boat advance, the official phrase being, ' to command the advanced guard both by land and water ' The double duty involved in these orders was arduous but interesting One had to keep an eye all round the compass , in front and on the right flank for the enemy, on the river to the left, and to the rear upon our own people By this time I had come to know the various values of the Nile waters pretty accurately, what our boats could do against the Nile, and what the Nile could do at its worst against our boats Thus I was able by noon each day to form an estimate of the spot on the river shore which a force of four companies of infantry would be able to reach by evening. I then looked about for the best camping-place on the shore, waited until the first boat had arrived there, gave orders for the thorn bushes to be cut, laid out the ground for the zereba, and then went forward again with the forty hussars and the score of camel-men to explore the rocks in front for six or eight miles, getting back at nightfall to find the advanced guard of four or six companies assembled there, and all made ready for the night. The main body of the River Column would be camped from two to six miles behind, according to the difficulties their boats had met in the day's ascent through the cataracts These latter were even more formidable than any we had encountered below Dongola, but our men were now thoroughly seasoned ; they had become exceedingly expert in all kinds of bad water, and, but for the necessities imposed by the presence of an active enemy always only a few miles in our front, it would have been possible for the column to make an average distance of perhaps eight or ten miles daily. With an enemy, however, in proximity, it became necessary to keep the battalions concentrated at night, excepting the advanced guard under my command, which had its separate camp some miles in front of the main body.

On the 5th and 6th February some strange things happened. I reached, early on the 5th, a high ridge of black rocks with a line of white quartz rock at top running at a right angle from the shore, and having an ugly pass choked with large boulders between its western end and the river A slave-boy, who had come to us from the Arabs, declared that his late owners were behind this ridge We, therefore, threaded the tumbled rocks with caution, passed the end of the ridge, and found clearer ground at its further side. The pass between ridge and river had breastworks of loose stones in it, and a rude hut of the same construction stood in its centre. I climbed the rock ridge to the right and had a lengthened survey of the rugged land in front. It was all a tossed and tumbled region of black and lighter coloured rocks, and the river, where it could be seen, deep sunken between its iron shores, was a tossing tumbling torrent of water. This ridge, Kirbekan, which rose about four hundred feet above the river, had been occupied by the Mahdists two days earlier ; they had left it for the real Shukook Pass, the entrance to which we could see two miles forward, marked by a particularly black and forbidding mass of rocks. I did not get back to the bivouac till after dark, and I found there an unusual order awaiting me. It was to halt horses and boats next morning, and await orders in camp. These came early They were of strange and fatal import. The end had come suddenly. The Desert Column had reached the Nile at Metemmeh ; Wilson had found Khartoum in the hands of the Mahdi. He had returned to Metemmeh with the greatest difficulty. Our column was to stand fast until further orders were received. Earle joined me next morning I took him to a high hill in the neighbourhood of the zereba, from the summit of which he could see Kerbekan and many other hills ahead. Seated there alone we talked of the future. We were old friends, dating back to the days of the Red River and Montreal in 1870. Earle was a man of very fine character. He had seen service in the Crimea, at Alma, Inkermann, and the Siege It was curious that now, when we had talked over all our present prospects and chances, his mind seemed prone to revert to these old scenes of Crimean service. He described, as we walked back to the zereba, the day of the Alma, thirty years earlier, ' the last of the old style of battles,' he called it, before the rifle in the hands of the infantry soldier had put an end to the pomp and circumstance of war for ever.

Two days later, on the 9th, I was ordered forward again, this time to find the black ridge of Kirbekan bristling with the Mahdi's spearmen. It didn't matter now. I had seen the land beyond the ridge on the 5th, had climbed the ridge itself, examined the pass between ridge and river ; there was nothing more to learn about it ; and when General Earle arrived with his staff at midday on the 9th, I had the plan of attack ready for him, the troops in position twelve hundred yards in front of the enemy's ridge.

Things had fallen out most fortunately for me. Had I been two days earlier at Kirbekan I should have found the Arabs there, and could not have examined the length and depth of the formidable position which they held. A day later it would have been the same, but on the 5th I had just hit off one of the two days in which the ridge was clear of the enemy. I had, in fact, eaten my midday biscuit and cheese on the very spot which, five days later, formed the key of the enemy's position.

But Earle and Brackenbury had a plan of their own for a front attack, and, of course, I said nothing about my plan until they asked me what I thought of theirs. Then I said my say. It was not to attack in front, for I knew every inch of the ground, having spent half an hour on foot stumbling over its maze of boulders four days before. ' What then ? ' they asked. ' March round the left flank of the ridge,' I said, ' and attack from the rear ; the ground is open on that side.' This plan was finally agreed to, provided I would run a line that evening round the flank I proposed to turn, and make assurance doubly sure that the ground was as feasible to the foot in practice as my eye, looking at it from the top of the ridge on the 5th, had deemed it to be. A couple of hours before sunset I took a small patrol out, and working round through the desert unobserved by the Arabs, got well in rear of their line on Kerbekan, so near to them that, looking over a lower spur on the reverse side of their position, I could see their movements on and behind the ridge, and count their numbers. I had got to within five hundred yards of their supper fires. I got back after sunset to the bivouac. Earle was alone, sitting on an old sakeyeh wheel. I told him that in an hour and a quarter his force could be in rear of the Arab position, marching over easy ground. He sent for Brackenbury. ' The account is so favourable,' he said when the latter officer appeared, ' that I think we must give up the idea of a front attack, move round the left flank of the ridge, and assault from the rear ' This manœuvre was done early the following morning with complete success. We turned the position on its left, got behind the ridge and the boulder kopjes near the river, cut the Arab force in two, isolated its vanguard, holding the rocks, from its main body and its reserves in the Shukook.

The moment the head of our column appeared round the enemy's left flank, a precipitate retreat of the main body began from behind the position to their camp, at the entrance of the Shukook Pass. Our little body of hussars pounded along as best their tired horses could go. Of the Dervishes, some jumped into the river on their left ; others hid in the clumps of boulders, and had a shot at us as we appeared. A few were killed, but by far the larger number reached the Shukook and got away into its labyrinths. Meanwhile the vanguard on the ridge and in the kopjes, about three hundred in number, abandoned to their fate, met their death bravely, and only succumbed to volleys of the infantry after they had inflicted a loss upon us very serious in its nature, although not great in number. Three officers and four men were killed, and four officers and forty-three men were wounded ; the officers lost were General Earle and Colonels Eyre and Coveney. At the mouth of the Shukook Pass we came upon the Dervish camp abandoned. We found in it eight or ten Arab standards, a lot of donkeys, and a few camels , but, as we had only about twenty hussars present, most of the animals could not be secured, and many of them got away, like their masters, into the rocks at the entrance of the Shukook Pass. I had here the closest shave of getting a bullet in the head I ever experienced. I had got to the top of a cluster of high rocks to have a better survey of the masses of rocks surrounding our little party, and I was leaning against a big one for a steadier sweep with the glass of the hills around when a bullet, fired from across the gorge within a hundred yards' range, flattened itself on the rock six inches above my head   The man was so near that the hit was simultaneous with the smoke and the report of the rifle. I was down from my perch in a jiffy, and got three men from below , then we went up again to the rocks. I had marked the exact spot on the opposite rock from which my friend had fired ; the three carbines were laid upon it , I put my helmet where I had first stood ; my friend fired again, and at the same instant three shots went off from our side. He fired no more

We buried our dead in the evening near the zereba from which we had marched in the morning.

The command of the River Column now fell to Brigadier-General Henry Brackenbury as next senior officer to Earle. On the morning of the 11th February we were going forward once more on the old familiar road. During the halt on this day's march I rode back over the scene of the fight on the previous day. ' Dead men,' they say, ' tell no tales ' ; but on a battlefield no more eloquent spokesman can call to him who will listen   Here the enemy's unburied dead told the story of their revolt—these old grey-bearded veterans, these mere boys, these strong men in the flower of their age, as they lay in every attitude of painful death   They had fought to the last cartridge for the homeland. Their ' punishment ' at our hands had been severe. The rocks glistened with the leaden splashes of our rifle bullets, where continuous volleys had searched every nook and crevice.

But here I come to an incident which gave the acutest point to the drama of this time. By merest chance, as the crew of one of the boats were at their old work of towing along the shore, a soldier of the Cornwalls noticed a small native saddle lying amongst the tumbled rocks, evidently dropped there by a fugitive from the fight of the day before. A black goatskin bag was fastened to the saddle, and in the bag the man found a scrap of soiled paper. He might well have thrown the crumpled scrap away, but his intelligence prompted him to bring it to his captain. From the captain it passed to the colonel of the battalion (Richardson). On my return to camp before sunset, I learnt that the Arabic writing on the bit of paper had been deciphered sufficiently to let us know it con-

tained ' bad news ' Later on, the whole was made clear. **This**
is what it said ·—

' On the night of the 26th January the army of the Mahdi entered
Khartoum and took the forts, city, and vessels in the river : the
traitor Gordon was killed Inform your troops of this signal
triumph which God has given to the arms of the Prophet of His
Prophet.'

This was a copy of an original letter sent from Berber by
Mohammed el Khier, the Emir of the Mahdi, to Abdul Wad
el Kailik, the head Emir opposed to us here. I took the letter
to the lower camp. It was the first news we had had of the
fate of Gordon We knew, six days previously, that Khartoum
had fallen ; now we knew Gordon was dead. He had written
a few months before .—

' Earle does not come to extricate me , he comes to extricate the
garrisons, which affects our national honour. I hope he may
succeed, and that the national honour will reward him ; but I am
not the rescued lamb, and will not be '

A strange chance had brought the first intimation of his death
to us almost on the very spot where Earle had fallen, and both
men had now passed beyond the reach of rescue and reward.

The receipt of this news had brought the Arabs out of the
Shukook fastness to fight us at Kerbekan in the very worst
position they could have selected for that purpose.

I must finish the record of the River Column. We passed
another group of cataracts above the Shukook Pass, and found
good water beyond them We passed also the place where the
steamer *Abbas* lay wrecked on the rocks of Hebbeh, the scene
of the murder of Stewart, Power, and Herbin, and on 24th
February reached Huella, a few miles below Mograt Island. All
the worst water on the Nile lay behind us ; we had started from
Hamdab with two hundred and seventeen boats ; two hundred
and fifteen had arrived at the top of the long-supposed impassable cataracts of Monassir, carrying still sixty days' food
supplies for the entire force. The men were in magnificent
condition ; the boats were as sound ·and fit for further work
as the day they had left England five months earlier. I was
taking the mounted troops forward for another day's work

when an express messenger arrived from Korti carrying urgent orders for the return to that place of the whole flotilla. The Desert Column had collapsed as an effective force It was returning on foot to Korti. The boats turned back to Hebbeh, and the mounted troops went forward for the last time towards Abu Hamed. This, the last day of our reconnaissance work, was the longest yet done. Between the forward march to within sight of Mograt Island and the return to El Kab we must have covered twenty-four miles, the greater part of which was in soft sand One horse and four camels died of exhaustion.

Nine days later we reached Meroë. I found an order there to take command of the force which was to hold the place during the summer. We were to tent the troops and prepare for six months of blinding heat. The Home Government had decided upon a campaign in the autumn, and ' to smash the Mahdi.'

I have sometimes thought that, for some inscrutable reason, the Almighty had given the English people a marvellous faculty of acquiring wealth in peace, only equalled by their wonderful power of wasting wealth in war—' muddling through,' 1 think they call it. I remember the Greeks in Cyprus used to exclaim as they watched our ways, ' Is it not a pity that God, who has given these people so much money, should not have also bestowed upon them some brains ? ' Or is it only

> ' A way we have in the Army ?
> A way we have in the Navy ?

And if this be the case, could not the many 'varsities which we now possess try their hands at mending that particular ' way,' lest it should end all our other ways ?

CHAPTER XVIII

HERE, then, at Meroë, or Abu Dom, I found myself on the 8th March, in command of another advance-guard — 'the farthest position up the river which we are to hold for the summer.' I write thence :—

'I have a battalion of the Royal Highlanders, two guns, a troop of cavalry, one hundred camel corps (Egyptian), a section of Engineers, fifty boats, and one hundred transport camels. We have to hut the men, put the place in a state of defence, and reduce what is now chaos to something like order. I shall, however, have some sort of a rest in other ways shall be able to take off my boots at night, get clean things, and lie down on something besides sand. We are on the left bank of the Nile, nearly opposite Gebel Barkal, the site of the old capital of Queen Candace's kingdom, which is still a perfect mine of relics, columns and capitals, broken pedestals, overturned tombs, stone lions, and strange sheep-faced animals, all lying in confused ruin, half or wholly buried in mounds of masonry and rubbish. The rock face to the east of the flat-topped mountain is hollowed into a temple, covered with hieroglyphics. The place is a mine of Egyptian art and antiquities as yet untouched ; it is fifteen hundred miles from the sea, and is, nevertheless, by no means the last remnant of that once mighty Empire. A group of eight pyramids lies a little way to the south of the hill ; some of them are very perfect, scarcely a stone being out of place ; they are small, only about forty feet in height, but beautifully built. If the Mahdi or his myrmidons give me time during the summer, I would like to clear away some of these piles of rubbish, and examine the ruins.'

A week later I wrote —

'A week of hut building, cleaning, scraping, entrenching. . . . We are here about one thousand Robinson Crusoes, building mud cabins, biscuit box lean-to's, and shelters of palm leaves and straw, the advanced sentinels in this great Soudan desert. Every one is bent upon making the best of it, and many an old trick of camp or lodgment learnt long ago in the North-West comes in handy now. . . . So far, the heat is not trying, the nights are pleasant, the thermometer ninety-three degrees to ninety-seven degrees in the afternoons. . . . If I were to let my pen run as to the twists and turns that led to the loss of Khartoum and the death of poor Gordon I would be writing for a month. Khartoum was lost in London, in Cairo, in Assouan, in Halfa, in Dongola . . . but there would be no use in speaking about it now. . . . How often I used to speculate upon the effect the news from the Soudan would have in England ; hopes raised to the highest pitch by partial successes—for they were only partial—of the march across the desert, and then, total collapse. Ah! you may well say the " wasted precious days of October and November," flung away through sheer stupidity, selfishness, and narrow-mindedness. Poor W. frantic, but unable to move a gigantic machine, the wheels of which had got clogged in the hands of men who sought only their own conceits, and saw only through the glass of their own vanities. Is it not strange that the very first war during the Victorian Era in which the object was entirely noble and worthy should have proved an utter and complete failure, beaten at the finish by forty-eight hours ? These things are not chances, they are *meant*, and the men and nations who realise that fact are fortunate, for then they can learn. What a lesson does the whole story of this Expedition teach ! Up to the last they were saying there would be little or no fighting. Poor T. thought the same. " I will believe in the Mahdi fighting when I hear the whistle of his soldiers' bullets," he said a day or two before leaving Korti. " It's a windbag," another remarked to me.'

Three weeks later, 28th March, I find the following :—

'I have been up half the night, owing to a violent sand-storm having made the sentries think the Arabs were coming on. . . . Even now the temperature goes up some days to a hundred and ten degrees. A telegram last evening brings news of the Reserves being called out, and fifteen thousand men ordered to India. The close of this nineteenth century seems likely to be as bad for England as that of the eighteenth was. I cannot think that, with war with Russia all but declared, the flower of our fighting force and the best of our thinking power will be left in the Soudan. If we are to fight Russia there must be no humbug this time. A defeat would mean National death. In the event of war between Russia and the Afghans we must either knuckle down or withdraw from the

Soudan   We can't keep half the army and all the staff up in this wilderness.

'1st May.—During the past week our mud roosts have been fluttered by news of sudden movement down-stream. Reuter gives us daily the heads of political and other news, and the first intimation of probable evacuation came in that way. What an extraordinary people we are ! For eight weeks we have been busy all day and every day building huts, and making ready for the hot season · now, when the huts are built and the hot season is upon us, we up anchors and away. The Arabs regard us as people possessed by " jins " or devils, and this change of front will not tend to lessen the idea   The Nile is now at its lowest stage of water, but our poor old boats will again do the work. All our camels are gone, the English boats alone remain . . My huts are real beauties. . . . So the Suakim bubble has burst and this railway is given up. It was sheer madness   These poor guides of ours are hopeless : they differ from the Bourbons inasmuch as they forget everything and learn nothing.

'22nd May.—This should be my last letter from Meroë. We march on the 26th for Dongola and Egypt. They have given me the hot job. I command the rearguard to Dongola, picking up as we go the various lots of horses, camels, guns, and men at the different stations   The weather has become excessively hot, one hundred and ten and one hundred and fifteen degrees in the shade, with a wind that seems to come from a furnace mouth   To-day we have the climax : first stifling heat, then a vast sand-storm ; and behind the storm came some most welcome rain, but not enough even to sprinkle the hard, hot lips of the fevered desert. All preparations are complete, and at daylight on Tuesday I blow up the fort and move off for Dongola '

So on the 26th May we blew up our little fort with gun-cotton and marched off from Abu Dom ('the father of Dom palms '). I was sorry to leave the place , no spot of greater interest and possessing more of what makes for real Nile beauty exists along the fifteen hundred miles from there to the sea

'You cannot live much with the Arabs,' I wrote, ' without learning to like them. They are quick, courteous, very brave, good-looking. As to their deceit, etc , of which we hear so much, I don't think they are a bit worse than the average acquaintance, I might even say " friend," one finds in clubs and professions in the daily intercourse of life in England. We call them " rebels," but right is wholly on their side. The abominations of the Egyptian rule were beyond words to express their atrocity.'

There is such a delightful paragraph in the *Official History of the Soudan Campaign*, dealing with our retreat at this time, that I cannot omit quoting it :—

'As it was certain that anarchy would immediately follow our withdrawal, and probable that a retreat on our part would allow the dormant hostility of the natives to find vent, it was necessary that the retreat, especially of the advanced portion of the force, should be conducted as rapidly and unexpectedly as possible. Jandet Effendi, the Vakil of Dongola, who had taken the place of the deposed Mudir, was at once informed of the intended retreat. He begged for fifteen days' start, before our policy was made generally known, in order that he might take what steps he could to mitigate the murder and the rapine for which he believed our retirement would be the signal. This was granted him and he at once started down the river.'

Unfortunately for the truth of the picture here given, it happened to be my duty to follow the excellent Vakil Jandet Effendi a few days after he had descended the river in his self-imposed mission of mercy and mitigation of suffering. Jandet, who was a Circassian of the well-known type, had literally swept both banks of the Nile of everything that he and his bashi-bazouks could lay hands on. The silver which these unfortunate peasants had gathered by selling us their provisions and their labour during the past six months, their camels and donkeys, had been carried clean off. Jandet travelled in a large house-boat on the river. His myrmidons scoured the palm patches and the dhourra plots on both banks. When Jandet reached Dongola his house-boat was loaded with chests of silver piastre coin thus gathered. Such is history 'as she is wrote.'

The march from Meroe to Dongola, two hundred miles, in end of May and early June, was the hottest work that had ever fallen to my lot. I had to pick up at each summer station in succession—Korti, Tani, Kurot, Abu Gus, and Handak—the horses, guns, camels, and transport of the whole force, all the remnants of the Desert Column that could not be put into our old boats. I can never forget the last day's march from Handak to Dongola. A desert blizzard blew straight in our faces, hot, strong, and bitterly biting with the grit, sand, and small stones that it hurled in our teeth. Camels and horses often turned aside, unable to face it. We had orders to leave no camels behind us The wretched animals that had been in the Desert Column were spectres, mere bones and sores. As they fell they had to be shot by the rearguard.

Two-thirds of the camels collected at Tani and Kurot thus perished. I had taken the precaution of feeding up my camels at Meroë for weeks before the move, giving them the large stores of grain laid in in anticipation of the autumn campaign, and ordered to be destroyed on evacuation, and although the camels had a double distance to travel to reach Dongola, I lost only one or two on the march down. But the strangest part of the proceeding was that the general officer in command of the force thought fit to report me to the commander-in-chief for not having obeyed the orders to destroy the grain by fire. Called on for an explanation, I replied that, although I had departed from the letter, I had still observed the spirit of the order, inasmuch as I had used the grain as extra fuel to keep the ebbing fire of life in my unfortunate camels, and while expressing regret at even the seeming departure from the letter of the regulation, I added that my penitential feelings were somewhat mitigated and consoled by the reflection that while the camels of the censorious commander had lost some eighty per cent. of their numbers on the short march, mine on the longer route had not lost above two per cent. My temporary commander at the time was an excellent but choleric little man, and I learnt afterwards from one of the staff that, as the thermometer was that day about one hundred and twenty degrees Fahrenheit in the shade, he was able to relieve his over-burdened feelings when perusing my letter, written on a sake-yeh wheel at Debbah in the middle of the night and left at his hut when I passed it at daybreak three hours later, only by making several short leaps into the air as he ejaculated, ' Consoled !—consoled !—mitigated !—mitigated !—d—— d—— ! '

At Dongola my rearguard duties ended, and I got once again into my old boat. I shall never forget the change from shore to river. The heat was terrific, but it felt as nothing on the water. As we sped down the shrunken but still lordly Nile, now changed in colour from the old muddy tint to a bright

green hue—the true ' eau du Nil ' of the Parisian fashion-plates
—our boats were still able to run the Third Cataract, Shaban,
Kaibar, and Amara down to Dal.

How strange these old scenes appeared ! It was only six
months since I had left them, but it seemed like as many years.

Finally, I reached Wady Halfa in mid-June, to find a telegram there from Lord Wolseley offering me the command of the
new frontier, henceforth to be fixed at Wady Halfa. I accepted the offer, with two months' leave of absence to England,
and was in London on the 30th June. In two months' time I
was back in Egypt again. On 9th September I reached Wady
Halfa. Things had changed all round. The Nile was at its
topmost flood. The Dervishes were at Dongola They had
followed our retreat closely ; their outposts were at the head
of the Third Cataract.

'You can imagine,' I wrote on the 11th September, ' how different
were the feelings with which I came to this place two days ago to
those of the 18th October 1884 Then everything was hopeful ;
no check had taken place ; I had caught up ten days of the time
estimate given to Lord Wolseley for the Secretary of State in
August, and I had every faith that, if left to myself, I could continue
to gain time on the long road still before us to Khartoum ; but from
that day forward began our delays and misfortunes. Little by little
the precious moments were allowed to drop, until the terrible words
" Too late " were stamped for ever upon our effort. But we must
not look back ; there is plenty of work to be done forward. I go
to Dal to-morrow to fix on a site for a small fort, which will be our
advanced station towards Dongola . . . The Dervishes are at
Abu Fatmeh All the wretched kinglets set up by us have fled :
our Intelligence officers now assert that the Mahdi is not dead,
but that he has retired into a cave, from which at the end of
three months he will come forth again What is certain is that
Mahdiism is not dead but is gaining ground daily . . . So the
Gazette (for the Soudan) is out. I feel sure that my absence from
it is all for the best, and I have so many things to be thankful for
that I can truly rejoice in the good fortune of those who have been
given honours and rewards.

' 12th of October.—The Dervishes are becoming demonstrative
at the Third Cataract, and I think that we shall shortly have them
this side of Kaibar. Think of the row there would have been last
year in the English papers if they had been even half so close !

But now the papers don't even notice the fact. They'll soon be playing another tune, I'm thinking.'

Meanwhile the problem before me was not an easy one to meet. The railway from Wady Halfa had been completed to Akasha, ninety miles. My orders were that this line was to be protected from attack   To hold these ninety miles and the base at Halfa I had one weak battalion of British infantry ; no cavalry, no guns, no mounted infantry ; one weak battalion of black troops, one ditto Egyptian battalion, and about eighty Egyptian camel corps. The Dervish gathering at Dongola was reported in numbers varying from eight to fifteen thousand men ; they had many guns and plenty of ammunition ; the capture of Khartoum had put all the resources of the arsenal there at their disposal. From Kaibar the rail-head at Akasha was, by desert route, not more than seventy miles. The advanced portion of the Dervish army was, therefore, within easy striking distance of our communications   it could cut the railway by a thirty-hour march on camels   The Nile was an exceptionally high one this year ; the desert wells were full.

I took in these main conditions and possibilities in the four days' visit to Dal. The first thing to do was to build a fort on the Nile twenty miles beyond the end of the railway at Akasha   This fort I counted upon to stop the first oncoming of the Dervishes when they came down from Kaibar. If they ' sat down ' before my fort I should have time to gather reinforcements in the ground between the fort, the head of the railway, and the angle made by the Nile in its course from Amara to Akasha, a rough and very broken piece of desert measuring some thirty-three miles along the Nile shore and about twenty-four across the desert   If they did not sit down before it, but left it and passed on into the Batn-el-Hager (' the womb of rocks '), through which our line of railway ran for sixty miles, then undoubtedly they would do a lot of damage to the line, give us plenty of hard work, and perhaps get even as far as Sarras. But they would never get back again   They might isolate my angle of ground between rail-head at Akasha and the advanced post at Kosheh, but if I could only get my fort built, garrisoned, and supplied in time, put a couple of hundred mounted men into the angle, and put another garrison at rail-head, I thought I would be able to play a fairly good game with the ten thousand Dervishes now in our front at Kaibar. Unfortunately, time and men were the chief factors in the problem, and both were against me. The men were far down the Nile—at Assouan, three hundred miles, and at Cairo, six hundred miles farther The Nile was against me in the matter of time : you could float down the river to Cairo on a log of wood in nine days ; you could not come up in a steamer from Cairo to Wady Halfa in twenty days. Nor was that the only difficulty. My masters were all down-stream too. I might propose, they disposed I might ask for men, guns, horses, and supplies, in ten minutes by telegraph ; they would decide in due time, and time paid many dues on the Nile. Egypt has always been the taxman's paradise. It is the same to-day. We shall see presently how it all worked out.

I set to work at once building the advance post at a place called Kosheh on the west shore of the Nile, six miles south of the Dal Cataract, where the river, making a sharp bend to the west, gave views up and down two reaches for six miles to north and west. The spot also marked the debouch of the desert road to Absarat and Kaibar, and it had the further advantage of having tolerably level and open ground around it. The plan of the fort was almost identical with that of the work at Meroé, which I had blown up three months earlier. It was built entirely of Nile mud, sun-dried into bricks of a very durable nature, exactly similar to those which the Israelites had declared to be the last straw (or absent straw) in the burden of their bondage some three thousand years earlier. On the present occasion, my Nile-mud brickmakers were Soudanese blacks, excellent fellows, who made mud pies by the thousand, and piled them one upon another at such a rapid rate that by the end of October the fort was already in a forward state, and early in November I had half a battalion of the Cameron Highlanders encamped there, followed a fortnight later by the remainder of the battalion.

The fort being finished, the black battalion (9th Soudanese) were moved across to the west bank of the river, where they soon built themselves another mud-pie fortification at that side. These works were only completed and garrisoned in the nick of time, for on the 28th November some eight or ten thousand Dervishes were on the river at Amara, six miles from

Kosheh. They had played their game very nicely, holding back at Kaibar until the last moment, and then coming on with a rush, covering fifty miles in two days. My railway was only a feeble thing : it was just capable of carrying one hundred and eighty men from Halfa to Akasha in one day ; then there was a two-days' march to Kosheh, so that to get a battalion to the point at which I hoped to stop the Dervishes from Wady Halfa would take ten days.

On 30th November I had in position at Kosheh two battalions of British infantry, fifty British cavalry, two battalions Egyptian infantry, twelve artillerymen, and one Krupp gun ; one company mounted infantry and eighty men of the camel corps, with sixty days' food, and four hundred rounds per man. Two small steamers, one of which was the *Lotus*, lay in the river off the fort. Two miles in rear of Kosheh I had an old ruined Nubian castle, Mograka, put into a state of defence—a zereba in front, walls loopholed, etc. Into this resuscitated ruin I put a weak battalion (the 3rd) of the Egyptian army.[1] It had been neck and neck the whole way between my old enemy of six months earlier in the Shukook Pass, Abd el Majid Wad el Kailik, and myself. He knew a good deal more of my dispositions and numbers than I knew of his. Every native Nubian along the Nile was friendly to him, and his spies were among us everywhere. Nevertheless, although I received a good deal of false information as to the Dervish plans, I also gathered sufficient accurate intelligence to make out their general purpose and intentions. The enemy meant to cut our railway, and then attack Kosheh and Akasha. They would hold us at Kosheh with their main body, while a flying column would swing round through the desert and cut the railway behind us. My game was exactly the reverse of this. It was to hold them before Kosheh, and hit their raiders along the railway in the Batn-el-Hager.

The ball opened on the 3rd of December. A raiding party of one thousand men, with one brass gun on a camel, suddenly appeared at Ambigol Wells on the railway at midnight, and tore up the line for more than a mile   At daybreak on the 4th they surrounded a small post which I had established at

---

[1] The British commanding officers were St. Leger, Everett, Barrow, Lloyd, Hunter, Bessant, Legge, and de Lisle.

Ambigol, and brought their brass gun to bear against it. There was an incident connected with this attack which deserves record. The officer in command, Lieutenant Annesley, West Kent Regiment, had kept his thirty-five men camped outside the little redoubt. It was his habit to go out every morning into the surrounding khor shooting sand grouse. On the morning of the 1st December he noticed that the birds killed had no food in their crops, whilst on other days it was the rule to find the bird well filled with the seeds of desert plants. Annesley, a bit of a naturalist, asked himself why the birds had not fed this morning—there must have been something to disturb them. He had been warned to be ready for a Dervish raid. There was a well at Haumagh, eight miles out in the desert. Were there Dervishes about to account for the empty stomachs of the grouse ? Anyway, he would get his men into the redoubt. A day earlier I had ordered a reinforcement of thirty rifles to Ambigol ; they arrived by train almost at the moment that the Dervishes began their attack. The train was a good target, and was repeatedly struck. Engine-drivers and men made for the fort, and got into it with trifling loss. The Dervishes now tore up the railway line in the rear of the train, as they had already torn up the rails a mile in front of it. Here, then, was the beginning of the test match I had been preparing for since September. So far the Dervishes had done well : they had demonstrated with five or six thousand men at Kosheh, and had struck my railway twenty-six miles from Akasha and fifty from Kosheh almost at the same time. It was now my turn to play. Had I even one hundred more mounted men the game was an easy one. All through October and November I had urgently asked for cavalry, but to no purpose. Macaulay wrote of the siege of Derry that ' even horse beans were doled out with a parsimonious hand ', in my case it was horsemen that were so treated. Almost from the day of my arrival at Wady Halfa I had howled for cavalry. In my diary I find .—

' Representations made to General Commanding that in order effectively to patrol roads, Kosheh should be held by five hundred men, half of them mounted, and that the railway and river transports should be made as effective as possible.'

I added that an advance of the Dervishes in force from Dongola appeared to be certain.

We had now reached 1st December. The Arabs had come down in force, but the only horsemen I had received in the two months' interval had been one hundred mounted infantry from Cairo, who arrived in November, and whose proficiency as horsemen was such that six of their number parted company with their steeds in marching half a mile to their camp

On 3rd December, when the ball opened, I had then but a small force to hold back an army of Mahdists flushed by their recent victories at Khartoum, well armed, and having seven guns ; I had also to protect a line of railway ninety miles in length through the Batn-el-Hager, the most broken bit of desert, save the Shukook, in all the Nile-land, and in the midst of an Arab population entirely hostile to us. But for that elbow or angle made by the Nile between Kosheh and Akasha, giving literally elbow-room behind the advanced post at the former place and before the rail-head at the latter, the job must have been an entirely impossible one. Cairo, even for a reinforcement of one battalion, was eighteen days distant ; Assouan, for the same strength, was seven days away. As things turned out, the little fort at Kosheh alone saved the situation It kept the Arabs far enough away from the railway to give the little movable column which I had scraped together, in the elbow behind it, room to hit the separated, long-distance attacks which the enemy could only make on that most vulnerable tail to our military position. It was curious to me to be obliged for two months to fight this fact with my military chiefs in Assouan and Cairo.

Neither of these excellent general officers had had any previous knowledge of Arab strategy, and I owed it altogether to the experience, gained six months earlier, of Arab methods in the Shukook region that my present little plan of campaign was based upon sound principles. The wilder the bird, the less he likes going behind even a mock barrier. Kosheh was not quite that, but it had some laths painted to look like iron.

Our Intelligence Department was at Assouan, and the Arab leaders in Khartoum had been careful to keep that place supplied with a thousand rumours of what they meant to do by marching direct upon Assouan from Berber and Abu Hamad.

These reports, coming from many directions, no doubt influenced the decision to keep back the bulk of the troops in Egypt, and hence the policy of 'doling out' supports to me on the exposed frontier. I think also it was calculated that if the worst came, and I was cut off from my base, a relief could be effected in due course. Nothing in our modern wars had sounded so well in the newspapers as the word 'Relief.' It is a most valuable journalistic asset; but at the time of which I am writing, to be cut off from one's base in war had something at least of the aspect of defeat, if not of disgrace; and I was in no mood to accept the position if it could possibly be helped.

To return to Ambigol Wells. After breaking the railway and burning a lot of the sleepers on the 3rd December the Arabs fell back again into the desert, and we were beginning to repair the damage when suddenly, on the 4th December, they came on us again in force, attacked the post, and brought their brass gun to bear upon it from a hill six hundred yards distant. At half-past four o'clock news of this attack was brought to me at Akasha by Lieutenant de Lisle of the mounted infantry, who had pluckily ridden out from the beleaguered post with two men under a very heavy fire. I had already drawn from my angle fifty mounted infantry, seventy camel corps, and fifty hussars to Akasha, and with these and two hundred and fifty infantry we started, on the evening of the 5th December, from Akasha, bringing also a camel gun, and a convoy of ninety camels with water, of which de Lisle said the garrison was running short. My telegraph wires were, of course, cut on the east side, but I had already laid a second line to Wady Halfa along the west shore of the Nile, and that was intact. By midnight we had collected at Tanjour road three hundred and fifty infantry, two hundred camel and horse men, and one gun; provisions, water, and ammunition on camels, and with these we started for Ambigol at 1 A.M. Four hours' steady marching brought us to the khor or defile leading into Ambigol Wells, and as day broke we were at the fort. The Dervishes had fled. A few deserters came in, and from them we heard the details of the attack. The Dervish force, about nine hundred strong, of whom four hundred had rifles, under Es Zain, an old enemy of ours on the Shukook, had left Amara on the 29th, half of them mounted. On the evening of the

1st December they were east of Ambigol. The nights of the 2nd and 3rd were spent tearing up the railway. When daylight came they retired into the desert. On the 4th they attacked the fort from all sides, hauled their gun on to a high hill five hundred yards away, and got off some dozen shots, fired with difficulty because of the continuous volleys directed at it from the fort. We had one man killed and one wounded : the Arabs lost about twenty all told. I left a gun and a company of the Berks Regiment at Ambigol, and we marched back to Akasha, where we arrived at sunset, having covered over fifty miles in twenty-four hours, thirty miles of it on foot.

In less than a week we had the railway repaired, and trains running through from Halfa to Akasha again. The work of that week never found outside record or acknowledgment, but I owe it to the brave fellows who freely gave me their toil and sweat to say something about it even now at this distance of time. We had literally to do the work of one hundred men with less than fifty. Watched from every side, and with seven or eight thousand Arabs in front and on our flanks for fifty miles, we held our own from Kosheh to Ambigol, repaired every damage as it occurred, and gave back shot for shot on both sides of the Nile ; for the Dervishes had now put two thousand men on the west bank, and reinforcements were daily arriving to them from Dongola east and west. Es Zain was soon astir again : this time he swooped round Kosheh with three thousand men at night through the hills, and struck at Mograka and Firket, where I had some Egyptian troops. I got word at Akasha late in the evening that he was on the swoop at Firket, and marched at sunrise next morning with five hundred men, half West Kent and half Berkshire Regiments, mounted men, and three guns, by the desert road to Firket ; but Es Zain and his merry men again vanished into the hills.

I left the column at Firket and rode on to Kosheh—all was right there. The Arabs were getting more active every day. I ran another gun and nine camel-loads of gun ammunition into the fort, got the wires going again, reinforced Mograka with a company of the West Kent and one gun, and rejoined the flying column at midnight at Firket—another long day.

As more troops were now coming up the Nile from Egypt I made my headquarters at Firket. It was a good point at which to concentrate the force now moving slowly up from Cairo, and meanwhile I could keep an eye on Kosheh and Mograka, and another on the desert route to Akasha and rail-head. Of course, the reports of alarms and excursions were incessant. Some of them were very funny. One evening a strong patrol of mounted infantry returned to Firket after dark reporting that they had found the fort of Mograka surrounded by Dervishes, whose banners were planted across the track leading from Firket to that post. They had engaged the Dervishes at close range ; the fire was hotly returned ; then the Arabs retreated, and the patrol had fallen back on Firket without loss. That of the enemy must have been very heavy I marched at daybreak next morning for Mograka There was no trace of any enemy ; but the commandant met me in front of his fort to report that he had been heavily attacked on the preceding evening by a large force of Arabs, that he had repulsed the attack with heavy loss to the assailants, and that his garrison had not suffered. I had many doubts the evening before about this mysterious Arab attack on Mograka, the banners, and the rest of the patrol story ; the commandant's account did not dispel them What had really happened was that the mounted infantry had volleyed at the Egyptian soldiers outside their fort while engaged in the dusk upon certain evening duties and ablutions, and the Egyptians in the fort had volleyed back at the patrol, each defeating the other, happily without wound or graze on either side.

Ten more days of firing, scouting, marching, moving convoys of stores from Akasha forward, sending sick and wounded down, and passing small reinforcements up, now went on ; and at last there seemed a prospect of bringing matters to a conclusion before Kosheh. That little post did its work splendidly. On 16th December two companies of the Camerons made a sortie at daybreak against the Arabs, who were daily creeping nearer the fort, finding cover along the shore as the waters of the Nile fell. Fourteen Dervishes were surprised and bayoneted in the rocks

The village of Absari, to the south of Kosheh, was found loop-holed and garrisoned. The Arabs came out from camp at Ginniss in large numbers, and the Camerons fell back upon the guns of the fort, which got many shots into the Arab groups.

This reconnaissance was to prove of great value to us later on, for it revealed the Arab strength and position and intentions in case of attack along the river Unfortunately, it was attended with loss. Major Chalmers and Lieutenant Cameron and four rank and file were wounded—Lieutenant Cameron mortally. Major Hunter of the 9th Battalion was also dangerously wounded. A few days later I tried another reconnaissance to discover what the Arabs would do if we attacked them from the broken and high ground lying a mile back from the river. About one hundred mounted men were to circle round behind the hills from Mograka and endeavour to approach Ginniss from the east. It was intensely interesting to watch the effect this movement had upon the Dervish camps for three miles south of Kosheh. First I saw an Arab rushing madly out of the broken ground towards Ginniss ; he had evidently caught sight of the cavalry movement in the hills, and was racing to give the alarm. I stood with watch in hand noting the exact time taken First fifty mounted men rode out at full gallop from the shore near Ginniss , then band after band of Dervishes passed streaming into the khors leading up to the higher ridges. What I wanted to find out was the exact time it would take the Arabs to gain a high dominating ridge which rose round the tangle of broken ground about three or four miles from Kosheh, and one or two from Ginniss. I got the time to a second · twenty minutes after the Arab vidette had given the first alarm I saw the heads and spears of many Dervishes on the skyline of the high ridge. Another body of mounted men, followed by footmen, moved obliquely as though to intercept our men, who were not visible to us, but whose general line of movement through the hills we could tell by the gallopings and racings of the Arabs.

Colonel Barrow's orders were not to commit the reconnaissance to close quarters, but to fall back on Mograka, passing the front of Kosheh, and retiring fighting. I sent out two companies of Camerons to threaten the Dervish flank. The Arab mounted men, followed by a couple of hundred of their foot, came on well. Barrow fell back across the front face of the fort. A wide khor opened into the hills directly in front of the fort, and across this our men passed, closely followed by the Arabs. One chief in particular pressed the pursuit very closely. He was shot near the khor. His horse galloped among our cavalry and was taken. This man proved to be the celebrated Kordofan Emir, Osman el Azreck, the best fighting leader in the Dervish army. The firing ceased suddenly, and presently we saw a party of Dervishes passing back over the khor, bearing the body of El Azreck on their shoulders.

A few days later the last of the reinforcements from Cairo reached Firket, and with them came Sir Frederick Stevenson, the commander-in-chief, General Grenfell, and large staffs. I had everything ready for them—food, ammunition, and plan of attack upon the Arabs at Ginniss. The fort at Kosheh had done its work. We were all tired of the long-drawn-out task which the delays and the lack of transport on the Nile had imposed upon us. For thirty days our little garrison in the angle had held some eight thousand Arabs, and preserved the railway to Wady Halfa.

On the 29th December a force of four thousand men was concentrated in the palm groves between Kosheh and Mograka, ready to move against the Arabs next morning. I suppose I ought to have been satisfied, but somehow I wasn't. As old people may live too long for younger men, so younger men may do too well for older people. That, at least, was what I thought; but it doesn't matter now. One most unlooked-for message of indirect approval of our work came to me about Christmas Day, when I bivouacked on the platform of an old sakeyeh wheel at Firket. It was a letter from our military attaché at Berlin telling of an interview he had just had with the great Von Moltke, who sent for him to discuss the situation on the Nile to the south of Wady Halfa.

'I do not see how it will be possible for your small force at and south of Wady Halfa to prevent the Arabs enveloping your positions, completely destroying the railway, and coming in force to Wady Halfa. Your line is far too long and your force much too small.'

General Stevenson held a meeting of officers that day near Mograka, and I was asked to state my idea of the next day's movements. I gave it, based altogether upon the Arab moves on the 22nd. If my brigade started from Kosheh one hour and a half before daybreak, I thought that it would be possible to gain the high ridge east of Ginniss at or near dawn. If that point was reached before the Arabs got to it from Ginniss, we held them in the hollow of our hands ; if not, they had every chance of holding *us*. The ground between us and the ridge was extremely broken and intersected with sudden ravines, but 1 thought I could take my three battalions there before daylight revealed our march to the Dervishes. I was told to do as I liked.

That evening I went out to the desert clear of Kosheh, and put two biggish stones to mark the front of an infantry battalion standing in quarter column. Thirty or forty yards behind the left-hand one of the two stones I placed a third and fourth stone, laid very carefully in a line bearing over the centre of the saw-back ridge, and full on the flat top of Gebel Abri, a mountain about eight miles distant to the south I said nothing to anybody, but ordered my three battalions and six camel guns to parade next morning. When night had quite fallen I went out to my stones again, and saw that the top of Gebel Abri was quite discernible over the centre of the saw-back ridge in the desert, east of Ginniss.

Before dawn I 'dressed' the Berkshire Battalion in quarter column squarely upon these stones. Two battalions, the West Kent and Durhams, fell in with their leading companies in line, on the rear company of the Berks, one to right and the other to left of that battalion. This formation gave three sides of a hollow square. Into that hollow I put the six Egyptian camel guns, ambulance stretchers, spare ammunition, water camels, etc., and I closed the rear face of the hollow with a scratch battalion of six companies, made up of two companies from the three battalions. This compact force was led by a sergeant of the Berks Regiment. On the left of the leading company. and behind this sergeant, I myself rode, to see that he led straight upon Gebel Abri. When everything was ready it was fifteen minutes to five ; no moon ; a misty, grey gloom was over the desert, but the dark top of Gebel Abri showed distinctly above the horizon nearly due south I sent back to the general, who, with his second brigade of British and Egyptian troops, was about six hundred yards in rear, that I was quite ready to advance. A message was returned asking me to wait, as the second brigade was not yet ready ; but as I had very closely timed the march to be done with the hour of dawn, I sent back again to say that it was imperatively necessary that my brigade should start at 5 A.M. ; and when that hour came, we moved forward. The line of march laid on Gebel Abri soon began to ascend from the lower levels near the river into the rocky ridges lying south of Ginniss and Amara. We were passing obliquely along the flank positions held by the Dervishes on the river south of Kosheh, diverging farther away from the Nile as we proceeded. We could see the enemy's fires in the palm groves and scattered mud houses by the shore, but beyond the barking of dogs to the right as we proceeded there was nothing as yet to indicate that the Arabs were aware of our movements. For quite an hour the march went on through very rough and broken ground. At times a ravine or khor of unusual steepness had to be crossed, in passing which the guiding cone of Gebel Abri disappeared from view ; but in these cases I took a star in the southern heavens in the line of the hill-top, and as we ascended on an opposite side of the ravine Gebel Abri was again in sight.

After about an hour's marching light began to show in the east, and one was able to see something of the surrounding desert, and the line of palms and houses along the river to our right. We were now abreast of Ginniss, about three-quarters of a mile from it. In our front, five or six hundred yards ahead, the razor-back ridge, to gain which was the entire object of the movement, was becoming more plainly visible in the increasing light. So far no shot, sound, or sign of movement had come from the Arabs. During the next quarter of a mile I made the battalions on the right and left of the Berkshires incline outwards from that battalion, which still kept its even pace to the front. When the flank battalions reached deploying distance they resumed the old direction again. The brigade was then in line of battalion columns at deploying distance, the guns, camels, etc., being in rear of the centre and guiding battalion, and behind them came the reserve battalion. The light grew rapidly, and by the time we reached the foot of the razor-back all the surrounding black and grey rocks and ravines were fully visible. Still no enemy showed anywhere, and the silence was still unbroken except by our footsteps on the rocky surface. I rode on to the top of the centre of the razor-back.

There the scene changed in an instant. The whole desert at the farther side of the ridge was outlaid before us : the long slopes leading down to the wide river, which stretched westward, dotted with the dark isles of the Amara rapids ; the endless Libyan desert at the farther side , the line of scattered palm groves and houses on the nearer shore, from which many groups of Arab horsemen and foot spearmen were streaming into the rocks and khors that lay immediately in our front.

For a moment I thought that we had won the race for the ridge by a mile ; but it was not so—we had only won it by a few hundred yards ; for as soon as some more figures of our people showed over the top, fire opened along a front of eight hundred or a thousand yards from numerous concealed enemies, some of whom were within two hundred paces of the height on which we stood. These riflemen were the leading scouts of the advancing Arab army, making for the ridge. I ordered the three battalions to line the ridge, for the sun was now rising at our backs, making things very visible to people on the lower ground to the west. The lower khors in our front were quickly filling with Arabs from the palm groves. The Berkshires got first into position on the crest, and while the two flank battalions were coming up I had time to look round and see where our supporting brigade was.

It was a long way behind, quite two miles, and it appeared to be halted, facing the village of Absari. The regiment of cavalry, which had orders to move on the left of my brigade, well out in the desert, was also visible about a mile to the southeast. It was quite evident that in a few minutes more I should have the entire Arab force on this bank of the river in our immediate front. The whole scene, as the sun came up, presented a very striking spectacle. For a few minutes the fire in our front went on, and the bullets came flying across the top of the ridge fast and thick, so far without reply. But it was now our turn to begin. The Berkshires opened the ball, and a hail of bullets soon swept the edges of the ravines in our front. The Durhams next took up the fire, and the West Kent followed, but before the infantry were all in line I called up the Egyptian camel Krupp battery under Colonel Woodhouse. Above the edges of a khor about a thousand yards in our front a large force of Arabs was gathering : we could see spear heads and

banners showing. One flag, particularly noticeable by its wide
folds, was carried by a man on horseback. Colonel Woodhouse
laid his first gun on this figure with aim so good that man,
horse, and flag disappeared from sight almost simultaneously
with the report of the little gun. For a quarter of an hour
the fire was hammer and tongs on both sides. When the
Berkshires first reached the hill crest they were met by so
strong a sweep of bullets that three or four men fell at once.
I therefore ordered the battalion to lie down on the inner slope
and fire over the ridge. The other battalions did the same
as they came up to the crest, and in a few moments a hail of
bullets was sweeping down the outer slopes and across the
khors and ravines, into which the spearmen and their leaders
were now rapidly gathering from the lower ground. Our
officers, mounted and on foot, did not dismount nor take cover,
for at that date it had not become the order or the habit to
do so.

One could now judge what the result would have been to us
had the Arabs got possession of this ridge before us—and we
had only saved it by a few minutes. It had been neck and
neck. If Gebel Abri had not been where it was, I don't think
it could have been done. Finding that they could not face a
front attack upon the ridge, the spearmen now began to move
towards our left, keeping within the shelter of several khors,
whose existence we could only tell by the spear heads and
banners showing at intervals above the edges. To check this
movement to the flank I sent the Egyptian camel corps out
beyond the left of our line, and moved the reserve battalion
to reinforce that flank.

I have already mentioned the name of Said Redwan of
Kordofan, a lieutenant in the camel corps. No bolder or finer
man ever carried sword than that officer He had now dismounted his men, tied down the camels, and the men were
firing away down the khors in their front Suddenly a group
of Dervishes rushed from some rocks nearer to our line and
began stabbing the camels. We could not fire at them, because
the men of the camel corps were in the line of fire just beyond
their camels. I shouted to the camel-men to clear off to the
left and leave us a clear field of fire ; they did so, all except
Said, who, seeing the Dervishes hacking at his camels, charged

singly into their midst, and began to hew and hack at them right and left. It was a strange sight, such a one as must have been frequently seen in Crusader times , and to make it still more of mediæval fashion, the Dervish swords were of the old straight, double-edged blade and two-handed type, precisely such as Sir Walter Scott's Nubian soldiers in the *Talisman* might have carried. On the present occasion the Dervish swords had the best of it, and Said Redwan got cut in several places, and went down among his camels; but this temporary fall saved his life, for his assailants were picked off by our men once the ground was clear. A few other fanatics now appeared from the rocks, hopping in the strangest fashion as they made straight for our men. One or two of them got so close to the line before they fell that one could see every feature of their faces distorted with the delirium of fanatical enthusiasm, the lips moving in prayer, the eyes rolling, their swords raised in both hands, twirling in a ceaseless circle above their heads. I could not discern any sign of rage in the expression of their faces; it seemed to be the ecstasy of self-martyrdom. The battle was soon over; we had had it all to ourselves.

I would now change front to the right and move down the slopes upon the Arab camps in and behind Ginniss. So, sending word to the generals and the Second Brigade, who were still more than a mile behind us, and sending an officer also to inform the cavalry on our left, another mile to the east, that I was about to move upon the river, I wheeled the line the eighth of a circle on its right, and, picking up our wounded men, began our march on Ginniss. I added to my message to the colonel of the cavalry that, so far as I could see, the Arabs were retreating along the Nile shore towards Atab; that he should conform to my movement, and thus place his regiment upon the line of the retreating enemy. Then we went straight for Ginniss. In half an hour we were there. The Arabs had fled along the palm patches and river shore beyond Atab, leaving two guns, fourteen standards, some wounded, and about two thousand medgideah dollars in our hands. The cavalry missed their chance. Although they were full on the flank of the retreating Dervishes, their commanding officer drew up his men at Atab and began firing at the fugitives.

Twenty minutes after we reached Ginniss, the Second Brigade came up, with the generals and their respective staffs. I loaded two Dervish donkeys with the Arab standards, took them to the generals, and presented them. That was the end of the battle of Ginniss. We lost only one officer killed—Lieutenant Soltau of the Berkshire Regiment. He was shot through the head a minute or two after we gained the razor-back ridge. He was a splendid specimen of youthful manhood as he stood behind the men of his company, who were lying against the top of the ridge , nor did he look one whit less splendid when, a moment later, he lay stretched on his back on the rocky desert with his sword still held firm in his hand. We buried him in the desert outside Ginniss. A touching thing happened at that simple funeral. Soltau had a pet dog, which he took with him wherever he went. It was a tiny thing, of the toy spaniel type, but, small as that animal was, it had the biggest heart of any dog I had ever seen. This was what happened. The body of the dead officer was carried on a stretcher behind the Berkshire Regiment as we marched from the ridge, and the stretcher, covered by a Union Jack, was put in a tent for a couple of hours while a grave was being dug in the desert. When all was ready, we followed the body to its last rest. The stretcher was laid on the ground a few feet from the grave, and the Union Jack lifted. The body, still in uniform, was then raised by four men and lowered into the grave ; but, cowering on one side of the blood-stained stretcher, in smaller shape than ever before, was the tiny dog. I have never forgotten the way in which that black atom dragged itself, crouching, from the stretcher along the few feet of sand to the edge of the pit, and lay there with its head hanging down into the grave. When some one lifted it away, it hung like a little dead thing, a sight sufficient to make strong men turn aside.

CHAPTER XIX

THE failure of the cavalry in pursuit, following the fight at
Ginniss, imposed extra work upon the infantry brigade. We
marched to Amara in the afternoon, and bivouacked in a palm-
grove by the river. In the middle of the night the sound of
heavy firing came from the direction of Kosheh, and was continued at short intervals until daybreak. Of course I could not
suppose that it arose from any real Dervish attack, and could
only attribute it to one of those night alarms or panics of which
the Zulu War of 1879 had given so many examples. The
volleys of musketry were undoubtedly fired by trained troops ;
but, as the men of my two battalions had had a very heavy
day's work, I did not disturb their bivouac.

A few minutes later, a mounted officer appeared from the
cavalry commander, who was camped with his regiment at
Atab, two miles nearer Kosheh. I had left one infantry
battalion at the same place the previous evening. The officer
brought an urgent demand for assistance : the firing, he said,
proceeded from Kosheh, four miles farther to the rear. I sent
back answer that it was quite impossible that there could be
any valid reason for this musketry outbreak at Kosheh ; that
the colonel should send an officer's patrol there to discover
what the firing meant. An hour or two later the same officer,
this time on a camel, appeared ; and again I had to get up from
my blankets. It was the same application for assistance
repeated. Kosheh was firing volleys at intervals. This time
I felt annoyed ; but the humour of the situation was too much
for other feelings, so I got some writing materials, and wrote
to the officer commanding cavalry :—

'There can be no cause at Kosheh for this firing. A few stragglers
may still be near that place. Your own position at Atab is abso-

lutely secure. You have an infantry battalion immediately on your right, two other infantry battalions are on your left at Ginniss; two batteries of artillery, two battalions of the Egyptian army, and the whole of the headquarter staffs are also there; while there is an unfordable river behind you and an impassable desert in your front. You should let your men lie down and rest.'

I was not disturbed again, and shortly after daybreak news came that the firing had been caused by the presence of a few Dervishes in a mud hut near Kosheh, which the Second Brigade was supposed to have captured the previous morning, after a heavy bombardment, when they first advanced from Kosheh. The volleys were fired by an Egyptian battalion to prevent these six Dervishes getting out! Meanwhile the Dervishes had fled south as fast as Arab legs could go. All their Nuggers had hoisted sail, and were already past the bend of the Nile at Sakt-el-Abd. I got a report from the cavalry commander after dark on the 31st that they had reconnoitred to Quake, which was found deserted; that the Arab Nuggers, with arms, wounded, etc., on board, were reported to be thirty miles south of Quake, and that he had not deemed it advisable to pursue them. I knew that part of the Nile well, for I had been over it frequently a year earlier. The currents ran swift in many places. There had been little wind that day, and I believed it was still possible, notwithstanding lost opportunities, to capture some, if not all, of the Dervish fleet.

Accordingly, at daylight on New Year's Day, having been supplied with two days' rations, a couple of hundred mounted men, horses, and camels, under Major Smith-Dorrien of the Egyptian army, started from Abri, the old *Lotus*, stern-wheeler, steaming up-stream with them.

I rode from Abri to the south, through Mahass and Sukkote. At Loarda I found the cavalry halted, and the *Lotus* beached, repairing damage from a sunken rock. At 2 P.M. she was under weigh again: at sunset I came up with the cavalry, halted near Kurtingo. One Nugger had already been captured, and others were only ten miles ahead. There was little wind: the Arabs were tracking. The capture of the boats was now assured. I sent the cavalry on to Kosheh. When night fell I found myself, with a single Egyptian orderly, no food, forage, or blankets, my little Arab pony dead-tired, at a spot some miles to the south of Eroë, where dwelt Ab-der-Rahman, the leading Arab sheikh in Sukkote. I had known this man before ; of course, he had played fast and loose with us, as he was bound to do, living between the upper and the lower mill-stones on the frontier ; but the sun was now on our side of the palm-trees, and Ab-der-Rahman professed warm friendship for us. I sent the orderly to ask a night's hospitality from this sheikh.

Ab-der-Rahman was profuse in his hospitality   His guest-house was at my service, and I had good food and excellent tea in a silver teapot for my supper.   The Dervishes had passed his house on the 30th at one o'clock in full flight for Dongola. There were many wounded put into Nuggers, some of the leading Emirs being among them.

Next morning (the 2nd) I was able to report the capture of nine Nuggers, arms, clothing, and grain.   I got back to Quake on the 3rd, remained there until all the captured boats arrived, and then marched to Kosheh.   Here I received the following message from the lieutenant-general commanding :—

'The Lieutenant-General desires to express to Br -General Butler the satisfaction with which he has read the report of his proceeding since the action of the 30th ulto., and of his activity and energy in following up the enemy, which has resulted in the important capture of nine laden Nuggers, which it is believed are the remainder of the enemy's river transport north of Kaibar. The Lieutenant-General wishes General Butler to convey to Major Smith-Dorrien, Major Lloyd, and Captain Page of the *Lotus* the expression of his satisfaction at the able and successful manner in which they have carried out his orders, as well as to Sergeant Sullivan, C. and T. Corps, for the efficient manner in which, under circumstances of some difficulty, he forwarded supplies to the mounted troops in advance.   The Lieutenant-General has forwarded General Butler's report to the Secretary of State for War.'

I got back to Wady Halfa in mid-January, and was glad to get a rest.   It had been two months of continuous going.   I must pass over the next couple of months, and come to the month of March.

The best thing about war is that it opens eyes in a mental sense, even as it closes them in a bodily one.   It was now clear, even to the English official in Cairo, that we had not a friend among the indigenous peoples of the Nile from Khartoum to the sea. The Greek, the Syrian, the outlander generally, the Jewish ' Shroff,' the semi-Christian inhabitants might wish to see us in a land which was no more theirs than it was ours, but the Mohammedan, whether Arab rover or Egyptian villager, regarded us as the children of sin and the accursed of God. The sole thing they liked about us was what the inhabitants of Cyprus used to call the ' English *livre sterling.*' It was this internal weakness in our position on the Nile, no matter what point we might choose for our frontier, that was the real difficulty. It resembled a bad sea-wall built to keep the tides in check, liable always to have the sea breaking through.

As soon as the little campaign at Koshch was over, the generals and their staffs departed for Cairo, where the winter season was at its height. Four British battalions were now left in my command, when there was no enemy in my front. Three months earlier, with ten thousand active enemies before me, I had to face the situation with a single battalion, slowly reinforced by a second one. But although I had no enemy in front, I had a very pressing and active one in my midst—sickness. I knew the Nile pretty well by this time. Keep the men moving, give them something to prevent their minds from rusting, and you get on fairly well in these Nubian deserts. Stop, form camps, remove the interests of active life, and immediately fevers in their worst form would show, increasing with the rising temperature of the summer months, until they decimated the ranks and sapped the strength of entire battalions. The usual drift of indecision was apparently now setting in in London.

A reoccupation of Dongola after Ginniss would have been a fortnight's work, but, in the then state of affairs in the Soudan and in Egypt, that occupation would have made our position only more costly, more difficult, and more insecure. Our soldiers would only have died in Dongola, when the hot weather came, instead of in Wady Halfa or at Assouan. For English troops and English gold this Soudan was only a bag without a bottom.

These, however, were the larger and more general aspects of the situation I had now to deal with. The particular thing in front of me was the rapid approach of the hot season, and the certainty, to my mind, of having in a few weeks to deal with a great outbreak of sickness among the three thousand troops at and south of Wady Halfa. At this distance of time I should not have written the word 'certainty,' if I had not had before me now some of the least among the warning words I then sent by telegraph and letter to my official superiors in Cairo and London. They may perhaps be of use to men in the future who are in positions similar to mine then. As early as 12th February I telegraphed the general in Assouan :—

'We are now approaching a very trying season for English troops we are occupying camping grounds which have been much fouled by previous occupation, and from which it is impossible to change. Our sick-list is exceptionally high, nearly ten per cent. being in hospital ; our barrack equipment is *nil*. We have neither bedsteads, mattresses, tables, nor forms. Three out of my four battalions are in tents, and to build huts for men will be a work of much time, since the district is almost destitute of timber and straw for roofs. I have now inspected the four battalions in this command in their new dispositions, and I beg the favour of the transmission of this telegram to Cairo, and if necessary to England, so that the fullest effort may be made, while there is time, for the provision of the requisites which will make life endurable during the hot season There have been fourteen deaths in the last four weeks, which are the coolest and healthiest in the year.'

These urgent messages only brought fresh queries, and demands for further reports. I had to show cause. I did so.

'I stated in my No. 199 that Kosheh hospital was being administered from Assouan, and hence there was delay in receiving medicines, which was detrimental to the sick Now for facts. I found many men (there) lying on the ground, and the reason given by medical officer was that he could not get a decision from Assouan as to the number of beds he was to keep up. He also said that he had asked Assouan on the 18th January for important medicines, but had not yet received them on the 7th February. Not a day passes that I do not find proof of the error of trying to administer these distant stations from Assouan instead of from the hospital here. I represented this months ago. All I asked was that the Medical Department should have the same measure of local administration given to it as was accorded to the Ordnance and Commissariat. I have no personal interest in the matter. I strive to do the best for the good of those under my command I can point

through five months to a long series of recommendations and proposals, many of which, opposed at first, are now admitted to have
been right.   Camerons and Durhams have over ten per cent sick
Staffords and Berks are more healthy ; but the sick-rate is increasing,
not diminishing.'

On 19th February I wired ·—

' I have again most urgently to call attention to the state of the
sick in this command   We have now two hundred and eight sick
here.   When I had only one battalion in brigade the evacuation
of the sick down the river was continuous ; now, with a heavy sick-
roll in four battalions, none are sent away, and more than two
hundred sick men are kept crowded in narrow spaces, amid the
noises of a camp ; even the wounded of Ginniss are kept here, losing
spirits daily amid the sad surroundings of numerous sick people.
Two deaths yesterday.   The hospital is so overcrowded that even
post mortem dissections were carried on in sight of the sick men.
While this state of things has been going on, the principal medical
officer is content to sit afar off (at Assouan) writing verbose objections to a better system, and opposing my repeated protests.   If we
had a single newspaper correspondent here, the system would not
last a day.'

It has been my misfortune in life to see a few things a long
way off, and to make some enemies by that foresight.   This
was one of these occasions.   All I got in reply was a demand to
put my opinions and requirements into the usual official form
of a letter, and to submit it for the consideration of my
superiors.   As we were already on the threshold of the hot
season, this altogether unnecessary delay made me feel angry,
but I sat down at once and wrote :—

·*5th March* 1886.

' SIR,—On many occasions during the past month I have put
forward by telegraph the requirements of the troops under my
command for the ensuing summer, as regards hutting, fuller provision of barrack equipment, protection from the sun, means of
supplying ice, solar hats, fuel (for boiling water), etc., etc.   These
demands were made in such ample form, and with such full recognition of the necessities of the Soudan summer, that a further report
upon them must, so far as the requirements are concerned, take the
form of recapitulation and of a progress report so far as it relates
to the work already accomplished.

' As the urgency of various matters involved appeared to me to override all other considerations, I deviated from the instructions contained in the adjutant-general's minute of the 25th January, which directed me to cause projects and estimates to be prepared. As I had had but too ample an experience, in eighteen months' service on the upper Nile, of the delays which are inseparable from the conditions of the transport service on the river, I took immediate steps to construct huts at Kosheh, Akasha, and Wady Halfa, and in order to induce rapid building, I fixed the scale of remuneration for troops and natives at so much per hut. if completed in a given time.

' This plan has resulted in the huts of the Durham Battalion at Kosheh being raised to an average elevation of nine feet in only a fortnight's labour, a result which presents a striking contrast to the erection of huts last year at Assouan, Korosko, and Halfa, at some of which places the troops were not hutted until the hot season was near its close.'

After treating in succession all the subjects already raised in my telegrams, and giving a list of our most pressing wants— ' three thousand bedsteads and paillasses, tables, forms, four thousand sun hats, burning glasses for boiling water, with proper kettles to suit them, similar to those used by the French troops in the Sahara '—I pointed out that as we were at that moment sending fuel by rail to Akasha, thence by boat to Dal, thence by camels to Sarkamotto, and finally by boat to Kosheh, at great cost and labour, these glasses would soon repay their cost. I alluded too to the sense of isolation which was felt by the soldiers of the brigade, who now regarded themselves as being ' almost beyond the outside edge of the Empire. They look in vain for any reference to them in the home newspapers, and the very existence of this distant frontier appears to be lost sight of at home.' No doubt there were reasons, political or other, for this state of seclusion, but soldiers could not be expected to understand these causes , and the sense of being forgotten or ignored, when men are engaged in very arduous work under trying conditions of climate upon a distant and exposed frontier, is not conducive to their health or contentment. I ended thus —

' In conclusion, I would desire to impress upon the authorities the gravity of the sense which I entertained of the medical and sanitary situation as it now presents itself here. Camping-places have been fouled by long-continued occupation, English and native. Chained as we are by the river and to particular situations on its banks by strategic, railway, and store considerations, it is impossible to abandon these sites or to move to ground free from contamination. Our sick-list is steadily on the increase, and is undoubtedly high in some battalions, being as much as twelve per cent. ; but what I regard as being far more serious is the fact that enteric fever, so far the British soldier's worst enemy in the Soudan, is showing marked tendency towards development. At Akasha the type of this disease has been peculiarly virulent, and, as already mentioned, five deaths have taken place in one day at that small station. There are some sixty cases of enteric fever now in the four battalions, yet the season has been the coolest and healthiest period of the year. Finally, I consider that, grave as the outlook for the summer must be, the only means of meeting it will be found in a full recognition of the fact that, while geographical isolation has raised insuperable obstacles in the way of distant centralised administration, it has also imposed upon the line of communications, upon Assouan and upon Cairo, very urgent necessities of supply.'

That letter brought matters to a climax. It must have reached Cairo about the 4th, and England, in some form, not later than the 20th March. On the 23rd March I received a telegram announcing that all the British troops at Halfa and to the south of it were to be immediately withdrawn. I had probably saved the lives of several hundred soldiers. The order for immediate withdrawal had come, but too late to save the lives of many poor fellows. The heat came early in April, and during the withdrawal the men began to sicken and die rapidly. Extracts from my private letters will best tell the tale :—

'HALFA, 18*th April.*

' I am still here, and at work removing stores and men. Another week should see this station (Halfa) closed. Only one battalion is now left, and the place begins to look very lonely. Yesterday we sent off seven hundred animals and about one thousand men. It is full time, as the heat is killing the poor sick men fast We have lost eight in the last few days. What a dreary prospect it would have been had we been condemned to remain on here during the whole hot season seven months from now.'

'HALFA, 25th April

'The weather has become frightfully hot. Thermometer one hundred and four degrees in the coolest part of the "Fostat" (dahabiyeh), and one hundred and twenty-two degrees in tents with a furnace wind blowing and clouds of dust. It has killed twenty-two of our poor fellows in fourteen days here. There are, besides, some four hundred sick men sent down the river of whose losses I don't yet know. How accurately I foretold what was coming, when —— and —— thought that I was exaggerating the prospects before us ! The last battalion leaves here to-morrow, but I am to stay behind. I shall be a general without any soldiers on a frontier which is supposed to be hostile ! '

'HALFA, 3rd May.

'This should be my last letter to you from Wady Halfa, but I cannot yet say for certain, as I can get no orders from Cairo. They are, I fear, treating me after their old manner, and they now want to detain me here without troops, commissariat, or occupation. The weather is as hot as it can be. It is an awful-looking place, glaring, burning, and baking The station grew more and more unhealthy, and I am glad that the poor fellows are out of it ; twenty-five died of heat and fever last month (April).'

All the Egyptian troops had now arrived, and the forts, stores, etc., had been handed over to them.

'WADY HALFA, 10th May

'When I last wrote I thought my letter was to be a final one to you from this place. It looks now as though I should be detained here for perhaps a long while. I do not know why ; there is no work for me to do, no troops to command. It is a week now since the last ton of stores and the last "detail" of men left here, yet I still remain all alone, and apparently for a long period. Up to the removal of the last battalion, I was allowed to think that I should go with the last of my troops, so I reduced my servants, sold my horse, and prepared to leave ; then at the last moment I am told that I must stay here. So here I am still. You cannot imagine the desolation and loneliness of the place now. Where " Biscuit Box Town " and " Bully Beef Tin City " once stood, all is vacant, wind-swept space We have had a month of terribly hot weather. In a fortnight our loss at Assouan, Korosko, and here has been forty men. Not a word of this is allowed to get out from Cairo, and while you can read telegrams from Burmah announcing the death of Private Jones from heat or fever, here there is profound silence over the deaths of forty poor Jones's from the same causes. As for

Y

a Ginniss gazette, I shall believe in it when I see it.   However, with
the help of God I hope to live through spites and flings as, with His
help, I have survived a few others before.   Poor Martin, " the big
man," died at Assouan of sunstroke two days ago '

'23rd May.

' Unless my health breaks I must stay until August.   It is possible
that, alarmed at the great mortality among the troops, the Government will order the removal of the English garrison from Assouan ;
but there are no newspaper men to let truth out or in, and the usual
silence is maintained as to what goes on here.'

' 30th May

' I must write you a short letter. . . . They are too many for
me , they are one thousand miles nearer home ; they have the
advantages of " interior lines," and they can warp words and twist
thoughts and actions as they like.   But what does it all matter ? '

' 7th June

' Do not expect a long letter this time.   I am wearing out the
summer. . . . The Nile has risen, but it may only be a temporary
rise ; the real one is not due for ten days.   When the afternoon
comes, with its long hot hours, I pace up and down in the dahabiyeh.
I fancy I have walked scores of miles now over those creaking
boards.   About four o'clock the woodwork becomes so hot that I
have to go up to the hut.   I read *Napoleon at St. Helena* by the
hour   Two days ago a very large crocodile put his head suddenly
up close to the stern of the dahabiyeh ; this could not be permitted,
so I gave him a bullet in his head when he came up again, and I
have not seen him since.'

'WADY HALFA, 14th June.

' In face of the intense heat now prevailing, you must only expect
short letters from me.   The last two nights have been nearly as
bad as the days, and last night sleep was not possible.   It was the
hottest night I ever remember   It was literally stifling.   One gasped
and struggled for breath.   I could not lie down.   I got at last into
the dinghy that was tied alongside the dahabiyeh, and dipping a
sponge into the Nile, kept pouring the water at intervals over my
head and body, sitting for hours on the boat thwarts in wet night-
clothes.   Nevertheless, I am keeping well, thank God, but our
poor officers and men are suffering terribly at Assouan.   In the
twenty-four hours ending at 3 P.M. yesterday, eleven officers and
men died there.   More than three months ago I told the authorities
what they might expect, but I wasn't listened to.   Not a word about
this mortality gets to England, and yet we have not had in this

generation such a rate of mortality as this among British soldiers. More than a hundred and thirty have died in two months, and six hundred sick men have been sent away , still the sick-rate goes up. I hope to leave here for Assouan to-morrow. [The prohibition had now been withdrawn.] I have urged the Cairo people to remove the remainder of the troops from Assouan while there is any remainder remaining. The temperature yesterday was one hundred and seventeen degrees in the shade.' [1]

The next glimpse of affairs is from Assouan :—

'24th June 1886.

'I got down from Wady Halfa a week ago. How long they intend to leave me here I don't know. I have been down with fever for the last three days, and writing is an effort It has been a bilious fever like those on the West Coast of Africa I suffered so much from twelve years ago. I am better to-day, but with the shade temperature at one hundred and seven degrees it is not easy to pick up. Our losses have been very severe. Things are now better ; six hundred weakly men have been sent down river, in addition to six hundred sick. What criminal folly it is keeping English soldiers here in the hot season ' '

That letter was to be my last from the Soudan. I had

[1] From the previous month of October, as soon as I had thoroughly examined the line of the railway through the Batn-el-Hager and the country lying to the south of its terminus at Akasha, I had decided against the possibility of maintaining our present position south of Wady Halfa We were bound either to advance or to retire To advance would mean the reconquest of the Soudan, a feat of arms which neither England nor Egypt was then prepared to undertake either with men or money To retire to Wady Halfa, giving up the line of railway, promised several advantages—first, the withdrawal of troops from a climate in which they could not live in the summer, except with immense loss of life and physical enfeeblement, and the substitution in their place at Assouan and Wady Halfa of the Egyptian army. Second, an enormous saving in the cost of the frontier garrisons Third, having the cataracts and the wilderness of the Batn-el-Hager in front of our troops instead of behind them, thus giving the Dervishes if they still wished to attack us, a present of those obstacles to transport, maintenance, and movement, which had proved so formidable to ourselves The experience gained in the four following months had strengthened these conclusions, all of which I had already communicated to the authorities in England With the approach of the hot season and our rapidly increasing sick-list, I saw that the question would not admit of further delay or postponement I saw too, that the Egyptian army was no longer to be regarded as a nursling and unfit to be trusted with frontier work Its English officers were of the best in our army The machine which Sir Evelyn Wood had designed and established four years earlier had now reached a very high degree of efficiency, and it seemed to be the most ordinary common sense that it should take its proper place on the frontier, and that, if English troops were still to be maintained in Egypt, they should be kept within the triangle Suez—Cairo—Alexandria, where at least the climate would allow them to live in summer.

managed, the day following my arrival, to get to the camp and the hospitals on Tagool heights, above the First Cataract. The heat was blinding, varying one day to another between one hundred and twelve and one hundred and twenty-two degrees in the shade. On the 13th June it reached the latter figure, and, as I have said, caused the deaths of eleven officers and men out of a garrison of about one thousand. The poor fellows were pitiable objects, lying like gasping, stranded fish in this killing heat ; a few degrees of higher temperature, and the whole must have perished. They were very patient, lying in a state of exhaustion, helpless and hopeless. The Dorset Regiment, recently arrived, and composed of very young soldiers, were the heaviest sufferers ; they were losing three and four men daily. A curious idea had got into the soldiers' minds. An old Coptic burying cavern of great size had been discovered in the hills above Assouan, and a vast number of wooden coffins were found in it. The usual tomb-rifling had taken place. It was said that the old dusty coffins had been utilised by the contractor who supplied the bread to the army for heating his ovens, and the epidemic was supposed to have had its source in this unhallowed fuel. But there was no need to seek for causes such as these : one hundred and twenty-two degrees Fahrenheit in the shade needs no occult help from dead men's dust or Coptic coffins to fill a new graveyard. The military cemetery at Assouan, begun a year and a half before this time, had now to shut its gates ; it was full.

When I was on the West Coast of Africa, twelve years before this time, a story used to be told of an Irish captain in some West Indian regiment stationed on the Upper Gambia, who had sent a despatch to our old friends the Authorities to the effect that he could not advise them to send any more white troops to his station, Bathurst, as the last man had died, and there was not room in the graveyard for any more. Such un-wonted words, when they reached home, quickened the languid senses of the officials who had to deal with this particular part of the Empire, and orders were issued to send a despatch boat to Bathurst for inquiry and report. It came in due time. The circumstances relative to the late garrison and the graveyard were as stated. Captain O'Filligan was found in his bungalow, seated in a ' Borneo ' chair ; at his right hand there was

a three-storied wooden tripod, holding three chatties placed
one above the other. A strong-smelling liquid was dropping
slowly from the uppermost chatty to the middle one, and
again from that vessel into the one underneath. Under this
last chatty a large wineglass received the final drips from the
third earthenware cooler. When this glass was full the captain
drank its contents, replacing the full glass by one already
emptied. After breakfast every morning the top chatty had
three bottles of brandy poured into it. By sunset all the
chatties were empty, and it was time for dinner. The story
went on to say that the O'Filligan was left at his post, and that
no more white troops were sent there. I relate this old West
Coast yarn, because it exemplifies a certain phase of human
nature which invariably comes out in crises of this nature.
Life will go on just the same as usual whether you bury ten
men or one in a day. Is not the bottle nose of the 'mute'
his red flag of no surrender?

Neither at Assouan nor at Wady Halfa did we, so far as I
know, hoist this flag, but I find in my notebooks many proofs
that the daily work knew no change of method ; and even in
Wady Halfa, after all the English troops were withdrawn, and I
was the last man of my brigade left, things of the most comical
nature occurred. In the last week in May news was brought
in from the desert of the approach of a party of Kabbabish
Arabs, with a large convoy of slaves in charge. The messenger
came to ask if they might bring the slaves, some eighty in
number, in to the station. I replied that if they brought the
convoy in, they must do so subject to my decision as to what
was to be done with the slaves after their arrival. This they
agreed to, and the next day saw the convoy arrived. It consisted of about sixty women and girls, and twenty youths and
men. All were from Central Africa. I had quarters and food
ready, and black soldiers for guards. The excitement in Wady
Halfa was intense. All the Arab and Greek traders, the owners
of whisky-shops, and the Bazaar people generally, had one
common bond of interest and sympathy uniting their otherwise
separate interests—slaves. The slave is to Africa what coin,
sport, capital, and labour are to other people in the world.
They are more than these things, for, where polygamy exists,
the marriage market and the slave market are one.

I think it was the celebrated De Lesseps who, as a boy with his father in Aleppo, was the abetter in a practical joke played upon a rich old Turk who had discarded one of his wives. The lady's sons, with the aid of De Lesseps, painted the discarded spouse a rich jet-black, and sent an emissary to the old Turk to say that a new slave negress had just arrived and was to be seen at a dealer's house in Aleppo. The Turk went at once to see the new arrival, and ended by paying a large sum for his former helpmeet under the belief that she was a new slave. I can believe this story from what I saw at Wady Halfa When the slave convoy arrived there I had already decided what the procedure was to be, and had obtained from the general in Cairo his approval. The slaves were taken from the Arabs and declared free, but as the poor things had to get food into their bodies, and raiment outside them before they were fit to be seen by an expectant public, I had them carefully housed in a large Government building, where they were washed and fed, and clothed in light and inexpensive drapery. Now came the question what was to be done with them. I proposed to Cairo that a present of three hundred pounds should be given to the chief of the Kabbabish, whose party would then be dismissed to their deserts : that the male slaves should be set free, but that the women, who had declared that they were helpless, should be given the offer of marrying each a man of the Black Battalion formerly stationed at Kosheh. The Black Battalion and the black ladies readily accepted this proposed solution. In order to carry it out with the fullest solemnity of the Mohammedan marriage rites, the Cadi and the Mamour of the district were summoned to attend and perform their several functions, religious and civil. The eventful day came. The Cadi, the Mamour, and an officer representing the Egyptian Government were present, seated at a table. The method of selection presented the chief difficulty. It was determined as follows A black lady stood in front of the Cadi's table ; three black soldiers from a list of specially selected men were marched in, halted by a word of command, and turned, facing the black lady, who was told to take her choice. She looked at them and they at her, the three black men showing much more confusion of mind and manners than the one black woman It was explained to her that she was not obliged to select any of the three put forward, and that there were several other threes in waiting ; but, in almost every case, she took her choice easily and without restraint. Then the Cadi and the Mamour performed their respective functions, and again and again the same process went on, with military precision. A piece of paper was handed to the sable couple, who usually disappeared through the doorway at the back, hand in hand. It took two or three hours to marry the whole female contingent, and when the proceedings terminated, it may safely be said that in all the long sad history of African slavery there had never been a happier ending to a slave convoy. But the most amusing incident in the proceedings immediately followed. All the married men vied with each other in decking their brides in the best European finery which the Bazaar in Wady Halfa could furnish, and within an hour or two of the conclusion of the marriage contracts the sable brides were resplendent in the brightest-coloured muslins and calicoes, many of them in high-heeled boots, and nearly all displaying, as they strutted about the Bazaar, parasols, scarves, and feathered hats in great variety. The process of civilisation in its most modern and advanced form had taken a matter of two hours. The pose of the parasol over the left or right ear was what pleased me most—it was perfect Who knows ? perhaps the French fashion-plate in the halfpenny papers is destined to do more for African civilisation than all the humanising efforts of minister, soldier, sailor, marine, and ordinary European trader in the past five hundred years.

As the month of June went on, the heat at Assouan, now unceasing, told more and more upon me. The old adage of the fish out of water was applicable for seven hours in every twenty-four, only that the fish was frying in a hot pan at the same time that he gasped for breath. It was curious to notice how the scorched brain, whenever it dozed off in a half-conscious state, began to see green fields and hear cool sounds and imagine rushes and brooks. The brain had its mirages as well as the desert. One's thoughts reverted to distant scenes in North America, snow-sheeted lakes, and nights of long ago when the Aurora flickered over great pine woods.

What strange extremes of heat and cold my life had seen ! Fifty-three degrees below zero on the North Saskatchewan, and here on the Nile one hundred and twenty-two degrees in the shade, above, or a range equal to that between the freezing point of water and its boiling point. Of the two extremes, I very much preferred the freezing stage. One might roast or boil oneself when freezing, but there was no possibility of freezing the boiling blood. I have known nothing sadder, in the course of my service, than the feeling that all those deaths and invalidings had been absolutely unnecessary—as much so, indeed, as though every one of these three hundred young soldiers had been pitched from the cliffs above the First Cataract into the Nile with a stone tied to his neck. To me it was in an especial degree irritating, because I had foreseen it in ample time to have it avoided.

Young man, if you would be happy in life, if you would die rich and respected, do not see too far ahead ! The rock. the wreck, the lighthouse are all steps in the same ladder, successive numbers in the catalogue ; but nobody will ever thank you for having discovered the rock before the ship was wrecked upon it, and you may be quite sure that when the Trinity Board erect the lighthouse, they will not put your name upon it. On the whole, summing it all up now, I should be disposed to think that the man fares best who does his best and leaves the rest. He is then like the man who is dealt two aces in 'vingt-et-un.' He stands to win on either card. If his prophecy has come true, he has made no enemies. If it has proved false, it is only his friends who will remind him of it.

For myself, the end of my work in the Soudan had now come. I had been losing strength for weeks, and the low fever which made food nauseous ran one down still quicker. I find no letter and no entry in a notebook from the 24th June to the 5th July, and I have only the haziest recollection of that interval I must have reached the condition of lethargic acceptation which I had noticed so often in the sick cases in hospital.

One day in the end of June at Assouan the senior army doctor came to see me. 'You must go down the river to a cooler climate,' he said ; 'you will not get better here.' 'But I can't go,' I said ; 'they have ordered me to remain here, and I won't ask them for leave.' 'Then I'll send you down,' he said. The next morning I was moved into a steamboat, and sent down river.

On the 5th July I wrote from Shephcard's Hotel, Cairo :—

'Here I am, thanks to the doctor, on my way home on four months' leave. In Assouan I had no chance, with the thermometer at one hundred and ten degrees, so they sent me down, and, a board having sat upon me here, I have been given four months' sick-leave to England. I am only weak, and have now no fever; all I want is rest. I am "played out," that is all. . . . Don't say anything to anybody . . .

'A week in Glencar would do more for me than all the doctors in Europe. It feels quite cool here after Assouan and Halfa. Don't expect a longer letter. Writing is troublesome'

And so ended the Soudan chapter in my life which, notwithstanding all its hard and rugged days and its disappointments, has remained a memory of lasting interest with me. All the books ever written about the Arab could not have taught me the tenth part of what I now knew of that oldest and youngest man on earth. I had come to be fond of this Arab, and of the deserts, and the river where he lived. We had been calling him all sorts of bad names for two years past, killing him whenever we got the chance, but, all the same, he was the better man of the two. Had the weapons been steel he would have licked us, one to our three. And this great river—what an endless lesson it was! A whole Bible in its palms and its reeds shaking in the desert winds. Cradle and grave of all things , beginning and end of empires, builder and leveller of human pride ; life in death and death in life ; earliest civiliser and latest destroyer ; old in the oldest days of which there is record, and young and vigorous to-day as when the Pyramids were born out of its 'womb of rocks.' I am not a believer in the success of any attempt to change the nature and alter the habits of life of the true Arabian race. Living side by side with the Arab, you are seeing the Old Testament as you never before saw it. Things are there still as they were. You imagine in England that you are the true inheritors, the rightful successors, of these old patriarchs and prophets and kings and people generally. You are in reality further removed even in your little Bethels and big conventicles from all sense and spirit of the old life of Jordan and Galilee, of Samaria and Judea, than are the inhabitants of Greenland from those of Peru. Arab Mohammedanism is a thousand times closer akin to the ways and days of David than you are; I am not quite sure that it is not even nearer to the early Christian idea of life, than are the present ideals and thoughts of the so-called Christian states of Western Europe ; but this is too big a matter to talk of here.

One little bit of experience of Arab or Arab-Nubian ways comes to mind in this connection. In 1884 I was given as interpreter, one Gamaul Ghindi by name, the most Europeanised Eastern I have ever come into contact with. His history was a strange one. Twenty years earlier a rich English lady, travelling on the Nile, had seen Gamaul on the river shore near Korosko, a naked brat of five or six years. The brother of Gamaul, a year older, had just been devoured by a crocodile ; and his mother, thinking, perhaps, that a similar fate might be in store for other members of her family, was willing to surrender this surviving imp for a consideration to the rich English ' sit.' Brought to England, and educated with the greatest care, Gamaul soon blossomed into a page-boy of exceptional sharpness. Then, growing older, he became valet ; was taken to travel over Europe, and rapidly acquired a practical knowledge of French, German, and Italian. He soon came to be looked upon as a marvel of civilised progress. Here was a real Ethiopian who, if his skin still retained its original colour, had at least shown himself amenable to the most advanced habits of Western civilisation He was presented in turn to the Pope and to the Emperor of Austria. When this man joined me at Korti I was delighted with him ; he seemed to be all things at once. He rode everything from a camel to a donkey ; he was a first-rate shot. Shot-gun cartridges were precious things on the Upper Nile, and Ghindi could manœuvre a flight of doves so ably that he could secure with a single shot a bag sufficient to give three persons a change of food at dinner from the everlasting tinned beef rations of Chicago.

One day I asked him how it was that, with such a record of triumphant career through the courts and capitals of Europe, he had come back again to this dreary desert world. He answered that he had come for the sake of the sport which he

had heard was to be had on the Upper Nile, and he added that
he was returning to Austria when the war was over to rejoin
a Viennese wife who was connected with a circus and travelling
menagerie business in that capital, which he was wont to
describe as by far the most enjoyable centre of civilised life in
Europe.

When we returned to Wady Halfa, I took a short leave of
absence to England ; and, before starting, I confided a horse,
a camel, and a large donkey to the care of Ghindi. After two
months I was back again at Halfa, but no trace of either
Gamaul, the camel, the horse, or the donkey could be found.
An escaped slave, whom Ghindi had taken under his especial
care and protection at Meroè, had also disappeared. About
the manumission of this negro Gamaul had professed the most
enlightened and philanthropic views ; so much so, indeed, that
it had more than once occurred to me to say that if he could
proceed to England and deliver a course of lectures before a
series of audiences, with the slave as a platform example, I
believed that highly remunerative results would follow.

After a month or two a rumour reached me as to the whereabouts of the missing Gamaul. He had not gone to Vienna,
nor was he lecturing in England. He was living quietly at
his old village near Korosko. I wrote to this village, but could
obtain no answer. Then I communicated with the commandant at Korosko. A police patrol was sent to the village, there
to arrest one Gamaul Ghindi, former interpreter to the River
Column. A week later, escort and prisoner arrived at Wady
Halfa, but whom had they brought as prisoner ? Not my well-
known guide, philosopher, and interpreter, whom I had last
seen in neat European dress, but a mean-looking native in blue
gallabeah, large white turban, with shaven face and head, and
shuffling gait. What stupid mistake had been made ? Then,
as I looked longer and closer, I saw that this Nubian native
was none other than my late traveller, valet, sportsman, and
guide, the incomparable Ghindi. He had gone back at one
fell swoop to his original native village ; he had flung off his
suit of English clothes, put on all the tokens and garb of
Ethiopic Islamism, sold my large Egyptian donkey, treated the
escaped slave in similar fashion, and he was now the proprietor
of a small sakeyeh and a growing harem in the place from

which he had been taken as an infant five-and-twenty years earlier. I suppose I should have had Ghindi prosecuted and incarcerated, and the rest of it. I did nothing of the kind. He went back to his village, and it is quite possible, if he is still alive, that he may be leading a life not much more reprehensible there than he would have led with the circus lady in Vienna.

I arrived home in the end of July. My friends at the War Office were cold but cautious. These two hundred poor fellows lying in the graveyard at Assouan, and the hundreds invalided and broken in health, whose cause I had written so strongly about while it was still possible to have saved them—these had now to be taken into account. So I was merely told that my letters had been too strong and too many ; to which I replied that, whatever might be their strength or their number, they had at least done some good, and might have done more if they had been listened to sooner. Later, I find a short mention of a visit paid to one in authority at headquarters, in order to find out if there was any probability of a gazette for Ginniss. There was none. I heard that N—— had gone back to Egypt quite in despair of getting anything, so I wrote to —— to say that what with N—— in despair, and poor Huyshe [1] dead, I felt that I should apologise to somebody for my tenacity of existence, after the manner of the Second Charles. Instead of a gazette I received a letter informing me that on the expiration of my sick-leave I would be placed on half-pay. The prospect was not too brilliant—less than two hundred pounds a year after close upon thirty years' service, hot and cold, in all parts of the Empire. The adage says that fools build houses for other men to live in. Certainly the men who build the big house of Empire for England usually get the attic or the underground story in it for their own lodgment.

A young man entering the Army, particularly if he should be blessed, or cursed, with that indefinable thing called ambition, should early in his life begin to build himself a mental citadel into which, when fortune goes counter to him, as in

---

[1] Colonel Huyshe was made an acting Brigadier-General for the action of Ginniss on 30th December. He died on his arrival in England from the effects of the heat in Korosko, in April 1886.

ninety-nine cases out of a hundred it will go, he can retire. It is in the lives of bygone great soldiers that he will find the material from which this citadel, this safe place against the 'slings and arrows,' can best be built. I am not speaking at random. I have often in life found doubts disappear, clouds lighten, and relaxing energies tighten again for the struggle, by turning to a chapter in the wonderful memoirs in which the captive of St. Helena has told in undying language the story of his early campaigns. And you need never be afraid of placing your heroes too high in this mental citadel, nor your villains too low. You may not be able to scale the heights, but neither will you so easily fall into the depths. It is a misfortune of the first magnitude in the lives of soldiers to-day that the majority of our recent wars should have had their origins in purely financial interests or sordid Stock Exchange ambitions.

With a few books and a very young family we took up a quiet life in France, where I read and wrote for the next eighteen months in a humble home among Breton orchards Here I received the K.C.B.

In spite of blank professional outlooks, and a constantly lowering balance at the military banker's, there is a good deal of sunshine to-day in the look back upon these eighteen months · the sunshine that was on a big magnolia-tree upon a house wall looking south ; in an apple orchard beyond , in a little garden, and in the bell-towers and tree-grown ramparts of an old city that was spick-and-span when Anne of Brittany was a girl ; and even the lessening balance at the banker's did not lessen the sunshine beaming from the eyes of the growing group of children who used to romp and play in the *terrain* between the old house and the railway, where the train to Dinard crossed a deep valley, through which a tiny rivulet sauntered leisurely on its way from the woods of La Garaye to the neighbouring Rance. Here again one lived among people not of the city : Sérot, *menuisier*, old Pierre, the orchard-owner, with his two old sisters, Marie and Pélagie, who milked the two cows, and knitted stockings as they led the animals to their daily pasturage , Simon, the rival farmer, whom we called Jules, who was wont to pay us sudden visits, generally to denounce the quality of the milk supplied to us by the cows of Marie and Pélagie ; and a wild sort of backwoodsman, name unknown, who used to come in the autumn or winter season, often at church hours on a Sunday morning, when he would haul out from baggy blouse or breeches pockets a brace of woodcock, a red-legged partridge, or a hare, going away as furtively as he had come.

CHAPTER XX

In the spring of 1888 we moved, family, bag and baggage,
from Brittany to Ireland, where, in a little nook among the
beautiful Wicklow hills, called Delgany, the home was again
established. The times were interesting   Mr. Gladstone's
first attempt, in 1885, to introduce Home Rule had resulted
in placing the Conservative Unionist party in power. The
twenty years of 'strong government' in Ireland had begun,
and coercion had again become the order of the day. Of
course it was all make-believe. Martial law, or its equivalent
in coercion, is bound to become ridiculous when lawyers and
philosophers attempt it. 'Don't hesitate to shoot,' spoken by
a tremulous police-officer, has almost invariably resulted in
sending a spluttering volley into a crowd of old men and
women and some small children

Parnell was at this time at the summit of his power. His
mountain home at Aughavanagh lay some twenty miles distant
from us at Delgany. When the grouse-shooting began in
August I got a letter from the Irish leader in London asking
me to join him at Aughavanagh. I accepted with delight.
I looked upon Parnell as one of the most remarkable men then
living in the Empire. To-day, twenty-two years later, I regard
him as the greatest leader of his time.

The Parliamentary session was late. The Government had
in the end of the session made up its mind to strike below the
belt at its great Irish antagonist. A wretched forger named
Pigott, for months before this date, had been hawking a
carpet-bag full of forged letters about London. Many fish had
nibbled at the bait, the *Times* swallowed it wholesale. It

published some of the concoctions in its columns ; actions at law followed, and finally the Government, thinking it had found an easy way of crushing Mr. Parnell, started a special commission of three English judges to investigate the allegations against the leader of his party

These matters had kept Mr. Parnell in London for a few days after the 12th August, and it was on the 16th that he arrived at Aughavanagh. Parnell was quite unlike any other man that I had ever met. Tall and strikingly handsome, there was in him something beyond definition or description. It was power utterly careless of its possession, seemingly unconscious of its own strength, unaggressive in its mastery, unstudied, impassive, without one touch of haughtiness. He was usually silent, but saying what he wanted to say in the straightest words ; never offensive, always fair ; always thinking, but never absorbed in his thoughts ; thoughtful of others ; alive to everything around him ; entirely without pose or pretence ; even in temper ; showing breeding to his finger-tips. You say all these things, and you might say fifty other things about him, and yet you are conscious that you have said nothing ; and the reason is this, that you might just as well attempt to describe the flight or passage of a Marconi telegram through space as to set down in words the secrets of this man's pre-eminence.

When he arrived at Aughavanagh no outward manifestation was visible that the master and owner of the place and shooting had come. Things went on as usual among the five or six guests—all political members of his party, except myself. No part of the large mountain area which was his property had been reserved for him. We had shot over it in detached parties on the two previous days. The weather was glorious.

The building in which we lived was an old three-company barrack, built in 1798 at a cross-roads in the lower part of the valley, which was then a rallying-point for the insurgents, Holt and Dwyer, and their daring bands. It was a gaunt, bare, stone structure, half-ruined, its central portion, the quarters for the officers, being still habitable. It stood about nine hundred feet above sea-level ; and, although not much of a view was obtainable from the old square limestone windows of the house, the moment one quitted the door great sweeps of heathery hill could be seen curving upward to Lugnaquilla to the west, or mixing themselves with lower mountains to the north and east.

From the shoulders of Lugnaquilla the eye was able to reach into great distances to the south-west The air was of indescribable freshness. The day following his arrival, Parnell asked me to shoot with him on a mountain to the south of the old barrack. We rode to the ground; the walking was exceedingly rough, the ground being full of tussocks in which grouse lay well but men fell easily. Parnell, who at this time was on a special regimen of food and liquid, and looked far from strong, nevertheless crossed these hummocky uplands with a light and easy step; shot surely and quickly, and seemed thoroughly to enjoy the sport. At halts he talked freely, sometimes of a parish priest in a neighbouring county who seemed to imagine that political support in the constituency carried some collateral right of poaching his (Parnell's) bog. ' As I knew that he would be out on the 12th, I sent ―― (one of my friends) down to join him, a year ago, so that I might get a few of my own birds; but the result of that attempt was that the reverend sportsman lodged a good deal of the shot of one of his barrels in my friend's knee, laying him up for six months.'

In the evenings we had pleasant conversation. He spoke little of politics; said no ill about anybody; and I can remember his giving unqualified praise to the manner in which the Governor of Kilmainham had carried out his duties towards him and his friends when he was a *détenu* in that gloomy prison. The quality in Parnell that most impressed me was the entire absence of sense or thought of superiority. Even in the most trifling details of life this was apparent When he opened his gun-case the gun was found rusty; but he would take no help in the cleaning of it; he did it himself. He did not seem to be self-conscious in anything.

When we were riding to the shooting-ground, he drew my attention to an occasional movement of one ear of the animal on which he was mounted, an oldish white horse. That peculiar droop of that particular ear in the animal, he said, indicated incipient lameness, and he went on at length to explain from the anatomy of the horse why this was so. Both

z

horses and mechanism of all kinds seemed to be favourite studies with him. We passed small groups of people on the road who had come out from neighbouring cottages to see him go by, and they were curtsying and cap-lifting to 'the Chief'; but it seemed as though they were not there, and when one of our party said that one of the most effusive cap-wavers had not paid any rent for five years, Parnell paid no more heed to the remark than he had to the waving. But if anything occurred to call for the exercise of his courtesy as host and master, it was given instantly. I was obliged to leave the party in the afternoon, and the car which was to take me home was on the road some distance away from the ground we were shooting over. When I had to say good-bye, he stopped shooting, took three or four brace of grouse from the bag, and, carrying them himself to the car, put the birds in the 'well' of the vehicle with a courteous message to my wife. When Mr. Gladstone, ten years after this time, was asked by the biographer of Mr. Parnell [1] to what causes he would ascribe the Irish leader's extraordinary ascendancy, the old man eloquently answered, 'To strength of will, self-reliance and self-command, clear knowledge of his own mind, no waste in word or act, and advantage of birth and education.' He covered completely the ground upon which this strange man's character was built. Despite the clamour of the modern Firbolg in Irish politics, the Irish people possess an instinctive knowledge of the attributes which go to make a great leader of men, and they will no more eliminate the factor of birth from this catalogue, when they can get it, than they would strike it from the pedigrees of their racehorses.

A month after this time I was summoned to London and asked to take up an inquiry into the administration, storehouses, organisation and personnel of the Army Ordnance Department in the United Kingdom. A Colonel Macgregor was associated with me in this attempt to probe a wound in the Army system which had been open ever since the Crimean War. Piles of Blue Books and Reports were supplied to us, sufficient to have given occupation to a lifetime ; but the Nile and Natal had given me a practical acquaintance with Ordnance matters of far more use to me than the dead liturgies of the

[1] Mr. Barry O'Brien.

preceding fifty years ; and by the aid of that experience I was able to run a line of suggested practical reform through the vast catalogue of congested compilations.

Our Report was ready within four months. It bore date 17th December 1888. It was all my own work, and I confess that I was rather proud of it. But alas for the vanity of human wishes ! I have dug it up now out of a mass of old papers, and I re-read it with mingled feelings. What buoyancy of hope, what heedlessness of personal profit there is in it ! But, all the same, there are passages in it that make my old heart rejoice, and make me bless my stars that I was able out of the destruction of the Report, which followed immediately upon its publication, to save just one single copy.

I received a peremptory order from the Secretary of State, Mr. Stanhope, to withdraw my report, all the printed copies of which were recalled and ordered in for immediate destruction. I spent a very uncomfortable Christmas holiday. The Civil side of the War Office was furious, the military officers silently rejoiced , but quietly, slowly, and imperceptibly our recommendations were eventually adopted. How much one's fortune turns upon the captain of the ship ! Mr. Stanhope knew very little about the army, or its stores, or its wants, and yet at this moment there was a Tory ex-Minister in London who, had he then been Secretary of State, would have had the ' Report of the Select Committee appointed by the Secretary of State for War to inquire into, and advise upon, Ordnance Store Department Questions ' crowned in Pall Mall. Only a few nights ago I was reading again with ever-increasing admiration the thoughts of Lord Randolph Churchill, as they are told in Mr. Winston Churchill's work, and I came upon a bit about the snapping swords and the bending bayonets of that time. But ' other men,' etc.

My unfortunate report having been given to the flames of the official furnaces in Pall Mall, the wrath of the authorities seemed to slacken, and early in January 1889 I was offered another odd job.

It had been decided to erect on the south and east sides of London, and at a general distance of twenty miles from the suburbs, a line of forts which would command the main routes from the sea to the capital on those sides. The sites for those works had still to be approved and purchased : this last business was my work. It opened up many new and, in some cases, interesting glimpses of English life to me. I dealt directly with the landlords and site-owners for the purchase of the six to ten particular acres selected at each place for Government acquisition

The legal experts of the War Office had drawn up an exhaustive document which recited in detail the powers given by several Acts of Parliament, made in the reigns of the Third and Fourth Georges, under which it was possible for the War Department to obtain land, whether the owner desired to sell it or not. The rules of these proceedings were elaborately laid down in particular by an Act under George IV. The officer accredited by the War Secretary (myself, in this instance) was to advance into the lands required, with lines of white tape and bundles of white wooden pegs, and with these he was to lay out and peg down the lines which marked the limits of the ground wanted. He was then to retire, having, of course, notified all the parties concerned. The next step to be taken was the summoning of a jury composed of the local yeomen, villagers, etc., etc., twenty-seven in number, whose impartial and intelligent verdict would decide the sum of money to be paid by the War Office to the owner. The erection of the defensive work could then be proceeded with. The whole thing appeared to be simplicity itself so far as the law was concerned ; but the lawyers had still to be reckoned with. My plan was to write to the different landlords informing them of the sites selected on their estates, and asking for an interview. The law of George the Fourth was necessarily alluded to, but in almost every instance my letters were met in a most courteous spirit by the owners, whose legal advisers soon entered the arena, and with these gentlemen I had many interesting interviews. I soon found that there was nothing they would have liked better than the enforcement of the enactment of George the Fourth. ' Only try it, Colonel,' one old and experienced city solicitor said to me, ' please try that Act of George the Fourth. Go in with your white pegs and tape into my client's land, mark out all you want, the more the better ; and then declare in the presence of accredited witnesses that in the name of the War Department you hereby annex and attach this particular plot, and that's all I ask. Then we'll begin to play ; that jury of twenty-seven local men will be our big drum ; then will follow placards, leaflets, paragraphs in the local journal—" Arbitrary and Tyrannical Proceedings on the part of the Military Authorities," etc., etc. But no ! it would probably end in the Government losing a dozen seats in the Home Counties at the next General Election. Colonel, take the advice of an old London solicitor. I must know something of my trade, because I have represented the *Daily* —— since it was started, and I don't want to lead you and your people into any trouble, but I will ask you to go to Mr. Stanhope—I'm a Tory and I wish well to this Government— and tell him from me that the less they say about that law of George the Fourth the better it will be for them. If they want the land, they can get it in the usual way by paying a good price for it. You can't go into a man's field and take six or eight acres in the centre of it and expect to get them for their agricultural or even park value ; you must be prepared to pay for a building site.' I soon found that my old friend was right. We had to pay from £200 to £300 the acre for land the agricultural annual value of which might have been seven shillings the acre.

One of our stations was on the top of Box Hill over Dorking. The owner lived in the valley beneath, in an historic mansion. He first drove me over the site required, and then we went to lunch in his beautiful house. There were six or eight Gainsboroughs and Joshua Reynoldses on the walls, and an adjoining room was lined from ceiling to floor with shelves holding Etruscan vases of immense value. The owner was a charming young man. I was to write to him about the War Office offer. ' Shall I address you here ? ' I asked. ' Oh no,' he answered, ' I can't live here : it is too awfully dull ; I should die. The —— Club, London, please.' Strange ! Here was London killing the old English country, and now we were expecting this same English country to save London from the foreign enemy !

Nearly a year passed in this work ; the sites were acquired, but it was then found that only a few of them could be built upon, as there was no money available for the erection of the works. There were many pleasant days during that time spent in company with Lord Wolseley, Sir Redvers Buller, General Nicholson, the Inspector-General of Fortifications, and Colonel Fraser. We used to go by train to Dorking and Reigate, Westerham, Merstham, or Dunton Green, and then drive ten or twenty miles over that beautiful down and valley country, lunching at some old village inn on the road. What delightful excursions these were ! I had just written a life of Gordon, and I was engaged upon a short biography of Sir Charles Napier. What stories of Crimean and Mutiny days, early memories of Burmah and Canada, anecdotes of the great Siege, used to enliven the drives along those lovely roads by leafy copse-woods that no motor's dust had then defiled! When this came to an end, early in 1890, I was offered by Lord Wolseley choice between the commands at Singapore and Alexandria. There could be no hesitation in the matter. I loved Egypt, despite the tricks of fortune she had played me Late in February I started for Alexandria, and travelling to Brindisi through an Italy lying for the most part in snow, got to Alexandria on March the 7th.

Although this was my fourth turn of service in Egypt, it was the first time that I had any leisure to look into the home life of the Delta. Hitherto it had always been a rush with me. One had met Arabs and Copts, Nubians and Dongolese, Greek and Syrian interpreters, but always under conditions where the enemy was more or less at the other side of the hill Now there would be time, one hoped, for a quieter study of all that had grown up out of the silt of Nile, that mighty earth-breast between the river's arms which had nourished human beings longer than any other world-bosom known to us, and given to man the seeds, plants, trees and flowers of his oldest and best civilisation.

That freshest of the Egyptian seasons, I will call it the ' Berseem ' time, was now beginning. All the level land is a vast sheet of waving green The animals are literally in clover, for berseem is the best of clovers ; and youngest kid and oldest camel are revellers in it. It is their easy, pleasant time ; the old blue buffalo munches berseem ; the Arab pony tosses and champs it , the goat goes quietly to sleep in the shade of the standing camel nibbling a sprig of it ; even the pigeon has a pull at it from under the donkey's nose. If the villagers want to turn the sakeyeh wheel while berseem is in, they put the bullock's head in a bag to hide from him the sight and perfume of so much sweetness and succulence. What I like best about this berseem clover is that it has outlived most of the other things Egyptian. It is really the blood rectifier of Egypt, and modern chemical research has discovered what the ancient people of Egypt knew six thousand years ago, viz. that this plant restores to the soil the properties which the other innumerable crops of the Delta take from it, so that we may truly say it holds Egypt together It is the elixir of Egyptian life, human and animal. Go on, old berseem ! While you sprout, all the rest may wither. The Jew, the Gentile, the Greek, the Levantine, the inhabitant of Britain, the Stock Exchange bounder, the Circassian and Turkish Pashas, will disappear from Egypt, unless they choose the better part , and the eternal fellah, he alone will survive, he and the Arab—one softened to his Delta home life by the sweet succulence of this wonderful clover, the other hardened to the asperities of the wilderness by the salts of the desert. All the animals in Egypt have to go through a regular spring course of berseem. It might be a good thing to start a human rest-cure based upon it.

Alexandria itself was everything except Egyptian ; but, once you were clear of the old mounds of broken bricks and the dust-heaps that surrounded it on the land side, you saw the fellah's life unchanged. You must get to Nile mud to find the fellah. You mount upon a ridge of sand with a palm-tree growing out of it : there you find the Arab. Both come in to the very outskirts of Alexandria, but each keeps intact his particular calling. The fellah is living in a low mud cabin with a plastered floor, and is dabbling in a bit of garden tillage, fed by a *shadouf*. The Arab is in his Bedouin tent of goat and camel hair ; he has a camel, ten goats, and two donkeys, and he sleeps upon the sand. He is ready to do a bit of garden work too, but it is like the popular song, ' Over the garden wall,' when the fruit is ripe.

There are many things to see inland from Alexandria. First, a series of immense shallow lakes of brackish water, the shores of which are very sparsely inhabited by a curious mixed race of fisher-folk—mud-waders and wildfowl-trappers. Where the waters of these great lakes merge into endless levels of chocolate-coloured mud, no drearier winter prospect could be imagined. But the scene is redeemed by the presence of enormous flights of aquatic birds: wild ducks in endless varieties, fisher birds of all kinds, long-legged 'waders' who can stand on one foot for hours, pelicans and flamingoes, kingfishers in great numbers; in fact, a whole world of fish, flesh, and fowl It would all be of endless interest to the naturalist if he could only get a bit of water that wasn't mud, or of mud upon which he could stand steady for an hour in order to study these queer fellows

These lakes are all that remain of the old, famous Nile mouths, long since closed up. I have read somewhere that they owe their origin to the Crusades. The Saracens cut the banks and flooded this coast district of the Delta to prevent their enemy's advance A Norman baron in armour would have made worse time over this region than I did with a fellah on either side of me, my arms round their necks, and their shoulders under my arm-pits, doing about a quarter of a mile an hour, with at least five pounds of red mud on each boot. All the birds had their heads up, apparently screaming with laughter at this approach of their enemy, until, when he had arrived to within one or two hundred yards of them, they rose with great flappings from the water, and flew away into remoter regions of this vast Serbonian bog Farther inland, behind these swamps, began the lands where the snipe dwelt , and these, when the autumn season arrived, I soon came to know well.

At Atfeh, on the Rosetta branch of the Nile, there was a little inn kept by an excellent Frenchman named Favre. His wife managed and cooked, and, like all her countrywomen, did both well Here, in company with my Engineer officer, Major Hare, I spent many pleasant days. Out all day, we tramped in swamps, cotton patches, rice fields ; on the brinks of old canals and choked watercourses ; in reeds and rushes ; along great dry banks of clay, where the acacia and the tamarisk flowers loaded the soft Egyptian air with indescribable fragrance ; in villages where the men and women dwelt in beehive structures, and the naked children ran like little black rabbits in a coney hutch ; through fields where the wooden plough (only a big forked stick) was dragged through the mud by a pair of buffaloes exactly as you can see it represented on the walls of some great Egyptian temple four thousand years old. All this was real Egypt, the land that ever lives. Rameses, Thothmes, Sethi, Ptolemy, Amenhotep ; Pinotem, Cambyses, Alexander, Cæsar, Amru, Soliman , Persian, Greek, Roman, Arab, Mameluke, they are as clouds that passed the sky thousands of years ago ; but here, in this brown-skinned mud-puddler, in that pitcher-carrying wife of his, and in these naked little pot-bellied children, Old Egypt and Middle Egypt and Young Egypt live, move, and have one continuous being.

In no other country does the woman of the land work harder than in Egypt, and in no other land does she win in the end such a complete victory.

Often, when we sat to rest for a while on a bank by one of those little mud warrens in the lower Delta called villages, my friend and I would laugh over the last report of the English consul-general and president upon the prosperity of Egypt, presented to both Houses of Parliament. And he would say to me, ' I wish we could take him just for one day with us. He might learn more of Egypt in a day's snipe shooting than if he sat for twenty years in his office chair in Cairo.'

When I had spent more than a year at Alexandria, the death of the Khedive Tewfik occurred, after a very short illness, in Cairo.

*   *   *   *   *

*   *   *   *   *

*   *   *   *   *

*   *   *   *   *

The death of the Khedive caused a political and financial
panic, but there was not the slightest reason why it should
have done so.   The troops in Cairo were confined to barracks.
I received urgent telegrams asking if I wanted troops ; our
consul, a kindly old gentleman who had suffered in the Arab
riots of 1882 in Alexandria, came to me in a state of nervous
excitement urging the necessity of getting reinforcements.
I declined to ask for them, seeing no reason whatever to
apprehend any demonstration in the city or elsewhere ; so he
appealed to his chief in Cairo, and I soon received a wire
offering a squadron of cavalry.   I replied :—

'Cavalry would be entirely useless in Alexandria streets, which
are all paved with large blocks of smooth lava stone from Naples,
and upon which the horses would slip and fall as upon ice.   I have
more troops than I want, and can spare you three companies of
infantry if you want them.'

But the Cairene fears were not to be allayed ; agents and
spies were sent out into the Arab quarters of the city to sound
the people.   The report brought back by the emissaries was
delightfully Syrio-Egyptian, 'All the people were saying
that the late Tewfik Pasha must have been a very good man,
because the English said so.'

When the warm weather came I paid several visits to Rosetta,
the favourite residence of Haroun al Raschid, whose name it
bore, and the Garden City so famed in Saracenic story.

Decayed, sand-heaped, and tumble-down, 'Raschid' was,
nevertheless, a spot always of delight to me.   The breaking of
Egypt and the building of her can be studied without let or
hindrance at this place.   At one end of the old town, the south,
the sand drifts are piling higher year by year ; on the north

side the growth of Egypt seawards can be read as one rides. Fifty years ago the lighthouse marked the end of the left shore of the Nile—the mouth of the river ; now the end is nearly three miles farther north. The low swamp-land is growing northwards at the rate of about a mile in ten or twelve years. The palm-trees end seven miles from the sea, and Fort St Julian is still farther back in a dense grove of palms. I have read that St. Julian, when it was built, was not far from the Mediterranean ; it is now about ten miles from it.

It was in the building of this fort that the celebrated Rosetta-stone was found by the French in 1798. In the centre of the fort there is an old Arab tomb of Tait Bey. I don't know who or what he was, but it would seem, from the study of the massive walls of his tomb, that its builders, having no stone quarries near them, chopped up any old stones they found, for in the walls of the mausoleum you can trace squares cut out of an obelisk with the cartouches of Rameses or Sethi upon them That they did not chop up the Rosetta-stone was perhaps owing to its being of the hardest black syenite, an almost unchoppable material. Will the Nile go on extending its banks farther into the Mediterranean ? Why not ? It pours down to the sea every year fifty million tons of solids, and holds another fifteen million tons in suspension.

In these years at Alexandria I had also time to carry out a far closer study of the life and thoughts of Napoleon than I had before been able to do. 1 got out all my Napoleonic books from home , was in constant communication with that excellent man, or firm, Georges Sons, of Bristol, and got from him every work which my purse could compass. Egypt, taken all the year round, lends itself in an especial manner to reading and study. That, I suppose, is the reason why it was the centre of so much literature and culture in the world for so many thousand years. When the warm weather comes in Alexandria there are six or seven hours of the daylight in which one can sit in the sea breeze near an open window and read, read, read. The thermometer varies in the room from seventy-eight to eighty-two degrees ; the air is saturated with the moisture of the sea ; and the sea is ever breaking in a low monotone of memory on a shore which is still haunted by half the great figures of the ancient world. We occupied a large flat in the Boulevard Ramleh, the back of which looked upon the old harbour of Alexandria. The site of the famous Pharos was just a mile distant across the water, there, too, was the so-called ' Tomb of Cleopatra,' at the other end of the ledge of rocks forming the eastern side of the harbour. As for the city itself, the European portion of it was only a base, new-born Italian copy of a town, surrounded by a rambling Arab quarter, outside of which vast mounds of desolation spread for miles. Upon the map of this tangle of town and graveyard I used to lay a plan of the ancient Alexandria made by a French savant, and thus it was possible to get approximate ideas of where the grand edifices of the Ptolemies and the Cæsars had stood. Of course, there was one lone and majestic monolith, Pompey's Pillar, still on its original site, but, as though it was left only to make the contrast between past and present more terribly telling, this glorious solitary column of Roman grandeur rises amid surroundings of indescribable filth and human wretchedness.

Alexandria and its neighbourhood was rich, however, in associations that have connected it with Napoleon, and to these I often went. It was near Point Marabout, on the west of the city, that he landed in July 1798. It was from the rock of the Phallarion, to the east of the old harbour, that he embarked for France in August 1799. Twelve miles away to the east was the battlefield of Aboukir, where he had, by one of the most splendid combinations ever made by him, swept into the sea a Turkish army three times more numerous than his own, and backed by an English fleet, in a couple of hours.

I caused inquiries to be made in Aboukir as to whether there were any very old people living there or in the neighbourhood who might at least have heard in their early days stories of the great Napoleon Bonaparte, or of the battle which had taken place in the bay nearly ninety years ago. There was one old sheik, I was told, who could speak about these times ; he lived in a palm grove on the shore of Aboukir Bay some five miles nearer Rosetta. One evening I rode to this group of palms ; I found there a very old Arab sufficiently aged in aspect to have reckoned a century. He was sitting outside his tent on a stool placed in the sand. Two, if not three, generations seemed to be about through the palms. The interpreter opened the proceedings ; a rough chair with goat's-hair seat was brought out and placed for me ; and the talk began. It came to this, that the old man had not seen the French at that time, for his mother afterwards had told him that when the French came to Aboukir she had taken him from the cradle and run away with all the family belongings towards the other side of the Lake Edku. But I said to the interpreter, 'Later on, as he grew to be a boy, this old man must often have heard his father and mother speak about these war times, and perhaps of Napoleon Bonaparte.' When this was duly rendered into Arabic the old sheik laughed an old toothless laugh, such as I once heard old Widdicombe the actor in Buckstone's Haymarket company laugh in the graveyard scene in *Hamlet* in the 'fifties. 'What does he say ? ' I inquired. 'He says,' answered the interpreter, 'that no doubt he must have heard his father and mother often speak of those times ; but he says that he paid no attention to what they said, and he laughed at the idea of any child having ever listened to anything that his father and mother had said.' I then caused him to be asked about the great naval battle in the bay, when so many ships were destroyed ; something about that he might perhaps have heard in his youth ? Alas ! this attempt to elicit the lore of bygone battle was even still more unfortunate, even though it began with much apparent promise After thinking, or trying to think, for some time, he replied that he had heard of that business. It took place just off the shore where we were then talking He remembered it, because ' a boat full of oranges went down in the bay in that storm ' ! I think this beats Southey's ' But 'twas a famous victory.' I afterwards found that the legend of there being an old Arab sheik in this part of the world who had seen Napoleon in his youth was founded upon the fact that there was a sheik at Ramanhieh, some ten or twenty years earlier, to whom the Great Captain had given an aigrette for his turban for some service rendered by him to the French, and this relic he had kept to the last.

One other little bit about the battle of the Nile before I quit Aboukir. A project was started in London at this time to recover the treasure which was supposed to have gone down in Admiral Brueys' flagship, *L'Orient*, in the battle. There was a company, shares, and the rest of it ; a considerable sum was collected, chiefly contributed by that large constituency of the public who are supposed to have more money than brains. Diving operations began at Aboukir ; several rusted skeletons of anchors, old chains, and bolts were dragged up, but not even a sea-eaten coin was found. Suddenly an extraordinary thing happened : a silver tankard appeared. The money for the diving operations was running short ; the news was wired to London, and more contributions came in. There was, however, considerable mystery about the tankard ; nobody was permitted to inspect it. The Alexandrian Greeks laughed a good deal. Nothing else was ever found. When I visited the treasure ' house ' in the village of Aboukir the scrap-heap was still there.

The despatch which Napoleon sent to the Directory announcing the result of the battle of the Nile, while it made the most ample acknowledgment of Brueys' bravery in the action, contained a paragraph expressing regret that he had not obeyed the orders given him by Napoleon after landing : to take his fleet into the harbour of Alexandria, where it would, from the nature of the anchorage, be perfectly secure from any attack by the British fleet. The vessel carrying this despatch was captured by the English, and the captured papers, even to the private letter, were made public in London. The publications of the time are full of denunciations against Bonaparte for the positive falsehood, as it was said, with which he had tried to screen his responsibility at the expense of Brueys for the loss of the fleet at Aboukir. It was said that no such passage for a ship of war as that stated by Napoleon existed leading into the Alexandrian harbour ; but truth will out, even in spite of politicians, statesmen, or history makers.

Admiral Sir Pulteney Malcolm had an interview with Mehemet Ali at Alexandria in the 'twenties, and the Egyptian ruler then told Malcolm that Bonaparte was right in giving Brueys the order to take his fleet into the harbour ; that there was a safe and practicable passage through which large ships of war could be brought into the harbour.

Palestine, the nearest to Alexandria of the centres of interest, had become the earliest object of a visit When my wife had come to Wady Halfa in 1886 we had planned this visit to

Palestine ; but the hot season that followed, and all that
followed it, had removed the project to an indefinite future ·
now it was near at hand.   We reached Jaffa early in April,
Jaffa, fitting gateway to that unequalled Land, fitting because
so unspoilt, so Eastern, so opposite to the spic-and-span—I shall
even say so Mohammedan, for it is to Mohammedan dominion
that we owe it that the Holy Land to-day *is* a holy land at all.
Had any European nation possessed this precious heritage
it would long ago have ceased to be itself : it must have
become English, German, or French—I will not say Russian,
for I believe that in Russian hands Palestine would probably
have been safe from at least the worst forms of Western outrage, that most fatal of all the devastations.

You leave Port Said at dusk in the evening, and at dawn
next day you are at Jaffa.   At Port Said you have seen all
that West and East and North and South could do to deface,
defile, and blotch.   It is ' hideosity ' in a cocoa-nut shell.
It is brutality boiled down, ugliness smoked and hung up to
dry in the sun.   The quaintest-looking passengers have embarked on board your steamer from Cairo, Brindisi, or Mar-
seilles, franked through by Cook or Gaze.   They are pilgrims,
mostly grim pilgrims—man-eyed English and Scottish women
in helmets and great puggarees, with husbands of a more
feminine type ;   clergymen of many persuasions , hopeless-
nosed men.   You ask yourself what would you take to be
tied by the link of a Gaze or Cook ' pilgrimage ticket ' to these
people ?   And no matter what the necessities of your pocket
might counsel, your whole inner conscience would go into stark,
raging rebellion at the proposal.   They are doubtless a thousand
times better than you are, more charitable, more kind, more
Christian ; but oh ! give me Arabians, Saracens, inhabitants
of Libya and Pamphylia, Pontus and Mesopotamia, the remoter
parts of Asia for company, ere you condemn me to go the round
of the Holy Land with these excellent unimaginative Western
peoples !

Well, as I have said, you are anchored off Jaffa.   You look
out and see a small, round, minareted, walled town, perched
up on a turtle-backed rock.   Between you and the shore a
raging sea is breaking on a ridge of rocks , around the town
there are gardens ; and beyond these again the old yellow

sand of the desert stretches south towards Ascalon and north to Cæsarea. We all got on shore somehow. It was a wonderful triumph for the Arab boatmen. Two or three of them stood on the ship's gangway ; three or four stood in the boat alongside , the steamer rolled heavily to her anchor ; the boat rose and fell with the great waves as they came surging shorewards. When the ship rolled towards the boat, and the boat was tossed up towards the deck of the ship, that was the psychological moment never missed by the Arabs. Whether the rigid man or woman liked it or not, out he or she went into apparent space, propelled by the strong men on the gangway, to be deftly caught in the naked arms of the Arabs in the boat and placed safely in the stern. Helmets and puggarees were flying, Arabs laughing and chattering, sea spray flying over everything.

Jaffa was even better on shore than it looked from the sea —steep, winding, narrow streets ; nooks, arches, lattices, and broken stairways , camels, donkeys, and crowds of people. Arabs, Jews, Christians, Turks, men with turbans and men with curls, women with yellow and white gauze veils ; the Latin convent, the Armenian convent, many small mosques—all seemed struggling to find a footing on this steep little hill. Wherever an orange-tree can get root space, there the golden fruit hangs ripe over the white walls, and its blossom fills the air with wonderful odours, until Jaffa dwells in the memory as a city of sweet scents. The Armenian convent was one of the French hospitals when Napoleon was here in 1798, and it has been made the scene of the supposed poisoning by Napoleon of the plague-stricken soldiers during the retreat of the army from before St. Jean d'Acre. Over and over again that most absurd of historical lies has been denied and refuted by unimpeachable testimony, but it is too good a bit of stage drapery to be allowed to be altogether removed from the theatre. And then history loves its lies, and carries them into a green old age ; they sell better than truth.

Leaving Jaffa for Jerusalem, the road lies through a succession of orange gardens. The earth smells of the East at its best , it yields olives, figs, pomegranates, almonds, mulberries, vines. In April everything is in blossom, and many things are in fruit. The road ascends gradually, and at Ramleh, ten miles out, we are in an open country. The most beautiful of all the scenes in Palestine is now before us—the plain of Sharon backed by all the mountains, from Carmel on the north to the hills of Hebron on the south-east. There is a very old and lofty square tower on the outskirts of Ramleh from the top of which a magnificent view, embracing the valleys and the summits of this mountain range, is outspread over Sharon What names are written on these blue hill-tops and hidden in these purple valleys ! The site hunter may be satisfied once for all in this prospect. It holds in that wide embrace from the hills of Nablous, southward to Olivet, and southward again to Hebron and Adoraim, enough to lay at rest the longings of all who ' come to see.'

From the top of this old Crusader tower, fully a hundred feet above the plain, you can trace, bit by bit, scene after scene, the little Land whose name and fame have filled the earth for two thousand years. It is a thing of wondrous beauty in itself, beauty of colour, space, light, and depth ; beauty far and near ; beauty of sound and silence ; beauty of the hour when ' the sun shifts the shadows of the mountains and takes the yokes from the tired oxen ' It was at this time we saw it. The sun was falling lower upon the western sea beyond the vale of Sorek, and the gold of his level beams was deepening upon the white villages that dot the valleys eastward where the waters of Sharon and Ajalon have their sources.

I forget now whether the tower of Ramleh sees into the vale of Ajalon, but I find in my notebook the following entry —

' Valley of Ajalon. The wonder is that the sun and moon do not often stand still to have a longer look at it.'

And so, through these valleys and rocks, you come at last upon Jerusalem. All grandeur gone from it, and nearly all verdure ; but the age of the place written everywhere over it— in the stones, in the caves, in the face of the earth, washed as it might be with cycles of the tears of men and women, and furrowed by the footsteps of human beings for æons of years. Ashes upon ashes, graves upon graves, ruins over ruins, all in so small a compass that a circle described from the centre with a radius of a thousand yards will enclose everything—

2 A

Tomb, Temple, Tower, Gate, Pool, and Wall. There on the east is the Mount of Olives ; there on the west the tower of Hippicus ; on the south the valley of Hinnom ; between Olivet and the city the valley of the brook Kedron. As to the verity of the sites, there is probably nothing more certain on earth than that the places shown are the true ones. All the churches and schisms are in agreement on this point , there was, in fact, no room for disagreement. The presence of tombs in the rocks proves that the traditional Calvary was outside the old walls, in an angle between the tower of David and that of Antonia, on the north face of the city. It was unintelligent of the latter-day non-Catholics to endeavour to discredit the authenticity of this site. The Moslems have been in Jerusalem since 630 A.D. They have never cast a doubt upon the sites ; these are as true to them as they are to the Christians. Is it probable that English or American Protestantism, now, when nineteen hundred years have gone, should find out more likely sites than these to which the East, that land of long memories, has given its unanimous assent in a continuous succession since the days of the Apostles ? Lightnings have struck those old scenes ; earthquakes have riven them ; wars and devastations have swept over them, as they have over Corinth and Athens, Rome and Palmyra. No one doubts the authenticity of *these* cities and their sites ; why, then, introduce doubt here, where the margin over which a human footstep could stray is incomparably more limited ?

Calvary was not a hill in the sense that we apply to that term ; it was a group of those same rough, rounded limestone boulders, with holes, crannies, and crevices in them, such as you can see everywhere around Jerusalem, and, indeed, in all parts of the Holy Land. The holes or crevices gave easy means of placing a rough piece of a tree upright in the ground, and the larger blocks of rock made the work of the tomb hewer more facile to his hammer and chisel.

Since the time of our visit they have made a railway to Jerusalem, and no doubt other railways will follow. These railways in the East always recall to my mind a delightful experience I once had of Western ideas applied to Eastern civilisation. A friend asked me to meet at dinner a Scottish acquaintance of his who was much interested in the pro-

gress of the East in general, and of civilisation in Asia
Minor in particular He was in outward semblance austerity
itself It occurred to some one in the party that it would
be a good thing to relate in the hearing of this stern old
progressive some of the lighter anecdotes and incidents of
European life in the East, where practical jokes were played
by young subalterns in India upon their native servants.
These stories, it was thought, would tend to ' draw ' the Scottish
elder, and would perhaps call from him severe terms of condemnation or reproof. The stories did not lack the element
of exaggeration. By this time the wine had circulated, and
to our surprise, and I think to our regret, an expression
of benevolent conviviality seemed to be overspreading the
countenance of our companion. At last it was his turn to say
something. ' Weel, noo,' he began, ' when we mad the reelway
from —— to ——, our dirrectors asked me to go out and see to
the running of it, for it wasn't paying its expenses, much less
a deevadend ; so I went to Smearna, and then on to the end
of the line. I soon found what was wrang. When the Arabs
cam doon on thar caa-mels to the coast with goats' hair or
wool, they just passed alang by our reelway, as though it hadna
been there at all. Weel, after a bit I just went to the Pashaw,
and I tauld him that the reelway was doin' nae bisness, and that
if he could mak it do a gude bisness my dirrectors wouldna
see him at ony loss. The next day he caught ten or a dozen
of these Arab men as they war goin' doun wi' their caa-mels,
and he had them all flogged in the Roonak. And when they
asked what for they war whippit, the Pashaw's seecretary said,
" For not using the reelway which the sublime Porte Sultan
had specially made and given them for their wool and goats'
hair." The next day he had another dozen Arabs of the same
sort whippit, and the day after that sax more. An' that
was enough. Thar was never ony mair trooble. The warking
expenses war covered that year, and the reelway is now paying
a handsome deevadend.'

We were silent. We felt awed by this unabashed avowal of
progressive ' reelway ' civilisation as applied to the East by
our severe Calvinist friend. Nothing that we had ever done
in the heedless days of youth, nothing that we had ever thought
of doing, could match the guilt and atrocity of this old sanc-

timonious Scotsman. O business! business! what crimes have
been committed in thy name !

We traversed the usual route to Bethlehem, to Hebron, to
the Dead Sea, and then northwards from Jerusalem to Nablous,
Samaria, and Galilee, and we had throughout the supreme
satisfaction of horses, mules, tents, bag and baggage, being all
our own. These four or five weeks' travel now lie in memory
shot with sunshine. A golden haze is over hill and valley ;
over lonely, rocky tracks that traversed lonelier, rockier hills ;
over noonday halting-places under solitary karoub-trees,
where little lizards, open-mouthed on bare brown rocks, drank
in the sunshine ; over desolate wildernesses in Judea, where
the track led round the ledge of steep white cliffs where some
of the earliest monks built themselves homes. Here in the
fissured hills that look down upon the Dead Sea they lived,
protests against the riches and corruptions of the Roman
Empire , and here, still, the foxes and jackals are the monks'
friends ; and the white paddy birds from the Dead Sea and
the blue rock pigeons from the surrounding precipices still
come in flights when the monks sound an evening horn to gather
them to supper. This old Christian religion of the East has a
charm about it that modern Christianity cannot rival. The
question, ' What went ye out into the wilderness to see ? ' they
answered thus, ' So that we might not see the city.' That
was all. It was a revolt against Rome, and all that Rome
meant.

At last an evening towards the end of April found us camped
on a hill at Ain Jennin, looking out over the plain of Esdraelon.
A great green level is this plain, eighteen miles across from
these hills of Samaria to those other hills of Galilee which
begin at Nazareth and run north until they lose themselves
in the loftier altitudes of the Great Hermon. Almost in the
centre of the green plain the Little Hermon rises, brown and
bare, out of the sea of corn ; and, farther to the right, Gilboa
divides Jezreel from Esdraelon, and marks the divide in the
plain between the waters flowing east into the Jordan, and those
which flow west into the Mediterranean.

A wonderful field of battle is all this green level land in the
setting of these bare mountains. From Saul to Napoleon—
what a catalogue ! I sat long looking at it from among the

oleanders that grow above the springs of Jennin until I had
the points clear for the morrow's ride.   Jezreel lay two hours'
ride to the north, then Fuleh one hour more.   The latter is
the central point from which the eye can sweep the entire
plain.

Our midday halt next day was near the half-ruined village
of El Fuleh. Eight miles of green corn, red hyacinths, purple
thistles, and innumerable wild flowers spread north to Nazareth,
west to Carmel, south to Jennin, and east to Gilboa, the Little
Hermon, and the dip in the plain where the waters of Hermon
lead eastwards to the Jordan Valley.

From Saul to Napoleon !   What a battle picture this plain
has been for three thousand known years, and perhaps as long
a time again of which we know nothing !   Here, too, is to be
fought the final fight.   The western half of the plain is still
called Mageddon, and there is a village up in the Carmel Hills
of the same name   Here the King of the South is some day,
they say, to form his line of battle against the King of the
North on Nazareth, Tabor, and the lower ridges of the Greater
Hermon.   It is almost ninety-two years to a day since
Napoleon's army came down from the heights of Nazareth in
three columns of attack, the centre bearing straight upon
Fuleh, the right column heading for Jennin, the left bearing
away to the foot of Tabor.   Murat is behind Mount Tabor,
waiting by the Sea of Galilee ; Junot lies nearer to Tiberias ;
Kleber is fighting hard at Fuleh, beset by ten times his own
force in the centre of the great plain ; Rampon is making for
Jennin.   It is a mighty net, the circumference of which is
nearly thirty miles ; and in the centre, at and around Fuleh,
all the armed Arab and Turkish cavalry and infantry from
Damascus to Jerusalem are gathered, intent only upon crushing
Kleber and his small division.

It must have been a glorious sight on that April morning
1799 when Napoleon, at the head of his little army from Acre,
reached the last hill overlooking Esdraelon, between Mount
Tabor and Nazareth, and saw in the centre of the great plain
the small squares of Kleber's division ' surrounded and pressed
by an enormous mass of cavalry and infantry.'   They were
the drops of honey put out to draw into the net all the floating swarms of Nablousian, Turkish, and Arab horse and foot.

Napoleon marched straight upon Fuleh with his main body, giving the signal to all his scattered columns by firing a cannon shot as he debouched into the plain. All was now confusion in the Turkish masses ; on every side they found the Franks were in the gorges through which only retreat was possible. The masses broke on every side and fled towards the Jordan along the spurs of Hermon, Tabor, and Gilboa ; but Murat met this headlong flight at the bridges of the Jordan north and south of the Sea of Galilee, and hundreds perished ere they could cross the river. All the Turkish magazines, stores, and arms were abandoned ; and never in all its long history of battle—Canaanite, Philistine, Egyptian, Chaldean, Jewish, Persian, Roman, or Crusader—had the plain of Esdraelon witnessed a victory more complete. It is not forgotten yet. As, later in the day, our little party, on its way from Fuleh to the foot of Mount Tabor, turned aside at the base of the Lesser Hermon and began to ascend to the little hamlet which is now all that remains of Naim, we met an old Arab sheik with his long gun balanced on his shoulder. I made the interpreter ask him about Napoleon Bonaparte and the battle. He knew all about it, and with many gestures expressive of attack and defence he pointed out the main sites of that memorable fight, and showed the lines by which the scattered host got finally to the Jordan, leaving five thousand of their own men dead on Esdraelon.

But to Esdraelon belongs a glory of another kind—its own peculiar property, shared by no other plain in the wide world.

Standing at Fuleh, and looking due north, you can see, some six or seven miles away, the green hills that embosom the village of Nazareth. How often from the hidden village, when the sun was sinking westwards over Carmel, must there have come to the top of the green hill overlooking the great plain the lone figure of a Young Man to look out over that great sea of beauty, and watch the slowly darkening plain, while Tabor, Hermon, Gilboa, Ebal, and the hills of Samaria still glowed in the sunset.

Skylarks to-day sing their sweetest over green Galilee ; a thousand wild herbs load the evening airs with perfumes ; the golden honeysuckles add their scent to that of the myrtle bushes along the pathways; and a sky of surpassing blue domes

the whole wondrous scene.   This village of the Nazarene is not
even mentioned in the Old Testament   Strange fact ! Yet
from it was to go forth one still small Voice which was to
shake the temples, waken the tombs, and bring the pillars of
empire to the ground.

It was here, on these grassy hills, that those wonderful Eyes
drank in, through three-and-twenty years, all that imagery of
fruit and flower, of seed and harvest time, all the secrets of
the trees, which afterwards became the theme of similitudes
and parables.   It was here the Master prepared to manifest
all that infinite knowledge of soul and sense, the pale reflection of which, as it is found in the Evangelists, has come as a
moonbeam over the troubled river of the lives of men, silvering
the turbid stream, lighting the gloomy headlands, and shedding
its benign rays far out upon the endless ocean in which the
fevered flood is at last to rest.

Looking south from the hills of Galilee over Esdraelon one
sees in a long line the blue mountains of Samaria, and at the
extreme range of vision—perhaps fifty miles distant—the hill-
tops of Ephraim.   How much of human destiny has lain
between these two points—Nazareth and Bethel !   It was at
the southernmost end of that long view that the mysterious
promise was given to the sleeper at the foot of his dream-
ladder, ' Thy seed shall be as the dust of the earth, and thou
shalt spread abroad to the west and to the east, and to the
north and to the south : and in thee and in thy seed shall all
the families of the earth be blessed.'   But stranger still was
it that here at Nazareth, fifteen hundred years later, the
' Son of the Carpenter,' looking out over Esdraelon, should be
silently awaiting the appointed time for the mighty mission
which was to be the final fulfilment of that promise of
benediction.

CHAPTER XXI

NOT the least of the advantages possessed by Alexandria was the variety of the routes that led to it from England. One could take many lines of travel going on, or returning from, leave of absence. The isles of Greece, Athens, Constantinople, the Crimea, Odessa, the Adriatic ports, Naples, and the Gulf of Genoa were all highways for the homeward or the outward bound. It was easy, moreover, for those that wished it to diverge from the beaten tracks to look at and study, history-book in hand, many of those fields of battle which the Great Captain had made for ever famous in the wars of the Revolution and the Empire. Thus, during the three years spent in Alexandria, I was able to visit the fields of Arcole, Marengo, Austerlitz, Aspern, Wagram. Of these, nearly all remain as they were one hundred years ago. One can stand on the ridge of the Pratzen and see at a glance how easily tactical genius laid the trap into which the Russian and Austrian columns precipitated themselves on that December morning, when from the low ground by Kobelnitz the central column of the French army scaled at sunrise the steep western face of the Pratzenberg and cut in two the Russian army on the plateau of Austerlitz Of all the incidents in Napoleon's wonderful life there is not one which, to my thinking, shows so completely the supreme military instinct of the man as his repeated exclamations of anger at the ignorance shown by the Russian general when, before daybreak on the 2nd December, news was brought to his bivouac that two-fifths of the Russian army were actually moving into the trap he had set. They were abandoning the ridge of the Pratzen and descending into the low ground of Solkonitz and Satschan, where they were utterly destroyed four hours later. Even the joy at seeing his enemy delivered into his hands could not quiet the instinctive rage that burned within him at the tactical ignorance and imbecility of his Russian antagonist. He was disgracing the great game!

How quiet they are now, these old scenes of bygone battle! These landscapes comprise vast stretches of stubble, potatoes, mangel-wurzle, ploughed lands and pasture, whitewashed village, meandering brook and little graveyard. Moravia is such a typical land of the village commune, with great open, tilled expanses; vast flocks of geese, herded like sheep outward from the great village green by the children in the morning, and homeward again at sunset, to sit all night in a white pack upon the same green ground. A very happy-looking land it is, sloping south towards the sun and the Danube, set in the centre of Europe, and caring not one mangel-wurzle to-day for the 'Day of the Three Emperors' up there on the Pratzen ridge.

My command at Alexandria ended in the autumn of 1893, and I went home to take command of a brigade of infantry at Aldershot.

At this time and for four years later, and for many years before, Aldershot was preparing the British army for the disasters of the South African War. I do not wish to be misunderstood. It was the fault of the system and not of a man. Aldershot was the child of the Crimean War, that war of the massed divisions, shoulder-to-shoulder tactics, parade, plumes, drums beating, and colours flying. It could not help itself. Never was the child more absolutely father to the man than was the Aldershot school of tactics the parent of Magersfontein, Stormberg, Nicholson's Nek, and Spion Kop. The Basingstoke Canal was the true source of the Tugela River, and batteries were lost in the Long Valley years before Long's guns fell an easy prey to the Boers at Colenso. Yet, when everything is said, it was the civil government of the army that must be held mainly responsible for the dismal failure of Aldershot to teach modern tactics to our army. When the site of the camp was first chosen, the land for miles and miles in every direction around Aldershot might have been had for the traditional song. But after a little while the vacant wastes lying contiguous to the military ground grew in value, towns and villa settlements sprang up, and land that could have been acquired at nominal rates in the late 'fifties or early 'sixties would have had to be bought at the rate of building sites twenty years later.

I remained at Aldershot two and a half years. We drilled and 'dressed,' marched and manœuvred, inspected and reported. 'The march past' was still the supreme test of tactical fitness for war, just as it had been nearly forty years earlier when I joined the army at Fermoy. When the summer season came militia and volunteer brigades were poured into the already too limited ground, making congestion more congested. At those times the inner springs of our military system came visibly to the surface. One could see both cause and effect, the strength as well as the weakness. Inspections, whether one had to make them or be made their object, were the most fruitful sources of knowledge. I have seldom known keener amusement than when I have had, either as a general followed by his staff, or as one of a staff following a general, to walk slowly up and down long lines of officers and men standing stiff as the old ramrods, and looking straight out at an imaginary horizon of infinite remoteness. I think that in my regimental and staff days generals were more irascible and far more faddish than they are at the present time. I remember an inspection once in the Nilgherry Hills, when the general, an old Indian officer, was particularly irate with everything he saw, and many things he didn't see. We had reached the hospital, and were passing by a low, mournful-looking building, the door of which appeared to have been recently battered in or out by some powerful agency 'What is that ? ' he asked. 'That, sir,' replied the medical officer, ' is the pathological institution.' ' The pathological devil, sir ! ' replied the angry inspector ; ' why, I can see from here that it is the hospital dead-house. What broke the door panels ? ' At this point the hospital sergeant intervened. ' Please, sir, Hospital Orderly Murphy came in drunk and riotous the night before last, and there being no place in which to confine him, he was put, lying on his back, for safety and security, into the dead-house. When he found where he was, sir, he kicked the lower panels of the door clean out, and

had finally to be taken on a stretcher to the main guard.'
Tableau !

On another occasion, also in Madras, it happened that this
same general, whose name was the lugubrious one of Coffin,
was, in all the pomp and circumstance of feathers and unnecessary anger, inspecting the men of a battery of artillery
drawn up in open formation. Suddenly stopping before a
gunner who, to the eye of the ordinary observer, did not
appear to differ in any marked degree from his fellow-men,
the general turned to the company officer and snorted out,
' Look at that man, sir ! ' The officer, who always wore a
large eyeglass firmly set in the triple environment of cheek,
nose, and eyebrow, at once directed his glassy stare full upon
the man to whom his attention was called, and then slowly
turned the same inscrutable glance upon the face of the inspecting general ; but he carefully refrained from making any
observation whatever. The vacuous stare through the glass
and the silence that accompanied it were more than the general
could stand. ' Is it possible, sir,' he exclaimed, ' that you can
find nothing to call for observation in the appearance of that
man ? ' The major turned his stony stare again upon the
soldier, surveyed him with even a closer scrutiny than before,
and then quietly observed, ' Well, sir, now that you have
particularly called my attention to this man, I do see that he
bears rather a strong resemblance to an old maiden aunt of
mine who lived at Cheltenham when I was a boy '

There were certainly terrible old dotterers going about in
those days as inspecting officers, and even in much later times.
One of the best regimental colonels I ever met nearly lost his
command through an unfavourable confidential report because
he failed to answer correctly the inspecting general's question,
put in the regimental coffee shop, as to the precise number of
currants which should be found in a penny bun. It was the
old man's favourite catch question, and it generally brought
down the colonel to his proper level. ' Thirteen, sir,' the dear
old dotterer would thunder ; ' there should be thirteen complete currants in every properly made penny bun.'

A year or two of my command at Aldershot went by, and
suddenly, in the midst of all this routine and red tape, a strange
thing happened. The incursion known as the Jameson Raid

occurred in South Africa in the very end of 1895. But before alluding further to this fruitful mother of so many disasters, I must relate one or two preliminary facts connected with the incursion which came under my personal notice. About a year before the Raid took place, an officer on the staff at Aldershot asked me one day if I could find time to see in London, at some office connected with the Chartered Company of South Africa, a new set of equipment for mounted infantry which had recently been completed, and of which the company were about to forward to South Africa some hundreds of sets. 'For what are they wanted ? ' was my first question. 'For some expedition which it is intended to make against a native chief,' was the reply. I did not go to see this equipment, but it struck me as somewhat strange that a matter of the kind should have been in preparation when one had not heard or read anything about it.

Some months passed, and Christmas 1895 came. The day after Christmas Day I told my brigade major to turn the brigade out for a route march, a useful exercise at that season of pudding and plenty. During the march, which was made on the 27th or 28th December, an officer who was riding with me said that he had been in London on the previous day and had heard that an event of the very highest importance was on the eve of taking place in the Transvaal—nothing less than an invasion across the border by a body of some six hundred mounted men, with guns and machine guns, moving on the Boer seat of government in Pretoria. 'The success of this flying column was assured : the Boers were unprepared. Great speculations were going on. All the knowing ones were confident of success.' More he said which I have forgotten. My answer was short and decided. 'You may go to London this afternoon or to-morrow,' I said, 'and you may tell all those fine fellows from me that their friends who are about to invade the Transvaal will get the most infernal dusting they ever had in their lives.' That was all. Three or four days later I was in London. Like a bolt from the blue came the news of the Jameson Raid. I had for some years past been following the course of South African affairs with a good deal of interest. A few years earlier, in 1889, I was approached by a general officer in high position and asked if I would go out to the then unnamed region lying to the north of the Transvaal, and take military and civil charge of the new colony which Mr. Rhodes was then about to establish to the south of the Zambesi River. The terms were simple and, to my mind, sufficient : twenty thousand pounds a year for five years, and unlimited scope of unchecked action. The proposal did not come to anything. The Alexandrian command was offered a little later, and I knew enough of the seamy side of South African native wars to make me unwilling to become their pioneer.

The news of the Raid and its collapse came to London almost at the same moment. I went to the War Office ; it was vibrant with mingled emotions. The Stock Exchange was still doing its best to maintain the fiction of the success of the filibusters. One officer showed me a telegram just received from that source which averred that Dr. Jameson had just entered Johannesburg in triumph. While I was reading it an official from the Secretary of State's office came in with a copy of the official despatch : Dr. Jameson and his officers, named one by one, and all his men, were prisoners in the hands of the Boers. The only thing remaining to be done was to pay the bill. That process is still going on even to this day.

A couple of months later I was offered, and I accepted, the command of the South-Eastern District, with residence in Dover Castle. I was sorry to leave Aldershot, notwithstanding inconveniences incidental to life in a small, old, wooden hut, very cold in winter and very hot in summer, of the era of the Crimean War—almost the last of its kind then standing in the camp. Like the Irishman, with his method of alternately starving and cramming his pig so as to produce ' streaky ' bacon, the War Department seemed to adopt a treatment of successive layers of hot and cold climates for their officers—I suppose with the object of fitting them for service either in Greenland or India as occasion might require. But, notwithstanding these little drawbacks, service at Aldershot under the command of His Royal Highness the Duke of Connaught was very pleasant.

Near to our North Camp was Farnborough Hill, where dwelt for half the year perhaps the most memorable, and certainly the most interesting, personage then living, the Empress Eugénie. In that house, and in the church and mausoleum, where stood the tombs of Napoleon the Third and his gloriously brave son, the Prince Imperial, I seemed to live again in the atmosphere of the Great Captain.   I had been at continuous work at this time, and for some years previously, upon chapters dealing with the Captivity at St. Helena and the recollections of the Captive spoken and written there ; and it now seemed something more than the mere accident of chance that I should have found, near Aldershot, a centre of so many gathered Napoleonic interests, such a mass of memorials of that vanished time—portraits, paintings, busts, names, and recollections of an unmatched epoch.

One day, in the summer of 1895, I had the honour of welcoming to my camp and hut three representatives of the greatest names on the roll of the marshal princes of the First Empire — Prince Murat ; Ney, Prince of the Moskowa, and Masséna, Prince of Essling.   Another day Prince Louis Napoleon, then a colonel of cavalry in the Russian army, did me the honour of attending a field practice of my brigade on the Fox Hills.   My orderly on that occasion was a man of the Scots Greys in the undress uniform of his regiment.   With a single exception the prince declared the man's dress perfect · the exception was the small round forage cap which was worn altogether over one ear—held on the head, in fact, solely by the chin strap.   The day was a grilling hot one, and the sun was beating full upon the oiled head of the trooper.   ' Why does he wear his cap only on one side of his head ? ' Prince Louis asked, after a long survey of the man and his horse.   ' Has he not got as much brain on the left side as on the right ? '

In March 1896 we moved to Dover, and took up our residence in the Constable's Tower, beneath which was the main entrance to the castle.   It was an ideal summer spot, but in winter and spring the winds howled about it often in furious fashion, making shrieks and whistles and various sounds which were probably the sources of the old stories of royal ghosts and other departed spirits said to perambulate the older portions of the pile.   King Stephen in particular was supposed to walk there ; John was also said to have a lingering fondness for the spot   Queen Mary's Tower was our garden house. There were walls of twelve and sixteen feet in thickness, secret circular stone staircases, and little octagonal wainscoted rooms,

from the windows of which one could follow the line of the
French coast for many miles, and see at night the flashing lights
across the Straits.   It was a delightful home.

During the years 1896 and 1897 I was induced to make a
lengthened study of the life of General George Pomeroy Colley.
I had known him intimately at times on and off service, and
I had formed a high opinion of his knowledge, his immense
energy, and powers of application.   I consented to write his
biography, the materials for which were voluminous.   I had
been twice in South Africa with Colley, on the first occasion in
very close relations with him.   It was, therefore, with deep
interest that I perused that inner story of a man's thoughts
which his private correspondence, even more than his spoken
words, often reveals.   But long before I first met Colley he
had been familiar with South African life and history : he had
served in Kaffraria and the Cape Colony in the 'fifties and
'sixties   A study of his papers and letters formed, therefore,
what was little short of a continuous field of South African
history, to which I was able to add my own experiences in 1875
and 1879, while it was possible also to see in many instances
the final results of particular lines of action and policy, civil
and military, in their relation to the races and peoples of the
southern continent.   The total trend of things—that is the
difficult matter to grasp in life · where is this thing going ?
If you once know that you will know much ; if you don't
know it, or can't correctly guess at it, you are more or less
in a balloon or in a rudderless ship, drifting where the wind
listeth

While my spare time was thus employed on the South African
past, the present was of course doubly interesting to me.   The
inquiry into the Raid had ended abortively ; but enough of
the waters had been stirred to show that financial intrigue
and sordid speculation and unblushing falsehood had played
their parts in introducing the final fiasco.   Out of all the mess
of pretence, simulated motive, and positive untruth that
marked the course of the inquiry, the unfortunate army man
had come off, as usual, second best.   The civilian conspirator
in high and low place had, conformably to custom, escaped.
It was poor Captain ' Bobby Black,' or equally simple Major
' Freddy Green,' who was doing time in gaol.

Although, for the moment, things looked tranquil in South Africa during 1896-97 and early 1898, and although many public utterances were made in those years by distinguished statesmen and others of a highly pacific character, there were at times curious indications that other forces and authorities were at work below the surface, as they had been at work previous to the Raid. In April 1897 considerable reinforcements of cavalry, infantry, and artillery were sent to South Africa—the very much larger portion of them being sent to Natal, where a camp of the three arms was fixed at Ladysmith, a place in sight of the Orange Free State and within a day's march of the Transvaal. At the same time officers were sent to South America to purchase horses for cavalry and artillery use. Two opposite forces seemed to be at work at home : the one, the Government, whole and entire, talking of peace and progress ; the other, a small section of two of the great public departments in London, in whose eyes the episode of the Raid seemed to be a meritorious and patriotic performance which had been marred only by the ill-natured freaks of fortune. An ' apple-cart had been upset,' that was all ; a few good and true men would soon set it on its wheels again. The optimism of these people appeared even then to be the most stupendous factor of folly I had ever known. It would not be reasoned with. One might as well try to influence the most pronounced lunatic in Colney Hatch as attempt to argue upon the basis of the Zulu War of 1879, the Boer War of 1880-81, the Basuto War of 1883-86, or the latest fiasco of the Jameson Raid. When the question arose in 1897 as to the place to be selected for the new military station in Natal to which the cavalry, artillery, and infantry reinforcements were to be sent from India and England, I was asked my opinion, privately and unofficially, upon a recommendation which I was told was made by a very high officer then at the War Office, that the new garrison should be placed at Laing's Nek. ' If you want immediate war with the Dutch,' I replied, ' put the garrison there.' That incident will suffice to show the wisdom of the wise two years before the war, and from that day forward up to the outbreak of hostilities the departmental heads continued to swell. The smallest word of doubt spoken made the mental congestion of the official brain only more manifest.

My labours upon the *Life of Colley* had reached their close, and the manuscript, revised many times, was at length ready for the publisher, when, late in October 1898, I received a cipher telegram at Dover from the War Office, asking if I would accept the command at the Cape rendered vacant by the sudden death of General Goodenough. I went to London, had interviews with the leading military authorities, and was informed that it would be necessary for the new general to proceed to South Africa with the least possible delay. I accepted the offer, not without reluctance. There were many difficulties inherent to the military position by itself, but in the present case it would be complicated by the new man's having to assume at once upon his arrival the entire civil duties of Governor of the Cape Colony and High Commissioner of South Africa, as Sir Alfred Milner had already left Cape Town for England upon leave of absence. These onerous civil duties had not even the monetary advantages attached to their performance which belong to them when held by civilians. On the principle which seems to have existed in England since the death of Oliver Cromwell, that the military labourer was wholly unworthy of his hire, a third only of the civil stipend was paid to the military *locum tenens*. I knew the move from Dover to South Africa would be a source of heavy personal expense, and it meant a disruption, at least for a time, of family ties. However, I followed my rule of military life, which is, ' Go where you are asked to go.' As I had not heard before that Sir A. Milner was coming to England, I asked the high official upon whom I called the not unnatural question, ' What is he coming home for ? ' The vague reply struck me at the moment as strange ; it seemed, in the tone and manner in which it was given, ambiguous, if not unreal.

I interviewed other high officials that day, but nowhere was any hint given me that war with the Dutch Republic was a probable contingency. Yet I have full reason to think now that even at that time a section of people, including several prominent persons in the War Office, were at work to bring that war about at an early date. A day or two later I received an intimation from the War Office that it was necessary I should see the Secretary of State for the Colonies before sailing. I wrote to Mr. Chamberlain's private secretary, putting myself at his chief's disposal. The 7th November was fixed for the interview; it lasted less than half an hour; and a gentleman whose name I did not catch—a permanent official—was also present. The Secretary of State passed in review many South African subjects—Basutoland; the war then going on between a Kaffir chief in the north of the Transvaal and the Boer Government; the balance of parties in the Cape; the general character of the leading men there The Dutch Republics were once mentioned. 'If they should force us to attack them,' said the Secretary, 'then the blow would have to be a crushing one'

I said little or nothing: I was there to listen Once or twice in the course of his rapid résumé of South African topics the name of some Basuto or Kaffir chief, with whom trouble had been or might be anticipated, came up for mention, and the Secretary had to ask the other gentleman present for the precise pronunciation. While the Secretary was speaking I continued to look steadily at the eager, white, sharp, anxious, tight-drawn face which was leaning towards me over the office table One had seen it so frequently in prints and newspapers that one seemed to be looking at some old-remembered friend from whom one had been long separated. While thus my eyes were fixed on that interesting face, I was conscious that the eyes of the third gentleman were as steadily fixed upon me. Indeed, so barren was the short interview of any expression of policy or plan, so negative in any indication of intention, any warning of possible trouble, any necessity for preparation or caution—the home-coming of Sir Alfred Milner not even mentioned, so far as its cause, objects, or duration were concerned—that when I came to think over it all afterwards I could only conclude that the object of the interview was solely for the purpose of inspecting and taking stock of the new Acting Governor and High Commissioner.

As the Secretary rose, signifying the conclusion of the visit, he said that it was only on civil matters he had desired to speak, adding that upon the military side of my work he, of course, would not presume to enter. As we shook hands, I asked him whether, if occasion should occur, he would wish me to write privately to him. He at once answered 'Yes,' and I left the room, the third party seeing me to the door.

Accompanied by a single staff-officer, I sailed from Southampton on 12th November in the *Hawarden Castle*. On the 15th we passed the *Scot*, after dark, homeward bound, with Sir Alfred Milner on board. Next morning we reached Madeira, and I found there a long and very interesting letter from the home-going Governor. In this letter, as in the London interviews already recorded, the mention of a likelihood of any trouble arising in South Africa during my temporary tenure of office was conspicuous by its absence. Everything in South Africa was 'fairly calm' 'There was nothing that should cause me serious embarrassment.' I should probably find the work before me 'rather interesting.'

We reached Cape Town on 30th November. At noon I took the oaths of office and began the work of administration immediately. My two first duties were typical in many respects of the South Africa then existing. I had to sign the extradition papers of an absconding fraudulent secretary of a London company, and I was called upon to approve a death sentence passed upon a Kaffir for a murder committed up country. Both incidents had the strangeness of things African attached to them. The absconding secretary had been a prominent personage among the passengers on board the *Hawarden Castle*, foremost in promoting all games and recreations on board I often discussed with my military secretary this individual We thought at first that he was a traveller in stockings from the richness and variety of colour of these articles displayed by him daily ; but gramophones were really his speciality. He had scores of them on board, intended for up-country markets, and one evening he gave us a performance in the saloon upon these excruciating instruments of torture. An evening or two before our arrival at Cape Town he gave a dinner party, to which he was pleased to invite my military secretary and myself. We did not accept the invitation. The night preceding our arrival, I said to my staff-officer, 'It is worth getting up at daylight to-morrow to see Table Mountain at sunrise.' We did so. The ship had anchored in the outer harbour ; the great mountain was in all its superb glory flushed with rose pink. A solitary boat had already approached the ship, carrying a couple of police-officers. While my staff-officer was regarding with admiration the glory

of the Cape peninsula, he saw the police-officers leading out
between them the gentleman of the gramophones, in handcuffs,
over the ship's side. I signed his extradition papers next
morning. Poor man ! those stockings had probably been the
cause of his ruin

The sentence of death upon the Kaffir was still more peculiar.
My acting predecessor in the Government had already signed
the man's death-warrant on the day of my arrival This proceeding was declared by the highest legal authorities to be so
utterly illegal that it would, had it been carried into execution,
have subjected my unfortunate representative to a charge of
murder. The case was brought up by the Attorney-General
at the first Council meeting. The first warrant was quashed.
Then my turn came I was determined that I would not in-
augurate my term of government by a death sentence ; besides,
the Kaffir had escaped his first execution by a fluke. To record
a second sentence against him seemed to me to be unfair.
Anyway, I refused to do it. I remembered the civil power in
Burmah hanging an unfortunate Burmese dacoit twenty miles
out from Tonghoo forty years earlier. The rope had broken
in their first attempt, and the unfortunate man fell upon the
ground dazed , after a while he revived, and while they were
preparing, under the orders of the Civil Commissioner, to tie
him up again, he asked that he might be allowed to chew
some betel-nut. They hanged him the second time, and then
it was found that he wasn't the dacoit whom they were after
at all, but another man of the same name. Our soldiers were
indignant, thinking that the law had had its chance and that
now ' the poor beggar should get his.' This Kaffir incident, I
thought, was such another case, and I was determined the man
should have his chance. His sentence was commuted.

I must pause a moment at this point in my narrative I am
conscious of the gravity of the issues with which I have now
to deal. Although twelve years have passed since I assumed
the acting offices of Governor and High Commissioner in South
Africa, all the momentous events which, so far as the public
were concerned, had then their beginning, are still in being.
The Boer War is still with us in the sense that our economic,
financial, and political systems are to-day as directly affected
by it as the constitution of a man who has suffered from a severe

malarial fever is subject to oft-recurring fits of ague, weakness and depression for years after his illness. Indeed, it may be quite possible that future historians will have to record many calamitous incidents in our history, the source of which could be directly traced to that war. The alliance with Japan, the tremendous new factors introduced into the larger spheres of international policies and politics by the issue of the Russo-Japanese War, the terrible alternatives of war or national bankruptcy with which nations are now confronted—these are only some of the effects originating in that small cloud of conflict which appeared above the political horizon in South Africa in the last year of the last century.

The last few pages of my story will have shown my readers how rapid was the transition of my life-work from the ordinary routine of military charge in England to what was undoubtedly at that time the central storm-spot of the world. I was sent upon that momentous errand at the shortest notice, without any warning, without any orders, without even the most casual indication of the possibility of my having to deal with un-expected events, still less with the developments of plans and purposes which I now know to have been then matured and arranged ; and it is now certain that there were persons high in the administrative and executive business of the Empire at the time who were cognisant of these plans and purposes. I may say at once that I have now no cause of complaint because I was then sent out without storm-chart, or direction of any kind Not even was the traditional finger of warning held up in any of the offices which I visited in the short interval previous to my departure from England. Indeed, when I re-read now the correspondence and the notes made at that time, I am struck by the fact that any indications of possible difficulties that might be before me were exactly opposite in their nature to those which were already awaiting me in South Africa I would furthermore desire to state that, although I felt very keenly, as will be hereafter seen, the attitude adopted towards me in the end of 1899, and all through 1900, by my official superiors, civil and military, in relation to the charges so freely laid against me in the press and in other places—charges that I had acted contrary to my orders, that I had neglected warnings, and that I was, in fact, the cause of the very mishaps and evils I had myself foretold—although, I say, I felt the conduct of those superiors to have been eminently time-serving and even cowardly, I can now make fuller allowance for their silences, their evasions, and even for their false statements.   Time has brought me some measure of atonement.

The question arises as to what documents I am now at liberty to publish in this book ?   Strictly speaking, I believe I am free to take from letters written to me in 1898-99 extracts dealing with statements of fact which I shall have to make, for I am aware that my own private correspondence was, on one occasion at least, used by a Cabinet Minister speaking in the House of Lords, and in a sense which was unfair both in time and in context to what I really had written in that letter. But I shall confine my references as much as possible to what I said and wrote myself.   The sun, as Wamba said to Gurth, is on my side of the hedge now, and he has been there for some years.   I can see little prospect that he will revert to the now shady side in a hurry again : it is more likely that side may become even more shady in the future.

I went out blindfold to South Africa in 1898 ; the bandages soon fell off ; and with these few preliminary words I will continue my narrative.

Heavy weather at the Cape did not at once set in after my arrival.   It was the southern summer, and beyond certain inconvenience occasioned by my supposed three official residences—Government House, Newlands, and my own military home at Rondebosch—being all in the contractors' hands for repairs, I had little to complain of for a fortnight or three weeks after my arrival   I pitched a tent at Rondebosch, had a room in an old bungalow in which Sir Harry Smith had lived with his Spanish wife in the 'thirties, and spent all my days in the Governor's office in Cape Town.   Within a couple of weeks following my arrival I began to perceive some strange signs of a state of things quite different from what I had anticipated. There seemed to be a positive rancour of expression against the Dutch in the Cape press as well as in the letters and despatches which came to me from our officials in the Transvaal. My acting predecessor had spoken on the day of my arrival of these strange ebullitions of temper : he had never seen anything resembling it in his experience of military correspondence. It was altogether new to me also. 'These scoundrels,' 'that blackguard, Blank,' was a frequent form of noun or adjective used to designate some Boer official in the Republics. I find among my papers the draft of a memo. which I wrote on this subject bearing date 10th December 1898. It runs thus :—

'Since taking over the duties of Acting High Commissioner in South Africa, Sir William Butler has had occasion to notice in some of the cipher despatches from —— certain forms of forcible language in the expression of that officer's opinions which do not appear to Sir William to be quite desirable either in relation to the matters to which they officially refer, or to the formation, by those to whom they are addressed, of a calm and deliberate judgment of the particular questions under discussion.   These questions affect important political interests in South Africa, and they might possibly become of great national and international concern in the future.

'Sir William feels assured that he has only to indicate this expression of his opinion to secure the cessation of what is probably only due to the exuberant nature of the existing political life in the Transvaal.'

I am almost certain that I did not send this memo. : probably my attention was called away to other matters , but the draft serves to show certain phases in the condition of affairs with which I had to deal within a fortnight of my arrival in South Africa.

I have not yet spoken of ' my ministers '—that delightful phrase in the make-believe of our Colonial system. I found them all excellent men. I had made the acquaintance of Mr. Schreiner, the Prime Minister, on board the steamer previous to landing, and in the next day or two all the other members of the ministry were introduced—Messrs. Merriman, Sauer, Herault, Tewater, and Solomon, the Attorney-General. I may say here, in regard to my acquaintance with these gentlemen that, from first to last, I had never come into official contact with men with whom it was easier to transact business, whose minds were fairer set to carry out the duties of their several offices, and who were less disposed to push any question that came before them to an unfair or one-sided issue. This ministry was what was called a Bond Ministry, although, so far as I can remember, the majority of its members were not members of the Bond. Mr. Schreiner, Mr. Merriman, and, I think, two others of the six, had been colleagues of Mr. Rhodes prior to the era of the Raid. That event was really the point of cleavage, social and political, in the entire fabric of life and politics in South Africa. It was this fact that was the principal revelation to me, newly arriving from England, where it was more or less assumed that matters had been patched over, or healed, in the two or three years following the Raid. But that was entirely erroneous. The fires were only slacked for the limit of three years, to which the chief actors in the rebellion, or the 'reform movement,' as it was called in Johannesburg, had been bound over to keep the peace towards the Government they had sought to destroy.

Among the officers of Sir Alfred Milner's staff who had remained in South Africa, and of whose knowledge, experience, and reliability I had been especially advised, was a Mr. W——. A day or two after my arrival this gentleman called to see me. I had a long and very interesting conversation with him as we drove together in a Cape cart through the beautiful oak and pine woods that fringe the eastern base of Table Mountain from Rondebosch to Newlands. We touched upon many topics connected with the political history of the last few years in South Africa—its parties, policies, and prospects. Alluding to the agents who had been and were still at active work in South Africa under the direction of Mr. Cecil Rhodes, Mr. W—— used words which were at once a revelation and a warning to me. 'The actions of these men,' he said, when at last we stood in the open grounds of the cricket club at Newlands, 'have made the government of the country on many occasions almost impossible to Sir Alfred Milner.'

Each passing day now developed some new aspect of these difficulties. There was an acerbity in political and journalistic life, a seeking for causes of offence, a girding and goading at the Dutch in and beyond the Cape Colony, that foreboded to me the development of very serious consequences. I found the English newspapers in Cape Town wholly under the influence of Mr. Rhodes The English journals in the Transvaal were outrageous in their language of insult and annoyance. Threats

Photogravure by Annan & Sons, Glasgow, from a photograph by Lambert & Weston, Dover.

Major General Sir W. F. Butler, K. C. B.
Taken in 1898. Commanding the South Eastern District.

and menaces were being used every day against the governments of the Republic and the people of Dutch race. The visit of Sir Alfred Milner to England was spoken of as having for its chief object the preparation and pickling of rods for the Republic, and I soon had no difficulty in tracing connections more or less close between the thoughts expressed in the letters which I received from the Transvaal, and the language used by the journals in Cape Town which were being worked in Mr. Rhodes's interest.

Things soon went farther. The editor of the leading journal at the Cape was a young and very able journalist and man of letters, who was also a member of the Cape legislature in strong opposition to the existing government of the Colony, and a devoted follower of Mr. Rhodes. One day there appeared on the Parliamentary notice paper a notice in this editor's name to ask the Prime Minister questions dealing with the alleged ill-treatment of Cape coloured people in Johannesburg by the police there ; and ' whether he has ascertained that the facts are substantially as stated, viz., that the British agent has made more than one representation ; whether he can inform the House if such representation had effected its purpose ; and if not, whether the Prime Minister can see his way to strengthen the hands of the imperial officials on behalf of these Cape Colonists, by an attitude of sympathetic interest on the part of this government ? ' If this notice had stood alone, there was nothing in it to take exception to, but it did not stand alone. The inquirer must have obtained the information upon which he based his question of the previous day in my office, where he had been for some time in a room next to that in which I sat.

It seemed to my politically unsophisticated mind that this procedure was scarcely fair either to me or to ' my ministers.' The fact of the editor of the leading journal in Mr. Rhodes's interest, and a prominent member of the Opposition, using my office as a base for the embarrassment of ' my ministers ' might be progressive policy, but it did not strike me as being precisely the game according to the military ' cocker.' I could not accept such a position, and I gave orders that the offender was to be informed in writing that he was not to enter my office again. This produced a fresh revelation. I was asked that the message might be delivered to him by word of mouth, otherwise, as wielding editorial powers, he would not fail to ' have his knife into me ' during the remaining portion of my time in South Africa. However, any harm that the newspaper could do to me seemed to be small compared to the humiliation of being the servant of Mr. Rhodes (for he was the real master of the position) in my own office. I was not then aware that it was this same journalist who had telegraphed, on the issue of proclamation by the High Commissioner on the 31st December 1895, the following message to the 'Reform Committee ' in Johannesburg, then in arms against their Government : ' You must expect and not misunderstand a proclamation putting Jameson formally in the wrong. Imperial authorities have no other course. Don't let this weaken or divide you.' And he had sent this message, according to his own admission upon oath, after he had visited the same office of the High Commissioner in Government House and read a draft of the proclamation there.

So far I have scarcely mentioned the man who, despite the partial exposures of the Raid, was at this moment, perhaps, as much as ever the mover of the destinies of South Africa.

Mr. Cecil Rhodes was a very remarkable man. A younger son in a family not blessed with an abundance of affluence, he had joined in the early 'seventies in the rush to Kimberley which the discovery of diamonds in that part of the Orange Free State had called forth. Constitutionally he was ill-fitted to take a merely physical part in the rough and tumble of a digger's life. But the white digger was from the first an anomaly in the pit at Kimberley the black man was the real miner. Mind, not muscle, was the white man's motor, and the peculiar mental nature of young Rhodes soon marked him for success among that strange conglomeration of Jew and Gentile which the diamond pit at Kimberley had rapidly formed.

When the name of Cecil Rhodes began to be used by the public tongue, a friend of mine asked the late Colonel Frank Rhodes to tell him something about this brother of his of whom the financial world was talking ' My brother is a strange man,' Frank replied. ' We were young chaps together, and there wasn't too much money or too many things among us. One day Cecil came and asked me to let him have one of my shirts, as he wanted to go to an evening party in London. Well, I wanted the shirt myself that evening, and I told him he couldn't have it. He said nothing, but I knew he didn't like losing a chance, so I watched him. I saw him off to the train. He had neither the shirt on him nor had he bag and baggage with him ; but I thought that I 'd go to the drawer and just make sure of my shirt. It was gone ! Cecil came back that night. "Well, Cecil," I said, "you won over that shirt of mine , but just tell me how you did it, for it wasn't on you when you left here, and you had no parcel with you. What did you do with it ? " He chuckled a little, and said drily, " I put it on under the old one " Now, that 's Cecil.'

He was a man of vast energy and long foresight. He soon had the diamond business at his finger ends He speculated, bought and sold. One of his earliest ventures was in a small steam engine of six horse-power which he had brought by waggon from Port Elizabeth. He used it for making ice-creams, a delicacy in prodigious demand among the diggers and thirsty denizens of Kimberley. He was in partnership with two other men, one of whom carried the water, and the other distributed the ice-creams to the community. Money came in. All at once a thunderstorm broke over Kimberley, and the diamond pit was flooded. The demand for ices ceased, but the pit had to be pumped out, and there was only one engine to do it Rhodes took the contract. It was for some thousands of pounds. A friend came and said, ' Take care about that water ; if you have not a secure place into which to pump it, it will all run back again into the mine ' A clause was inserted in the contract, stipulating that the mine management was to be responsible for storing the water when it was pumped out. Just as the last buckets were up, the dam of the temporary reservoir burst, and the whole volume ran back into the pit again. Another contract to pump followed, at twice the amount of the first. That was the beginning of Mr. Rhodes's fortune , the rest is known. With wealth came the wish to win more than wealth. One by one obstacles were bought off, or beaten off. He was a bitter enemy and a generous friend. Every man had his price, he thought, and if he was worth buying, he was bought. The history of the Rhodesian concession will probably never be accurately known. Strange stories were told about it, and about the wars that followed it. At the time that I was approached by the general officer in London about taking charge of the new colony on the Zambesi, my visitor said : ' This Rhodes is an extraordinary man. He said quite quietly to me the other day, " All the fellows that go in there to settle as farmers will be massacred by the natives." '

When Rhodesia proved a failure, the Transvaal became the next necessary acquisition to save the market Millions had been lost by the outer public in Chartered stock ; they might be won again in the Rand mines ; so the Raid was organised and looked upon as a certainty, for was not the Transvaal a nut between the nutcrackers of De Beers and Rhodesia ? To get the cracker into working order the railway to Bulawayo had to be built. In these things you must have a cry ready to catch the public ear. ' The Cape to Cairo ' gave the necessary key for turning on the money-taps. One great obstacle stood in Mr. Rhodes's path—an old, rugged lion-hunter, a stout Boer fighter named Paul Kruger, a man of seventy years or thereabouts when the Raid was planned and carried out. Mr. Rhodes was a most astute calculator ; he knew the buying price of a great many men and women A cheque for ten thousand pounds, a thousand shares in a gold mine or a new company, a diamond tiara—these things were as tickets given for the honour people pawned in the shop of his success. But that old Boer of seventy beat him in the end, and when that end came the master of gold and diamonds could only repeat the mournful words of the poet, ' So much to do, so little done.'

At the time of my arrival in South Africa, Mr. Rhodes was at his magnificent residence at the foot of the Devil's Peak above Rondebosch ; but as he did not call upon the Acting Governor and High Commissioner, I never had the pleasure of making his personal acquaintance.

I had to leave Cape Town on 12th December to open a large South African Exhibition in Grahamstown. The occasion was of some importance. All the South African states and territories were to be represented there. There were public dinners, many speeches, and the rest of it. What would I speak about ? I thought over it during the railway journey, and decided upon

my line   I would preach peace to these unfortunate people
who were being now lashed towards war by so many hands.
A special train carried me, together with a staff of ten persons,
on our route   It was a long journey, some forty-four hours,
but I would have had it even longer.   In old days I had never
tired of South Africa outside its towns and cities   It was the
same with me still.   I saw again with pleasure the hot blazing
wastes of the karroo, the great plains of the upper plateaux,
the far-apart river valleys with their yellow streams, the green
mimosa fringings, the huge table-topped hills, with glimpses
beyond those hills of blue mountain ranges, and over all that
wondrous sky, with its atmosphere of arm-stretching and lung-
expanding freedom, the glory of space everywhere visible.
Well, it was worth coming all those miles of ocean, and finding
oneself condemned to the desk of a thankless office, just to see
it all once again.   The special train reached Grahamstown on
the evening of 14th December, and on the following day the
formal opening of the Exhibition took place.   There were many
addresses, much speechifying, walking round, and the rest of
it.   The heat was intense.   On the 16th there were various
functions of an official nature, and on the 17th a public luncheon
was given in the drill-shed to about two hundred and fifty
persons.

I had no set speech prepared, but my mind was full
of a few salient matters.   Here was this vast land, still but
half-occupied by man.   How lavish had Nature been to it !
What plains, forests, fertile valleys, and mimosa-covered glens
she had given it !   What gold and diamonds she had stowed
away in it in kloof and ridge !   How she had mixed her favours
of pastoral and mineral riches, so that all whose home it was
could take their share !   That was the South Africa as it lay
under the incomparable sky—a land worth working for, worth
thinking for, worth loving.   What were its people doing with
it ?   How could all these gifts of Nature be best turned to benefit and increase the happiness of the people ?   I saw the rivers
flowing out to the sea, their waters lost to the enrichment of
the soil ; I saw the gold and precious stones passing to the
coast for shipment to another hemisphere for the profit of the
alien

This was my third visit to South Africa   Years had come

and gone since I was last here. What changes were those which I saw on every side ?   Extended railways, new streets, large public buildings, great docks at the seaports ; these were evidences of progress. But there was another change that I could not account for. I turn to the public prints, and there, side by side with this increased progress, so tangibly displayed, I discern a strange alteration. The old amity of life, the social harmony between race and race, seems largely to have disappeared ; suspicion and distrust seem to have taken the place of former confidence and assurance. Is there any reason why this should be ? Is not the land wide enough for all ? Are populations jostling against each other in these vast empty uplands ? Why should the flag be narrowed down to cover a single interest ? It is elsewhere a broad and far-spreading ensign , it is not a narrow emblem ; its folds cover and shield varied races over the earth. I could find no reason why its character should change upon this continent. Was it not possible to get back again to the friendship of old times, to the union of hearts, to a confederation which would be natural, spontaneous, unforced ?

I concluded by saying :—

' South Africa, in my opinion, does not need a surgical operation ; she needs peace, progress, and the development which is only possible through the union of many hearts and the labour of many hands. Perhaps, Mr. Mayor, I ought to offer you an apology for what may be deemed this short excursion into the borderland of politics. But I venture to regard this question from another, and I hope a higher, standpoint ; and I do not think it is inconsistent with the season we are now approaching, which for more than eighteen hundred years has repeated to men its first message of goodwill, or incongruous to this city which, prominent beyond all other cities in the land, has identified itself with education and civilisation, if now I lift my glass and drink with all my heart to the peace, the brotherhood, as well as to the progress and prosperity of this country.'

I had received that day a letter from a British resident in the Transvaal which appeared to be so important that I determined not to lose an hour in sending it to England. I take the subjoined extracts from that letter, but must preface them by saying that the question of the treatment of the persons of colour known in South Africa as ' Cape Boys ' had for months past been a prominent subject of correspondence with the Colonial Office. There had been a vast amount of reference to it in the Cape and Transvaal newspapers, and Parliamentary questions asked, as we have seen. The Secretary for the Colonies had desired that he should be kept closely informed on all matters connected with the subject, and all the reports received from our agent in the Transvaal were forwarded to him, many of them by cable. It was in connection with these ' Cape Boys ' that the opprobrious epithets in correspondence, which I have already spoken of as having been applied to the Transvaal officials, had occurred , and it was also in relation to it that the editor of the leading Cape Town paper had taken his strange line of action a week prior to this time I now give my letter containing the extracts above mentioned :—

'GRAHAMSTOWN, 18th December 1898.

'DEAR MR. ——,—I think it right to send you a private letter which will go home with the despatch dealing with the position of Cape coloured persons and British Indians in the South African Republic, because I cannot put into official form the real facts which have come to my knowledge upon this subject. That the whole question has been worked by what might be justly termed a syndicate of systematic misrepresentation I have not the slightest doubt. Upon receipt of your telegram asking for full particulars of these alleged outrages, I called upon —— to furnish all information. After much delay, I have received from him a private letter ; but I cannot admit the privacy from you of any knowledge coming to me in any form, when the subject-matter is of such importance as that now under consideration. I therefore send you two extracts from Mr. ——'s letter, in the shape of communications received by him from the —— Vice-Consul in Johannesburg. The latter wrote as follows .—

' " Mr. Dodd (secretary of the South African League of Johannesburg) has not yet brought more affidavits nor the details he promised to supply from the Landdrost's Court Rolls as to the number of Boys fined or discharged I saw Daniels (a leader of the Cape Boys) and urged him to bring as many ' Boys ' to me as he could who had been fined for not wearing the badge, in order that they might make the necessary affidavits before me But these people are indifferent, and are slow to assist us, although they are perpetually asking for assistance."

' Again : " The South African League have not yet sent me the promised details, and I cannot understand the delay, for, as a rule, they are only too glad to fish out any information that may be used against the Transvaal Government."

' This, then, is the result of all the telegrams and despatches, the questions asked in the Cape Parliament, and the newspaper " leaders " on the subject. I have no doubt that cases of rough usage by police have occurred in Johannesburg ; but we must bear in mind that that town is probably the most corrupt, immoral, and untruthful assemblage of beings at present in the world. All political questions in South Africa, and nearly all the information sent from Cape Town to England, are now being worked by what I have already termed a colossal syndicate for the spread of systematic misrepresentation, and I am therefore very careful to insist upon the verification of intelligence before transmitting it to you. The bane of South Africa in the last twenty-four years has been the false information sent home. There has never been a time in that long period when that disease reached greater depth than now. The bitterness of political feeling in this colony is extreme, and there can be little doubt that at least a section of one party, and a powerful section too, is doing its utmost to push matters to a conflagration. I do not think these people will succeed in their aim, but they have immense means at their disposal ; and the naturally inflammable nature of political thought, the absence of habits of steady industrial life, and the loose social customs prevailing, give additional power to their efforts   I take advantage of a quiet hour to write this note. I am here opening a Colonial Exhibition, and my time is very fully occupied.

(Signed) ' W. F. BUTLER.'

I had written strongly in describing at that moment what seemed to me to be the true condition of affairs in South Africa. Nearly twelve years have passed since I penned that hurried letter in the midst of a dozen functions   I see no reason to be ashamed of it to-day.

I left Grahamstown very early the next morning, travelling by Cape cart to King Williamstown, and, after further visits and functions there, took the special train again, and passing by Queenstown, Naaupoort, Stormberg, and De Aar, reached Cape Town on 23rd December. The year was not destined to close without further complications. A man of British nationality had been shot by a policeman in a midnight brawl in a low quarter of Johannesburg. The man's name was Edgar ;

the man who fired the shot which killed him was named Jones. Edgar had already knocked another Englishman to pieces, maltreating him to such an extent that he soon after died of his wounds. Had this drunken brawl occurred in any other city in the world out of the Transvaal it would have occasioned no excitement outside of the people immediately concerned in it. The time, after midnight; a drunken brawl; a man left dead, or mortally hurt, in the street; his assailant is a fugitive in a house The police are called for; the fugitive is pursued; a door is broken open; the fugitive shows fight; a shot is fired; the man is killed The policeman is arrested, and charged next morning with culpable homicide. On this foundation the South African League seized with avidity, and built upon it a huge international question. Indignation meetings were immediately organised; a petition to the Queen was prepared, all the wires were pulled at once. Telegrams, cablegrams, letters, and despatches flew like leaves in a November storm. All the newspapers in Mr. Rhodes's interest in South Africa double leaded their types. So well had the organisation been arranged, that the so-called petition to the Queen had already appeared in sensational type in Mr. G——'s newspaper, and the London journals were in receipt of sensational cablegrams from South Africa before the meeting had been even held which was to denounce the slaying of an unoffending citizen.

As early as Christmas Day I wrote a warning note to London. I said :—

'The state of unrest which men, far more than events, had succeeded in producing in South Africa has been notably exemplified this week in the case of the shooting of a man in Johannesburg by a policeman. I am yet without details of the occurrence, and I am therefore unable to speak fully upon it; but already the affair has been seized upon with the usual avidity by the press to make political capital, and further to inflame passions already sufficiently excited, and to raise suspicions among the Dutch You will see by the headlines of the newspaper paragraph attached how unscrupulous are the means used The usual military drafts for Cape Colony and Natal, the constitution and members of which have been arranged more than a year ago, are made to appear as special reinforcements to be sent out in connection with some new development of the political situation, and they are quoted as fresh

2 c

proofs of increased tension between England and the South African Republic.   I cannot tell you of the difficulties which I daily experience in obtaining really accurate information upon the true state of affairs here.   The press is almost wholly in the hands of men who are bent upon one persistent policy, that which is vulgarly known as " getting the fat in the fire." '

Again, on the day following Christmas, I find myself writing to another very high Government official in London in the following terms :—

' I take advantage of a quiet day to write you something about affairs here as they strike my mind, coming back to this country after the lapse of years. . . . The ship of State appears to me to be sailing through a sea in which the steering would be easy enough but for the ever-present pressure of a side current, set in force, controlled, and continued by the will of one man, acting through a number of subordinate agencies.   In times past this force has been moved in various directions, sometimes favourable to imperial interests, oftentimes opposed to them, but at all times based upon self-interested considerations.   This game, for it is, I believe, a game, and not a policy, still less a lofty purpose, is now directed solely to one end—a constant effort to bring the Government ship into stormy weather by embittering the relations between races, and taking advantage of every passing incident to produce, maintain, and increase unrest, suspicion, and discontent.   Everywhere around the High Commissioner's horizon I find the evidences of this set purpose and intention.   I find every passing event magnified and distorted, and men so influenced and surrounded that it is almost impossible to look for a calm or dispassionate opinion from them.   I can trace curious links of connection between the inner currents of official reports which I receive and the outer agencies of so-called popular opinion. . . . The Transvaal continues to send out its usual crop of reported Cape Boy grievances   An unfortunate incident has recently occurred in Johannesburg : a man named Edgar was shot by a policeman in a night scuffle.   The matter is in the hands of justice, and must take its course. . . . So far I have no reason to think that the shooting of Edgar had anything in it of a political or premeditated nature, but, of course, the case must be closely watched, and full justice insisted upon. . . .'

The end of the year came.   During the past thirty days I had travelled a couple of thousand miles through the Cape Colony, seen a great many of its people, and conversed with numbers of its politicians, clergymen, and public men. Situated, as I was, at the inner circle of authority, seeing, as forty years of army life had accustomed me to see, both sides of the South African hill, I was in a position to compare reports, weigh facts, measure quantities, and estimate values as few others could have done. No man knew better than I did all that we had suffered from false information during the preceding quarter century. It had been the root of all our past trouble. Now, all at once, I was brought face to face with this old evil, multiplied to a degree I could not have imagined possible ; no longer sporadic, but systematised, gigantic, unscrupulous ; powerful in means of execution ; directed to one end, that end fraught with possibilities of the gravest kind.

If I had been sent out, or had come out myself, blindfolded to South Africa, I was determined that those persons at home to whom I was responsible should at least know what I was now looking at with the bandage off.

Almost on the last day of the old year, I went to the Docks to see some friends away by the outgoing mail steamer to England Mr. Rhodes and many of his intimate friends were passengers by this steamer. As I was leaving the vessel I passed Mr. Rhodes near the gangway. Our eyes met for an instant. He was speaking to somebody in what seemed to me a sharp falsetto tone of voice. The expression of his face struck me as one of peculiar mental pain. I seemed to have seen it once before.

That evening there was a remarkable eclipse of the moon. We stood outside of the verandah at ' Charlie's Hope ' at Rondebosch watching the shadow slowly creeping over the great disc of the moon until the eclipse became total There were two or three officers with me, and we all agreed that never before had we witnessed such an extraordinary colour as that which suffused the moon at the moment of totality, or the equally strange, shadowy, and spectral light which fell upon the earth at the same moment. The face of the moon seemed to have been washed over with a blood-stained cloth, and the old garden round ' Charlie's Hope,' with its lofty cypress-trees, looked in the sombre light like a nocturnal graveyard.

CHAPTER XXII

THE beginning of the year 1899 found me engaged in keeping the Colonial Office informed by cable of the events developing in Johannesburg in connection with the Edgar affair. It became increasingly evident that the South African League and the agitation in Johannesburg were one and the same thing, and that the efforts of the combined forces were directed not upon South Africa, but upon England. A stream of misleading cablegrams were being sent to the London press. The editor of the *Cape Times* was also the special correspondent at Cape Town of two important London daily papers. The editors of the leading Johannesburg journals had been specially imported from England after the close of the abortive inquiry into the Raid, to carry out the 'Constitutional methods' which Mr. Rhodes had declared at that inquiry to be his future purpose. It would have been difficult to determine which of these journals now played higher, with words as counters, in the game of insult to the Government under which they lived, and against the people of the land out of which they and their backers were at that moment making their fortunes. Calumnies, contempt, taunts, and insults were the everyday comments upon all things Dutch in the land. Persistent efforts were made to induce or compel the acting High Commissioner to add his inner quota of misrepresentation to the general outside flow of constitutional cable-current which was going on. I was constantly receiving copies of resolutions said to have been passed by corporations in the eastern provinces, with requests that I would cable them at once to the Secretary of State. To these I invariably replied that the resolutions did

not appear to me to warrant the cost of cabling, but that they
would be duly transmitted by the first outgoing mail steamer.
One of these cases will suffice to illustrate the worth of all
The Cape journals had noticed one morning in their usual
style that the mayor and municipal council of Cape Town
had carried without opposition a strongly-worded resolution
condemnatory of the Government in the Transvaal, but a day
or two later it transpired that the resolution had not even
been presented to the council ; and when it *was* presented,
the presenter was found to be the only member in its favour—
all the others were opposed to it. This absurd instance was
only one among many others of a similar kind , the end sought
was to get the falsehood once on its way to England, and trust
to the twenty days' start the cables would have in misleading
public opinion at home before any refutation could overtake
it. I had got an early hint about the manner in which the
preparation of the telegraphic information was manufactured
for transmission on Sunday evenings to London for the Monday
morning papers by the inner circle of the ' Constitutionalists '
in their mansion near Cape Town. One of the leading spirits
assembled at the supper board held the pen on these occasions ;
the guests added their varying sparks of imaginative composition ; and from these there would be compiled some bits of
sensational news, the final reading of which would be the signal
for uproarious applause from the other members present. As
this information came to me from one who was himself often
a guest on these occasions, I was not too readily disposed to
take seriously all the resolutions that came to me, nor to send
them by cable to the Colonial Office.

At first it had seemed to me that I occupied almost an
intolerable position in being the administrative chief of Government, working my office under conditions such as I have already
described as existing between my office and the editor of the
leading Cape journal But a little further reflection showed
me that the worst conditions of life will be found to possess
some compensations. It seemed to me that this strange state
of things could be turned to account. If Mr. Rhodes's agents
and partisans were within my doors, might it not be possible
for me to know something, at least, of what Mr. Rhodes and
his friends were doing ?

South Africa is a land of strange contradictions. Under its gorgeous sunshine and the alternately depressing and exhilarating influence of its atmosphere, the European mind seems to be subject to sudden outbursts of confidential communicativeness. I had about me some officers upon whose loyalty and good service I could entirely rely. It was not long before they were approached by the Constitutionalists, who were anxious to find out what I was doing.

My Grahamstown speech had been received throughout South Africa with marked approval, except in one quarter. To the inner circle of the party working for war it had come like a shell ; but while their journals could not openly denounce the policy I had outlined in that address, they were, nevertheless, bitterly opposed to me. When one of my staff was approached by an old English college acquaintance who was now acting as an imported Constitutionalist in South Africa, he came to ask me what he might say to this former school chum. ' Say anything you like,' was my reply, ' but bear in mind that it is more essential for me to know what they are doing than for them to know what I am doing. So, give me away, provided you get an equivalent for the gift.' Thus it came to pass that I knew a good deal more of the inner springs and workings of the South African League, its ramifications and intentions than they knew about me, for in truth there was nothing to know about me that I was not perfectly content they should know. The cards were altogether new to me ; but that was the stronger reason why I played them as they came—without combination or contrivance.

Writing on 11th January to the Colonial Office on the Cape Boy question, I closed my despatch thus :—

' I am convinced by the knowledge of facts (in relation to this matter) that it is necessary to receive with caution, and even with a large measure of suspicion, statements emanating from the officials of the South African League.'

On the same date I wrote privately to a high Government official :—

' The despatches going by this mail will tell you what has been happening here during the past couple of weeks. More and more the conviction grows upon me that the small and noisy group of men who have got all the telegraphic and most of the press power into their hands are steadily intent upon the production of friction, and nothing but friction, in this country. It is not the situation that is difficult in South Africa, it is the men who are doing their utmost to make the situation impossible who have to be reckoned with. What we want are honest men   If you could induce a few of that class to emigrate here, we might have hope in the future, but I fear that neither Houndsditch nor even the Stock Exchange will help us much in that line.'

In this month of January I received many visitors, from the Transvaal, Natal, Rhodesia, Kaffraria, and different parts of the Cape Colony.   I also visited the old Dutch settlements of the Paarl and Stellenbosch to open stock, agricultural, and fruit shows ; and I was able to see with my own eyes and hear with my own ears the real condition of things in the Cape Colony, and to gather the true opinions of the people.   And what a world of difference there was between the South Africa of one's senses and that other South Africa of the 'Constitutional' press ! The latter was a pandemonium of hatred, unrest, and contention, which that press never tired of presenting as the natural outcome of every grievance, real or imaginary, under which any portion of the community was supposed to suffer in any part of the sub-continent.

One saw in these old settlements the true life of the land : the vineyard, the fruit orchard, the garden, the stock farm ; all the simple surroundings of the village, the church everywhere the centre round which the community had grown up, the old thatched or tiled houses ; the tree-lined streets ; the cool ' spruits ' running along the roadsides ; the ' stoops ' ; the white gables shadowed by the bright green oak-trees ; the flocks of white geese on the village common   Beyond these circles of shade, verdure, and cultivation, which man has made in the wilderness by turning the waters of the Berg river over the level spaces of the valleys, the eye rested on the great steep mountains, purple, opal-coloured, and red-brown, according as nearness or distance showed their ridges through the parched midsummer atmosphere.   One saw at those gatherings the Dutch people of South Africa at their best—big broad-shouldered men, matrons fat and fair, youths and girls healthy, fresh, and rosy   A sober, steady, peaceable people were they, utterly destitute of swagger or pretension, yet having plenty of resolution ; at home in every work of horse, cart, saddle, and harness ; knowing the secrets of the beasts, the fowls of the air, and the fruits of the earth, and experts in the things of food and raiment that could be made from them.

These outings were only chance days in the otherwise unbroken record of office life, a life to which the cable had now added its daily obligations of cipher message, receipt and despatch, making the High Commissioner a kind of pointsman on the railway of thought and action between two stations. One station was a centralised office six thousand miles away in London, which knew nothing of the truth about South Africa, has never known it, and apparently will never know it ; the other station was a district lying between two circumferences, one a hundred yards, and the other a thousand miles distant from my office, where most of the sources of information and the springs of action were already set and arranged, with the intention of manipulating intelligence so as to mislead public opinion in England, and inflame passion throughout the empire.

I did not flatter myself into the belief that I could change this state of things, which had all the power of great wealth and deep persistent purpose behind it. All I could hope to do was to try to make a few of the men who were my chiefs see South Africa as I then saw it. Nearly forty years earlier I had been given a practical lesson in what might be called the art of moving a crowd. It was a very simple matter. My regiment, then stationed at Aldershot, had attached to it a medical officer of great natural physical strength. He proposed to some half-dozen of us that we should go to London on the evening of Derby Day and take part in the festivities which were then a common feature in the celebration of that great racing event. He had a sort of undress rehearsal at Aldershot. He placed four of us to mark the corners of an imaginary square, the sides of which were eight or ten feet in length. He himself stood in the centre, and at a signal from him we were to sway together in one particular direction, to the right or to the left, according as he might indicate by his raised arm. By eleven o'clock at night there was a dense crowd at the top of Waterloo Place or the Haymarket—I forget which, for the locality is now so altered that it is not easy to identify its old boundaries. Under the leadership of our medical brother officer we had soon wedged our way into the centre of the thickest crowd, and taken up, more or less accurately, the positions practised earlier. After a bit our fugleman gave his signal, and we quietly pressed in the direction indicated by him. At first the effect was scarcely perceptible, but after a little time one saw the pack of people moving in obedience to our impulse. Then our leader swayed in another direction, and again the crowd seemed to respond without apparently being aware of the force to which they were conforming. A sort of rocking undulatory movement began in the pack, and it increased so rapidly that in a very few minutes the crowd was trooping whither it scarcely knew, carrying everything, including policemen, before it. These guardians of the public order were apparently as ignorant of the source from which the motion had originated as were the members of the crowd themselves. So it was in relation to the action of public opinion which I was now beholding in South Africa A few men, a very few men, were setting in motion waves of apparent opinion—resolutions, protests, proclamations, and petitions—which had their sole origin and inwardness among the agents of Mr. Rhodes's league.

To me who, seeing the machinery by which this apparently big business was being worked, had only in view the enlightenment of my chiefs in England, the task was a simple one in principle, though arduous enough and costly enough to me in details. I put aside the ideas of possible personal interest, professional advancement, the opinions of friends, the certainty of creating powerful enemies, in my desire to do this service by the men whose advanced sentinel I was.

The root question in my mind was, how shall I make these responsible people at home understand the hollowness of all these intrigues which are everywhere working to bring about what I am convinced will be a vast national calamity ?

'It is easy enough to see,' I cabled on the 14th or 15th January, 'that the present agitation in Johannesburg is a prepared business. The machinery is fully visible here, and the immediate movers are only clumsily concealed.   The objects sought are, first, political and financial effect in London ; second, to make government in Johannesburg impossible ; third, to cast discredit upon the ministry now in office here.   It is needless,' I added, ' to indicate the original train layers : they are nearer to you than to me.'

Mr. Rhodes and his henchmen had left Cape Town on 28th December ; they were reported at Madeira on 10th January, and they would be due to reach England about the day this telegram was sent by me.   A general shaking of the scenery had been arranged to take place in South Africa to synchronise with the arrival of the war envoys in England. It was even proposed to send two of the Rhodes members of the Cape Parliament to Johannesburg to make incendiary speeches there, in order that the Transvaal Government would feel itself compelled to arrest and put these gentlemen over the frontiers.   ' That would bring matters to a crisis.'

While I was thus working to keep my chiefs informed of the state of affairs, I received, towards the end of January, a most satisfactory assurance from a very high Government authority that my efforts were fully appreciated by him ; and he added a remarkable expression of opinion, that he had ' long felt that the difficulties in South Africa were greatly increased by the untrustworthiness of the information furnished,' and that he ' approved of my decision to insist on reliable evidence of grievances reported.'

I did not receive this most gratifying expression of approval until the end of January, but previous to the receipt of that approval, on the 22nd January, there arrived a long cipher message couched in very different language and of a totally different character.   I am not in possession of a copy of this message, but I remember only too well its substance.   It asked in almost rude language for proofs of what I had stated in my telegrams as to the action of the South African League and their agents with reference to the Edgar case and to other matters.   It called for detailed despatches on this question, which was described as an outrage of the grossest character, as well as upon the other questions dwelt upon in my telegrams for some weeks past.   It was not difficult to discern, I thought, in the faces of one or two among my official entourage an ex-pression which seemed to indicate that the message, when it stood at last in its deciphered nudity, was not altogether displeasing to them.

Perhaps the most noteworthy document which I find among my papers of that time is the copy of a communication I made in that month of January 1899 to our agents in the Transvaal. It runs thus :—

' I regret to be obliged to record the fact that I find it extremely difficult to arrive at accurate information in relation to events happening within the limits of the S. A. Republic. I cannot avoid drawing comparisons between the first accounts which I receive of these occurrences, and the subsequent details which come to hand later on. It should be steadily borne in mind that it is not a coloured version of events which I require, nor one in which the story is but partly told ; the adjuncts of communication by steam and electricity become only more fatal instruments of misinformation and of subsequent disaster if the news sent through them from the circumference to the centre be not the truth, the whole truth, and nothing but the truth. This has been the lesson of the past history of our relations with the Transvaal, and it is a lesson which has every chance of repeating itself in still more deplorable characters, if the necessity of the fullest, the most unbiassed, and the most accurate information, uncontrolled by any outside agency, and unprompted by any organisation, be not absolutely adhered to.'

The 22nd January was a Sunday, and the mail steamer was to leave for England on the following Wednesday ; I had therefore three days in which to write the explanatory despatch which the cipher message had called for in angry haste. I sat down at once to reply, and three days later the despatch, a very long one, left for London. I will not now inflict it *in extenso* upon the reader : it can be found at page 204, Appendix to the Report of the Royal Commission upon the War in South Africa, published in 1903. After tracing the history of the Edgar case, and the political agitation which arose out of it, I summarised the situation as it then appeared to me as follows :—

' 1. The (Edgar) case, so far as I have been able to trace it, presented no features which removed it from the catalogue of unfortunate night conflicts, too often ending in homicide or murder, which occur in cities such as Johannesburg, where the presence of gold in immense quantities has collected so many representatives of the greed and the need of human society ; and above all, that the case itself, whatever might be its form of demerit, was still *sub judice.*

'2. That although the state of feeling in Johannesburg had doubtless many elements in it of natural and spontaneous origin, those elements had, at least for the moment, been allayed by the action of the State Prosecutor of the South African Republic in re-committing the prisoner Jones on a charge of murder instead of one of culpable homicide ; and that the agitation which produced the meetings of the 24th December and the 14th January was largely, if not wholly, of exterior origin, held under the auspices of the South African League, and therefore to be regarded as being artificially engineered, and to be misleading in the sense that they represented the full body of public opinion ; though by no means misleading or unreal in the sense that they were liable to occasion scenes of riot, disturbance, and possible loss of life in Johannesburg, where there already existed so many elements of danger, both in the population and its outside environments.

' Of the larger question of the factor dominating all other subjects in Johannesburg, and now largely entering into this Edgar question, I would now speak.

' I do not think I err when I say that it is easy to discern in many quarters of this country traces of influences which are being steadily directed, I will not say to the promotion of racial antagonism, but certainly to the evolution of aims which cannot fail to evolve that end. This policy, in my opinion, can only terminate, if it is persisted in, in producing a war of races, the ultimate consequences of which no one could adequately estimate.

' I do not believe that such a conflict is necessary to our interests here. On the contrary, I believe that these interests can be best advanced by the steadily applied forces of peace and progress acting upon two races which are not in their institutions or beliefs naturally antagonistic to each other. I believe that education, the spread of enlightenment and social well-being will bring about closer interests between the states and peoples of South Africa, producing either the desire or the necessity for a confederated form of government, and gradually leading to union on a closer basis, such as exists in Canada.

' I believe that this union would ere now have taken place, but for mistakes in the past, which are mainly traceable to wrong information and to the precipitate action of influences similar to those I have been dealing with.

' In my estimate of the forces bearing upon the Edgar affair, and matters cognate to it in Johannesburg, I found it impossible to shut out from consideration the fact that the South African League was to a large extent the direct descendant and at least the part-inheritor of the traditions and aspirations of the combination of persons and principles which had so nearly led the Government of this colony into grave trouble only three years ago ; that the passions of that unfortunate period were still existing beneath the surface here ; and that the same influences were to-day at work for the futherance of the same objects then contemplated.

'It is quite possible that I am mistaken in these beliefs and opinions   I do not claim to possess any special insight into the deep and complicated problem of the South African difficulty ; I regard it from the point of view of a soldier who has known the country for nearly a quarter of a century, and who has seen the rise and results of many attempts towards the solution of the problem.

' As a soldier, too, I have looked upon my duty in relation to the information, or expression of opinion, I have sent by telegram ; I felt as one who, placed in some sense at the outposts, was bound to give his chief the full and free expression of his opinion upon the situation confronting him.

' I regret that the short interval at my disposal between the receipt of your telegram asking for further information and reasons for statements, and the departure of the outgoing mail should have left me no time for the revision or correction of this despatch ; but I deem it necessary to send it in this incomplete and crude state in preference to losing a mail.

(Signed) ' W F BUTLER,
' Administrator and Acting High Commissioner.'

Three weeks after this despatch left Cape Town, Sir Alfred Milner arrived there from England   I met him at the steamer, followed him to Government House, and we went through the papers which dealt with matters occurring during his voyage out.   I submitted a full copy of the document above quoted. I was disappointed to observe that he perused it with un-disguised impatience.   I rose to take my leave, saying, ' I envy you only the books in your library.'

I have already spoken of the entire absence of any instructions regarding the military position in South Africa previous to my departure from England , and during the two months which followed it the subject received no mention, either official or private.   The surprise with which I found, within a fortnight of my arrival, that the party of the Raid were actually engaged in fanning into flame the embers of racial ill-feeling was therefore all the greater ; and hence it was that I dwelt so strongly in my letters and despatches upon this dangerous aspect of the agitation.   Could it be possible, I asked myself, that this extraordinary supineness on the part of the governing people at home was existing together with a policy of active aggression on the part of the old raiders and their new association, the South African League—the one side six thousand miles away, and apparently blind to the possibility of war ; the other actively engaged under my eyes in preparing the way for civil conflict of the worst type ?   Two things were clear to me in this strange dualism of contradiction : first, I would do everything that lay in my power to put my chief in possession of the exact position in South Africa; and secondly, I would guarantee, as I alone was in a position to guarantee, that neither act nor word of mine would enable the party of the Raid to claim me as a sympathiser with their aims or objects, or, on the other hand, would give the Dutch people in the Cape Colony any reason to apprehend I was not perfectly fair and open in my action towards them.   As commander of the troops in the Cape Colony and Natal, I held the balance.   There would be no war while I was there.   If the Raiders raided I would inexorably run them in ; if the Boers raided, I would as inevitably run them out ; but I knew that the chances were a thousand to one that the Boers would not do anything of the sort while I held the helm, and I was equally confident that the Raiders would hesitate to shoot while there was a chance of their finding themselves between two fires.

But how about the future ?   How long could the situation continue ?   Supposing that the unexpected happened, and the war party broke bounds, how did I, the officer commanding the troops, stand ?   To answer this question I was now free The return of the High Commissioner relegated me to my own job, and I set off at once to study it where it could alone be studied—on the frontier.

I took a single staff-officer with me, and I made a severe outbreak of enteric fever in the garrison at Ladysmith the ostensible reason of my visit to Natal.   We went direct to Johannesburg.   I need not say with what interest I saw the place the ethics and politics of which had been the cause of so much of my official labours for nearly two months. The scene was a revelation to me. I had known in old days in Western America many mining centres, but Johannesburg, or Jewburg, as its denizens preferred to name it, was wholly different from any of these. Outward order was admirably maintained by the 'zarps,'[1] of whom one saw only a few about One did not observe outward rowdyism or intemperance, but the more fashionable forms of gambling and immorality were everywhere to be seen. Liquor bars served by cosmopolitan ladies with straw-coloured hair were to be seen at every corner; the Stock Exchange had four of these establishments contiguous to it There were clubs, betting dens, brokers' offices everywhere. 'It is Monte Carlo superimposed upon Sodom and Gomorrah,' a well-known Cape politician had recently described it to me. 'It is the central sin spot of civilisation,' another man had defined it. Such was the city, but outside one saw stretching, far beyond the mounds of ashen grey silt and crushed reef slag, and the long lines of black iron chimneys vomiting blacker smoke into the clear, bright atmosphere, the great sky-bordered plains of the Transvaal, lost in space What strange freak of demon or destiny was it that had dumped down here a great gold mine to draw together in the interior of a land, so far peopled by a race of primitive Christian farmers, all these human products of greed and gambling ? 'Houndsditch and the Stock Exchange,' I had written to a distinguished statesman a few weeks earlier, 'are not the sources from which the redemption of South Africa is to be looked for.' Here in Johannesburg these two places, or their equivalents in the world, seemed to have pre-empted the right of human settlement.

After a day or two I passed on to Natal. This was all old ground to me. Majuba, the Ingogo, Newcastle, Ladysmith, the Tugela, the high ground at Mooi River and Estcourt; twenty-three years earlier I had ridden, driven, and I might say thriven, over them all, for to their splendid upland air in the winter season of the southern hemisphere I had owed a rapid recovery to health and strength after the tropical fevers of the West Coast.

Ladysmith, and the country north and south of it, became

[1] Boer police.

the chief object of my study.   The new feature in the landscape
was the railway from the sea at Durban to Johannesburg.
This line crossed the River Tugela at Colenso ; twelve miles
north of that river it touched Ladysmith ; some twenty miles
farther north it passed through the ridge of the Biggarsberg ;
thence it traversed a fairly open country to Newcastle ; and,
still following a northern course, it climbed, in a series of curves
and deep loops, the high grounds at the base of the lofty Majuba
table mountain ; until, passing through a tunnel at Laing's
Nek, it emerged upon the plateaux of the Transvaal, at an
average elevation of some five thousand feet above the level
of the sea.

From its point of crossing the Tugela at Colenso to the
tunnel at Laing's Nek this single line of meandering railway
traversed the north angle of Natal.   It had to its right and left
the Orange Free State on one side, and the territory of the
Transvaal Republic on the other—both states drawing in
to a point just north of Laing's Nek, where they met the
apex of the diamond-shaped figure which Natal forms.   In
the centre stood Ladysmith, set in a hollow between the
Biggarsberg mountain and the Tugela River.   Perhaps, in the
whole history of modern strategic selection, no more unfortunate choice had been made than when, two or three years
before this time, the town of Ladysmith was selected by the
military authorities in the War Office for the new body of troops
which it had suddenly determined to send to Natal.

As early as February 1896, that is, within two months of
the Jameson Raid, the formation of a garrison in Northern
Natal was urged by the military authorities in London   This
force, it was said, ' Would always enable us, in case of need, to
take up a strong forward position near Ladysmith (in Natal),
or on Transvaal territory beyond Newcastle, on what is locally
known as " the Berg," or at Harrismith in the Orange Free
State '   This memo. was virtually the beginning of the Anglo-
Boer War.

After visiting Ladysmith, and inspecting the troops there,
I passed south over the Tugela, saw Estcourt and Nottingham Road (to which last-named place I had moved half the
troops from the fever-stricken hole at Ladysmith), and then
went north again to examine the Biggarsberg, Laing's Nek, and

Majuba. The visit to the last-named place was one of the most interesting events in my life My memoir of Sir George Colley had just appeared in London, and I had an advance copy of the book with me It was from this great vantage point of Majuba, and because I had in my mind a fixed picture of everything that had produced the disaster there—the faith Colley had in the man in the ranks, who had long left the ranks ; the belief in a destiny which was based on the exploits and genius of a wholly different race of men and women from that which now existed in our social system ; above all, the extraordinary lengths to which the teaching of false history had been carried in our schools, our press, and on our public platforms, that I was able to judge of a possible war between us and the Boers with a power of forecast of a quite exceptional character. These things were driven deeper into my mind by a document which I had received from the War Office before my departure from Cape Town.

The document in question was a letter, dated 21st December 1898, asking me to take up the question of the defence scheme for Cape Colony and Natal, and to formulate a detailed plan for the disposition of the troops then stationed in the two colonies in the event of a sudden outbreak of hostilities in South Africa. Had the letter ended there, all would have been easy work for me ; but it had a widely different purport as it went on. It recommended to me the initial occupation, both in Natal and in the Cape Colony, before an outbreak of hostilities, of advanced positions upon, and even over, the frontiers, the adoption of which must, to my mind, have led to the earliest and most complete initial disasters. It pressed upon me the necessity of at once seizing, in my plan of campaign, all the bridges over the Orange River between Cape Colony and the Orange Free State ; and, with regard to Natal, it also impressed upon me the necessity of seizing Van Reenan's Pass in the Drakensberg, and of pushing my weak forces in both colonies at once to, and over, the frontiers, where, of course, their capture or annihilation by even small bodies of active mounted riflemen must have been the work of a few hours. There were to be no supports behind these troops, which were thus, as it were, shot into hostile space, having behind them military voids many hundreds of miles in length, peopled by a strong and active population of Dutch farmers, the cousins and brothers of the men who lived beyond these frontiers. Here, then, had suddenly come upon me, from the point least expected, by far the most formidable force I had yet met in South Africa. The party of the Raid, the intrigues of the South African League, the Boer enemy—these I could all reckon and cope with in my plan of defence. But the War Office friend, the latest staff college strategist, fed to his eyebrows on false military history, with his plan of campaign cut and dried, signed, sealed, and delivered in that terrible congeries of confused opinion and congested clerkship which I had so long known in Pall Mall—that was something wholly unexpected by me.

As I sat on the summit of Majuba, while memory went back into times of bygone disaster to our arms, and my eyes ran over the far-stretching panorama of Northern Natal, with all its traps and dangers to an army moving from the south, I realised that there was one way, and one way only, by which I might hope to save the land committed to my charge from the enemies that were within its borders and from the friends at headquarters in England. That way was to make in my own mind my own plan of defence, say nothing to the War Office about it as yet, and await events.

' It was comparatively easy,' I wrote later, ' to frame in my own mind my own scheme of defence for Natal and the Cape Colony ; but it was another matter to formulate reasons for my dissent—to show cause for not pushing forward my weak force into the Drakensberg passes on one side, or to within a half rifle-shot distance of the Orange Free State on the other.'

I have spoken of Ladysmith and its new garrison planted there early in 1897. It was said in the correspondence dealing with the establishment of this increased garrison that its cavalry and artillery arms ' *would have a steadying effect upon the Boers.*' It certainly had that effect, although in a sense not quite the one expected. One incident in connection with that ' steadying effect ' comes to my mind as I write.

The new garrison was strong in one arm—artillery. It had an entire brigade division of eighteen field guns of the most recent pattern. It was, of course, expected that this strong

unit would impress the minds of the Boer farmers around
Ladysmith, as well as those in the Orange Free State, from the
frontiers of which Ladysmith was in sight twenty miles away.
The British officer and the Boer farmer have always been by
nature and inclination good friends Both were open-air
sportsmen, neither belonged to what is known as the shop-
keeping class. Within a few weeks of the establishment of
Ladysmith as a military garrison at the door of the Free State
friendly feelings were established between the farmers and the
officers ; the latter were asked to shoot bucks on the surrounding farms, the farmer came freely to see the officer It was
thought a good idea that the Boer visitors should see the power
of the new weapon—the destructive nature of its projectiles at
long ranges—for they would thus be impressed by the hopelessness of trying conclusions with their rifles against such
powerful artillery weapons.

The day came The eighteen breechloading guns were drawn
up outside the camp at Ladysmith facing a well-known ridge
called Waggon Hill, from which the firing point was distant
about three thousand yards. Some one had conceived a bright
idea : it was to buy a number of Kaffir goats from a neighbouring kraal and picket these animals on Waggon Hill. The
annihilation of these goats under shrapnel fire at this long
range would no doubt add immensely to the lesson which the
Boer farmers were about to learn All this had been arranged
to everybody's satisfaction Goats and guns were in position,
the guests and the gunners were assembled, everything was
ready. Fire began Men with binoculars averred that they
could see signs of perturbation among the goats , all the
shrapnel burst at or over the hill. After twenty minutes the
' cease fire ' sounded. The visitors and their hosts mounted
and rode to Waggon Hill As they neared it some goats
could be discerned still in being ; a few, perhaps, were alive ;
twenty had been bought for the trial. The order was given
to count the dead. Lo ! a miracle had occurred : there were
no dead , twenty-two goats were found alive on the hill !
Two newly born kids were among them ; one old nanny-goat
was still showing signs of maternal excitement, but even she
and her premature twins were doing well.

This was all very funny, but for me it had another aspect.

To whatever side I turned I found elements of future trouble. Here was an instance : a blind belief amongst our own people, alike at Ladysmith and in London, that these guns, together with their infantry and cavalry adjuncts of two regiments, could be shot forward at any given moment to Laing's Nek, to Van Reenan's Pass, perhaps to end at one blow the Boer resistance.

Taking everything I saw and heard into consideration, I determined, as I have said, to hang back from the frontier in case of war, instead of advancing forward to it or over it. But this plan had to be carefully hidden from possible enemies over the Berg as well as from all my own people. For various reasons I must pretend to go forward. In this narrowing angle of North Natal there were nearly one hundred and twenty miles of railway ; that line could not be abandoned all at once to the enemy. There were three courses open to him. He would (1) either raid into Natal and destroy the line ; or (2) he would remain entirely on the defensive within his own territory ; or (3) he would invade North Natal in force. In either of the two first alternatives it would be necessary to hold the line of railway, and even in the event of an invasion in force it would be necessary for us to hold it long enough to effect the destruction of its most vulnerable points by the rearguard of a retreating force.

I had, therefore, arranged to push the garrison at Ladysmith to the gorge through the Biggarsberg which had the railway running through it to Glencoe ; to entrench that naturally splendid position ; to send light troops forward to the Ingagane, and possibly to Newcastle, and to use my two regiments of cavalry and the Natal Mounted Police for scouting widely to the east and west of the railway, watching the passes of the Drakensberg on the west and the drifts over the Buffalo River on the east, getting instant news of all Boer movements, and standing ready to face back from Glencoe to Ladysmith if seriously threatened upon either flank, and to retire entirely from Ladysmith over the Tugela to Estcourt, and even to Nottingham Road, if the forces of the two Republics crossed the Berg and the Buffalo, and descended from Laing's Nek along the railway upon Glencoe in strength. The essence of my plan of campaign was defensive : an easy retirement in

face of superior numbers; blowing up of culverts; breaking
of bridges; carrying along by means of the railway, which was
the centre of the movement, my stores, supplies, and ammunition.   Later on an entirely fatuous use was made of this simple
scheme, changing its whole nature, essence, and design.

So much for Natal.   In the Cape Colony the nature of my
plan was nearly the same.   The three railway junctions of
De Aar, Naaupoort, and Stormberg were to have garrisons;
in the first instance only one river bridge was to be held, that
known as Orange River Bridge, on the main railway route to
Kimberley and Rhodesia.

All these plans and purposes, however, I put away in my
own mind, quite as fearful of my friends in the War Office,
with their plans for seizing the very ends of the sub-continent
by spreading out my poor little force of five or six thousand
men over fifteen hundred miles of frontier, as I was of the
Boers beyond the Bergs and rivers and the great plateaux of
the central continent.

I went back to Natal, stopping again for a day or two in
Johannesburg.   Everything in that great gold centre was
humming of peace and prosperity.   A great 'boom' in stocks
and shares was in full swing.   The Stock Exchange howled
with excitement.   'A man was poor in the morning and rich
in the evening,' they told me—they did not say what happened
to him the day after.   I was taken to see one of the largest
of the racing stables belonging to one of the many cosmopolitan millionaires on the Rand   Among the animals produced some had cost prices running well into four figures.
That horse was for the Kimberley Derby in the following
August or September; this animal was entered for the
Kroonstadt Newmarket: this again for the Johannesburg
Oaks in November.

When I got back to Cape Town I found the same serenity
of life and prospect everywhere prevailing.   Indeed, I found
something more.   Here is the picture of the British army as
it stood at that moment in England in the eyes of the best
judge of the soldier I had found in the course of my service.
The letter awaiting me bore date 8th February 1899 :—

'We are doing little here (the War Office).   I struggle to get the army into fighting efficiency ; but it is no easy work under present conditions ; more and more the W. O. clerk is becoming the real ruler of the army, and views and objects are paid less and less attention to. We offer only boys' wages, and consequently we only obtain boy recruits, and of those we accept, *over* one-third are below even the low physical standard laid down for recruits In fact, at this moment over one-half of the *Home* army are unfit to carry a pack or do a week's, I might perhaps say a day's, hard work in the field ' '

This *exposé* of our military weakness was given at the end of a letter in which the life of the late General Colley was dealt with by the writer. Its significance was the more impressive taken in that context , and it certainly did not tend to lead one to think that a policy of diplomatic aggression against the Dutch Republics could have been then even remotely possible. All the more, however, did it confirm me in the necessity of framing my scheme of defence in South Africa upon the lines I have already indicated. March and April ran out without anything occurring in the apparent situation. It was only later, when things assumed other aspects, that, looking back upon these months, one was able to see beneath their outward calm signs that had a subsequent significance. Individual members of the most advanced section of the old Raider group began to arrive from England Some of these persons went to Rhodesia, others to Johannesburg Some of the ladies whose husbands filled prominent positions in the Chartered Company in Rhodesia departed for England Mr. Rhodes was still in England. But the movements of individuals above mentioned had reference solely to the financial groups known as the Chartered Company, ' De Beers Co.,' and the largest of Anglo-German syndicates in Johannesburg. Not one word of warning, official or private, was coming from the War Office. Indeed, things were running quite in the other direction. We received orders to reduce expenditure ; to give up ordnance and other storehouse accommodation. The propositions to complete the field transport for the troops in Natal and the Cape Colony, sanctioned two years earlier, were negatived Our estimates for repeating the small field trainings and marchings which had been given in other years were reduced. Our proposals to purchase land for military practice and for remount establishments were refused And, so far as the mind of the military advisers of the Home Government could be read in the despatches, letters, and decisions coming to us from London, the outlook was one of profound peace.

When, within a year of the time I am now dealing with, the mendacities of the political and financial world were let loose against me in London, and I was charged with having wilfully neglected my duty of warning the Home authorities of the condition of affairs in South Africa, I went back among my old papers and letters to seek for any traces, in these early months of 1899, showing that I had received intimations from my superiors of a disposition on their part to bring matters to a climax in South Africa It is almost absurd to read now the items which I then exhumed from this correspondence.

' I am afraid,' wrote one headquarters staff-officer in high position, ' that you will find a good deal of work in front of you in connection with defence matters—this has been caused partly by a certain amount of misunderstanding at headquarters '

Again, as late as the month of May 1899, I find the problem of South African defence thus referred to :—

' It is difficult to unravel the various directions sent to you from the different branches here, each without the knowledge of the other branches concerned ! '

Again, another high authority at the War Office wrote :—

' There has been a good deal of confusion at headquarters from various branches having taken action without reference to the Commander-in-Chief's department. Neither —— nor —— knew what was going on.'

The official document which I had received about the time of Sir Alfred Milner's return to the Cape, on the subject of the usual defence scheme for my command, had in its earlier paragraphs this sentence —

' Her Majesty's Government has no special reason to apprehend any hostilities with the Republics in the immediate future.'

A grandiloquent statement of opinion which was reiterated to me five months later, viz. in June 1899, in the following enlightening sentiment .—

' Without entering into any close consideration of the political situation, we cannot shut our eyes to the fact that the possibility of war in South Africa has not yet been eliminated '

It would not be easy, I think, to beat that ' yet,' written from the source and centre of all military authority three months before the actual outbreak of war—an outbreak which was solely caused by our determination to press the diplomatic initiative during that and the two following months, leaving the case of the military initiative to be entirely unconsidered. It will scarcely be credited that a Secretary for War three years after this time had the temerity (I shall not use a stronger term) to say that the orders sent to me at the Cape relative to a defence scheme had been of a clear and helpful nature   This, too, was despite Sir Redvers Buller's statement before the War Commission when he gave that body the inner, or War Office, account of what was happening at that moment in the War Office   This is what he said, ' What really happened was this . I came up from Aldershot early in July (1899) and I told the Under Secretary for War that if the War Office telegrams were published hereafter he would be hanged. I said every head of every department of the War Office is sending out telegrams on the same subject, but in a different sense, to that poor unfortunate general at the Cape, and you will drive him mad.' Well, though the telegrams and letters were even more muddling than poor Buller had any idea of (because, although he was at that moment secretly designated to succeed me in the command of South Africa, he had only a partial knowledge of the confusion), the conflicting orders did not drive me mad. They only drove me into a silent resolution to form my own scheme of defence quite independent of what I called ' the tangled thread of former plans and orders.'

All at once, early in the month of May, the scene changed. I think it will be desirable that I should treat this change not as I can see it with so much clearer vision now, but as my letters and memoranda of the time show, as in a series of ' snapshots,' the effect produced on my mind by each fresh development of the situation.

' 3rd May 1899.—We are getting our South African news from London as we get much of our meat and all our drink from it.   But there is a difference between the mental and bodily sustenance thus received. The news is first made up here by the syndicate for the transmission of false information, which has such enormous resources at its disposal, and is then cabled to London to produce alarm on the Stock Exchange or unrest in the Cabinet. Here nothing is known about this alarming state of things, and in Johannesburg it is even less apparent. Our Johannesburg has more prosperity in it, as that word is understood in modern life, than any place in the world. Nowhere is there so much betting, gambling. drinking ; so much eating of good things ; in no other place are wages so high ; nowhere does the lady with the straw-coloured hair reap larger harvests, the publican sell so many drinks, or the Jew find so many avenues open to him. But your *London* Johannesburg is quite another place.'

' 10*th May.*—Saw Governor to-day. He spoke at some length upon state of affairs here. Having held reins of civil government for nearly three months in his absence, I resolved, on giving up my seat, not to speak of civil affairs unless he spoke first to me. He said the situation had considerable amount of danger in it, although not the danger the newspapers appeared desirous of giving it , that out of, say, ten chances, there were nine that matters would not reach the stage of armed intervention, but that remaining one should be considered. "Supposing," he said, "it was necessary by and by to bring pressure to bear upon the Transvaäl Government in a matter such as the franchise, could anything be done in that line by moving the troops in Natal forward to the frontier ? " I laughed openly at the idea. The existing force, I said, could only be relied on to hold certain positions in Natal and the Cape Colony which I had already fixed upon in my own mind, but for obvious reasons kept to myself. To bring pressure on the Dutch Republics would require forty thousand men (that was a sudden offhand answer to a question put offhandedly ; later on, as events developed, I put the numbers very much higher) We then touched upon many matters of controversy then going on between Colonial Office and Transvaal. I said that in my opinion " the real danger lay in the suspicions entertained by the Boers and by all the Dutch in South Africa about our real intentions ; that since the Raid they suspected everything we did and said to be merely a plot to work on the old lines ; that if they could be persuaded the demand was honestly put forward, without ulterior objects, things I thought would be right ; that a few honest men meeting could probably solve the existing situation in a few hours ; and that the real danger lay also in the occult influences at work, backed by enormous means and quite without conscience, to produce war in South Africa for selfish ends '

' *Sunday*, 14*th May*.—Governor called in afternoon. Had long conversation with him A despatch is on its way out which he thinks will cause immense sensation ; he had only a cable summary of it, and he did not speak in any detail of it. It probably recounted under ten or a dozen heads the Uitlander case as based upon the petition recently sent from Johannesburg. Thought that if he met Kruger in Council either in Pretoria or Bloemfontein they would be able to settle matters ; but would the Transvaal agree to meet him and discuss these questions, or would they say, " This is our matter, not yours ; you have no right to interfere with us," etc. ? If that line were adopted, it would mean war. If the conference took place, he thought he would have no friend in it ; President Steyn and the present Cape Ministry would be against him.

' I said that if the object was to settle existing differences on a just basis he would find many friends , that, provided the despatch of which he spoke was not in the form of an ultimatum, and did not demand a yea or nay answer, I saw no reason to think Kruger would decline to negotiate—such a course would be unwise from the Dutch point of view. Suspicion of our intentions was the chief difficulty with them I spoke again of the hidden influences at work in the Colony, —— and ——, etc. These he appeared to minimise The *Cape Times*, he thought, was not identical with Rhodes He frequently reverted to the weak state of Kimberley, but agreed with me that any reinforcements now sent there would be fatal in their effects upon the Boer suspicions, already too highly excited. He struck me as being considerably perturbed at the prospect which would be produced by the despatch, and I gathered from his manner as much as from his words that it overstepped what he thought was prudent

' " I know," he said, " that Chamberlain won't put things in the most conciliatory manner. You remember his speech about doubting Kruger's desire to settle matters ? " " Yes," I replied, " and his allusion to the necessity of supping with the devil with a long spoon (the Czar being the devil)."—We spoke more to this effect.—" Nothing could persuade the Boers," he said, " that Chamberlain was not a party to the Raid," and although they hated him (the Governor), yet he thought they would believe what he said. This again led him to the idea that if he was left to himself he could settle matters with Kruger if they met ; but would they meet ? He spoke of the possibility of raids, into Basutoland, and elsewhere. The interview lasted the better part of an hour. I

went to the train with him. He looked ill and excited, or rather,
I should say, worried, and in want of sleep and rest. I felt pity
for him.'

The above *précis* deals only with salient subjects spoken of.
A couple of days following I wrote a full account of the interview to the highest military authority in the War Office. In
that letter I said :—

'If he (the Governor) had a clear, unhampered hand, I believe
he could settle the Uitlander difficulty as it stands in a few days,
and I have reason to believe that he thinks so himself. But, will
he be allowed that free hand, or will the fatal habit of Home interference, which has so often, in the past fifty years, dashed the cup
of peace from the lips of unfortunate South Africa, again mar the
situation ? The question is one of flesh and blood, capable of
being solved by common-sense and honest effort. It does not need
any deep diplomacy to settle it. The Jameson Raid and the subsequent move of troops into Cape Colony and Natal are the two
factors chiefly responsible for the present situation. We seem to
be always bent upon attempting to forestall the action of time by
feverish and not too straightforward efforts to snatch at results
before they are ripe, and to anticipate the gradual flow of events
It is now nearly six months since I arrived here. I have had many
glimpses behind the scenes, as well as in front of them. I have
read much and travelled much in that interval   You know my old
experiences of twenty and twenty-five years ago. The things I tell
you are not hastily gathered or lightly sifted · I know what I am
speaking about. So far as I can now read the signs of the times
here, I can see no small danger that a situation of affairs in itself
perfectly capable of solution by ordinary peaceful methods may
become, through false, incomplete, or inaccurate information on
one side, and through distrust and suspicion on the other (the
latter engendered by the sorry and sordid action of Dec. 1895),
may become, I say, a possibility of deeper national discredit at
home, and a certainty of misery and misfortune to this country
greater than it has heretofore known in its history.'

'*25th May.*—Called at Government House 12.30 o'clock at
request of Governor. He read extracts from documents which he
had received from Natal—petitions from Ingogo and Newcastle
people asking for protection in the event of war. The Natal
Ministers had forwarded these to their Governor, saying that they
had no information from him about war , they ask for information

and seem to protest against being left in ignorance of the situation. Natal Governor informs them that he has no information, and he in turn asks High Commissioner for it. This led to talk as to what might happen in Natal if crisis came   I described the nature of the country from Newcastle to the frontier, and said that Boers could easily be at Laing's Nek before we could get there, etc., etc. I said that railway in Natal was like a figure of eight in many places, and that it could not be protected from sudden inroad from two sides.   Governor then went on to speak of general situation.   He was not hopeful of his coming meeting with Kruger ; thought the latter would talk, but would not come to an issue, etc.   He then passed to probabilities of Boers fighting.   He thought they would not fight, etc.   I said they would fight for their independence, but not on lesser matters.   I said that Mr. Chamberlain's recent state-ment in Commons that there could not be a dual allegiance (*i.e.* Uitlanders must take Transvaal citizenship and give up their own) seemed to me to sweep away the chief difficulty as to the extension of the Franchise to Johannesburg people.   He agreed, but said he was sorry Mr. C had spoken thus, as it took from him (the Governor) a trump card which he might have played with good effect when meeting President Kruger, etc.

'He spoke of what the Johannesburg people would do in the event of war.   They would be loud in howls against him for the war ; many people would quit Johannesburg, etc.   He spoke of the capitalists, said —— was only kept hostile to the Transvaal by ——, who, he said, is "a rebel, an irreconcilable."   Many of the capitalists were desirous of coming to terms with the Boer Government.   I gathered, although it was not actually said, that Mr. C.'s aim had been to prevent this agreement   He said that the people of Johannesburg were like a man having a bad tooth, afraid to get it out, but glad when it was out.   My own impression is that behind all this lies a plot to force war on the Transvaal.   I am not sure that the work they are doing will not be as opposed to the true interests of the Empire as was that done one hundred and twenty years ago by our Government in North America ; and that Mr. C. will not live in history as Lord North lives, but without even the excuse of having had a bad king to lead him on the road to ruin There was as yet no ultimatum, he said, nor was there any im-mediate likelihood of one, and for himself he thought that "troops should be on the sea" before an ultimatum was sent   Interview lasted about forty minutes   When taking my leave I gave him my reply to Mr. C.'s proposal to excise my despatches.   I of course refused my consent.'

The subjoined draft of a letter which I wrote later on the same day explains more fully the last sentence above given :—

' DEAR SIR ALFRED MILNER,—From a passing observation of yours made towards the close of our interview to-day, I have thought it possible that you might have slightly misunderstood my meaning with reference to the subject of your letter of the 23rd inst. What I desired to express was that I did not know to what extent the Secretary of State had the right to hold back despatches (from publication in Blue Book) , but that I could not be even a silent consenting factor to the proposed elimination from my despatches of sentences which conveyed my opinion of the extent of certain forces at work in South Africa in December and January last. I believed then, and I still believe, that these forces, both in Johannesburg and elsewhere, did not represent even in a small degree the real opinion of this country ; that they were all working under the direction of one man, in whom recent defeat at the polls in this Colony had accentuated the bitterness of his defeat in the Transvaal three and a half years ago, and whose set purpose was now, as it was then, to bring on war between England and the Transvaal.'

Comparing the record of the conversations of 25th May with those of 14th May, a marked change will be noticed in my estimate of what was being done. Reluctantly, I was now forced to conclude that the work of misleading the public at home was to be carried on by additional hands in the future. This Blue Book business had a suspicious aspect. It was, in my opinion, becoming increasingly evident that the flow of false intelligence to England met with neither check nor disapproval The thing that puzzled me most was that, while the work of making up the diplomatic case against the Transvaal had the apparent support of some powerful men, not one word of preparation or warning, not even a query, was coming to me from my own chiefs at the War Office. From this silence it was clear that no decision had yet been come to by the Government on the question of war with the Transvaal. Even if war was anticipated by the Cabinet as a whole, surely the general commanding in South Africa would receive some intimation—even a private hint—of the approaching possibility ?

My line of duty appeared clear. I must not agree to any proposed excisions of the despatches sent by me five months earlier. Let them do it if they wished, but not with my approval.

This decision appeared to cause some difficulty, because on the 26th May a clerk came to see me in the castle at Cape Town, where I was transacting my usual military work, and asked if I would myself draft the cablegram for the Colonial Office. I did so at once. It ran thus :—

'THE CASTLE,
'CAPE TOWN, 26th May 1899.

' To SECRETARY OF STATE FOR COLONIES.

' General could only regard his concurrence in proposed omission of passages from his despatches as a stultification by himself of his own opinions, to which he still adheres   He begs to thank you for the courtesy of question, and quite understands that publication of parliamentary papers rests with you alone.'

A few days later the Conference at Bloemfontein began.

CHAPTER XXIII

The Bloemfontein Conference Two interesting letters. Further interviews and correspondence. Proposed raid from Tuli. Despatch of 22nd June to the Secretary of State Some cablegrams from and to the War Office Increased difficulty of the position Resignation of the Command Departure from South Africa

THE Conference at Bloemfontein began on 31st May Great expectations were entertained by five-sixths of the people that it would lead to a peaceful settlement of the matters in dispute , but the remaining one-sixth made no secret of their hostility to any peaceful solution. The organs of the Raiders were more violent than ever. If hard words and insults to the Dutch could break up the meeting, they were not wanting. But neither were they wanted · its fate was foredoomed.

The Conference met on five days. The franchise question had been selected by the Colonial Office as the test subject. If the franchise was refused to the Uitlanders, war would have followed at once ; if, on the other hand, the franchise was given to the extent demanded—a five years' residence in the Transvaal—then the destruction of the Boer Republic would only be a question of a few years, or perhaps of a few months, with the South African League always present to manipulate the scheme and to agitate for rebellion But, of the two courses, that of the out-and-out refusal of the franchise was the one most desired by the Raiders That course would leave the road open for the much-desired ultimatum , troops would then be on the sea, and the resort to force could no longer be delayed.

Very little is known of the inner history of the Conference. Our representative dumped down a proposal for a five years' franchise, and refused to entertain or discuss any other matter put forward by the Republics. He spent one entire afternoon in debating the dynamite concession, putting questions to President Kruger thereon which, when they were read later on in the light of the Kynoch revelations, resembled the queries of an advocate acting in the interests of a rival dynamite syndicate

An episode in the Conference comes to mind as I now write. At one of the meetings there occurred some observation on the part of the English representative which showed the real drift of the franchise question, viz. the subversion of the Republic either by force or through the new franchise. Old Kruger's feelings overcame him, and he exclaimed bitterly, 'It is our country you want. It is our country you want.' The old man bent his head between his hands, and the tears flowed down the weather-beaten face A young officer who was on the staff of the High Commissioner, describing the scene to my family, added his opinion that they were ' crocodile's tears ' I have wondered whether the solemn declaration of the English representative, as given at page 23 of the Bloemfontein Conference Blue Book, that ' neither he nor his Government had any wish to take away the independence of the Transvaal,' was occasioned by this outburst of feeling.

Two letters were written to me about this time which are interesting lights upon the thoughts of men at this crisis of their country's fortunes. The first was written by Mr. Schreiner, the Cape Premier.

'PRIME MINISTER'S OFFICE,
'CAPE TOWN, 27th May 1899

' MY DEAR SIR WILLIAM BUTLER,—I have finished reading, but not finished thinking over, the volume of Trevelyan's *History of the American Revolution*, which you kindly lent me. It will go back on Monday, just in time to keep my contract. It has been a real pleasure in all ways to read this book, though I could wish that it took me more completely away from grooves of thought which are growing painfully familiar to some of us in South Africa I do now and then hope that I may wake one morning to find that I have only suffered from bad dreams , but it is hard to realise that one is powerless to arrest the growth of any disease which one fancies threatens what one dearly loves.

' The Americans were at any rate so far in the wrong technically that they refused to render to Cæsar the things that were his, but God keep the Empire and South Africa if the subterfuge for a racial war is to be the refusal by the people of an inland state to part quickly enough with their own lawful and treaty-guaranteed rights and privileges.

'In these wonderful days one might at times be pardoned for forgetting that Her Majesty has any subjects in South Africa except those who are supposed to be anxious to throw off their allegiance and become Republicans—for whom it would seem the open door of free commerce must be *made* to connect, through broken walls, if necessary, with the inmost chambers of the National and Constitutional privileges and reserves. To decline to introduce your friend into a spare bedroom is truly the act of a churl; but to hasten to open the door of your own private chamber to a stranger armed with a bludgeon is the act of a man very magnanimous or very pusillanimous.

'In 1895 the man with the bludgeon obtained the order of the boot, and was sent out of the house. Let us hope that in 1899 it will be a friend who will ask for the spare bedroom. I suppose I have no business to write to you as I feel; but then you lent me the book, for which many thanks.—I am, etc.,

'(Sgd.)   W. P. SCHREINER.'

I sent this letter to a very high personage, and I asked that it should be laid before Her Majesty the Queen. I wrote :—

'The writer is the Prime Minister of this Colony—a gentleman whose honesty and ability have never been questioned, even by political opponents, and whose devotion to Her Majesty and to the Throne I would not insult by comparison with that of the financial exponents of loyalty now so loud in protestation and apparently so keen in their efforts to bring on a racial strife in this country.'

The idea of sending this letter to the highest source of power itself came suddenly to me, without consultation or advice from anybody. How could I succeed in awakening the crew and passengers of a ship that I saw steering straight upon breakers ? I had tried the steersman, but without result. I had tried, as this record shows, some persons very high in authority in England ; but in vain. A fortnight earlier I had received a letter from a gentleman in Pretoria, a man who for thirty years had had the politics and the history of South Africa at his finger-tips I had known the writer for twenty-five years. He had been editor of the *Cape Times* and proprietor of the *Natal Times* in old days No man had a better knowledge of men and affairs in all South Africa than he possessed. I considered his views of the gravest importance, and I handed the letter to the High

Commissioner. Later on I sent it to the War Office. Here it is :—

'PRETORIA, 8th May 1899.

' MY DEAR SIR WILLIAM,—I only received your book this afternoon. The reason is my fault and not yours. All the officials in this country are most courteous, and as they think I have a bit of human sympathy with them—never forgetting that I am an Englishman from the top of my head to my heels—they do all sorts of kindness to me. These people do so crave for sympathy. They have been hounded into fear They like their land as we like ours. We must respect their homes as we respect ours It would, I am sure, have been a great pleasure for you, and especially Lady Butler, to have seen the well-dressed people at this hotel this night. To-morrow there is to be an agricultural show, and the town is crowded with good-looking women and pretty children and sturdily-built men. They are all so well-mannered. The whole population has so much improved that you would hardly know them. There are lovely homes, sweetly pretty gardens, and placid prosperity. I am speaking of Pretoria.

' Johannesburg, with all its wealth and the exuberance of the display of it, I am not greatly in love with. There does not appear to me to be any moral rectitude there in any of the walks of life. They forge petitions and would do anything else without compunction. In Pretoria there is absolutely a more moral tone, though no doubt many things have been done by their legislators, as Galatea said to Pygmalion, in innocence.

' (Pardon my scribble, but I am writing with a lot of people talking round me)

' To return to my thoughts. What I was endeavouring to say was, how cruel I thought it would be if these quietly, well-dressed women were to lose their homes through the ravages of an unprovoked war ; and then I wondered how you were to replace these stalwart men when every white man in this country is needed for its peaceful occupation.

' The Native Question has yet to be dealt with. With rest and peace that can be effected perhaps When the Whites get fighting then the black man—poor wretch '—thinks his chance has come It is wonderful how well the Natives are informed , they are already talking of war between the Whites My sources of information are more than fairly good. It is impossible for me in a letter to you to do more than state facts without arguments.

' The white races of the Transvaal are loyal to Queen Victoria . you find some picture of her in nearly every home, especially among

the Boer homes, in the Transvaal.   They say, these Boers and their
wives, that they do not believe in the words of English Ministers,
but they do in the words of Queen Victoria   That is very pretty,
is it not ?   The women of the country are its backbone, and their
absolute confidence in Queen Victoria is now keeping the peace.
The men are ready to fight ; they are tired of being nagged at.
I wish England could peacefully re-annex the Transvaal, and a
precious bad time the Capitalists would have .   .

'It has been most difficult to write this with the chattering going
on around me. . . . The Parliament here was in secret session to-
day.   I don't absolutely know the result, but it goes thus far :
they will not be hastened, and will make laws which they think
are necessary.—Yours, etc.,

'(Sgd)   R. W. Murray.'

May was now closing.   The war of words was louder than
ever.   If hard names levelled against the Dutch could make
war, they were flying about thickly enough ; but of themselves
they would break no bones.   The question I had to ask myself
was, What was the War Office about ?   What did the Government mean ?   Was it all bluster or business ?   If business,
why were our garrisons being reduced, our best officers taken
away, our proposals for camps, storehouses, exercise grounds,
hospitals—insufficient to meet the wants of even our small
garrisons—negatived or diminished ?   Why was Natal, the most
vulnerable point in the South African colonies, left without
a general to command it for five months ?   Why were the
reserve men of the battalions being sent to England, and the
experienced artillery officer who had been commanding at
Ladysmith for two years, also removed ?   Here were two
streams of Home authority apparently running in opposite
courses : the supposed peaceful, diplomatic, cautious Colonial
Office running mad for war , the warlike War Office seemingly
bent upon profound peace.

What did it all mean ?   To me it meant this, that I would
not budge one inch from the line I had marked out until I had
War Office sanction for action   Mr Rhodes and his agents
might shake all the scenes in the varied repertoire of Raid and
Revolution ; all kinds of pressure—official, social, and popular
—might be brought to bear upon me to join in , but without
a clear and explicit mandate for movement, my merry men—

some seven thousand all told—would stay where they were. As I told the Royal Commission four years later than the time I am now dealing with, while ' I held the neck of the bottle ' Rhodes and his Raiders would have no countenance from me. If Cæsar, seated in Pall Mall, told me to move, action would be taken at once ; but the orders must be Cæsar's and not Cecil's. In the middle of June I find that I wrote to the War Office as follows .—

' If the Jews were out of the question, it would be easy enough to come to an agreement ; but they are apparently intent upon plunging the country into civil strife. . . . Indications are too evident here to allow one to doubt the existence of strong undercurrents, the movers of which are bent upon war at all costs for their own selfish ends. It has been my aim since I came here to keep myself clear of this gang. They brought many of our people into their slime and grime a few years since. Carlyle writing fifty years ago could only see one honest man in the crowd . " It is the drill-sergeant." Let us stick to that, and leave the Jews and their gold alone. The history I was taught as a boy showed me that the patriot's road led often to the scaffold · now it leads to a house in Park Lane, a box at the opera, and a yacht in the Mediterranean. " Take care," Ruskin said to the boys at the Woolwich Academy, " that they do not make of you young soldiers sentries only, to stand at the door of their big shop while they are cheating inside." '

The High Commissioner sent for me on Sunday, 11th June, a day or two after his return from Bloemfontein. A *précis* of what occurred at the interview has interest now :—

' Saw the Governor for an hour at the Mount Nelson Hotel. He appeared to be anxious over situation, and to have more on his mind than he wished me to know. He spoke of Kimberley , the difficulty of doing anything with Volunteers ; the difficulty of the Government here ; the small supplies of food at Bulawayo ; the chances of railroad interruption. He said that the opening of a war in which the Orange Free State joined the Transvaal would probably see a rolling back of our authority up to the Great Range—*i.e.* the Dutch overrunning the country to within a hundred and fifty miles of King Williamstown and two hundred and fifty of here ' Spoke of opinion in England being ignorant of the real state of affairs. (Query . Why was it so ?)

' His Secretary afterwards spoke warmly about Rhodes having had a meeting with Chamberlain yesterday (as had been telegraphed from London), saying, "At such a moment to embarrass His Excellency by such an act ¹ " He also spoke of the cable syndicates and the difficulties they occasioned. I took advantage of this to press my point of the influences at work to get the "fat in the fire," etc. His Excellency spoke a good deal of Johannesburg, what its people would do in the event of war. He seemed to have had many interviews with a certain Mr. Sampson, who wanted to fight the Boers *coûte que coûte.* (If I had my way I would let him do as he wished, and I would back even old Kruger to give him fits with a rifle at three hundred and fifty yards) I gathered that H. E. wanted me to propose something to him ; but I told him exactly the situation as it appeared to me. I did not know the War Office mind, still less did I know the Government mind, and so far I had no reason to think they meant anything. They would tell me, I supposed, when they thought fit to do so. I had told them exactly my plans in the event of their declaring war (How strange appeared the telegram of the Director of Military Intelligence in the light of what H. E said about the Dutch "rolling us up to the Great Range" !) The Secretary also spoke about Rhodes having told him or others at home that the Dutch would be divided among themselves in the event of war. (I think they begin to see more clearly every day now. It is a pity they did not do so before.)

' H. E. asked me to let him know any political news that I might hear. Altogether, both he and his Secretary impressed me with the idea of being much depressed by the situation now reached. They must see the awful volume of lies which the syndicate gangs have so long passed off as truth upon the British public.

' From the singular mixture of forces now at work here and in England, I cannot avoid the conclusion that an extremely virulent and active faction is at work to bring on hostilities at all costs with the Transvaal. Rhodes's frequent interviews with Chamberlain at such a moment, when every straw in the balance between peace and war counts, is of itself sufficient to make the Dutch believe that they are again to be " rushed." '

The above short *précis*, written on the evening of the interview, contains some remarks that deserve explanation. I gathered that His Excellency wanted me to propose something. When speaking of Johannesburg, the High Commissioner made reference to a Mr. Sampson, whom he described as an intense hater of the Boers. Sampson had had several interviews with him. He, Sampson, had lately arrived from

England, had been to Johannesburg and to other parts of the
Transvaal, feeling the temper of things. He had proposals
to make, and His Excellency thought they might be deserving
of consideration by me.

I knew Sampson to have been one of the few ‘ fighting
reformers ’ of the Raid time, and that he had served with
distinction in the Boer War of 1880-1881 ; but I was also aware
that he was exactly what His Excellency had described. To
such a man at such a moment I must be cautious in making
any proposition. His Excellency had more than hinted that he
was ready to go anywhere, and he said that he himself had
dissuaded him from visiting Johannesburg again. The ‘ something ’ which His Excellency seemed to wish me to propose
appeared to be entirely connected with this gentleman.   I
had replied, as stated in the *précis*, ‘ I did not know the War
Office mind or the Government mind.’   Would I see Mr.
Sampson ?   I replied I would, of course, see him if His Excellency desired   ‘ Then I shall direct him to call upon you,
and he will explain his views personally to you.’   The idea
of forming a ‘ ring ’ with the troops round the Republics was
again mentioned in this interview, and was again met by the
same objections. ‘ So far I had no reason to think the Government meant anything ; they would doubtless tell me when
they thought fit to do so,’ etc , etc.

It seemed more than strange that this idea of a ‘ ring ’
round a frontier of some twelve or fourteen hundred miles
should have come up, when the force in South Africa was only
some seven thousand or eight thousand all told, the ‘ ring ’
comprising places seven hundred or one thousand miles from
Cape Town   Hence the remark which alludes to the Boers
believing that they would again be ‘ rushed.’

Another point requiring comment is the allusion to a telegram received on the 8th or 9th June, a day or two prior to
this interview, from the Director of Military Intelligence   I
had sent this officer by telegram a statement of the dispositions
which I proposed for the troops in the event of hostilities being
declared. These proposals followed exactly the lines already
stated. Briefly put, the advanced positions were held back
from the frontier for reasons which, of course, have long been
obvious to everybody, but which at that time were entirely

unknown to people in England, and even in South Africa. A day or two after my cable giving the initial dispositions had been received in London, I received a message from the Director of Military Intelligence asking why I had not included the occupation of Van Reenan's Pass and all the bridges over the Orange River in my initial plans.   Hence the exclamation of surprise with which I heard the High Commissioner's assertion about our being 'rolled up to the Great Range.'   It came to this, that while I was being urged, from London, to go forward with my puny detachments into the Republics, they were, if I did so, to roll us up two hundred miles within our own limits

Two days later I wrote to —— at the War Office this letter :—

' The cable will long since have given you our news. It comes back to us like the image of a man's figure reflected in one of those absurd distorting mirrors often seen in old country houses in England. . . . I have sent by cable and mail full details of what I would propose to do in the event of a crisis and have given my reasons for the proposed dispositions. It seemed to me that in the letter from the War Office (21st Dec. last) and the telegram now received from the Director of Military Intelligence the fact of the difference between the conditions of our frontiers and those of ordinary Military Powers and of other countries has not been quite understood.

' In talking to the High Commissioner a day or two ago I asked him what he thought would be the state of our frontier Provinces in this Colony in the event of war between us and the two Republics. "An immediate rolling up of our authority as far as the Great Range," he answered   If he is even half within the truth, then the pushing forward of infantry detachments to the Orange River bridges at Bithuli, Norval's Pont, and near Aliwal North would be a very doubtful movement.

' If you look at the map you will see this " Great Range " marks, speaking generally, the south and south-east rim of the upland plateau region—the southern watershed of the Orange River , and that between it and that river there is a wide extent of country. That intervening district holds a numerous and active Dutch population. If the Orange Free State declared for the Transvaal the people of this district within our frontier would, I think, largely act against us. and, although I do not go so far as Sir Alfred Milner

goes, still I think they might easily be able to cut the communications of relatively small bodies of infantry pushed on to hold weak
positions in the Valley of the Orange River. .   .

'Here are words Froude spoke at Port Elizabeth nearly a quarter
of a century ago, before he visited you at Maritzburg, "There are
three courses open to Great Britain in this country · there is open
force ; there is a second course open to her (and this, I venture to
tell you, will not succeed) : it is to fasten on the soil of the Free
States, to involve yourself with them in small and exasperating
disputes, to advance one claim here and another there, to continue
a series of provocations until you irritate them into violent language
or some precipitate act which will form a pretext for attack, and
proceed upon the plea that they have begun the quarrel [1] Trans-
actions of this kind are bills of credit drawn on the moral Government of the world · you get some immediate object, but by and by
it comes in for payment, and it will have to be paid with interest
and with compound interest to the very last cent. The third
method is conciliation, and if ever South Africa is to be really
united in any wholesome bond of unity conciliation is the course you
ought to follow.' "

.   .   .   .

[Here occurs the break in the MS.—E. B.]

The week succeeding the abortive end of the Bloemfontein
Conference had seen many developments Demands had
come from Rhodesia to me for arms and ammunition ; these
I had sent to the High Commissioner for his approval The
stormy petrels of the time of the Raid were again moving
mysteriously about the country. There were constant rumours
in the newspapers of reconnaissances on the Natal frontier,
and movements near Tuli in Rhodesia.

About the 10th June a mysterious document had been sent
to my office by the High Commissioner's private secretary.
When it was submitted to me I saw that it contained every
possible element of foolishness and of danger. It was a proposal,
dated prior to the Bloemfontein Conference, to make, in the
event of a war with the Transvaal Boers, a raid from Rhodesia
near Tuli upon Pietersburg and, if possible, Pretoria, in the

---

[1] This was precisely what the South African League were working to bring
about Their chief in Cape Town admitted it twelve months later when the
capture of Pretoria appeared to mark the end of the war

Transvaal. This document came, in the first instance, from the senior Imperial officer in the service of the Chartered Company, and was addressed to the High Commissioner's secretary.

The numbers to take part in this second edition of the Jameson venture were quite inconsiderable, and the idea was that the raiders, coming down in rear of the Boers, might be able to achieve wonders—capture Pietersburg, cut the railway between that place and Pretoria, and exercise what was described to be a very decisive influence on the general campaign. One reading of the scheme sufficed to show its imbecile nature, but that was not its chief fault. Once countenance such a proposal at a place some fifteen hundred miles distant from Cape Town, and with officers and men not in the least degree under my command, or answerable in any way to me, and the danger of having the Jameson fiasco repeated with graver results was evident. I put the paper aside as a thing too silly for official language to deal with calmly.

Side by side with the appearance of this dubious document came applications from the Rhodesian Government for arms, ammunition, and warlike equipment already mentioned. Those applications I sent to the High Commissioner, declining to act upon them except by his authority.

Mr. Sampson, whom I have already mentioned, called upon me one afternoon, and I received him in the presence of my military secretary. He had come, he said, at the instance of Sir Alfred Milner, with whom he had had several interviews. He was unreserved as to his previous history and present desires. He had fought against the Boers in 1881, had done his best to fight them in 1895, and was now very desirous of fighting them again. He knew the Transvaal from end to end; he could serve without pay. He ended with a question whether I could do anything to assist him in his desire of fighting the Boers. I replied that it was impossible I could do anything of the kind; I knew only what he himself knew of the existing situation—that was, what I read in the newspapers. I had received no instructions to raise troops or reinforce garrisons. I had no doubt that, if the Government were compelled to resort to active measures, his former services would not be forgotten.

On 17th June I wrote a letter to Sir Alfred Milner which

marks with absolute fidelity the chart of the moment at which it was written.

'DEAR SIR ALFRED MILNER,—Thinking over what you told me yesterday as to rumours, etc., which have reached you of purchases or attempted purchases of horses and provisions by the Boers, I think inferences which might be drawn therefrom should take account of certain facts now existing on the frontier of the Free State and the Transvaal, and of the apprehensions and suspicions of the Dutch which these facts can scarcely fail to produce among them—for instance, the presence at Ladysmith of a strong and partly mobilised force of the three arms within sight of the Orange Free State border. The fears, too, of the Dutch in both Republics cannot fail to be accentuated by the presence on their western borders of many of the influences used against them in 1895 at the time of the Raid, and by the movement towards Rhodesia in the last few weeks of some of the active agents such as Mr. Sampson, who recently called upon me at your request. Then we find the press telegrams with their strange omissions and additions, etc. These things would make it easy to imagine that they—the Boers—were threatened with a repetition of the raids, excursions, and alarms of a few years ago.

'I can find in the balance of things no reason to suppose that there could be a Dutch party in South Africa *desirous* of war with us : can they think the same about us ?—Yours, etc '

On the same day, 17th June, I sent the following telegram to the officer commanding in Natal .—

'COLONEL CHISHOLME,—Having received from His Excellency your letter of 26th May, General requires full explanation by telegraph as to recent proposals and recommendations made by you to the Governor Natal, involving important military action on the frontier without any previous reference to him. This action has been taken in the face of orders and rules to the contrary. Send by mail detailed statement of your proposals for mobilisation No movement is to be made or orders issued without G.O.C.'s authority.'

A good deal of history is behind this telegram It will be seen by it that it was from the High Commissioner, on the 16th June, that I had received intimation of what my lieutenant, Colonel Chisholme, had been doing in Natal without any reference to me But it was eight months later that I read in the Blue Book Defence of Natal that the High Commissioner in Cape Town and the Governor of Natal had been arranging, also without reference to me, what was to be done. On the very day that I had informed Sir Alfred Milner of the dangers and difficulties of the country he was telegraphing to the Governor of Natal —

'You can tell Minister from me that it is out of the question that any invasion of Natal should be tolerated by Her Majesty's Government,' that 'such an event is highly improbable, I think ; but Natal would be defended with the whole force of the Empire if it occurred.'

When one reads this in the light of what followed, one wonders at nothing. What infatuation ! Sir Alfred Milner and Governor Hely-Hutchinson settle between them the whole plan of campaign, and the General Officer Commanding in South Africa is altogether ignored   And so the farce, so soon to change to tragedy, goes on, until on the 3rd of August we read as follows :—

'Mr. Chamberlain to Sir W. Hely-Hutchinson :
'Propriety of moving troops nearer to the frontier so as to watch Laing's Nek is being considered by Her Majesty's Government.'

And again :—

'If it is desired to garrison Laing's Nek would Colonial troops be sent with British ? '

This proposition which, had it been carried into effect, would certainly have produced immediate war, was never communicated to the General Commanding in South Africa. I was only aware of it six months later when I read it in the Blue Book.

But to understand the full measure of the optimism existing in the middle of June on the question of 'the ring theory,' so dear to the High Commissioner, and destined later on to prove in practice so dear to the British Empire, we must revert to the suggested raid from Rhodesia towards Pretoria. I had, as I have already said, put the paper by as something too foolish to be dealt with seriously, when I received a letter from London suggesting the self-same project.

I went to Government House, told Sir Alfred Milner the purport of the letter I had received from London, and told him also my opinion of it : ' A wild, useless scheme, certain to be brought to naught by twenty or thirty Boers after the raiding party had got some distance into the Transvaal, but even still more objectionable by reason of the danger of its becoming a counterpart in every respect of the scandalous experiment of four years before, for while I was asked to organise and equip the proposed raiders, I could not interfere to prevent its coming off on its own account, whether a state of war existed with the Transvaal or not. That a break in the communications with Rhodesia, such as was most likely to occur, would leave the raiding party free to imagine orders for itself, and give it the means of precipitating a conflict whether the British Government wished or did not wish for war.'

The more I considered the question the less I liked its look. Not a word from the War Office ; nothing to indicate to me that the Government had any thought of war ; no response to my many messages showing our unpreparedness in every respect ; and still these continued promptings of the civilian element to push up troops, to ' make a ring ' round the Dutch States, and even to organise another raid on the old discredited plan. What were the forces at work behind it all ? I knew some of them for months past. I could now no longer doubt that more powerful forces than I had imagined were joined with the old agencies in the effort to force a racial war upon South Africa.

On the 21st June I had a second interview with Sir Alfred Milner. Again came the old suggestion. I told him exactly my position. I had no instructions from the Secretary of State for War ; I was now asked to organise this raid ; unless he, as High Commissioner, would give me his authority to do so, I would not do it. Any orders in writing, signed by him, would be implicitly obeyed, but without such orders I must use my own judgment in matters for which I was alone responsible, and my judgment was, moreover, absolutely opposed to the ' ring theory ' under the conditions of numbers and distances then existing in South Africa. ' It would be said afterwards,' I remarked, ' that by my action and through my foolish disregard of facts I had precipitated a conflict before we were prepared for it ; perhaps brought on a war when the Home Government desired peace.' He caught at this. ' It can never be said, Sir William Butler, that *you* precipitated a conflict with the Dutch.' ' I understand your meaning,' I said ; ' there can be no further use in my continuing the interview.'

On 22nd June I was shown for the first time a letter, dated the 1st of the preceding February, which left no further doubt in my mind as to the men who were engineering the Tuli raid and the methods they were employing, and threw a flood of light upon the hitherto dark places of this work. Here was the explanation of all the enigmas of the last two months —the arms constantly demanded by the Chartered Company ; the questions asked by the High Commissioner's private secretary about men of the Reserve living in Rhodesia ; the striving after the ' ring policy,' which was for putting troops in widely separated posts on the very borders of the Dutch States, leaving six or seven hundred miles behind them destitute of all support or posts—' not to give the Boers a chance,' as it used to be defined by these sapient strategists.

But before following out the series of events which this letter, shown to me on the 22nd June, gave rise to, I will go back in the record one day, and give here the despatch which I addressed to the Secretary of State, of the 21st. It ran as follows :—

'CAPE TOWN, 21*st June* 1899

' SIR,—I have the honour to inform you that on the 12th instant I forwarded a cipher message of which the following is a copy :

' " I have now the honour to explain in fuller detail, which time did not allow of my doing by last mail, some at least of the circumstances which hold and govern the military situation existing in South Africa at the present moment—circumstances which, so far as I can see them reflected in recent official telegrams and in the public press, do not appear to be fully recognised in England."

' I stated in the above message that in the event of the crisis of war being reached, the situation which would probably have to be met would be more one of civil conflict than of regular military operations, carried on between two nations at war, where the respective lines of frontier might be expected to define the limits of, at least, the opening operations. What I desired to indicate was that, although the Orange River geographically formed the boundary between the Cape Colony and the Orange Free State, and in Natal the Drakensberg range and the Buffalo River marked the same divisions between that Colony and the Republics, these natural features did not affect the population, which certainly on both sides of the Orange River, and in a lesser but still considerable degree in Natal, was composed of similar elements.

'In this statement of a factor which had to be recognised in any proposed dispositions of troops for defence or protection of frontier in the opening phases of hostilities, I by no means wished to convey that the Dutch population on our side of the borders was disaffected towards British rule, still less that it was disloyal to Her Majesty. I believe that the sentiment of personal devotion to Her Majesty is not only strong throughout the Dutch of this Colony, but that it exists in a much greater degree than is usually supposed in both of the Dutch Republics; but I believe that side by side with this feeling of loyalty and devotion to our Sovereign there has been produced of late years in the mind of the whole Dutch race throughout South Africa a deep feeling of suspicion, of insecurity, of doubt as to the sincerity of our intentions towards them and of the honesty of the means that have been employed against them. These suspicions and these doubts have all had their source in the events which culminated in the Jameson Raid of 1895   They have been continued since that unfortunate epoch by many untoward occurrences both in England and in South Africa, and they are especially strong at this moment throughout South Africa.

'That there has been cause for these feelings and suspicions few men who have followed the events of the past years would be able to deny.   Many of the influences of 1895 seem to be again at work as open or hidden forces in the business of provocation of the Dutch people, and the estrangement of the two races.   It apparently matters little to the agents of this dangerous propaganda what the consequences may be so long as the object they have in view may be obtained.

'It is not my province to inquire too deeply what that ultimate object may be , it will be enough to say that its pursuit has produced a larger amount of distrust and suspicion in the minds of people within the Dutch Republics, and outside them, than I believe has ever before existed , and that there is a growing apprehension among a vast majority of the Dutch race, that it is hopeless for them to attempt to break through the barriers of misrepresentation by which financial agencies and Stock Exchange syndicates have apparently surrounded them.   How closely all this now affects the possible military situation will be better understood when it is remembered that some of the most active agents in the events of three and a half years ago have recently arrived upon the scenes of

their former exploits ; that there has been of late a rapid recrudes-
cence of the crop of rumour and sensational report, and that many
of the " stormy petrels " of the time of the Raid are once more
moving in and around the Transvaal. It is my earnest effort to do
all in my power to prevent, by any act or movement of the troops
under my command, the situation becoming still more strained and
excited I cannot ignore the fact that the same forces and influences
whose unrestrained action led to so much misfortune in 1895 are
present, and it is impossible to avoid the conclusion that the aid of
these influences is to-day, as it was then, the forcing on of a racial
war in this country. Some of the elements which such a strife would
set loose are aptly described in the subjoined extract taken from
a report recently written by Major Scott Turner, 42nd Highlanders,
an officer of some six years' experience in Rhodesia ·

' " There is always in South Africa a floating population of
loafers, mostly men who have made Europe too hot for them, who
are ready to join any corps raised for any service.
' " The absence of any fighting in South Africa since 1897 renders
this class exceptionally large at the present moment, and Johannesburg is especially full of this class of person. Unless there is time it is
often difficult to avoid enlisting these people."

The employment of such persons in a war against whites, where
regular military supervision would be difficult, if not impossible, is
a contingency not to be contemplated without misgiving
' It would be a mistake to imagine that there exists in South
Africa a political question as distinct from the military one. There
is no abstract military question, neither is there a political one, as
these names have significance elsewhere both are involved together
and cannot be separated, at least at a time such as the present.
' From all these reasons, as well as because I am convinced that
the true condition of affairs here has been gravely misunderstood in
England, I have deemed it my duty to write this despatch I am
unable to avoid the conclusion that powerful and persistent influences are at work here and in England to produce strife in South
Africa, between the white races, at all costs. That these costs will
not be small, if once the result is arrived at, I am deeply convinced
of. The whole social fabric of life in South Africa is too closely
interwoven together to allow the sword to be the arbiter of the
differences between the white races without endangering the very
existence of the social body itself.
' Outside and within the limits of the white race, there is still an
enormous preponderating mass of black humanity. In the Trans-

keian Territories the total black and coloured population number seven hundred and eighty thousand souls, the white population is only sixteen thousand.

'In Basutoland the disproportion between the races is greater, so is it in Zululand and Natal. In the Transvaal and throughout this Colony the black races still outnumber the whites, down even to Cape Town itself.

'Such facts appear to me to deserve the fullest consideration in any proposed solutions of difficulties which might commit the white races in South Africa to a possible internecine struggle wherein about one million of men and women, scattered over an area nearly as large as Europe, might be involved.

'I can see no reason why practical solutions should not be otherwise attainable.

'The presence of suspicion and the influences which have produced it, are, in my opinion, the chief obstacles in the path of such solutions.

'Whether these opinions are correct time only can show, but I have felt it my duty to put them before you, and their expression may at least tend towards a clearer appreciation of the situation.

'Whether my views be right or wrong they have not been hastily formed. It is now all but a quarter of a century since I was first sent to study and report upon questions in South Africa of similar import to those treated of in this letter.—I have the honour to be, Sir, Your most obedient Servant,

'W. F. BUTLER, LIEUTENANT-GENERAL,
'*Commanding Troops South Africa.*'

This despatch was written before my interview with Sir Alfred Milner on the 21st June, and, of course, before I had seen the extraordinary document dated 1st February and handed to me 22nd June. The despatch was therefore penned under impressions and beliefs which still drew a distinction between the work of the Rhodes faction in South Africa and that of the Government in South Africa, and still more the Government in England.

When I reviewed the situation in the light of the new knowledge introduced into it, the gravity of the position in which I then stood appeared to me to be very great. To what extent had the English Government sanctioned, or been aware of, what was now going on in South Africa ? What was the strict line of my duty towards the Government six thousand miles away ?

To the question which I had so often put to myself, ' Was the policy of the Home Government peace or war ? ' the first indication of an answer soon came. On 22nd June, the date upon which I became aware of the consultation in London in January about the proposed Tuli raid, a cable cipher message arrived from the War Office of considerable significance. It directed transport mules to be bought for all the troops now in South Africa. It also directed the completion in waggons and harness of all similar transport. It asked many questions as to further provision in very large numbers of mules, horses, oxen, waggons, etc. ; and finally, after demanding the times at which these requirements could be met, it asked if I had ' any observations ' which I might wish to offer.

On the 23rd June I replied in full detail to all the specific inquiries contained in the War Office cablegram ; and then turning to the last query I wrote :—

' You ask my observations. They might fill many pages, but they could be summarised thus : I believe that a war between the white races, coming as a sequel to Jameson Raid and the subsequent events of last three years, *would be the greatest calamity that ever occurred in South Africa.*'

I sent Sir Alfred Milner a copy of the War Office telegram of 22nd June and of my reply to it, being desirous that in every step I now took it should not be said I had exercised my command in possible opposition to his views without informing him of the line I had taken.

In his reply, given in the War Commission Blue Book, p. 87, Sir Alfred informed me that in his opinion the tendency of my remarks was calculated to convey a wrong impression of the actual situation and of the effect likely to be produced by a resolute attitude on the part of Her Majesty's Government, and that he entirely demurred to these observations.

To this I replied that I made them in what ' I believed to be the highest interests of the Empire, and for the honour of Her Majesty's Army.'

Three days later the following cipher cablegram reached me :—

'LONDON, 6 P.M., *27th June.*

' GENERAL, CAPE TOWN,—Concluding paragraph of your telegram of 23rd June. You have evidently misunderstood my telegram of 21st June.

' You were invited to offer observations as to suitability of War Office proposals for securing object in view, viz. increased efficiency in existing forces, not as to the general merits of policy adopted by H.M. Government.

' You cannot understand too clearly that, whatever your private opinions, it is your duty to be guided in all questions of policy by those who are fully aware of our views, and whom you will, of course, loyally support.   SECRETARY OF STATE.'

Again I took stock of the position, and again the more I looked at it the more hopeless it grew   The one thought in my mind, once I knew what was being done, had been to tell the people at home of their danger, and of their ignorance as to what this war would mean, and now they would not take my warning.   I was ' to be guided in all matters of policy by those who are fully aware of our views '; but there was no section of policy possible in all this South Africa that was not, in eight parts out of ten, a military matter.   Two alternatives were before me : either I must resign, or go on as the dumb follower of Sir Alfred Milner   I drafted a cipher message on 29th June, placing my resignation in the hands of the Secretary of State ; but on reading it again next morning, I decided not to send it.   Perhaps something would turn up, I thought, that would change the situation and throw more light upon it.   So three days went by, during which nothing came from the War Office of any moment.

On the 3rd July I received a private letter from the War Office telling me of certain reports that were current in London regarding my attitude towards the South African question, and advising me, if these reports were true, not to continue in my command.   From this letter it was clear to me that a campaign of calumny was on foot against me in London, which I calculated must have begun shortly after my refusal to consent to an excision in one of my despatches.   A similar campaign of abuse had been worked in Cape Town during the past few weeks.

All this did not matter much. I knew that I had told the truth right along these seven months, and I believed that in doing so I was giving my chiefs the best service possible.

Having read attentively this private letter received the 3rd July, and before replying to it, I went to Government House, saw Sir Alfred Milner, and put the question to him : ' Have I, in my official capacity here, been a hindrance or embarrassment to you in the prosecution of your designs ? ' He replied without hesitation that undoubtedly on some occasions I had so hindered him ; and he named three of the occasions in question—viz , when I declined to correspond with Colonel Nicholson direct as to the arrangements for the prospective raid from Tuli ; when I had added to my telegram of the 23rd June to the Secretary of State, in reply to his query for ' any observations ' ; and when he had sent Sampson to me, and I had not proposed anything to him.

I replied that if I had been a cause of embarrassment to him it was easy to remove the cause , and I added that in all these and other matters in which we had differed I had used my own right of judgment in regard to my own action, but that in all things I had told him I was ready to take any step indicated by him in writing and signed by him, no matter how much I might differ from him as to its desirability.

I went back to my office and wrote a despatch to the Secretary of State reviewing my line of action since I came out to South Africa, and stating that, since I now found it was possible that I might have been moving in opposition to the policy of Her Majesty's Government, and that my action since my arrival had been a cause of embarrassment to Her Majesty's representative here, I was prepared to place in the hands of the Secretary of State the resignation of my present appointment, to be dealt with as he thought fit.

I now give some extracts from my answer to the private letter from the War Office —

' You say that " if reports are true I have in some way or other caused it to be generally felt in South Africa that my sympathies are with England's possible enemies," that I " consider the claims of the British subjects upon the Transvaal Boers for equal political rights to be unjustifiable, and the resistance of the Boers to those claims for political rights to be fair and right." You add that you

" have no evidence to quote in support of this report, but it is a fact that it is current here."

'I do not know who has spread these reports about me and my opinions. It is true that I have, and long have had, sympathy with the people of Dutch race in South Africa. Long ago I studied their history and formed my opinion about them, and these opinions I have openly stated in my writings for years past ; but I have never held the opinion that the claims of British subjects upon the Transvaal Boers were unjustifiable, nor that resistance of the Boers to those claims was fair and right

'I have written very openly to you during the last three or four months, but I think you will look in vain for any such statement. I have held all along since my arrival here the view that powerful agencies were at work in England and in South Africa to nag at the whole Dutch race, to inflame racial differences, and to provoke or produce strife with the Transvaal.

'These agencies I considered were the real causes of the tension, for they were the origin of most of the suspicion and mistrust existing among the Dutch people as to the intentions and demands of the British Government   Ever since I had time to write to you about the situation in South Africa that has been the unvarying line of my opinion, and to others I have expressed the same views.

'In official despatches to the Secretary of State for the Colonies, as well as in private letters to Mr. Chamberlain, and again to the Secretary of State for War in recent despatches, I have held to the same language and expressed the same views.'

.   .   .   .

The events which now followed—the embarkation of Colonels Baden-Powell and Hore in July, with the object of raising irregular forces on the Transvaal frontier ; the arrival of eight or ten staff-officers ; the purchase of eighteen hundred mules ; the sending out of six million rounds of small arms ammunition —were given full publicity by the Rhodesite press, and set the Boers in a state of unrest greater than they had been in before.

All this filibuster preparation seemed the more incomprehensible when one knew that nothing in the whole catalogue of caution could altogether abolish the danger of the hiatus which would exist between the moment that the Boers knew our Government meant war, and the time when our army in South Africa would be strong enough to assume the offensive.

There was one course possible for the Government, if it

intended to go to war with the Dutch Republics, or even if it suspected that it might be dragged into war by the efforts of the Jingo section , this was to take advantage of the summer manœuvres at Aldershot and Salisbury Plain, and quietly to prepare in every detail two or three divisions complete in transport, etc. These would have been ready at a day's notice for embarkation to South Africa, and could have been landed there under four weeks' time. Another division might have been similarly prepared in India to be thrown into Natal in a fortnight.

This course would not have had a hundredth part of the publicity of the one adopted, and the inevitable hiatus would then have been reduced to the shortest possible limits.

On the 19th July the London *Times* announced officially that the diplomatic crisis was satisfactorily ended by the concessions of the Boer Government on the question of the Franchise. This announcement made the Jingo party redouble their efforts.

. . . .

On the morning of 9th August I received the following cablegram from the War Office :—

'LONDON, 8 P M., *8th August.*

' Your letter 4th July. Her Majesty's Government has come to the conclusion that Imperial interests would suffer if situation described by you were to be prolonged. Your resignation is, therefore, accepted, and you should come home as soon as possible. You will hand over, provisionally, command in the Cape of Good Hope to Colonel Morris, R.E., and command in South Africa to Major-General Symons, who will remain in Natal. Commander-in-Chief has recommended you for appointment as General Officer commanding Western District. Inform me by telegram whether you accept.

' SECRETARY OF STATE.'

To this I sent my reply on 10th August In it I detailed the steps I was about to take to carry out the instructions as to the command I thanked the Secretary of State and the Commander-in-Chief for the offer of the command of the Western District, which I begged permission respectfully to decline, not desiring to be the cause of possible embarrassment to the Government, and I commended my personal staff to the

favourable consideration of the Secretary of State. I then
wrote to inform Sir Alfred Milner that my resignation had been
accepted, and the next morning I called upon him at his request.
In a *précis* written at the moment, I find the following :—

'Governor said he thought ring round Free State, troops in
Kimberley, De Aar, etc., would awe Free State and prevent civil
war. I heard him through, and then said that he had my views
already on this question of strategy. I said that the whole Aldershot Division would not suffice to hold line of railway alone from
Kimberley to Palachwé.'

I had previously opposed the idea of placing Imperial troops
in Kimberley, on account of its false strategic position, and
had repeatedly urged my reasons for my opposition. My views
regarding this Kimberley question, upon which so much de-
pended later on, and upon which hinged the whole series of
disasters in the following December and early months of 1900,
I again gave in this interview.

On 12th August I received the following :—

'LONDON, 12th *August*
'Your telegram of 10th August. You need have no misgivings
as to possible embarrassment here. Commander-in-Chief and I
discussed the question in all its aspects before making proposal
which represented our opinion carefully arrived at. Please tell me,
under these circumstances, if you adhere to your resolve as to
Western District. I shall take no steps until I hear from you again,
but an early decision is necessary. Your recommendation of personal
staff shall be noted. (Signed) LANSDOWNE.'

This renewed offer of the Western District I now accepted.
I arranged to sail on the 29th August, but I got two or three
telegrams from the War Office hastening my departure to the
23rd. One of these threw light upon the object of the hurry
to get me away from South Africa : it advised me, 'above all
things, to avoid any sort of demonstration by those hostile to
English views.' How little they knew the principle upon which
I had guided my conduct of affairs through all these months !
They could not understand that there had not been a 'gallery '
all the time to which I was playing, and that now my audience
would not descend *en masse* and escort me to the ship with
bands and banners. The pity and the poverty of it all !

Mr. Hofmeyer called in the forenoon to say good-bye. He said that he and the Dutch community of Cape Town would have liked to go on board to make their adieux, but they knew their doing so would be misunderstood.

Before proceeding to the vessel I went to Government House, took a formal farewell of the Governor, and then joined my family on board the steamer, where I found my own officers and almost all of our English friends.

The rain, which from daybreak had descended in torrents, had now ceased, but masses of clouds continued to roll in from the sea, shrouding Table Mountain, and capping the summit of the 'Lion's Head,' that lofty landmark which, from the earliest times of their settlement, the Dutch have connected with their fortunes in South Africa.

AFTERWORD

On his return from South Africa, my father found that, as a friend at the War Office informed him, he was ' the best abused man in England ' ; and the persistent attacks that were made by a section of the press upon his character as an officer and as a servant of the Crown increased in violence after the opening of hostilities in October. The repeated reverses to our arms at the beginning of the war were attributed to his neglect of warning to the Government during his late command . and in consequence of the assertion that he was thus responsible for the surrender of the Gloucester Regiment at Ladysmith at the end of October, he, the General in Command of the Western District, was requested not to be present during the Queen's visit to Bristol in November, for fear that the violence and insult threatened against him might cause inconvenience to Her Majesty. Of all these and many other libellous accusations my father took no notice, in accordance with the rules of the Service, beyond submitting that some vindication of his character should be made by his military superiors. It was not until four years later. when the Royal Commission on the war had been appointed, that he had the opportunity of speaking for himself.

There is one incident which I think is little if at all known, and which I mention here as being significant of what my father's patriotism, so slandered at the moment, really was. In the midst of the initial disasters of October and November 1899 he offered to go out ' in any capacity,' to do what he could to help to retrieve the Empire's losses. The offer was not accepted, however, and he continued in the peaceful home commands of Aldershot and Devonport all through the war and up to January 1905. It is interesting in this connection to remember how, during an unofficial visit which my father subsequently paid to South Africa, one of the Boer generals who had given us the greatest trouble during the war greeted him with the bluff compliment, ' It was lucky for us, General, that you were not against us in the field ! '

In the spring of 1905 he was made President of the War Office Committee appointed to inquire into the ' War Stores Scandals ' , and his Report, disquieting in its revelations, and unconventional in its picturesque phraseology, whereby he gave occasional play to his Irish humour, which he could seldom quite repress, again brought him criticism.

About the same time he was invited by the Liberals of East Leeds to become their candidate in the approaching General Election, and he was about to accept an offer which opened to him a field of such novel interest now that his soldiering was at an end, when the difficulty which the Education Question, then so prominent, placed in his way as a Catholic confronted him, and he withdrew.

In October 1905, at the age of sixty-seven, he was placed upon the Retired List, and he established our home at Bansha, Co. Tipperary, close to the home of his childhood. Here he lived until his death on 7th June 1910.

In the June of 1906 he was appointed Knight Grand Cross of the Order of the Bath as a King's Birthday honour ; and three years later he was made a member of the Privy Council of Ireland.

On the occasion of my father's marriage, Ruskin had written to him : ' What could you two not do for England ? ' He gave her his best soldier's service, and now, during the term of his retired life, he strove for Ireland with all the endeavour of his declining years   He was frequently invited from the capital and the provinces to lecture to the people on certain social and economic questions ; and ever genial and full of tact, though he never spared his hearers when unpalatable truths were necessary, he was everywhere received with enthusiasm.

The keen interest he took in the question of National Education was given ample scope in the positions which he held as member of the Statutory Commission for the National University of Ireland, created under the Irish Universities Act of 1908 ; as member of the Senate of this University ; and as Commissioner of the Board of National Education in Ireland.

The following very kind tributes that came to my mother from these institutions after his death testify to the services he rendered them :—

RESOLUTION OF THE SENATE OF THE NATIONAL UNIVERSITY OF IRELAND.

' That the Senate desires to record its deep regret at the death of the Right Hon. Sir William Butler, G C.B., at a time when his sagacious counsel and ripe judgment were of such inestimable value in shaping the policy of this University from the earliest period of its existence ; and that the Senate tenders to Lady Butler and the other members of her family its heartfelt sympathy with them in their profound sorrow.'

RESOLUTION OF THE COMMISSIONERS OF NATIONAL EDUCATION.

' That we, the Commissioners of National Education, desire to place on record our great sorrow at the loss we have sustained by the death of Lieut.-General the Right Hon. Sir William Butler, G.C.B.

' Sir William Butler was a valuable member of our Board, on account of many qualities which are seldom found united in a single person.   He possessed a deep knowledge of Irish history which was illuminated by a genuine patriotism.   His insight into the manners of the people, and his practical acquaintance with some of the more obscure aspects of Irish life, gave weight to his judgment in dealing with many of the difficult problems of National Education.   His love of children and his sympathy with their ways taught him to view education not as a mere collection of precepts but as a living reality.   He was particularly interested in the physical well-being of the young.

' By his country, which he served with rare devotion, his loss will be long felt : to his colleagues who loved him for the brightness of his intellect and the sweetness and simplicity of his character he has left the memory of a life without fear and without reproach, and the sense of an irreparable loss.'

The end, sanctified by the Rites of the Church, came very peacefully after a brief illness in which a recent affection of the heart, unsuspected because never complained of, was brought to a crisis by a chill.

Of my father's great worth in private life it is perhaps not the place here to speak ; but with regard to the courage with which he met the trials of life and its ending I may not inappropriately quote my mother's words to me after he was gone : ' He taught me how to live, and now he has taught me how to die ' ; nor yet the following fragment of verse found among his writings :—

> ' On the dim tombs of time I see
> The names of men who strove in vain
> To lift the load, to break the chain .
> Then why a better grave for me ?
>
> O Thou the First and Last, the Whole,
> Thou who from toil and tears of man
> Dost shape on earth Thy mighty plan
> And build while all the ages roll,
>
> Enough it is for me to know
> That all the travail of the years,
> The gleams of hope, the clouds of tears,
> Add something to Thy work below '

He was buried with full military honours in the remote little country cemetery of Killardrigh, of which he speaks in the opening chapter of this book. Thus were the two ends of his life's long thread brought close together : the river and the mountain and the glen that formed his earliest recollections form, too, the scene of his last resting-place.

INDEX

Printed by T. and A. Constable, Printers to His Majesty
at the Edinburgh University Press